The Wonder Weeks

"This is a very practical and entertaining window into the babies' first year and a half. Van de Rijt and Plooij have observed and found the vulnerable times in an infant's development. . . . Wonderful."

—T. Berry Brazelton,† MD, Professor Emeritus, Harvard Medical School

"Van de Rijt and Plooij's work on infant development has enormous value for clinical use and scientific application. Not only have they explained the periods of puzzling, difficult behavior in infancy which so worry parents, they have also shown how these behaviors mark developmental leaps and have described the stages in the infant's understanding. What's more, van de Rijt and Plooij have described the play and communication that work best with babies at different ages and thus helped parents understand and connect sensitively with their babies. This parent-child connection is the major prerequisite for the development of secure, well-adjusted children. *The Wonder Weeks* is essential reading for everyone who works with infants—pediatricians, social workers, psychologists, and, of course, parents."

—John Richer, MA (Oxon), PhD, Dipl Clin Psych. Honorary Consultant, Pediatric Psychology, Oxford University Hospitals NHS Foundation Trust, Oxford, England, and Department of Physiology, Anatomy and Genetics, University of Oxford

"Anyone who deals with infants and young children will want to read *The Wonder Weeks*. The book will open parents' eyes to aspects of their children's growth, development, changing behavior, and emotional responsiveness that they might otherwise not notice or find puzzling and distressing."

—Catherine Snow, PhD, Shattuck Professor of Education, Harvard Graduate School of Education

Portrait of Hetty van de Rijt, created by her grandson Thomas on September 12, 1998, when he was two years old. She and Thomas had a very close relationship, and during her last seven years, he was the sunshine in Hetty's life, which was restricted by disease.

Hetty paid a high price for the research she undertook with her husband and coauthor, Frans Plooij. She contracted a tropical disease during their stay in Tanzania, and following a long, brave battle with the disease, passed away in 2003.

Through her life's work, Hetty hoped to give parents across the world peace of mind and self-confidence to give all babies a chance of "a smart start for a happy beginning." She lives on through *The Wonder Weeks*.

With the
10 Predictable Leaps

The Wonder Weeks

A Stress-Free Guide to Your Baby's Behavior

Hetty van de Rijt, PhD, Frans X. Plooij, PhD,
and Xaviera Plas-Plooij

Countryman Press

An Imprint of W. W. Norton & Company
Independent Publishers Since 1923

For information about permission to reproduce selections from this book, write to
Permissions, Countryman Press, 500 Fifth Avenue, New York, NY 10110

For information about special discounts for bulk purchases, please contact
W. W. Norton Special Sales at specialsales@wwnorton.com or 800-233-4830

Manufacturing by LSC Communications, Harrisonburg
Book design by Anna Reich
Production manager: Devon Zahn

Countryman Press
www.countrymanpress.com

An imprint of W. W. Norton & Company, Inc.
500 Fifth Avenue, New York, NY 10110
www.wwnorton.com

Library of Congress Cataloging-in-Publication Data

Names: Vanderijt, Hetty, author. | Plooij, Frans X., author. | Plas-Plooij, Xaviera,
1976– author.
Title: The wonder weeks : a stress-free guide to your baby's behavior / Hetty van
der Rijt, Frans X. Plooji, and Xaviera Plas-Plooji.
Other titles: Oei, ik groei! English
Description: Sixth edition. | New York, NY : The Countryman Press, a division
of W. W. Norton & Company, [2019] | "First published in 1992 as Oei, ik groei!
By Zomer & Keuning Boeken BV, Ede and Antwerp." | Includes bibliographical
references and index.
Identifiers: LCCN 2019029570 | ISBN 9781682684276 (paperback) |
ISBN 9781682684283 (epub)
Subjects: LCSH: Infant psychology. | Newborn infants—Psychology. |
Infants—Development. | Child rearing.
Classification: LCC BF719 .V3713 2019 | DDC 649/.122—dc23
LC record available at https://lccn.loc.gov/2019029570

10 9 8 7 6 5 4

For our sweethearts, heroes, and examples:
Marco, Thomas, Victoria, and Sarah

Important Note

This book is intended as a general information resource about how babies behave at various points during the normal development process, and why they behave that way, so you can have a better idea of what to expect along the way. Neither the publisher, authors, nor anyone else involved in the development, production, marketing, or distribution of this book makes or can make any promises at all about how your particular baby or toddler will develop or behave, or about whether any suggestion or recommendation in this book will work for you and your particular baby or toddler.

This book is *not* a substitute for individual medical diagnosis or treatment of your particular baby or toddler. If you have any doubt or concern about the behavior, development, or physical wellbeing of your child, always consult your child's pediatrician or another appropriately trained medical professional. Do not hesitate to seek emergency care for your child or yourself if you think it may be needed.

Neither the publisher nor any author controls the content of any third-party website that may be mentioned in this book. You should always do your own research before adopting any new practices or using any new products.

Contents

Preface to the Sixth Edition

Having a baby is at the top of the list of things you'll never forget. It's likely you'll always remember things like what you ate the night before "it all" started, the exact time of the delivery, who you called first to tell the news. Your baby arrived and you are suddenly a parent. And whether this is your first time or you have had a baby before, it is always special.

I feel that way toward *The Wonder Weeks*—it was born to my parents, Hetty van de Rijt and Frans Plooij, but it has become mine, too, in the last decade or so. The three of us, in addition to the entire Wonder Weeks team, are proud that we have been able to help millions of parents globally. Every email, post, or message we receive from parents gives us a sense of joy. It is just like someone complimenting you on your baby! We receive such satisfaction from being able to help parents, so if you ever find yourself searching for answers, we are here to help you!

There have been many changes since *The Wonder Weeks* was first published in 1992. Snail mail has been replaced by social media and emails, parents have a different view of parenthood, and fathers are now just as involved with the upbringing as mothers are. When my mother and father started their original research, fathers went to work and mothers cared for the baby. There were always exceptions, of course, my father being one. For the two years my mother worked on her PhD at Cambridge University, he stayed at home with me. He would then go on to work a full day until 10 p.m. while my mother took over at home.

Fortunately, fathers and mothers play more equal roles these days. The way we deal with the postnatal period and breastfeeding has also changed drastically over the years. In the past, for instance, mothers often felt pressured about their choices, whether to breastfeed or use formula, how long to nurse, when to wean, and so forth. Nowadays, as a mother you can feed your child for as long as you choose, on demand (and not at set times!), and openly. Businesses are even required to offer new mothers pumping rooms for privacy. Hopefully you feel less like you need to follow arbitrary rules about leaving your baby to cry, or feeding them on a schedule, and other things that feel completely unnatural, and instead can follow your natural instincts more than ever before.

When you sell millions of books worldwide and have so much contact with parents, you learn a lot, too. My father and I have taken readers' comments and suggestions to heart and made the message in this book even clearer. In this revised edition of *The Wonder Weeks*, you will find:

- All the latest insights into the developmental leaps

- Increased interaction: check off what applies to your baby and discover the patterns in their personality

- Renewed lists with the changes you notice in your baby: a unique account of your baby's most important milestones per leap in their development

- Fresh, recent insights and commentary directly from new parents who've used Wonder Weeks

- A new chapter on how parents can better care for themselves, especially when they are exhausted and discouraged

- Ways in which to experience the world through your baby's eyes

- The 10 things you really need to know about developmental leaps

The Wonder Weeks has never before been so complete and accessible. It's been a pleasure and honor to work closely with my father on this revision, with my mother's words also at hand.

We wish you and your baby all the joy in the world as you share the challenges of growing up and have "a smart start for a happy beginning."

—Xaviera Plas-Plooij

Introduction

Some people have all the luck: they find each other in love and also in their work.

In 1971, having completed our studies in educational psychology, physical anthropology, and behavioral biology, and just married, my wife, Hetty, and I left for Gombe National Park, Tanzania, East Africa, to study chimpanzees with Jane Goodall. When we arrived there (with a large wooden chest containing equipment and some clothes), we soon realized the particular research project we had prepared for proved impossible under the prevailing circumstances. And there you are, then . . . powerless. But it was precisely that feeling of powerlessness that led to the discovery of our lives.

We had to pick another research topic. We realized that Gombe National Park was the only place on earth where we could observe free-living chimpanzee mothers and their newborn babies at such close range. We did not have any theory or hypothesis at hand for testing, but we were trained in systematic, direct observation of animal behavior in the field, in the tradition of our compatriot and Nobel Laureate Niko Tinbergen. We decided to observe the developments in behavior of chimpanzee babies in their interaction with their mothers, in the hope of finding something interesting. It was an incredibly risky investment in time and effort. There was a chance we would have nothing to show after two years there.

We spent the first six months familiarizing ourselves with the chimpanzees and their surroundings. That usually takes years when you are dealing with a completely unknown species, but the years of experience in Gombe were passed on from one researcher to the next. During those six months, we gradually built up a list of characteristic and recurrent behaviors. During the final year and a half, we observed the chimpanzee babies and their mothers in terms of the list. The advantage of this method of observation is that you can be sure that a certain behavior hasn't occurred if you haven't observed it. You know how often certain behaviors occur, how long they take, and can see how they change with age.

When our African adventure was over, we went to work in Robert Hinde's Medical Research Council Unit on the Development and Integration of Behavior, at the University of Cambridge, England, and we had reams of data to analyze.

Out of this analysis emerged the notion of what we now know as "developmental leaps." The data showed clear phases of "regression" in independence—difficult phases when the baby clings more closely to the mother, when they want to be nursed more often, and let out "whimpering sounds" more frequently than before. Before our research, such regression phases had been found by others in 12 other primate species and two lower mammalian species, indicating that this appears to be an old phenomenon, perhaps emerging during the very evolution of life on earth.

The results of the data analysis also supported the idea that in the course of early ontogeny, a hierarchical organization emerges in the central nervous system that underlies the behavioral development of free-living chimpanzee babies and infants.

Once we had earned our PhD degrees—Hetty in Cambridge, England, and myself in Groningen, the Netherlands—we went on to observe and film human mothers and their infants in their home environment in the Netherlands. These studies clearly demonstrated that human babies, too, go through difficult, age-linked regression phases in a similar way. With each difficult phase, babies make a leap in their mental development. Each time, a sudden, drastic, age-linked brain change enables babies to enter a new perceptual world. Thereby they discover more complex aspects both within and outside their own body, and master new, more complex skills.

When our initial research results were published in scientific journals, Hetty and I wrote the first Dutch version of *The Wonder Weeks*, which was published in 1992. Our research with babies clearly struck a chord with new parents time and again, and our original research with babies in the Netherlands has been replicated and confirmed by research teams in Spain, Britain, and Sweden.

The Wonder Weeks is now a worldwide bestseller and can be read in more than 20 languages. My research partner and wife, Hetty, lives on through these words.

—Frans X. Plooij

Your Baby's 10 Leaps in Mental Development

Jolted from a deep sleep, the new mother leaps from her bed and runs down the hall to the nursery. Her tiny infant, red-faced, fists clenched, screams in their crib. On instinct, the mother picks up the baby, cradling them* in her arms. The baby continues to shriek. The mother nurses the baby, changes their diaper, then rocks them, trying every trick to ease their discomfort, but nothing seems to work. "Is there something wrong with the baby?" the mother wonders. "Am I doing something wrong?"

A crying baby is no fun for anyone. You want to see a healthy and happy baby. Parents** frequently worry about their baby and they often think that they are the only ones not walking around with permanent smiles on their faces. That they are the only ones who feel insecure, fearful, desperate, or aggravated when their baby is troublesome and cannot be comforted. Parents commonly experience a mixture of worry, fatigue, frustration, guilt, and sometimes even uncomfortable feelings of anger toward their inconsolable infants. We can tell you now: you are certainly not alone. Reading that other parents have felt this way in *The Wonder Weeks* can help, although you should certainly seek professional help if you feel completely overwhelmed or aggressive.

A baby's crying can also cause tension between the parents, especially when they disagree on how to deal with it. The well-meant but unwelcome advice from family, friends, neighbors, and even complete strangers only serves to make things worse. "Let them cry; it's good for the lungs," is likely not a solution parents will want to hear. Disregarding the problem does not make it go away, either.

THE GOOD NEWS: THERE IS A REASON

We have conducted 35 years of research into the development of babies and the way their fathers and mothers respond to the changes. Our research was done in homes, where we observed the daily activities of parents and children. We gleaned further information from more formal interviews. We discovered that, from time to time, all parents are plagued by a baby who won't stop crying. In fact, we found that, surprisingly, all normal, healthy babies are more tearful, troublesome, demanding, and fussy at roughly the same ages, and when this occurs, they may drive the parents to despair. At this point, we have figured out the rhythm of these ups and downs, and can predict, almost to the week, when a baby will go through another one of these difficult phases. English, Spanish, and Swedish researchers have replicated our research and found the same results. Parents the world over will agree that being prepared for a fussy baby may not be as good as skipping the fussy phase altogether, but it certainly helps.

* This book is gender neutral. We do not use "he" or "she," we use "they" to refer to both girls and boys.
** We use the word "parent" throughout the book to keep it legible. It could just as well say "mother/father/caregiver."

There is a reason babies cry: they are upset. Their brain is undergoing sudden and drastic changes and that, in turn, changes the way the baby perceives the world around them. These changes enable a baby to learn many new skills and should therefore be a reason for celebration. After all, it's a sign that they are making wonderful progress. But as far as your baby is concerned, these changes are bewildering. They are taken aback—everything has changed overnight. It is as if they have entered a whole new world.

THEY CAN DO A LOT MORE ALL OF A SUDDEN!

THE LEAPS IN MENTAL DEVELOPMENT

It is well accepted that children's physical development progresses in what we commonly call "growth spurts." A baby may not grow at all, or very little, for some time but then all of sudden grow a quarter of an inch overnight. It appears that the same thing happens in a child's mental development. Parents notice that, all of a sudden, their baby can do or understand all kinds of new things. Neurological studies have shown that such leaps are accompanied by changes in the brain. (To read more about these studies, see our reading list at the end of this book.) The leaps in mental development are not necessarily in sync with the physical growth spurts. The latter are more numerous. Many milestones, such as cutting teeth, are unrelated to these leaps in development. This book outlines the 10 leaps in mental development that all babies go through in the first 20 months of life. It tells you what each of these leaps means for your baby's understanding of the world around them and how they use this understanding to develop new skills, skills they need for their further development.

Parents can use this understanding of their baby's developmental leaps to help them through these often confusing times in their new lives. You will better understand the way your baby is thinking and why they act as they do at certain times. You will be able to choose the right kind of help to give them when they need it and the right kind of environment to help them make the most of every leap in their development.

This is not a book about how to make your child into a genius, however. We firmly believe that every child is unique and intelligent in their own way. It is a book on how to understand and cope with your baby when they are difficult and how to enjoy them most as they grow. It is about the joys and sorrows of growing with your baby.

All that's required to use this book is:

- One (or two) loving parent(s)

- One active, vocal, growing baby

- A willingness to grow along with your baby

- Patience

THE MAGICAL LEAP FORWARD

With every mental leap your baby makes, they gain a new perceptive ability. That new ability enables them to perceive, see, hear, taste, smell, and feel many new things that your baby was unable to perceive before. With their new cognitive skills, your baby's whole life changes. It is as if they have to rediscover the world, and your baby could use your help with that!

TIP

Before your baby goes through a developmental leap, read what the next leap entails. It will help you to understand what they are about to go through, what is about to change in their perceptive ability, and how you can help them to discover this new world. You can guide them on their voyage of discovery.

One of our readers compared a leap to an update on your laptop or phone: it happens all of a sudden and you have no control over it, but then afterward your phone can do many new things.

We can take that comparison a step further. After such an update, the user often has trouble with all the new functions. Imagine your baby as this person, trying to deal with the "updated" brain they have suddenly acquired. Even your beloved apps don't work the same way they used to!

ONE SMALL STEP BACK AND A GIANT LEAP FORWARD

Each leap in development comprises three parts—a brain change and two phases—which are then followed by an "easy" period. You will see throughout the book that the "fussy phase" is quite similar for every leap. It may feel repetitive to read through it every time, but it's important to recognize this. Certainly your family will become accustomed to it.

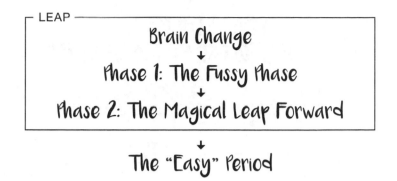

Brain Change

All of a sudden, there it is: a new mental ability. And the only one to notice is your baby. Their brain is suddenly able to perceive new things. Almost nothing is as it was before.

Phase 1: The Fussy Phase

When a baby takes a leap in their mental development, it is an intense experience for them, as so much changes! That is why the first thing you notice about a leap is the *fussy phase*. This phase is the onset of a leap. Characteristic behaviors during this phase are:

The three Cs: Crying, Clinginess, and Crankiness

Your baby cries more often, hangs (almost literally) on you, and they are not themselves. This happens with every leap. There are also characteristics in this troublesome phase that are not the same during all leaps, and babies may only display some of them. You can find these characteristics in each chapter about a leap. As a parent, when you notice "something is wrong," you start to get concerned. Some parents worry that their baby is sick or they get irritated because they don't understand why baby is so "fussy." This phase is also marked by a small "regression." It seems as if your baby's development has taken a step back . . . as if their behavior is more babyish, they can't do certain things anymore, they are less independent than before. Add that to the three Cs and you will understand why we call this the difficult phase of a leap. It is difficult for your baby and difficult for you.

When Do These Fussy Phases Start?

The good news is, you know when your baby will make a leap! There are 10 leaps during the first 20 months of a baby's life. The initial fussy phases don't last long, and the intervals between these early phases are also short. The schedule for these leaps is on page 22. The bars indicate the weeks from the due date.

LEAP SCHEDULE:
YOUR BABY'S 10 GREAT FUSSY PHASES *

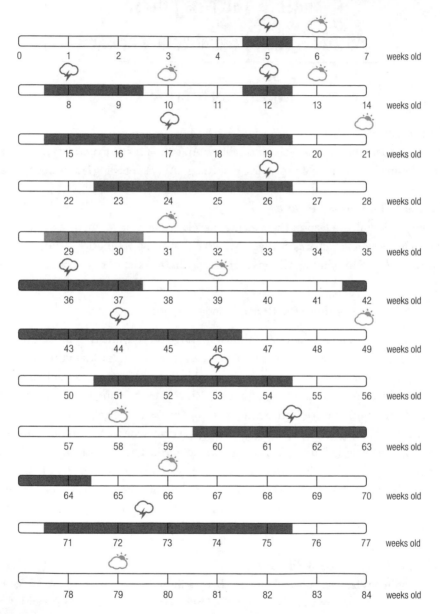

* The bars indicating the difficult periods may appear long, but we have good news for you: the bars indicate that a baby could be fussy in that period. It doesn't have to last the entire time! But you will notice the difficult phase of the leap during that time. For other babies, the fussy phase may last longer but will be less intense; all combinations and variations are possible.

If you know when the troublesome phase can occur, it will be easier to recognize it and it will not come as a total surprise.

■ Your baby may be fussier now than before.

■ **C**rying, **c**linginess, and **c**rankiness (the three **C**s) at around 29 or 30 weeks are not telltale signs of another leap. Your baby has simply discovered that their mommy or daddy can walk away and leave them behind. As funny as it sounds, this is progress. It is a new skill: they are learning about distances.

☐ Your baby is probably going through a comparatively uncomplicated phase.

⚡ Around this week, a "stormy" period is most likely to occur.

☁ Around this week, it is most likely that your baby's sunny side will shine through.

NOT A SINGLE BABY ESCAPES

All babies experience fussy phases, although it can affect some more than others. Not surprisingly, temperamental babies will have more difficulty dealing with them than will their calmer counterparts. These babies will have the greatest need for their mommy and daddy, yet also might have the most conflict with their parents. If you have an especially hard time with the first leap, though, don't worry. The intensity can differ from leap to leap. One round might be a nightmare, whereas another is merely a headache.

The Timing of the Fussy Phases!
To make your life that bit easier, it's good to know exactly when to expect what. And that is actually quite simple.

1. Place the leap schedule on page 22 next to your calendar and count the weeks.

2. Write down the date under the bars in the leaps schedule and transcribe them to your calendar, paper or digital. Both work!

3. You can also use the Wonder Weeks app to help you keep track of the dates. The app works beautifully in tandem with the deeper information in this book.

The Due Date: Because Brain Development Starts at Conception
We base our calendar on your baby's due date, not the date on which your baby was born. This is because the brain develops at the same rate, whether your baby

is still in the womb or out in the world. For the first year, you cannot expect a premature baby's brain to develop at a faster speed and therefore "catch up." You wouldn't want this to happen, either. They need time to develop. Likewise, when a baby is born a few weeks after their due date, their brain is naturally more developed. So it makes sense that the developmental leaps are based on the due date. For example, if your baby was born two weeks late, their first fussy period will probably occur two weeks earlier than we show here. If they were four weeks early, it will occur four weeks later. This phenomenon indicates that each fussy period is accompanied by a growth in a baby's brain. The date of birth is all about birthdays and cake; the due date says something about your baby's mental development.

Your Baby Needs You. Now, More Than Ever!

Now that you know when a fussy phase is on its way, you can help your baby.

As a new world opens up to your baby, you are the best person to guide them through the changes they are undergoing. We hope that each chapter about a specific leap will provide you with an understanding of what your baby is experiencing, the way they see the world, what interests them, and what they want to discover. Because you are aware of what happens in the "new world," you can help your child get the most out of what the leap has to offer.

You Are Your Baby's Safe Base

Your baby's familiar world is turned upside down as they go through these changes. The only thing they want is to be near you. You know your baby better than anyone else. They trust you more and have known you longer than anyone else. They will cry, sometimes incessantly, and will like nothing better than to be carried in your arms all day long. As they grow into toddlers, they will do anything to stay near you. Sometimes they will cling to you and hold on for dear life. They may want to be treated like a tiny baby again. Give them that comfort and security as best you can.

Phase 2: The Magical Leap Forward

When your baby suddenly becomes fussy, you may feel worried at first and then even a bit annoyed by their behavior. If you are following the Wonder Weeks leaps schedule, though, hopefully you'll realize what's going on. You may notice that they're attempting to do things you have never seen them do before. This is the phase we look forward to: the magical leap forward! This phase starts at the end of the fussy phase, or just after it has peaked. You will be able to see magical leaps forward from weeks 5, 8, 12, 19, 26, 37, 46, 55, 64, and 75.

Take Note!

In the schedule of fussy phases, you see that the bolt of lightning (when the chance your baby is going through a fussy phase is at its greatest) sometimes coincides with the times you will see the magical leap forward. The phases do not always follow one another from one day to the next, so your baby won't necessarily be fussy on Monday and wake up on Tuesday as if nothing is wrong. It is also quite normal that the peak of frustration can stimulate your baby enough that they can suddenly do a number of new things (after all, their new perceptive ability, the brain change, already started at the beginning of this fussy phase). In short, there is a chance that you will see your baby trying new things during the last days or week of the fussy phase. They may start to learn some new skills, but the magical leap forward refers to the full array of skills for phase 2.

Time to Explore the New World

Your baby is more or less over the shock of entering a whole new world. Now they start to explore, and want you close by as they do.

Each new ability enables your baby to perceive different, more complex aspects and consequently learn new things. For example, they may now see and feel how a hand can curl around an object and develop the skill to grasp. With practice they will learn to put that into action, reaching for and holding on to a toy. The brain change opened the way to a new ability that leads to skills they couldn't develop before that leap. Some skills will be completely new to them, whereas others will be an improvement on skills they acquired earlier. The question is: which parts of this new world will your baby explore first? Each baby has their own preferences, temperament, and physical characteristics, and these will lead them to select the things they find interesting. Whereas one baby will quickly sample everything, another will be captivated by one specific skill. These differences are what make babies unique, after all. If you watch, you will see your baby's unique personality emerging as they grow. And it is important to remember that your baby will make choices. What is your baby going to do with this new ability? What new skills are they going to master first? Mind you, it is physically impossible for a baby to master all of the new skills that they are theoretically able to master during this magical leap forward all at once. Every skill takes practice and time.

Your Baby Needs Your Help

You are the one who can give your baby what they need and what suits them. You know your baby better than anyone else, so you can help them get the most out of each new experience. Your baby is not the only one making choices; you are experiencing this new world alongside your baby. Some parts of that world will be less interesting, so pay attention to where your baby's interests lie. In the chapters about a specific leap, you can read all about the new world that is opening up for your baby. You can prepare yourself and know what you can do to help and guide your baby at this time. They will enjoy it if you share these new discoveries, and this will accelerate their learning progress. Admittedly, the troublesome phase has passed and your baby will not cling to you all day, but they still prefer to be very close to you. They want to discover the new world with you—or in any case, know you are not far away from them.

You Can Set Limits

When a baby learns something new, we want to encourage them and make it stick so they can build on that new skill. To crawl instead of being carried means unlearning the habit of reaching "up" for their mommy or daddy. Like the earlier example of a phone update, the old way of doing things is no longer available. Once they can crawl, they can get their own toys. After each leap, a baby can do more and will also be more independent. The more they do themselves, the more their self-confidence and self-esteem will grow.

The Easy Period: After the Leap

After a period of being bombarded with all the new perceptions and the reactions that follow, a period of relative peace should set in, a more relaxing time. Your baby will still be busy putting the new things into practice, learning and trying out new skills. You will notice your baby is less clingy now, and some of the pressure you felt to provide constant attention is off. They will be able to play independently when you need to do other things. Your baby is again the sunshine in the house. Unfortunately, this period of relative peace and quiet doesn't last long—it's just a lull before the next storm. Growing up is hard work!

HOW TO USE THIS BOOK

The chapter on page 45, "Newborn: Welcome to the World," describes what a newborn's world is like and how they perceive the new sensations that surround them. And we can let you in on one thing: it is so different from our perception of the world that it is a real eye-opener!

The Leap Chapters

As you know by now, this book will review the 10 leaps that happen in a baby's first 20 months of life. Organized by leaps, each chapter contains the information you need. You may recognize some things from a previous leap, as development builds on knowledge and experience. Each leap chapter contains the following sections:

The Fussy Phase: The Announcement of the Magical Leap: This section describes the clues that your baby is about to make a developmental leap. Reflections from other parents about their babies' troublesome times offer sympathetic support as you experience your baby's fussy phase.

In this section, you'll also find a list of habits, characteristics, emotions, and more signals that your baby is changing, called "This is how you let me know the leap has started." Check off what you've noticed that indicates your baby is about to experience a big change. You will probably see a pattern in their behavior. But don't let the idea of a checklist stress you out. These are changes you might observe, not milestones that your baby should be meeting.

The World of . . . : This section describes the new type of perception that your baby has acquired through the change in their brain. Read it and absorb the information. Although no one can know for certain, research indicates that a baby experiences the world in vastly different ways than we, as adults, do. But if you're curious as to what might be going on in there, we've designed activities that may mimic your baby's perception at the specific time of the leap, so you can imagine what they're seeing, hearing, and feeling.

The Magical Leap Forward: The Discovery of the New World: This section describes the new skills and things babies of this age may find interesting and might do. It is important that you gain an insight into the world your baby is going to discover so you can help and guide them. As you complete the lists at the end of each chapter and check off your baby's patterns and preferences, you will discover your baby's unique developing character! You may wind up adding a few entries of your own. As always, try not to have expectations or compare your baby's skills to those of others. Each baby is unique and special. Your baby may not be waving goodbye, but they can understand your request for them to clap their hands.

The Easy Period: After the Leap: This section describes the easy period. Baby is easier again, more independent and more cheerful again. Keep in mind, though, a theory is just that. We can't promise that after each leap, the sun will shine. You will see that for yourself when you read the quotes from parents we've included in the book. They are not only fun to read, but will probably also be very recognizable and, especially during the last two leaps, they may give you ideas to help you when observing your baby.

What This Book Offers You

Support in Times of Trouble: During the times you have to cope with crying problems, it helps to know that you are not alone, that there is a reason for the crying, and that a fussy phase never lasts more than a few weeks, and sometimes no longer than several days. This book tells you what other parents experienced when their babies were the same age as yours. You will learn that all parents struggle with feelings of anxiety, aggravation, and a whole range of other emotions. You will come to understand that these feelings are all part of the process, and that they will help your baby progress.

Confidence: You will understand that feelings of worry, frustration, and joy are essential. They are the driving force behind your baby's progress. You will be convinced that as a parent, you know better than anyone else what your baby needs at any given time. No one else can tell you. You are the expert, the leading authority on your baby. You know your baby best.

Understanding Your Baby: This book tells you what your baby endures during each fussy phase. It explains that they will be difficult when they are on the verge of learning new skills, because the brain change upsets them. Once you understand this, you will be less concerned and less resentful of their behavior. This knowledge will give you more peace of mind to be able to help them through each of the fussy phases.

Hints on How to Help Your Baby Play and Learn: After each fussy phase, your baby will be able to learn new skills. They will learn more quickly, more easily, and with more pleasure if you help them. We supply a range of ideas for different games, activities, and toys so that you can choose those best suited to your baby.

A Unique Account of Your Baby's Development: You can track your baby's fussy phases and progress throughout this book. We have incorporated a number of lists to fill in or check off. They will only take a few minutes to complete per leap, but they will provide you with a unique insight into your baby's personal character, traits, and preferences during the first 20 months of their life.

FROM US TO YOU

We hope that this book answers all your questions about your baby's mental development. Should you still have any questions, want to tell us something, or even treat us to a great photo of your baby, then please feel free to do so! You can also sign up for our monthly baby news and the free leaps alarm at www.thewonder weeks.com This very handy tool sends you a message a week before a leap so you can read up on the coming leap before it happens!

Experience the World Through your Baby's Eyes

Every leap chapter contains activities especially for you as a parent. We know you have your hands full already and may not feel like doing what may feel silly. But try and make the time, because you will really understand what effect discovering that new world has on your baby when you experience it for yourself.

#Blessed and #Stressed

Becoming a parent is the most wonderful experience in the world. You have been blessed with the most beautiful little being and you feel a new kind of love that you have never felt or given before. You are responsible for the life you hold in your arms and you will need to help and guide them as they grow through childhood and far beyond. The relationship with your partner also takes on a new level: you are now united forever through your child. It is as if you have been reborn, your relationship has been reborn and, on top of that, you have a newborn life in your arms. #blessed. But changes are always accompanied by some form of stress, no matter how wonderful life is. Having a baby is quite something, and that's an understatement. Life with a brand-new baby is a roller-coaster ride going from #blessed to #stressed. All very normal, in fact.

Things You Need to Know:
Stress is normal, and it even has a function: it makes you more alert as a parent and more receptive to changes your baby is going through!

- It is not only women who experience stress in the months after birth; men do, too! Unfortunately, however, the postpartum and stress-related ailments men have are often not recognized or acknowledged.

- Having a baby increases the chances of developing stress-related ailments.

- Feeling stressed is not a sign of weakness. Hormones play a role.

- No matter how long you dreamed of having a child, once you have given birth it can feel quite overwhelming, as if it has suddenly "happened to you." And it is all happening so quickly!

FROM GOOD STRESS TO BAD STRESS
Every parent experiences some kind of stress. It doesn't mean that you are unhappy or anxious, or that you will eventually become depressed. However, it becomes an issue if that stress starts affecting you, your family, or your health adversely. We can distinguish three forms of stress:

- Postpartum parental stress (which we all experience)

- Postpartum anxiety (1 out of 5 people may experience this, according to some studies)

- Postpartum depression (the most extreme form, but the least prevalent)

Postpartum Parental Stress

Stress has a function, and let's be honest, a life without any form of stress simply doesn't exist. As a brand-new parent, your stress levels peak, and we call that postpartum parental stress. So much changes in your life—everything really—and that is accompanied by worries, anxieties, and, therefore, stress. There is nothing wrong with that as long as the stress is at a manageable level.

However, it does pay to be conscious of the fact that you are going through a stressful period, so you can prevent that stress from taking over and negatively affecting your life.

Two scientists, Thomas Holmes and Richard Rahe, have researched a list of life events that can cause people stress. Some life events are more stressful than others. If you add up the events from this list and score under 150 points, then you are doing okay and there is only a slight chance you will get a stress-related ailment. As soon as you get above 150 points, the chances increase. The higher your score, the more vulnerable you are. This list includes a whole range of life events that you might or could encounter as a parent. Take a look:

Pregnancy:	40 points
Welcoming a new family member:	39 points
Change in financial situation:	38 points
Change of job:	36 points
More frequent disagreements:	35 points
Difficulties with family-in-law:	29 points
Change in responsibilities at work:	29 points
Spouse stops or starts working:	26 points
Change of personal habits:	24 points
Changes to working hours or conditions:	20 points
Moving house:	20 points
Change in social activities:	19 points
Mortgage or small loan:	17 points
Change in sleeping habits:	16 points
Change in eating habits:	15 points

Add up all the things from the list that have happened in your life in the last six months and see how you score on this stress scale. As an example: a woman has a three-month-old baby and she goes back to work. She works fewer hours than before her pregnancy and has taken out a small loan to renovate the nursery. Plus, she no longer sleeps as deeply through the night as she used to. This is all a very normal and typical situation. By adding up all these points, she scores 179.

Pregnancy:	40
Welcoming new family member:	39
Change in financial situation:	38
Change in responsibilities at work:	29
Mortgage or small loan:	17
Change in sleeping habits:	16
TOTAL:	179

And let's not forget the men. It's not only new mommies who experience increased stress; new daddies do, too. They are also involved, and their life changes just as drastically. Imagine that a man became a father four months ago. He and his wife have agreed she will work fewer hours or even stop working. The man now has more or all of the financial burden on his shoulders. During the pregnancy, he and his wife disagreed more often than before. There was nothing wrong with their relationship, but hormonal fluctuations can affect moods and how often words are exchanged. And he is a modern father, so he also takes care of the baby when they wake in the night. All these things together add up to a score of 154 points. (Welcoming a new family member: 39 points + change in financial situation: 38 points + more frequent disagreements: 35 points + spouse stops or starts working: 26 points + change in sleeping habits: 16 points = 154 points.)

As you can see, having a child and everything that comes with it brings changes in your life, which can cause stress. So it's quite easy to reach 150 points. And every new life event on top increases the risk that things can become too much to cope with. Do not forget, you may be a new mommy or daddy, but everyday life continues, and there is no guarantee that it will not throw a few more stressful events at you around the time you have just had a baby. A family member could become ill, there might be a death, or you could get into financial difficulties. After having a baby, if even one of these types of situations occurs, it can send stress levels through the roof.

The number of points you score only says something about your chances of getting stress-related ailments. Some people are able to function perfectly well, physically and mentally, while scoring 200 points on the stress scale. It all boils down to the fact that everyone is different and people deal with stress in their own way. Some people cope better with it, and some have better support networks around them. And that's without even mentioning how hormonal changes can affect people.

> *Life changes require an effort to adapt followed by an effort to regain and obtain stability.*—**Instagram post**

CAREGIVING & STRESS OVERLAP

Did you know that the area of the brain responsible for maternal care overlaps with the part playing a role in stress? When the maternal care region is activated, the stress region is automatically turned on.

Even If You're Not Stressed

The stress scale is not intended to scare the living daylights out of you. On the contrary, we only want to show you that:

- What you are going through, doing, and managing is an enormous feat.

- It is very normal to be stressed by the situation every so often.

- Everyone who has a child faces difficulties at some point or another. You can't always see the silver lining.

- You deserve to pamper yourself and take a moment for yourself every now and then.

THE WONDER WEEKS AND STRESS: ANCHOR MOMENTS

The primary aims of this book are to reassure you and to give you insight into the mental changes your baby goes through as they grow. It is not easy when your baby takes a leap in their development and it affects your baby, you, and your family. We hope that *The Wonder Weeks* will help alleviate your doubts and concerns because you will know why your baby is upset during certain periods. We cannot eradicate the stress that accompanies a leap, and we wouldn't want to, either. Stress is all part of life and parenthood, and it shapes us, making us more alert and more receptive to the changes our baby is going through. And that latter is important. What we can do, however, is offer you a helping hand by reminding you of the importance of taking time for yourself and suggesting ways to do that, with 5-minute, 10-minute, and longer "anchor moments." These are simple things that you can do, or not do, that anchor you in the here and now. They take you away from the roller coaster of events and emotions and help you regain balance; they provide a moment of calm. When you integrate regular anchor moments in your day, you give your body time to reset itself and to come to rest. Those moments are a great help in reducing stress!

Below, you'll find a list of simple suggestions. Every leap chapter contains three anchor moments specifically designed for the stresses that particular leap might cause. But feel free to come back to any of these, to repeat what has worked in the past, or make up your own. Read a story, go shoot some hoops, paint your nails, whatever you want, as long as you take brief moments of rest that will anchor you and bring you back to the here and now. You really deserve to take and enjoy these moments.

"Tea break": It may not be tea, but having a drink, such as an herbal tea or other relaxing beverage, makes you sit down and relax. Don't rush it. Avoid stimulants—such as coffee, ordinary tea (which contains caffeine), energy drinks, and the like—in these "tea breaks."

Meditation: It's not for everyone, but even the most down-to-earth among us can find a way to meditate that will suit us. Meditation teaches you how to control feelings of panic, to slow down your heartbeat, and to manage disconcerting emotions. You learn breathing techniques and to focus your thoughts in a way that totally resets your mind. You will instantly feel better and more alert after meditating, even if you only meditate for a few minutes. There are numerous apps that show you how you can integrate meditation into your daily routine.

A less formal exercise is just sitting and staring into space or at something like a plant (and knowing that it is okay to do so). As the joke about an old English farmworker in his own vegetable garden goes, "Sometimes I sits on my wheelbarrow and thinks, and sometimes I just sits."

Reflection: But you have a lot of wonderful new experiences, and it's important to savor these and let them sink in, because before you know it, your newborn is a few months old. Each day can bring many amazing and intense feelings, so cherish them. Sit on the couch with your baby, look at them, and think about all the wonderful times you have already spent together. Take a moment to really think about and cherish them.

You might also think about your own body, and what an amazing job it did. Or about the shared joys with your partner that your baby has brought you both.

Mindfulness: You may have heard of mindfulness therapies. These are ways of helping people who are, for instance, anxious. Essentially, they focus on the here and now, such as sitting comfortably just focusing on your own slow breathing or something else that is immediate. Focusing on breathing can be very helpful.

Breathing and "Breath-FS": We breathe all day long and take it for granted. We rarely take time to focus on our breathing. Make sure your baby is in a safe place first, so you don't have to keep opening your eyes to check on them. Then sit down quietly, close your eyes, and concentrate on your breathing. Breathe deeply in and out 10 times. Your heartbeat will slow down. Think of nothing but your breathing.

Taking a "breath-FS" has an even greater effect. This exercise is based on the fact that inhaling is similar to putting tension on your body (think about it: you hold your breath when you lift something heavy) and exhaling releases that tension (when you have a fright, you hold your breath; and when you relax, you breathe out again). To release the most tension possible through breathing, say FFFFFF while breathing out. When you have almost completely exhaled, say SSSSS. You will exhale more deeply than you usually do. As you completely exhale, hold it for a moment before breathing in again. Take 10 breaths saying FFFFSSS and you will instantly feel more relaxed than before.

Music: Much classical music relaxes, even if it's not to your taste. Try to listen to one or two pieces. Many Mozart works are particularly good for this.

Dancing: Or put on your favorite music and dance around your living room. Music and dancing are good stress releasers. You can really feel yourself let go and enjoy the moment. You can even dance with your baby in your arms!

Puttering: Some people find it relaxing to do simple tasks that require little or no thought but are satisfying, and to do them without rushing, just enjoying the simple pleasures.

Exercise: With modern lifestyles, it is a cliché to say we do not exercise enough. But many people don't, and it is not only our physical health that suffers. Exercise is now often "prescribed" as a treatment for mild depression and anxiety. For many of us, simply going for a walk can be relaxing; again, we are doing something simple, active, and natural.

Oxygen: It is so very important to unwind, and surely everyone is aware of how calming it is to take a walk, especially in the countryside. A quick walk can replenish your oxygen, and it's something you can do with your baby, family, or on you own. Fifteen minutes is usually enough to get that oxygen boost. That vacuum cleaner will just have to wait, that housekeeping can be done later; you are your number one priority.

Prioritize: So, you're too busy to think about yourself, as almost all parents say at some point. But let's be honest: it often simply comes down to changing your priorities. There is nothing more important than you and your health; your baby and your family depend on your being well. So, don't forget to take those anchor moments. They don't take much time. Setting priorities does not necessarily mean that you have to exclude things; it's simply about doing the most important things first. If you are stubbornly convinced that you really do not have any time for yourself or for those quiet moments, set yourself a challenge. Write down all the things you have to do that are "more important" than taking time for yourself. Then read your list, and be honest: are they really so much more important than you?

Take a Longer Break: You and your partner, often with the assistance of others, can help each other to look after yourselves. Other family and friends can also be involved in whatever ways feel appropriate for you. Remember, children are brought up not just by parents but, as someone once said, "by the village." That starts from birth.

Most babies can happily be looked after for short periods by other people. But this person should be well known to your baby and your baby should have seen that the person has your "stamp of approval." That means that these other people, often grandparents, other relations, or very close friends, will have spent a lot of time, hours and hours, with your baby and you together, so your baby can see you trust that person. This is always important, but especially so after about six months, which is after the relationships regression period.

Having this help can give you a break to look after yourself. This is natural: babies are born with the expectation of having one or two special caretakers, but also of having a few other caretakers who can help from time to time for brief periods.

But expect to find it difficult to leave your baby, however much you trust the other person! That's natural, too.

What to do when you have a little more time? Your list may be a long one, although you may well find yourself at a loss and be thinking about your baby. Here we shall give just a few suggestions specific to relaxing and "recharging your batteries."

Don't Forget Talking: Just talking about your baby with your partner can help the reflection process and promote sharing and consolidating of feelings and memories.

Sometimes relationships get neglected in the effort of looking after your baby. Spending time together, just you and your partner, can be important in keeping the relationship close. And that is good for your baby.

Sport: Playing sports helps some people relax. Some prefer team sports; others, solo or one-on-one. Whichever is your preferred activity, it helps relax you, and reminds you of the other parts of yourself that are not focused on your baby, and that will help you focus all the better on your baby.

Massage: Massages make you feel good in your skin. They ground you. The nicest thing, of course, is to visit a good massage therapist who will treat you from head to toe, but if you don't have the luxury to do that, you can massage yourself. Spread out your fingers, grasp your head in your hands, and massage it. Close your eyes and relax. Or massage your feet and your ankles. A well-known saying reminds us of the importance of "keeping our feet on solid ground"; feet are key to grounding and calming ourselves.

⚓ THREE ANCHORS A DAY KEEPS THE STRESS AT BAY!

Try to incorporate three anchor moments into each day—one in the morning, one in the afternoon, and one in the evening. Do what suits you. Just because your baby is asleep or quiet does not mean you have to rush about doing jobs or thinking you have to stimulate your baby. You want to do the best for your baby, but it is important to have time to focus on your own well-being, and that will help you help your baby. It is not selfish to do so—quite the opposite. It is natural for moms to "slow up" after their baby is born; this is an important natural way of helping them go at baby's pace. Go with the flow of it.

YOUR REGRESSION PERIOD

Just as your baby goes through the stress of each regression period, so you are going through a period of major change. And just as a regression period stresses different babies differently, having a baby stresses different parents differently.

Postpartum Anxiety

We hope the "anchor moments" will help you find some calm during a very stressful time. You should be aware, however, that normal anxieties and stress can sometimes take on a more extreme form and affect how you function. You will perhaps not be surprised to hear that 1 in 5 women experience this type of anxiety, because having a baby, in itself, tests their stress limits to the maximum. And yet, postpartum anxiety is not readily discussed. It is also difficult to recognize and hard to distinguish from the normal stress and worries parents go through.

At some point, almost every parent worries that they will drop their child when going down the stairs, so how do you differentiate between normal anxiety and the type of irrational fear you have when you are suffering from postpartum anxiety? On top of that, there is no rigid line between normal, tolerable stress, and a stress level that is too high.

Characteristics of postpartum anxiety are:

- The worrying thoughts are present continually or frequently; they control your thoughts, to a certain degree.

- You may have panic attacks: you are suddenly overwhelmed by anxieties and fears, and they control your mind and even your body at times.

- You may feel constantly restless, irritated, and rushed.

- You may have difficulty in getting to sleep, or wake often even when your baby is not crying.

- You may feel stress physically: pressure on your chest, extremely tense muscles, churning feelings in the stomach, or queasiness.

If you recognize yourself here and you are plagued by unsettling thoughts and anxieties that seem to be taking the upper hand, be reassured that there is usually nothing to fear. Parents who worry they may leave their baby behind somewhere generally never do. Parents who are concerned about accidently hurting their baby usually don't hurt them. Another reassuring fact is that many parents experience these feelings. As mentioned earlier, studies have indicated that 1 in 5 women and roughly 1 in 10 men may experience some form of postpartum anxiety or postpartum depression. Because, let's not forget: you are both going through major changes and today's men are just as big a part of parenting as women are and go through it all, too. Men also have emotions and feel doubts and stress.

WARNING

If you see yourself facing what feels like overwhelming anxieties and you are finding it difficult to cope, then reach out for help. You need support, and your baby and partner will only benefit if you are feeling at your best. The quicker you get help, the easier it will be to clear those thoughts from your mind. The longer you walk around with them, the more they will pull you down. Talk to your friends and family about how you are feeling and clearly tell them that you need some support and that what you are feeling is more than normal anxiety. Go to your doctor and ask for advice. Talking anonymously on online chat groups can help. Look for the help you need and don't be embarrassed to ask for it.

Postpartum Depression

There are times when the anxieties and stress go even further, and then we are talking about postpartum depression—when those occasional concerns and worries have become constant and overwhelming. Postpartum depression is similar to depression that can occur in any phase of life. Characteristics are:

- Moods of despondency

- Crying fits

- Feeling empty or dead inside

- No interest in your baby, or even a dislike of them

- Touchiness, irritation, feelings of aggression

- Fretting

- Lack of self-confidence, feeling of helplessness

Postpartum depression can also be accompanied by postpartum anxiety. And just to make it a little more complicated, not all doctors and scientists agree about the term "postpartum." Some say that the essential difference between postpartum depression and another type of depression is the hormonal aspect, and therefore the term "postpartum depression" only applies to women. Others believe that because testosterone levels in men who are heavily involved in their partner's pregnancy decrease in the initial period after the birth, men can also be affected by postpartum depression. And another group states that postpartum depression doesn't necessarily have anything to do with hormones because parents of adopted children can also suffer from it. Whatever term or cause we decide to pin on it, many parents come to feel depressed.

If you are suffering from depression, you should seek professional help. And take care of yourself as best you can.

THE MOST IMPORTANT TIP OF ALL!

Your life is changing. Period. Things will never be the same again after giving birth. There's no point in trying to pretend that you can simply carry on as before, just with a little one in tow. Life simply doesn't work that way. Accept that your life has changed and that you will need to get used to the new situation and that you, both of you, will have to rediscover your life and make it yours again. You may have less time for things you used to do and realize you can no longer spontaneously pop out of the house now that your baby has come along. Nowadays, it takes you at least 10 minutes to pack everything up and then check you've not forgotten anything. And you will not be the first, or the last, parent to get a whiff of a dirty diaper just as you take a step outside. Life is different. It's blessed, but let's be honest: you also have to get used to every new blessing that comes your way, and that takes time.

Newborn:
Welcome to
the World

Watch any new parent when they hold their baby for the first time. Chances are, they will follow a particular pattern. First, they will run their fingertips through the baby's hair. Then they will run a finger around the baby's head and over their face. After this, they will feel the baby's nails, fingers, and toes. Then they will slowly move toward the baby's middle, along their arms, legs, and neck. Finally, they will touch the baby's tummy and chest. The way in which parents generally touch their newborn baby's body is often very similar, too. First, a new parent will touch their infant with only their fingertips, stroking and handling them very gently. Slowly but surely, as they become more comfortable, they will use all of their fingers and may sometimes squeeze their baby's skin. Finally, they will touch them with the palm of their hand. When they eventually dare to hold their baby by the chest or tummy, the new parent will be so delighted that they may exclaim what a miracle it is that they have produced something as precious as this.

Ideally, this discovery process should occur as close to birth as possible, but don't worry if your baby is not ready to be held right away. Sometimes there are medical reasons to hold off on this, and it doesn't mean you will not be able to bond in the same way. Whenever you hold your baby for the first time, it will be one of the most special moments of your lives. After a mother and father's first encounter with their baby, they will no longer be afraid to pick them up, turn them around, or put them down. They will know how their little one feels to the touch.

Every baby looks and feels different. Try holding someone else's baby and you will notice it's a strange experience. You have become so accustomed to your own baby that you forget all babies are different. It will take you a minute or two to get used to it.

GOOD TO KNOW

- Most mothers feel extremely close to their newborn baby in the first hours after birth, but the experience can be overwhelming. This feeling of closeness can happen more gradually but when it does, mothers are extremely perceptive about their babies' needs at that moment.

- When it's possible, if fathers can also hold their baby in the first hours after birth, they build a strong bond with their baby.

- Most babies are wide awake during this period. They are aware of their surroundings, they turn toward quiet sounds, and they fix their gaze on the face that happens to hover above them.

TAKE CHARGE EARLY

As we said in the preface: you will never forget those first moments and days with your baby. They make a deep impression on you and they are also essential for bonding with your baby. This is your time. Think about yourself and your brand-new family. Be sure to speak up if you want to have your baby near you, or if you want to be alone with them for a while. You decide how often you want to pick up and cuddle your infant. Unless there are medical complications, don't worry about the social rules of "how it should be done," or take others' opinions too much on board.

"I felt very possessive when my daughter was being passed from one person to the next, but I kept it to myself. I now wish I had spoken up."
About Laura, newborn

"With my first child, I was so concerned with other people's feelings that I often couldn't breastfeed how and when I wanted to. That's all changed. This is my baby and my breast in my home. It's up to me how I nurse my baby."
About Victoria, newborn

"I became very possessive of my son and I really didn't like other people holding him too often and too long. It was secretly happy when he cried in their arms and then stopped the moment I held him."
About Kevin, newborn

DO REMEMBER

Cuddle, rock, caress, and massage your baby when they are in a good mood, because this is the best time to find out what suits them and what relaxes them most. When you know their preferences, you will be able to use these methods to comfort them later on when they are upset. If you only cuddle, rock, caress, and massage them when they are in a bad mood, your "comforting" can cause them to cry even longer and louder when you try to comfort them in such a way at a later time.

GETTING TO KNOW AND UNDERSTAND YOUR BABY

As a mother, you are intrigued by your baby. In some ways, you already know them. After all, they have been with you for the past nine months, but once they are born it is different—totally different, in fact. You see your baby for the first time, and your baby also finds themselves in completely new surroundings. You look for familiar traits in your tiny newborn, ones you were used to when they were in your belly.

Seeing, hearing, smelling, and feeling your baby during those first few days has a tremendous impact on the parent-child relationship. Most parents instinctively know how important these intimate moments are. They want to experience everything their baby does. Just looking at their child gives them immense pleasure. They want to watch them when they sleep and listen to them breathe. They want to be there when baby wakes up. They want to caress them, cuddle them, and smell them whenever they feel like it.

> *"My son's breathing changes whenever he hears a sudden noise or sees a light. When I first noticed this irregular breathing, I was really concerned, but then I realized he was just reacting to sound and light. Now I don't worry about it at all. I think it's wonderful to see when his breathing changes."*
> **About Bob, newborn**

Most mothers consider what they experienced during their pregnancy. Is their baby the peaceful little person that they expected them to be? Do they kick at certain times of the day as they did before they were born? Do they have a special bond with their dad? Do they recognize his voice? Often parents want to "test" their baby's reactions. They want to figure out the best way to do things. They want to get to know their baby for themselves, how to respond to them, and how their baby responds in turn. Parents will appreciate advice, but not rules and regulations. And when they are right about their baby's likes and dislikes, they are pleased, as it shows how well they know their baby. This increases their self-confidence as parents and they will feel they are able to cope with their baby on their own when they take them home.

A WORD ABOUT SLEEP

Sleep: only five letters, but you only notice the massive impact of sleep on your life once you've had a baby. . . . Every day we get hundreds of emails from parents from all over the world, and most are about sleep. Or rather, about their baby not sleeping, not sleeping enough, or sleeping restlessly. Fathers, mothers, brothers, and sisters will all notice: when a baby arrives, their sleep patterns are disturbed. As a new parent, no doubt you would love a magic formula to make your baby fall asleep at night or a calendar to reveal what to expect and when. But we must disappoint you right now: there is no such list. We're not saying this to discourage you, but to remind you that when you're looking out for your baby's best interests, you might have to sacrifice your own comfort. The reasons?

- Babies have different sleep needs than we do. And in case you haven't noticed, a baby's sleep needs and sleep cycle and ours are like fire and water: they don't mix that well.

- A quick fix is rarely a good long-term solution.

- An average number of hours doesn't say anything about your baby in your circumstances.

After you read this "spoiler" and you feel that you've had cold water thrown on you: don't worry, there is hope, and we have a lot of good news to share with you. We hope to give you an insight into the challenging but beautiful and healthy sleeping pattern of your baby. We will give you tips that will help your baby, as long as your baby is open to them and you let your baby set the pace. But what we really want to get across is how important it is to value the natural development of the sleep process without intervening.

We will focus on the link between sleep and leaps in the next chapter, to give you an insight into the sleep development of your baby, just as we do about your baby's mental development. Armed with this information, you can make the right choice for your baby, yourself, and your family.

I've discovered a game. It's called "never sleep again."
The steps are: have a baby. That's it . . . that's the game.
Admittedly it's not a very good one. —**Instagram post**

YOUR BABY GETS TO KNOW AND UNDERSTAND YOU

During the first weeks after birth, your baby slowly becomes familiar with the world around them. You will get to know each other more intimately than anyone else in your shared world at this time. Your baby will soon be taking their first leap in their mental development.

But before you are able to understand what your baby will experience at five weeks after the due date, when they take their first leap, you need to know how your newborn baby perceives their world and the role physical contact plays in that world of perception.

YOUR BABY'S NEW WORLD

Babies are interested in the world around them from the moment they are born. They look and listen, taking in their surroundings. They try very hard to focus their eyes, which is why babies often look cross-eyed as they strain to get a better look. Sometimes they tremble or gasp in sheer exhaustion from the effort. Parents often say their baby looks at them as if they are staring, transfixed with interest. And that is exactly what they are doing.

A baby has an excellent memory, and they are quick to recognize voices, people, and even toys. They also clearly anticipate specific situations, such as bath time, cuddle time, or nursing time!

Even at this age, a baby mimics facial expressions. Try sticking your tongue out at them while you sit and talk to them, or open your mouth wide as if you are going to call out. Make sure that they are really looking at you when you try this, and give them plenty of time to respond. A young baby is able to "tell" their parents just how they feel—whether they are happy, angry, or surprised. And they use body language, which their parents soon understand. Besides which, a baby will make it perfectly clear that they expect to be understood. If they aren't, they will cry angrily or sob as if heartbroken.

Your newborn baby already has preferences. Most babies prefer to look at people rather than toys. You will also find that if presented with two playthings, they are able to express a preference by fixing their gaze on one of them.

Babies are quick to respond to encouragement. They will enjoy being praised for the lovely smell of their skin, their looks, and their actions. You will hold their interest for longer if you shower them with compliments.

Young babies can already see, hear, smell, taste, and feel a variety of things. And they are able to remember these sensations. However, a newborn's perception of these sensations is very different from the way they will experience them as they get older.

WHAT BABIES SEE

Scientists and doctors used to believe that newborn babies were unable to see. It's not true. Your newborn can see perfectly clearly, up to a distance of about 8 inches. Beyond that, their vision is probably blurred. Sometimes they will also have difficulty focusing both eyes on whatever they are looking at, but once they have, they can stare at the object intently. And they will even stop moving briefly. All their attention will be focused on the object. If they are very alert, they will sometimes be able to follow a moving toy with their eyes and/or head. They can do this whether the object is moving horizontally or vertically. The important thing is that the object is moved very slowly.

The object that your baby will be able to follow best is a simple pattern with the basic characteristics of a human face—two large dots at the top for the eyes and one below for the mouth. Babies are able to do this within an hour of birth. Many of them have their eyes wide open and are very alert. Parents are often completely fascinated by their newborn baby's big, beautiful eyes. It is possible that babies are attracted to anything that even vaguely resembles a human face when they are this young.

Your baby will be particularly interested in colorful objects, rather than dull, plain surfaces. They will probably prefer red above all the other colors. The brighter the color contrast, the more interested they will be. They prefer defined stripes and corners to round shapes.

WHAT BABIES HEAR

Your newborn baby can already clearly distinguish between different sounds. They will recognize their mother's voice shortly after birth. They may like music, the hum of an engine, and soft, rhythmic drumming. This makes sense because these sounds are already familiar to them. In the womb, they were surrounded by the constant thump, rustle, grumble, and wheeze of their mother's veins, heart, lungs, stomach, and intestines. They also have a built-in interest in people's voices and find them soothing. Your baby recognizes the difference between deep and high-pitched (female) voices. High-pitched sounds will draw their attention more quickly. Adults sense this and speak to babies in high-pitched voices, so there is no need to feel embarrassed by your "oochy-koochy-cooing." Your baby is also able to differentiate between soft and loud sounds and does not like sudden loud noises. Some babies are easily frightened, and if this is the case for your baby, it is important that you don't do anything that will frighten them.

WHAT BABIES SMELL

Your new baby is very sensitive to smells. They do not like pungent or sharp odors. These smells will make them overactive. They will try to turn away from the source of the smell, and they may start to cry, too. Your baby can smell the difference between your body scent and that of other people. If they are presented with several items of worn clothing, they will turn toward the article that you have worn.

WHAT BABIES TASTE

Your baby can already distinguish between several different flavors. They have a distinct preference for sweet things and will dislike anything that tastes sour or acidic. If something tastes bitter, they will spit it out as fast as they can.

WHAT BABIES FEEL

Your baby can sense changes in temperature. They can feel heat, which they put to good use when searching for a nipple if it is not put in their mouth, since the nipple is much warmer than the breast. They simply move their head in the direction of the warmest spot, as long as their face is already near.

Your baby can also sense cold. But if they are allowed to become cold, they will be unable to warm themselves, because at this age they can't shiver to get warm as a means of controlling their own body temperature. Their parents need to consider their body warmth. For instance, it's not very sensible to take a baby in their stroller for a long walk through snow and ice, no matter how well wrapped up they are, because they may become too cold. Better to keep them bundled up against you so your own body warms them. If your baby shows distress of any kind, hurry inside where it is warm.

Your baby is extremely sensitive to being touched. Generally, they love skin contact, whether it's soft or firm. Find out what your baby prefers. They will usually enjoy a body massage in a nice warm room, too. Physical contact is simply the best possible comfort and amusement for them. Try to find out what type of contact makes your baby sleepy or alert, since you can put this knowledge to good use in troublesome times.

YOUR NEW BABY'S SENSES
Your Baby Experiences the World as a Mishmash of Sensations

Your baby cannot process all the impressions sent to the brain by the senses as adults can. They experience the world in their own baby way. We smell a scent, see the flower giving off the scent, feel the soft petals, and hear a bee buzzing toward the flower. We can distinguish between these senses, we know where they originate. Your baby experiences the world as a mishmash of sensations that changes drastically as soon as a single element changes. They receive these impressions but cannot distinguish among them. They do not realize that their world is made up of signals from individual senses and that each sense conveys messages about a single aspect of it.

They Perceive the World and Themselves as One and the Same

Your baby is unable to make a distinction between sensations that originate within their own body and those that come from outside it. They assume everyone and everything else feels what their body feels. If your baby is hungry, warm, wet, tired, or happy, so is the world. To them, the world is one big smell-sound-and-cuddle sensation, a whole.

Because a baby perceives the world in this way, it is often difficult to discover the reason that they are crying. It could be anything inside or out of them. The baby's crying may drive parents to distraction when faced with this dilemma, and they can lose confidence.

Your Baby's New Tool Kit

If you were to experience the world in the same way your baby does, you, too, would be incapable of acting independently. You would not know that you have hands to grasp things with and a mouth to suck with. Only when you understand these things will you be able to do things deliberately.

This does not mean, however, that newborn babies are completely incapable of reacting to the world. Fortunately, Mother Nature has equipped your baby with several special features to compensate for these "shortcomings" and help them survive this initial period.

Their Reflexes Tell Them What to Do

Babies have several reflex reactions to keep them safe. For example, a newborn baby will automatically turn their head to one side to breathe freely when lying facedown. However, you won't want to put your baby on their belly and walk away, especially not at first. Place them across your lap or on your chest and admire the way they settle in. In some ways, this reflex is similar to the way a puppet reacts to its strings being pulled. They do not stop to think, "I'm going to turn my head"—it simply happens. As soon as a baby learns to think and respond, this reflex disappears. It is a perfect system.

Newborn babies also turn their heads toward sound. This automatic reaction ensures that a baby will shift their attention to the nearest place of interest. For many years, doctors overlooked this reaction because a newborn's response to sound is delayed. It takes 5 to 7 seconds before a baby starts to move their head, and it takes another 3 to 4 seconds to complete the movement. This reflex disappears when a baby is between one and two months old.

They have the sucking reflex. As soon as the mouth of a hungry newborn comes in contact with an object, their mouth will close around it, and they will start to suck. This reflex provides the baby with an incredibly strong sucking ability. It disappears as soon as a baby no longer needs to suckle.

A baby has the gripping reflex. If you want your baby to grasp your finger, just stroke the palm of their hand. They will automatically grab your finger. If you do the same with their feet, they will use their toes to grab your finger. This gripping reflex is thought to date back to prehistoric times, when hominid mothers were covered with thick body hair. Because of this reflex, babies were able to cling to their mother's hair shortly after birth. A baby will use this gripping reflex during the first two months of life, especially if they sense that you want to put them down when they would much rather stay with you!

A baby shows a reaction called the Moro reflex when they are frightened. It is more commonly known as the startle reflex. They arch their back, throw their head back, and wave their arms and legs about, outward at first, then inward, before crossing them across their chest and stomach. They look as if they are trying to grab at something during a fall.

All of these baby reflexes disappear when they are replaced by voluntary responses. But there are other automatic reflexes that remain for life, such as breathing, sneezing, coughing, blinking, and jerking back a hand from a hot surface.

Their Cries Get Your Attention

You likely don't think of your baby's cries as a reflex, but they are the first line of defense in situations when they can't do anything to solve a problem, such as a wet diaper. In these cases, your baby employs another strategy: they wait until *someone else* rectifies the situation, because they are unable to do it for themselves. If no one helps them, the baby will cry incessantly until they are completely exhausted.

"My son's crying fits started in his second week. He cried day and night, even though he was nursing and growing steadily. I thought he was perhaps bored. Last week, I put a rattle in his crib. It seems to be helping. He was certainly crying less!"
About Paul, 4th week

Their Appearance Melts Your Heart

In order to survive, your baby has to rely on someone else to attend to their every need, morning, noon, and night. They usually have a good set of lungs to inform you when it's time to jump in, but luckily nature has also supplied them with a powerful weapon that they continually put to use—their appearance.

Nothing is cuter than a baby. Their extraordinarily large head makes up almost one-third of their total length. Their eyes and forehead are also "too big," and their cheeks are "too chubby" in relation to the rest of their body. Their cute looks are endearing. Designers of dolls, soft toys, and comic books are quick to copy them. This look sells! This is exactly how your baby sells themselves, too. They are sweet, tiny, and helpless—a little cutie, just begging for attention. Their cute appearance charms you into picking them up, cuddling them, and taking care of them.

Throughout the world, babies have been seen looking as if they are smiling before they are six weeks old. Smiling babies have even been filmed in the womb. Newborn babies "smile" when touched, when a breath of fresh air brushes their cheeks, when they hear human voices or other sounds, when they see faces hovering over their cribs, or simply when they are full of milk and feeling content. Sometimes they even smile in their sleep. Parents are very enthusiastic when they see this and are quick to call it a smile. And it looks like one. Later on, when your baby starts using their smile in social contact, you will see the difference. Those initial smiles change from something superficial, almost robot-like, into social smiles. But that doesn't detract from the joy those smiles bring.

Your Baby's Biggest Need

Even before they were born, your baby perceived their world as one whole. At birth, they left their familiar surroundings, and for the first time were exposed to all kinds of unknown, completely new things. This new world is made up of many new sensations, things they couldn't experience in the womb. Suddenly, they are able to move freely, sense heat and cold, hear a whole range of different and loud noises, see bright lights, and feel clothes wrapped around their body. Besides these impressions, they also have to breathe by themselves and get used to drinking milk, and their digestive organs have to process this new food, too. All these things are new to them. Because they suddenly have to cope with these enormous changes in lifestyle, it's easy to understand why they need to feel safe and secure and why they desire physical contact.

We've talked about how babies react to their environment and what nature has provided to help them, but what can you do to help them feel safe and secure?

BABIES GET BORED, TOO

Your baby is not yet able to amuse themselves. Lively, temperamental babies in particular make no secret about wanting some action as soon as they are awake. Here are some ways to keep your baby entertained.

Try to figure out what your baby likes. Explore the house with them. Give them the opportunity to see, hear, smell, and touch whatever they find interesting. Explain the items you come across while exploring. No matter what it is, they will enjoy listening to your voice. Pretty soon, they will start recognizing objects themselves.

- Have a quiet "chat." Your baby enjoys listening to your voice. But if you also have a podcast or video playing in the background, they will have difficulty concentrating on your voice. Although young babies are able to make a distinction between different voices when they hear them one at a time, they cannot distinguish one from the other when hearing them simultaneously.

- Place interesting objects in convenient places for your baby to look at when they are awake. At this age, they won't be able to search for them by themselves, so for them it's "out of sight, out of mind."

- Experiment with music. Try to discover their favorite music and play it to them. They may find it to be very soothing.

Say It With Cuddles!

Close physical contact is the best way of imitating your baby's secure world inside the womb. It makes them feel safe. After all, your womb hugged their body, and your movements kneaded it, as far back as they can remember. It was their home. They were part of whatever took place in there—the rhythmic beating of your heart, the flow of your blood, and the rumbling of your stomach. Therefore, it makes perfect sense that they will enjoy feeling the old, familiar physical contact and hearing those well-known sounds once more. It is their way of "touching base."

TOUCH: SIMPLY THE BEST COMFORT

Besides food and warmth, nothing is more important to your infant than snuggling close to their mommy or daddy during the first four months of their life. As long as they experience lots of physical contact, their development will not be delayed, even if you don't have much opportunity to play with them.

- A young baby generally loves lying close to you and being carried around. At the same time, this is also a good opportunity for them to learn to control their body. If you really want your hands free, then carry them in a baby sling. A baby can lie down in a baby sling, so you can use one shortly after birth.

- Another idea is to give them a relaxing massage. Make sure the room is warm. Pour some baby oil into your hands and softly massage every part of their naked body. This is a nice way of helping them grow accustomed to their body, and it will make them wonderfully drowsy.

- At this age, a baby loves to be picked up, cuddled, caressed, and rocked. They may even enjoy soft pats on their back. They can't get enough physical contact now. Don't worry about whether you're doing the right thing—they will soon let you know what they like best and what comforts them most. In the meantime, they are learning that they have a wonderful home base to which they can safely return when they are upset, and they will need that when they make a leap in their development.

Sleeps and Leaps

As we mentioned in the previous chapter, questions about sleep come to us from parents all over the world. We hope this chapter will help you navigate that important subject. To remind you again:

- Babies have different sleep needs than we do.

- A quick fix is rarely a good long-term solution.

- There's no such thing as "an average number of hours," since every baby is unique.

SLEEP IS IMPORTANT!

Few adults really get enough sleep, whether they have children or not, even though they know how important it is for them. Good sleep contributes to concentration, healthy weight, healthy skin and hair, a positive outlook, and we could go on. Yet good, consistent sleep is elusive. Maybe it's because we can still function even when we steal an hour or two from our body's sleep requirements. Studies have shown time and again that we need at least seven to eight hours of sleep per night, and sometimes even more. We are, of course, talking about consecutive sleeping hours. So why is it hard to find our own sleep time during these hours? You can guess what's coming . . .

Just like us, your baby needs sleep. Without enough sleep, they don't develop as well as they should physically, emotionally, and mentally. The quantity of sleep your baby needs depends on their age and personality. Some children need far more sleep than others, just like adults. But one thing's for sure: the sleep rhythm is faster; the sleep cycle is shorter—and that makes their sleep needs very different from those of an adult. If a baby wakes up after a few hours and then falls asleep again, they had a perfect sleep, if you are only looking at their needs from their viewpoint! As an adult, you quickly tend to think that your little one didn't have enough sleep and that not sleeping has immediate, negative consequences for their development. It doesn't have to be like that at all: the idea that your baby has a problem comes up because we, as adults, project our sleep needs and rhythm onto the baby, and that is unfair.

FROM SLEEP PROBLEMS TO DIFFERENT SLEEPING

In this book, we will speak about "different" sleep. Yes, we get that in day-to-day life, it may feel as though the sleeping "problem" is your baby's, but what if you turn it around and see that you're the one who's going to need to adjust, at least at first? It is not fair to the baby to call their completely normal sleeping behavior problematic. That's why we talk about "different" sleep.

Your Sleep and Your Baby's Sleep: Not a Great Match

Your baby and you have different sleeping needs, and they clash. Usually you are the one who suffers, and not your baby (fortunately). Your baby's sleep requirements often indirectly define your sleep rhythm, and that can be really difficult. Your little one is perfectly fine waking up three times a night (it's normal during the first 12 weeks, in fact). But you have to get out of bed, disturbing your sleeping cycle, and then fall asleep again, leaving you completely exhausted in the morning. Often, you likely feel that you're falling asleep just as your baby is waking up again. Not to mention that your morning starts earlier than before you were a parent. If you also have an older child who also wakes during the night, you are dealing with three different sleep rhythms, sleep cycles, and sleep requirements, and it becomes even more difficult for you and your partner, often not so much for your children. If we don't sleep enough, we become moody, irritated—in short, extremely tired, so tired that it will affect our daily life in a negative way. Of course, you need to prevent this, or at least minimize it. If you understand your baby's sleep behavior, know what to expect, and what to do to make it easier for yourself, you prevent real sleep problems. There are dozens of books that offer solutions, and we encourage you to explore those. Here we just want to reassure you that it's okay to feel frustrated and tired, and to suggest some reasons behind the cycles that cause these issues.

Now and then, it is time for a reality check. Before you, there have been countless generations of parents and babies who survived this. You will, too!

NICE TO KNOW AND NEED TO KNOW

During the months after having a baby, 90 percent of parents have sleep problems. It's not you. It's not your baby. It's just nature.

Day-Night Rhythms and Sleep-Wake Rhythm

To understand what your baby's sleep entails, you also need to understand what "sleeping" is. Sleeping is much more than closing your eyes and letting go. Sleep is a very complicated process that directly influences our health and development. To sleep as we adults do, you need the part of your brain that is not fully developed yet in babies, and that is the actual "problem."

When we think of the day-night rhythm, we automatically think of sleeping and waking up. But that sleep-wake rhythm is only one of the many day-night rhythms!

EXAMPLES OF DAY-NIGHT RHYTHMS IN ADULTS

- Change in the heart rate during the day and at night (faster during the day, slower at night)

- Change in temperature during the day and at night (drops slightly at dusk)

- Change in the volume of urine production (less at night)

- Production of the sleep hormone at night and decrease in the stress hormone at night

- Difference between day and night in the quantity of growth hormones or testosterone produced

- . . . And last, but not least: the sleep-wake rhythm

Our Biological Clock: Reset Every 24 Hours!

In the center of an adult brain is an element that underlies all those different day-night rhythms. That part of the brain is called the "biological clock" and has a rhythm of just under 24 hours that goes up and down (or "oscillates"), without outside influence. This part is connected to the eyes and registers when there is light and when it is night or day. And that's fine, because if the biological clock is left alone, it will progressively deviate more and more from the earth's light-dark cycle that lasts 24 hours. The biological clock is "reset" every day and runs in synchronicity with the earth's light-dark cycle.

Melatonin: The Sleep Hormone

One of the day-night rhythms in adults concerns the production of melatonin, a.k.a. the sleep hormone. Your brain (specifically, its pineal gland) produces this as soon as it gets dark. And when babies are born, they cannot yet produce that substance! Your body produces less of other substances, too, when you go to sleep; e.g., cortisol. Cortisol is a stress hormone that makes you alert. Once you produce less of it, you automatically relax more, and the decrease in this hormone makes sure you fall asleep and stay asleep more easily.

In short, to have a lovely night's rest, you need—among other things—a sleep-wake rhythm and the production of specific substances in the brain. When it's dark at night, you are sleepy; and when it's light during the day, you are awake. You let go, or on the contrary, you are alert. And you know what? Your newborn baby does not have that sleep-wake rhythm and hormonal regulation yet. Your baby is biologically not able to have a day-night rhythm until they are close to three months old. It's just not possible! That knowledge can be reassuring. You aren't doing anything wrong, nor is your baby doing anything wrong; it's just biologically impossible during the first weeks and months.

A Biological Process: The Development of a Sleep-Wake Rhythm

The question now is: when does a child have a full sleep-wake rhythm along with all the other day-night rhythms? That's why we have listed the various elements of a mature sleep-wake rhythm for you.

Pregnancy

In the womb, your baby does not yet contribute to a sleep-wake rhythm or other day-night rhythms. The day-night rhythms they display are caused by substances, such as melatonin, that enter their body through the mother's blood via the umbilical cord.

Halfway Through Pregnancy

The first form of the biological clock appears in your baby's brain halfway through pregnancy, but it is still far from complete. It seems that the eyes already have a connection to the part of the brain that we call the biological clock.

BIOLOGICAL CLOCK AND PREMATURE BABIES

The fact that the biological clock emerges halfway through the pregnancy is important to know for very premature babies. Because the foundation of day-night rhythms is already present in a certain form and the eyes are probably already connected to the biological clock, premature babies could get a certain day-night rhythm earlier than full-term babies. That's why there is a lot of debate as to whether or not it is better for premature babies to quickly get used to the light and darkness of day and night.

Newborn Babies

After cutting the umbilical cord, there is no longer a melatonin supply through the mother's blood, there is no reserve, and a baby is not able to produce it yet. A newborn baby does not display day-night rhythms yet, and that's why the sleep-wake rhythm is chaotic. Short sleeps, long sleeps, in daytime, at night; your baby sleeps when they feel like it. The difference between dark and light has no effect (yet) on them when it comes to producing sleep hormones.

Birth Up to Six Weeks

Your baby takes naps spread over the 24 hours of the day. You do not notice a difference in the hours and times they sleep during the day or at night. They are not yet guided by the presence of light or darkness. They sleep when they want to sleep.

Week One

The day-night rhythm of your baby's body temperature starts. You don't notice that as a sleep-wake rhythm, but it is the first step in that direction. To obtain a good sleep-wake rhythm, your baby first needs the day-night rhythm of the body temperature. You could say that the day-night rhythm of the body temperature is the mold in which the sleep-wake rhythm is shaped.

Six Weeks

Your baby now has the foundations of a waking rhythm. Not a sleep rhythm yet! The waking rhythm develops earlier than the sleep rhythm. But the sleep-wake rhythm has developed a bit further. Also, researchers have already found a small concentration of melatonin (the substance produced at night to sleep through the night) in seven-week-old babies. You will notice that the times of being really awake and the times of being tired cannot be so clearly distinguished anymore. Whereas, at first, your baby's wakeful and sleepy times were spread out in complete disarray over the day and night, those short chaotic moments now seem to get closer together. This is far from a true pattern, but the process has started!

Two Months

Your baby begins to develop the very first precursors of a sleep-wake rhythm. You won't notice that immediately, but it is great to know that, biologically, the night rhythm has started in the developmental process! Don't expect miracles, but observe the subtle progress in the development of a healthy day-night rhythm.

Three Months

The time your baby sleeps during the day decreases and the time they sleep at night increases. Always remember: right now, it's only about the number of minutes, the sum of time. This doesn't say anything about how often your baby wakes up. Even if a baby sleeps six hours (and that almost never happens), it doesn't mean that these are consecutive hours. In short, your baby wakes up a few times, and that is completely normal at this age. At a biochemical level, you can only measure a day-night rhythm if it concerns melatonin production.

Three to Six Months

A pattern increasingly develops in the production of melatonin at night. From now on, a difference in cortisol levels between night and day can also be measured. From 15 weeks onward, you will notice that your baby has a clear sleep pattern over 24 hours. Your baby has set sleeping hours during the day and night. You will also notice that the new pattern acquired around three months will be greatly disturbed when they reach the fourth leap at about four months. Apart from that (temporary) disruption, it is great to see that your baby has started to develop a rhythm. But be warned, all this applies to the majority of babies, but . . . every baby is unique and there's nothing wrong if your baby doesn't yet have set sleeping and waking hours.

Actually, you can learn two important things here. First, a newborn baby can't sleep through the night yet, as they simply don't have a day-night rhythm—it is biologically impossible. Second, of all the different day-night rhythms (difference in body temperature, difference in heart rate, difference in urine production, difference in alertness, etc.), the sleep-wake rhythm that is so often important to parents always develops last. So your baby already has a number of day-night rhythms long before we notice them in the form of sleep.

DAY-NIGHT RHYTHMS: SLEEPING THROUGH THE NIGHT?

It's just not that simple. Every baby is different and every baby sleeps differently. Some fall asleep by themselves without waking you up. Those babies do not need you to comfort them if they wake up from time to time during the night. Other babies only sleep well if they are with you all the time. Why is that good to know? Because you then realize that any lists with times and averages are simply irrelevant, and you can't expect a young baby to sleep through the night. Lists with averages and times can be more frustrating than reassuring, and you could even say that they are not honest or respectful of your baby. These types of lists could suggest that your baby falls outside the margin and is "lacking." And, of course, that's not true.

Does anyone have daydreams about the revenge they will play on their kids when they're older? Like wake them up hourly, cry loudly in their ear, and play nursery rhymes on repeat for 12 hours? Frannie has been all sorts of crazy in the sleep department lately. —**Instagram post**

BABIES SLEEP DIFFERENTLY THAN WE DO

It's not just the day-night rhythm of babies that is different from ours; there also are numerous differences in the way we sleep and the way a baby sleeps. One of the major differences is your baby's sleep cycle. Those differences from ours exist for a reason: they are biological advantages for your little one and they help them survive. In short, you don't want to change the sleep cycle, even if that means that your baby wakes up in the night more often than you do. But it is still good to understand the background of the sleep cycle. You start to understand your baby's sleep behavior, and by understanding it, you get to know when you can put your baby down, or leave the room without them waking up and then having to start again from scratch. The biggest differences in the way babies and adults sleep are in the sleep cycle and the sleep phases.

Everyone has roughly two types of sleep: non-REM sleep (non-rapid eye movement) and REM sleep (rapid eye movement). The non-REM sleep is the tranquil sleep. We are not stimulating the brain in a special way, we are not busy processing things—we are just resting deeply. But then again, not all phases of the non-REM sleep are equally deep. Your child has three different non-REM sleep phases:

Non-REM Sleep Phase 1

Sleep is very light. You could almost call it a phase of very intense relaxation or lethargy. The eyes are shut, but it is very easy to wake from this phase. You can recognize that phase in yourself when your eyes are closing—when you nod off while watching a movie, for example. It is the phase just between being awake and asleep, but leaning more toward sleep.

Non-REM Sleep Phase 2

The body starts to reach "sleep status" in this phase. The heartbeat slows, the body temperature starts lowering slightly, and the muscles relax even more.

Non-REM Sleep Phase 3

This is the phase of very deep sleep. It is difficult to wake up in this phase. The body relaxes completely and the body temperature and heartbeat are considerably lower. This phase is followed by REM sleep.

REM: Extremely Important for Good Development!

The REM sleep is also called "active sleep," and that actually explains everything. During this phase, people sleep lightly and wake easily. Your mind is actively processing and learning. When you look at the eyes, you see just how active the mind is: the eyes move very fast, faster than you could move them when awake. Hence the name: rapid eye movement. The strange thing is that the rest of your body is completely at rest. The activity is really focused in your head at this time. It's the same for babies. Sometimes, you can even see the eyes move. That shows how actively your baby is processing everything in this sleep!

In the past, it was thought that the REM sleep was only important for processing your day in your dreams. But more recent research has increasingly shown many other crucial benefits of REM sleep in babies. During the REM sleep, the neurons in the brain are further stimulated. The blood flow to the brain almost doubles in REM sleep! That stimulation may well be essential to the creation of new brain connections. Therefore, the REM sleep is thought to hugely influence brain development.

There are "activity- or experience-independent" brain connections and "activity- or experience-dependent" brain connections. To put it more simply: for the first, you don't have to do anything (the independent variant); and for the other, you have to do or experience something (the dependent variant). A leap in mental development is an example of an independent variant. Your baby makes a leap, whether they want to or not, and the leaps will occur neither earlier nor later, no matter what you do. So, actually, you don't have to do anything. Those brain connections are generated spontaneously and that leads to the new ability, the new type of perception.

Those spontaneously generated brain connections are plentiful. If they are not used, they disappear again. But . . . the connections that are used remain. In other words: with appropriate stimulation, your baby maintains the many brain con-

nections that have been created. Or, as the saying goes: "Use it or lose it." As a parent, if you respond to the leaps and play the games that help your baby process the leaps and the skills they bring, they will keep as many brain connections as possible. These are of the dependent variant. They depend on your little one's activities and experiences. The good news is that if you facilitate your baby's learning efforts during the leaps, you will maintain as many brain connections as possible. Very good news when you consider that the creation of brain connections is especially crucial in those first two years.

REM SLEEP AND LEAPS

During a leap, most babies don't sleep as well as they normally do. The slightest thing wakes them. Parents say they daren't put their baby down, because their baby wakes up and the parents have to start all over again. In a leap, babies often do not seem to reach the restful, deep sleep. It may be that babies enjoy a relatively longer period in REM sleep during leaps in order to create new brain connections. So it's no wonder that your little one is woken by the slightest thing: they are in REM sleep, and humans wake more easily in that sleep. Give your child the chance to grab those extra periods of REM sleep, especially during the leaps. If they only want to do so on the familiar lap of a parent, let them. It is tempting to put them down for a while and quickly finish something you'd been planning to do, but just pick up a book instead. If your baby wakes up more relaxed, because they can more easily process the leaps after those superficial REM sleep-naps, it is not only they who benefit, but ultimately you and your family, too.

NON-REM + REM = SLEEP CYCLE

And now comes the first part in which you as a parent can really "do something." If you understand the theory and take the time to get to know your baby's sleep cycle, you will know when you can put your little one down without waking them. You then know when it is "safe" to leave the room. The sleep cycle is simply the non-REM sleep + REM sleep, one after the other. After these two, humans start the non-REM again, then the REM (second cycle), then the non-REM again, then the REM again (third cycle), until they wake.

Difference Between a Baby's and Adult's Sleep Cycle

Even though both babies and adults go through the same sleep cycle, the time duration differs enormously. Whereas a newborn baby has a cycle of some 40 minutes, and a baby a few months old (up to about nine months) has a sleep cycle of 50 to 60 minutes, an adult has one of 120 minutes. Also remember that the ratio of non-REM to REM is completely different in babies than in adults; babies spend more than twice as much time in REM sleep and much less time in non-REM sleep.

Even Children's Sleep Cycles Differ from Adults'

The change in sleep cycle is a progressive process. It takes years before your little one's sleep cycle looks like yours. It is only when children reach school age that their sleep cycle approaches ours, lasting some 90 to 100 minutes. The difference in the number of minutes someone spends in non-REM and REM sleep does not disappear after infancy, either. Even by the time your child is three years old, they still spend 50 percent of the time in REM sleep, whereas we are only in REM sleep for 20 percent of the time. So sleep is not something that you "fix" in infancy. It takes a lot of time before children sleep as we do. And that's as it should be, because the way babies sleep is good for them. It has survival benefits and makes them healthy and strong.

DID YOU KNOW...?

- Your baby wakes up more easily in REM sleep and when entering non-REM sleep.

- A baby spends more than twice as much time in REM sleep as adults do.

- Day-night rhythm is more than just being awake or asleep. It's physical. During sleep, the body temperature decreases, the heart rate slows, less urine is produced, the stress hormone levels drop, and there is increased blood supply to the brain.

- The non-REM sleep (nonactive sleep) has three phases.

- Non-REM + REM = sleep cycle.

- The sleep cycle is a lot shorter in babies than in adults.

- You experience several sleep cycles during the night.

- At the end of a sleep cycle, you wake up or a new sleep cycle begins.

SLEEP CYCLE

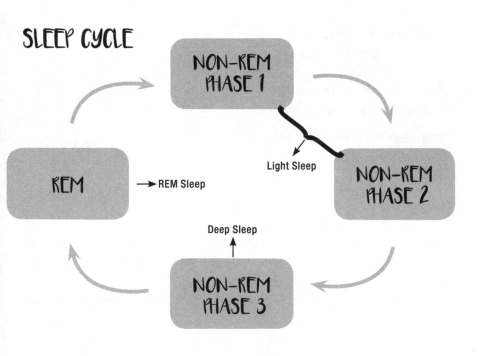

SLEEP CYCLE NEED-TO-KNOW

NON-REM SLEEP PHASE 1

- Sleeps very lightly.
- Eyes are closed.
- Very easy (extremely easy) to wake up.

Differences Between Baby and Adult

- This phase is a lot shorter in adults than in babies (only 2 to 4 percent of sleep time).
- In adults, this is often seen as lethargy or napping on the couch.
- Babies often only have a moment of non-REM sleep phase 1.

What It Means:

- The baby wakes up easily, so there isn't enough time to put them down or slip away.

REM SLEEP

- Active sleep.
- A lot of dreams in this phase.
- Body stationary, eyes moving a lot.
- Active brain stimulation.
- Creation of many brain connections.
- Blood supply to the brain doubles!

Differences Between Baby and Adult

- Babies in REM sleep twice as long.
- In babies, you see the eyes moving quickly under the eyelids.

Good to Know:

- REM sleep helps babies process leaps.
- Does your baby appear to have more short REM sleeps for an extended period of time during a leap? That is normal and good for them. Don't try to make them sleep longer or deeper.
- Your baby wakes up easily, so this is not the right time to put them down or sneak away.

NON-REM SLEEP PHASE 2

- Body relaxes more, feels limper.
- Heart rate slows.
- Body temperature decreases further.

Differences Between Baby and Adult
- An adult spends 45 to 55 percent of the time in this phase; a baby, much less than this.
- The older a child gets, the more time is spent in this phase and less in the REM phase.

Try This:
- Test whether your baby is already sleeping deeply enough to put them down/ leave the room, etc., by lifting an arm and "dropping" it. If it falls limply, your baby is in the end of phase 2 or even already in phase 3 and is deeply asleep. If the arm falls but is still "under control," not really limp yet, they are still in phase 2 and you have to be very careful when you put them down to leave the room. Or you have to wait a few minutes until phase 3 starts.

NON-REM SLEEP PHASE 3

- Deep sleep.
- The whole body relaxes.
- Sleep talking and sleepwalking are possible at the start of this phase.
- Possible nightmares and night terrors at the end of this phase .
- Even when you relax very deeply, this phase doesn't last very long.

Differences Between Baby and Adult
- Adults have a deeper and longer sleep in this phase.

Keep in Mind:
- It is now very easy to put your baby down to leave the room, etc. Your baby is in a deep sleep.
- This phase starts approximately halfway into the whole sleep cycle of a baby.
- Keep in mind that a new cycle starts after this phase and the sleep (if your baby does not wake up) becomes a light sleep again!

KEEP TRACK OF YOUR BABY'S SLEEP CYCLE

If you frequently "test" how long it takes until your baby sleeps deeply, how many minutes they sleep more lightly, and when they wake or continue to sleep, you can act on it. You will then know when to put your little one down or to leave the room to do something. Then, you know for how many minutes you must carry on quietly and when you can rest assured that you can start vacuuming without waking your baby. Don't forget, another rhythm starts with every leap, so you will have to learn about new cycles and rhythms regularly.

1. Check and write down how many minutes after closing their eyes your baby's body seems to relax completely.

2. Do the "arm test": carefully lift an arm, then let it "fall" (it sounds more dramatic than it is!). If it drops limply, the baby is in a deep sleep. Write down the number of minutes it took after they closed their eyes. If the arm drops, but is still controlled by the muscles and not completely limp, they are not in a deep sleep yet.

3. Check your baby's movements regularly. If you notice body movements, they have come out of a deep sleep and are sleeping more lightly. This phase is "do or die," as it were: start another sleep cycle, or wake up.

4. By writing down all times for three days, you will be able to predict your baby's sleep cycle.

5. NOTE: This does not work for babies younger than 15 weeks and it is not an absolute prediction like calculating leaps. This can only give you an idea of your baby's rhythm so you can respond to it more easily.

Waking Up: For the Safety of Your Baby?

You would think that we would be made in such a way that the sleep cycles of parents and babies would seamlessly adapt to each other to create a beautiful, harmonious start in life. But no . . . So why does this difference in sleep cycle and sleep rhythm exist? It looks like frequently waking during the night is a kind of safety advantage for your baby. Babies are vulnerable, and the younger they are, the more vulnerable they are. A few survival factors can explain why a baby wakes up a few times at night:

- Their stomachs are still very small and milk digests rather quickly. A baby needs milk to survive and because milk digests quickly, they need a "ration" more often than we need food. If a baby didn't wake, they wouldn't get food during those hours, which is not good for growth. We are talking about young babies who are not eating solid food yet. Solid food, including puree, is a lot heavier to digest. You will notice that a baby old enough to eat solids will wake from hunger less frequently.

- Being in a deep sleep for a shorter time also has safety advantages. It is important that a baby wakes up if there is something that causes discomfort or something that could harm their body. Think here of "simple" things, such as a dirty diaper. If worn for too long, it causes irritation, and your little one can be in discomfort due to the acidic substances in urine. So it's good that their deep sleep is not so long that their skin could suffer from wearing the wet diaper.

- Also consider a little nose full of mucus that obstructs breathing. Since their breathing is not as developed as ours, it is important that your baby can wake easily if something bothers them in their sleep.

- Babies seem to sleep best when they are with you and not when they're completely alone. That, too, seems to have a logical explanation, if you think about the fact that a baby can't survive without you. A baby depends completely on you. And they "know" it. Not consciously, of course, but it is a primeval instinct. They are safe with you; alone is just alone. Hearing your voice or feeling your hand, etc., can be enough. The amount of contact a baby wants to sleep peacefully depends on the baby and their age. The older they are, the less need for direct contact. But there are no guidelines here. Many (self-appointed) sleep professionals are wary of body contact or talking to your baby, because they believe that babies then never learn to fall or stay asleep on their own. But experience shows that if you let nature run its course, babies can increasingly be on their own, and fall and stay asleep by themselves. You can look at it in a different way: if a baby feels from the start that they are safe, that you are there for them, they become more self-confident and in the long term that leads to very strong self-confidence. This allows them to fall asleep and stay asleep by themselves with a safe feeling.

- Another reason that your baby wakes up easily is the fact that they can't yet control their body temperature as adults can. If we get cold, it's not that bad. But it is for your baby. It is important that they wake if they are too hot or cold. But remember, by the time your baby starts crying, they may already be feeling discomfort. That's why checking the temperature frequently is very important.

- Also, think of little things that could cause discomfort; e.g., a small toe getting stuck in a loose stitch of the blanket. We would feel it, immediately disentangle the toe, etc. Your baby "puts up with" a lot more and doesn't protest immediately. When they start crying, it often already hurts. You have to be quick, and that would be impossible if your little one didn't wake up and cry to indicate there really is something wrong. It should be added—maybe unnecessarily—that crying is a real sign of discomfort: something doesn't feel right. A baby never cries without reason. As adults, we might think the reason is exaggerated, but for your baby the reason is real, and that's what it's all about, right? Of course, a stuck toe is obvious, but not feeling well is also a reason. A reason that is very real to your baby, and that we must handle with love.

This is all intended to reassure you and to make you understand that waking up during the night has benefits for your baby. You mustn't read it the other way around and become scared when your baby seems to sleep longer and more soundly once in a while. With all our experience, and that of thousands of pediatricians all over the world, we can say: a baby seems to be preprogrammed in such a way that they feel what is best for them. There always seems to be a good explanation for all the natural rhythms, a natural explanation.

Increasingly, more physicians and professionals are opposing certain types of sleep training that keeps your baby in a deep sleep for longer than your baby may need by nature. Many professionals state that this sleep training comes at a price, and perhaps at a risk. Helping your baby get the sleep they need at that time is good all around. That's how you respond to your baby. You create the conditions your baby needs to give them the chance to do what they need. If you rely on sleep training to solve your "problem" and teach your child almost unnaturally to sleep when forced, this is not beneficial to your baby. You then disturb the natural processes, which doesn't help build a tight bond with your baby.

KEY TIP

Not everything you hear is equally true: not all parents are equally open about the sleep behavior of their baby. Some parents make the story sound better than it is in reality. Parents don't do this out of malice, but we live in a society in which a baby sleeping well or not is often considered proof of good or bad parenting. And here, too, we can honestly tell you: the fact that your baby sleeps "well" or "badly" says more about their personality and age than about your parenting!

SLEEP AND LEAPS

Once your baby has developed a day-night rhythm, you will notice that the rhythm and the way your baby sleeps will change during a leap. We also have to point out that there are exceptions: babies who sleep marvelously during a leap. But these are really exceptions. It is also not that strange that a leap affects your baby's sleep; there is a lot going on in their mind. They go through a difficult phase and experience stress. These are enough ingredients to considerably affect sleep.

DO REMEMBER!

Let this become your mantra, because it is what it is really all about: no one sleeps the whole night through. Not even you. After the sleep cycle is completed, you enter the twilight zone between being asleep and being awake, but you continue into the next sleep cycle. Your baby cannot—we repeat: cannot (!)—sleep through the night. Not a single baby. However, some babies will start another sleep cycle by themselves. But that doesn't mean these babies sleep through the night. That is simply impossible!

Sleep Disturbance: Unfortunately Not Only During Leaps

During each leap, your little one suffers from the three Cs: crying, clinginess, and crankiness. They eat differently, feed differently from the breast (your baby will often want to breastfeed a lot more), and sleep differently (often more lightly and superficially). When the leap is over, you will notice that your little one doesn't cry as much anymore, is in a better mood, eats and sleeps better, but . . . as far as sleep is concerned, the sleep disturbance is still there after the end of the leap. Sleep disturbance is more prevalent during a leap, but it is also there when the difficult phase of a leap is over, albeit to a lesser extent. This is also a reason why parents experience so many problems with sleep disturbance.

Sleep and the First Three Leaps

Because your baby doesn't yet have a day-night rhythm during the first three leaps, you will find it difficult to determine that the rhythm was disturbed by the leap. How can you detect a change in rhythm if there is no rhythm yet? Still, you will notice changes in your baby's sleep during those leaps, especially with daytime naps. Your baby sleeps more lightly, for shorter periods, or even longer than normal! Some babies are continuously busy with getting to know the world in their heads. Those babies sleep more lightly and for shorter periods at this time. Babies who sleep longer know they have enough to deal with already and they know how to create a good balance, including a good portion of sleep. The way your baby deals with these leaps is influenced by their personality and their circumstances. On the one hand, you have no influence over this (with regards to personality), but on the other hand, you do! It is good for the baby to have the chance to sleep. It seems unnecessary to mention this, but it isn't. During a leap, you need to bear in mind that things can quickly become too much for them, as they are very open to all the stimuli around them. So take the time to quietly sit or lie on the couch with your baby. Do you notice that your baby is tired? Do not overstimulate them; give them the chance to get some sleep when they want it.

Sleep Regression Periods? Or, Welcome to Leaps 4, 6, and 10

Many people mention sleep regression periods. These are longer periods in which a child suddenly sleeps much "worse" than before. It is clear we don't want to link it to the term "worse," but of course we get what they mean by the term. The periods people refer to when speaking about sleep regression do not appear out of thin air. Those periods are much easier understood when you look at the leaps. All leaps are a step forward for your baby. After making a leap, they can observe more complex aspects of the world and understand the world at a higher level. With each leap, they are mentally able to do things they did not have the mental capacity for before that leap. Some leaps seem to bring about even more than others. These are sort of "overarching" leaps through which the previous leaps are even better integrated.

Compare it with building a brick wall. Every brick is a part added, but the brick that is finally placed on the bottom bricks is not just a part of the wall, but keeps the rest connected and sturdy. This is a simplistic representation, but it clarifies it well. These leaps are 4, 6, and 10, which occur at 4, 8, and 17 months, respectively. These leaps are experienced by parents throughout the world, irrespective of culture and religion, as the most difficult in every way: in terms of crying, clinginess, and crankiness, but also with regard to eating or breastfeeding and . . . sleeping. Because the effect of the sleep rhythm is twofold (not only on your baby, but on your mood, too), it is experienced as particularly difficult during these leaps.

SLEEP REGRESSION

Sleep regression periods (although the word choice is unfortunate) contrary to what you often read, do not appear out of thin air, and they are there for a reason. Your baby does not have a problem that needs resolving, but needs your love and help to get through the leap. Once the leap is over, sleeping is a lot easier.

Sometimes your little one will experience more sleep regression after the difficult phase of this leap, too. Therefore, the sleep regression phase can last somewhat longer than the difficult phase of the leap. This is due to two other reasons that affect these periods of "worse" sleep. First, the outcomes of those leaps have huge consequences. Your baby can do more things mentally following the leaps, but need to practice with their body to do what they can already do in their mind. This varies from learning how to use their hands (in particular, during Leap 4); to learning to crawl, or in a few cases to already take the first steps in Leap 6; and learning to run, wriggle, and perform other physical antics by Leap 10. So not only is your baby's sleep affected by the mental leaps, but also by the physical consequences of practicing the new skills. And second, as if that weren't enough, biology plays a role, too. Think, for example, of teething. In short, enough reasons to explain that your little one may enter a period in which they will sleep a bit "worse" for a while.

For All Babies and Parents in Leap 4 and the Weeks Thereafter . . .
We won't sugarcoat it: of all the leaps and sleep regression periods, this is the one experienced as the most intense. Sleep problems, sleep questions, and sleep dramas and despair hit a high here. Remember: after this, you have made it through the worst.

> *"Usually she fell asleep as long as I touched her. Now that she is in the fourth leap, it's no longer enough. I have to talk to her, too. When she feels and hears me, she falls asleep, although it's more difficult than normal and she sleeps worse than normal."*
> **About Angelica, 17th week**

Bad Sleep . . . Has the Leap Started?
Out of all the characteristics of a leap (crying, clinginess, crankiness, wanting to breastfeed more often, being more shy with strangers, etc.), there is one that you notice virtually immediately when your little one enters a leap. A kind of first signal. You guessed it: "worse" sleep. You can notice it from the fourth leap, when there truly is a day-night rhythm. With each further leap, it becomes increasingly clearer because your child invariably develops a more stable rhythm. Remember: your baby can't help that they wake up more often and cry more often or just want to be close to you more. Nights are difficult; there is so much to discover! And the world is so new, different, and scary in your baby's perception. So they want to be with you. As a parent, you are their rock, their safe base to rely on in times of trouble.

Daytime Naps and Leaps
You will also notice from the fourth leap that daytime naps are influenced by the leaps. Your baby faces so much that they sleep more lightly and for shorter periods or find it harder to fall asleep. On the one hand, that's because your little one does not stop processing everything; there is so much to be discovered. On the other hand, it is because, during those light REM sleeps, extra blood is pumped to the brain and there is extra brain activity to create good brain connections. Fine for the brain, but this biological process keeps the baby active, which influences the

daytime naps during the leap. After a leap, you may notice a new pattern in their daytime naps. That does not happen from one day to the next, but progressively. Until another leap occurs that influences the daytime naps (temporarily).

> Leap 4 is well and truly hitting us at the moment. Massive progress in cognition for Peter is making him wired and struggling to settle. Lots of tears that say "I just want to be asleep" during the day and then only mummy naps will do.—**Instagram post**

Nightmares and Night Terrors

A good day or night rest can be terribly disturbed by a nightmare or a night terror. A night terror is something that you generally see around three years of age, but can also happen earlier, sometimes from the second year of life. A night terror is a real panic attack during sleep. Your little one cries, screams, or may even lash out and is inconsolable. You can't get through to them and whatever you do only seems to make it worse. This is contrary to a nightmare. Your baby could have those much earlier, sometimes even at four months. With a nightmare, you can get through to them and they are not in a completely deep sleep. Another difference between these two things is that a child can remember a nightmare the next day, but not a night terror. You then come up against the following problem with regard to your baby: it is not possible to "talk it over" the next day. Neither can you ask them what the matter is. And that can make you feel quite desperate. Especially if your little one goes through a period in which they often have nightmares.

"He will just begin crying out in his sleep. It doesn't wake him up, so he will cry for a bit as I shush him and put a hand on him to calm him. Then he stops crying, all while remaining asleep."
About Desmond, 23rd week

"Sometimes my baby girl wakes up screaming with all her might. I literally jump out of the bed to pick her up and comfort her. It usually takes a couple minutes till she opens her eyes and realizes that I am holding her. Then she settles down and goes back to sleep. However, sometimes it doesn't help at all because it looks like she can't wake up—she keeps her eyes closed and keeps screaming. Then I put her down and gently stroke her cheeks, calling her by name till she opens her eyes and sees me."
About Ivy, 22nd week

Nightmares and Separation Anxiety

During the period when separation anxiety plays a part, babies will have more nightmares. You can't prevent separation anxiety, and you don't want to prevent it, as it's a part of normal development. Of course, you can make sure that the intensity of the fear is as low as possible. And that your baby gets through this period as easily as possible, a period in which they learn that you can in fact leave, but that this doesn't mean that you will never come back. You can do this from the leap of relationships (when your baby is around six months old) by playing the games we describe on page 234. By assisting them from that moment, the peak of separation anxiety between 8 and 10 months will be less severe, which also influences the nightmares that a child can have during that period. You can't completely prevent nightmares, and you don't have to; they are completely normal things to have. And so long as your little one knows you are there for them, everything will be fine.

> *"She has screamed in her sleep during this most recent leap (the seventh), but when we looked on the monitor, it was clear she wasn't awake."*
> **About Sarah, 46th week**

To Wake Them or Not to Wake Them?

Should you wake your baby up when they are having a nightmare? Opinions differ—among physicians, too—but the majority still think that the smartest thing to do is to let your baby sleep when they are having a nightmare. You could place a reassuring hand on their tummy or head or soothingly say that everything is okay, but that is different from waking them. You then reassure them and try to bring them back to the peaceful phase of sleep. But don't underestimate your intuition! If you think it is so bad that it's better to wake them, then do so; you need to follow your instincts. Ultimately, the combination of you and your baby is unique, and you have to find out what works best for you both.

"She screamed in her sleep and I saw the pain and fear in her face. It happens to her quite often and every time I picked her up and calmed her down, it seemed to just get worse, until she woke up abruptly, and that did not feel good, either. I now let her be and only talk to her soothingly. That seems to work better. She continues to have nightmares, even though she is always happy and cheerful during the day. I'm glad I found a way that seems to work for her."
About Mindy, 37th week

NIGHTMARE STATS

Some parents noticed that their baby had already had a nightmare at four months. By the time babies are in Leap 6 (the second difficult sleep period, known as the second sleep regression period), around 40 percent of them have had a nightmare. At Leap 10 (17 months) it's more than half. The percentage rises steadily because ultimately, we all have nightmares now and then.

By Parents for Parents

Okay, now you know that your baby sleeps differently than you do as an adult, and that yes, it can be really exhausting. Due to the natural benefits, you don't want to, and can't, change anything about their sleep. Your child sleeps in a different way and at different times than you do, and they do so for various good reasons. The solution, therefore, is to adjust your (sleep) behavior. Here are some tips by parents for parents. These have helped them and could help you, too. See what suits you and try it. It's worth it!

- Take turns sleeping in the guest room for a night, or even on the couch. Express milk, and get a night's rest.

- Try giving baby a bath during the day. Usually a child sleeps more soundly after a warm bath, and you can do that during the day, too, instead of only in the evening!

- Ask for help. This is an important one! Even if there is nothing wrong with your baby, even if it is normal that you are tired, it's not easy. Everyone with children knows this and will be glad to help. Sometimes an hour is enough. Just taking a nice shower, taking a walk, exercising, doing something for yourself. Don't be embarrassed; everyone will understand!

- Some babies love being swaddled. You need to get lots of information if you want to try this. Choose a good cloth and find videos that show you how to do it.

- A sling can work wonders, too. Your baby feels safe close to you and you can still do things because your hands are free. Your baby will wake up less quickly and fall asleep faster because they can feel you.

- Eat healthy. Yes, coffee, sugar, and energy drinks seem like a good solution, but only in the short term. The good effect is followed by a dip, and then you are twice as tired. You can't cope with those kinds of dips now because you're already living on your reserves. Healthy eating does wonders and you will soon feel the difference in energy. Eat lots of whole-grain products, fruit, and vegetables.

- One of the most effective tips is to rest during the day, too. Is your baby going to sleep? Take a nap, too. Yes, that means you can't do those things you wanted to do while they are sleeping. Just do them later. Sometimes it's smart to leave the mess be for a while. And you know, with that new energy from those extra daytime naps, you'll do the things you have to do a lot faster afterward!

Fresh air helps! Go for a walk on your own regularly, after you've fed your little one and if someone stays with them, of course. Fresh air does wonders, especially if you are very tired.—**Instagram post**

Have a power nap when your partner is home. A half-hour nap is often enough to recharge your batteries.—**Instagram post**

So: Does Your Baby Sleep Yet? Mine Sleeps like a Dream!

We hope we have given you more insight into the normal, natural pattern of your baby and their sleep. We hope you understand that we can't give you ready-made, quick fix answers, and that wouldn't be good for your baby anyway. We hope you find strength in this information and that it helps you not let others' comments drive you mad.

Trust yourself, trust your baby, and trust your interaction. Give yourself space to accept that you simply have to go through this phase together and that ultimately everything will be fine. Try the tips that helped other parents. And don't be afraid to ask for help from family and friends, but also from doctors if you feel the need.

Once you have read this, you may ask yourself: who actually came up with the saying, "Sleep like a baby"???

Leap 1

The World of Changing Sensations

**AS IF YOUR BABY
HAS BEEN REBORN**

round five weeks and sometimes as early as four weeks, or about one month, your baby will take their first leap in their development. As described in the first chapter, you'll know this is happening because your baby will become fussier than usual. The three Cs of fussy behavior—crying, clinginess, and crankiness—will appear in earnest. Although you may feel helpless when this happens, remember what your baby is going through. The best thing you can do is to be there for them. Something new and strange is happening in their world and it bewilders them, so it's natural to want to return to the safe, warm, familiar world, a world with their parents at its center. Around this age, all babies desire more cuddles and attention than they usually do. It is therefore normal that you notice your baby is more demanding. This period may last only a day, but with some babies, it lasts a whole week.

THE FUSSY PHASE:
THE ANNOUNCEMENT OF THE MAGICAL LEAP

Babies can't ask for help at this age, nor can they move closer to you or reach out their arms to you. What a baby can do is yell. So they will whine, cry, or scream until perhaps they have driven the entire household to despair. With a bit of luck, though, their distress will have the desired effect, and have you running to them and letting them snuggle up to you. Give them all the cuddling they need and all the contact you feel you can handle at times like these. They need time to adjust to these new changes and grow into their new world. They are accustomed to your body scent, warmth, voice, and touch, so with you, they will relax a little and feel contented again. You can provide the tender loving care they really need during this trying period.

A baby may refuse to sleep alone in their crib. You could try bringing the crib or a bassinet into your room, or use a specially designed co-sleeper bed that is actually attached to your mattress. At the end of the day, you may decide that taking them into your bed is the only solution. We know this is a good solution for many parents, but it's a controversial and very personal one that you may want to discuss with your baby's pediatrician. If you are interested in learning more, see www .cosleeping.nd.edu.

Baby may also want to sleep on their belly, which they didn't before now. Lying on their belly may give them the feeling of the belly-to-belly contact with you and the security they so badly need at this point. However, it is not safe for a baby to sleep in the prone position until they are able to roll over by themselves.

It's Not Your Fault—It's Just a Leap!

All parents want desperately to find out why their baby is having crying fits. Usually, they will first see if their baby is hungry. Then they check if the diaper has come loose. They change the diaper, as it may be wet. Pretty soon, they discover that all the comforting in the world doesn't really stop their little bundle from resuming their relentless crying. No parent enjoys having their baby cry, especially when they can't do anything about it. It undermines their confidence and is very distressing. Often, parents are afraid that something is wrong with their tiny baby. They think they are in pain, or that they might be suffering from some abnormality or disorder that has gone undetected until now. Others worry that the milk supply from breastfeeding alone is not sufficient. This is because the baby seems to crave the breast constantly and is always hungry. Some parents take their babies to a doctor for a checkup. Of course, most babies are pronounced perfectly healthy and they are sent home.

"My son was very clingy, and I had him on my lap a lot of the time, even when we had company. I was terribly concerned. One night, I hardly slept at all. I just spent the whole night holding and cuddling him. Then my sister came and took over for a night. I went in the other bedroom and slept like a log the whole night. I felt reborn when I woke up the next day."
About Bob, 5th week

"Normally, she is very easy, but she suddenly started crying nonstop for almost two days. At first I thought it was just stomach cramps. But then I noticed she stopped whenever I had her on my lap, or when I let her lie between us. She fell asleep right away then. I kept asking myself if I was spoiling her too much by allowing it. But the crying period stopped just as suddenly as it had started. And now she is as easygoing as she was before."
About Eve, 5th week

"My daughter was crying so much that I was afraid something was terribly wrong. She wanted to breastfeed constantly. I took her to see the pediatrician, but he couldn't find anything wrong with her. He said that many infants went through a similar crying phase at five weeks."
About Juliette, 5th week

GOOD TO KNOW

It is very normal that your baby wants to nurse more often when they are making a leap in their development. There is nothing wrong with your milk. When the fussy phase lasts a bit long, you may feel that you need to call the pediatrician for reassurance that you are producing enough milk. Most of the time, your baby is simply upset and has a greater need for physical contact and comfort. A pediatrician may suggest these are the "regulating days" and advise you to continue breastfeeding. Calling the pediatrician is most likely to happen around six weeks, and then three and six months. No coincidence really, when you consider that a baby goes through a fussy phase around those ages.

If It All Becomes Too Much

A leap is an intense, stressful experience for both baby and the parents, and you may find the strain unbearable at times. You may become exhausted from the lack of sleep or because anxieties are preventing you from sleeping well. A baby who is confused and crying constantly can make any parent feel insecure and anxious. The tension builds and parents find themselves unable to cope. Feeling that tension, the baby becomes even fussier and cries even louder than before. It's a never-ending circle. Both the baby and their parents can find relief from that added stress if they receive support and compassion.

- Comfort your baby with physical contact and attention. It will make it easier for them to adapt to all the changes at their own pace. It will also give them self-confidence, knowing that someone is there for them whenever they need comfort.

- As parents, you need support too, not criticism, from family and friends. Criticism will only undermine your already battered self-confidence; support will enable you both to cope better with the difficult phases.

Spit up, breastmilk, formula, poop, and diaper ointment—that's how I smell these days! And somehow she just loves to curl up under my neck. We have good days and we have bad days. We have restless nights and sometimes restless days. Parenting is not easy. This new lifestyle is not easy. It's completely new and totally unknown. So all I can do is take one day at a time. We will find our rhythm eventually; I mean, she's only 23 days old! Let's cut each other some slack!—**Instagram post**

 **ANCHOR MOMENTS** *

Only a couple of weeks ago, you brought new life to this amazing world, making it even more beautiful. You did an amazing job! Don't ever forget that. Take some well-deserved anchor moments for yourself. To relax, to be a better you.

In 5 minutes: Breathe consciously. Count to five breathing in, and five breathing out. Take time to do this.

In 10 minutes: Do some solo reflection: sit on the couch with your baby, look at them, and think about all the wonderful times you have already spent together. Take a moment to really think about and savor them. Think about your body, and what an incredible thing it has acheived.

More time: Take a bath or footbath and put some Epsom salts in the water. Epsom salts are full of minerals, such as magnesium; dissolved in water, these will enter your body, charging it with all kinds of good stuff.

Does Your Baby Calm Down When Close to Their Daddy or Mommy?

Most parents notice that close physical contact helps when their baby is not feeling "themselves," and that their baby responds better and more quickly when they are in physical contact with one of their parents.

Parents who carry their babies around whenever they are in a fussy mood may label them "extremely dependent." These babies like nothing better than lying quietly against their mother or father and being stroked, rocked, or cuddled. They might fall asleep on a parent's lap, but start crying again as soon as furtive attempts are made to sneak them back into their cribs.

* For more anchor moments, see page 36.

Parents who stick to feeding and sleeping schedules often notice their babies fall asleep during feeding. Some wonder if this is because the baby is so exhausted from crying and the lack of sleep that they have no energy left to nurse. This may seem logical, but it may not be the whole story. It's more likely that the baby falls asleep because they are where they want to be.

"Velcro baby! Little Hank is going through a leap and has me baby-trapped. Even with him in the carrier it's been hard to do much this week, and I've had to rely on family support.
About Hank, 7th week

"When my baby was crying all the time, she seemed so lost. I had to massage her for a long time before she calmed down a bit. I felt exhausted but extremely satisfied. Something changed after that. It doesn't seem to take as long to soothe her now. When she cries now, I don't find it such an effort to put her world to rights again."
About Nina, 4th week

SOOTHING TIPS

When you want to comfort your baby, a gentle rhythm and warmth can play a very important role. Hold your baby upright against you, with their bottom resting on one arm while your other arm supports their head resting against your shoulder. When your baby is in this position, they can feel the soothing beat of your heart.

Here are a few other things you can do:

- Cuddle and caress them.

- Rock them gently back and forth.

- Walk around slowly with them.

- Hum a song.

- Pat them gently on the bottom.

- The most successful way of comforting a crying baby is to remember what they enjoy most when they are in a cheerful mood, and try it even during a fussy phase.

The World of Changing Sensations

There are a number of indications in babies aged approximately four to five weeks that show they are undergoing enormous changes that affect their metabolism, internal organs, and senses. For instance, at this age, your baby is likely to outgrow problems with their digestive system that they may have had initially.

The metabolism of a baby also changes at this age. You may notice that they're crying real tears for the first time. Furthermore, parents notice that their baby stays awake for longer periods now.

Finally, everything points to the senses going through a period of rapid growth. Your baby is clearly more interested in the world around them. Just after birth, they were only able to focus on objects that were up to 8 inches away, but now they can focus at a longer distance. It's not surprising then that a baby feels it's time for some action, as they are more sensitive to outside stimulation.

Five- to six-week-old babies are even prepared to work in order to experience interesting sensations. In a laboratory experiment, babies showed that they could adjust the focus of a color movie by sucking harder on a pacifier. As soon as the baby stopped sucking, the picture blurred. Babies at this age have difficulty sucking and watching at the same time, so they could keep this up only for a few seconds. To check that this was really what they were trying to do, the babies were then required to stop sucking to bring the picture into focus. They could do that, too!

The dramatic growth of your baby's senses does not mean they have acquired a new type of perception. They still cannot process all the impressions that their senses, even improved, send to their brain in the same way we as adults can. In fact, at this point your baby is losing some of their newborn skills. The inborn tendency to follow a schematic face (oval with three dots) with their eyes and/or head suddenly disappears. They will no longer turn toward a sound slowly or imitate facial expressions. These early skills were controlled by primitive centers in the lower brain, and they disappear to make way for developments in the higher levels of the brain. Soon you will see similar behaviors emerge, but this time they will seem to be much more under your baby's control than ever before.

"Toward the end of a breastfeeding, my son behaves a bit peculiarly. He suckles really fast and then stares into the distance with a glorified expression on his face. And then he starts sucking again. He looks really voracious, as if he is very keen being on my breast."
About Matt, 5th week

This week is Nomi's first mental leap—when she becomes more aware of her senses. She has been extra clingy the past two days. We all have good days and bad days. There are times when we need to slow down and allow our growth to catch up, no matter what age. There are days when we need our mama or a close friend a little extra. Pay attention to that. Honor those emotions and follow where they take you.—**Instagram post**

Experience the World Through Your Baby's Eyes

Squint your eyes so that everything is a blur. Then look at someone's face and take note of the contrasts and main forms and features of the face. That is what fascinates your baby so much at this time! Look around and try to find 10 contrasts in your direct vicinity. The light behind your screen against the dark edge of the screen. The cuff of your dark sleeve against the light background of your skin, or vice versa. The black lines on your blouse against the white background. The dark lines between your fingers when they are placed together. And so on. Try this activity when you are outside, too. As you become more aware of the contrasts surrounding you, you'll be better able to imagine what your baby's world is like.

BRAIN CHANGES

At approximately three to four weeks, there is a dramatic increase in a baby's head circumference. Their glucose metabolism, in the brain, also changes.

Your Baby's Choices: A Key to Their Personality

All babies' senses develop rapidly at this time, and it will become apparent that they are now more interested in their surroundings. But every baby will have their own preferences. Some bright-eyed infants really enjoy looking at and watching everything and everyone around them. Others will listen keenly to music and sounds around them and will find sound-producing objects, such as rattles, more appealing than anything else. Another group of babies will love to be touched, and they would like nothing better than to play games all day that involve being touched and caressed by someone. Some babies don't have any clear preference. Even at this very young age, you will find that every baby is different.

> *"I take my daughter along to my singing classes every day. During the first few weeks, she hardly reacted to sounds at all, and I felt quite concerned, to be honest. Now, suddenly, she's totally preoccupied by noises of any kind when she is awake. If she wakes up crying and I sing to her, she stops immediately. She doesn't stop when my friends sing, though."*
> **About Hannah, 6th week**

THE MAGICAL LEAP FORWARD: THE DISCOVERY OF THE NEW WORLD

The very best way to help your baby is to give them support and tender loving care. It is impossible to spoil a baby at this age, so comfort them especially when they cry. The development in their senses offers a new opportunity for baby to discover new things. Give your baby the chance to enjoy their senses. Try to find out what your baby likes best by watching their reactions carefully and responding to them. Once you know what your baby likes, you can gradually introduce new things to them.

Watch That Smile to Discover Your Baby's "Likes"

Your baby will smile when experiencing things they enjoy. That could be through something they see, hear, smell, taste, or feel. Because their senses are more acute now and they are able to perceive a little more of their world, they will also smile more often. It will be very rewarding to experiment and discover which activities produce these wonderful smiles.

"A major moment for the day! Hell, a major moment for the past few days. Not crying when not being held or nursing. Okay, or crying just because. This moment quickly ended following discontentment and actual tears. But there's great things that are happening. She's looking at things longer, not just seeing them but looking at them. Listening to the changing sounds around her. And giving more social smiles. I'll take lots of those!"

About Lynn, 5th week

"I dance around with my baby, and when I stop, he smiles."

About John, 6th week

"When I put my face close to my daughter's and smile and talk to her, she makes eye contact and grins. It's wonderful."

About Laura, 5th week

"My daughter smiles at her dolls and teddy bears."

About Jenny, 6th week

"The last few days, my daughter has refused to nap during the day unless one of us is holding her. Yesterday, though, she fell asleep on her own. Now we know what was going on these past days: she made her first leap. She has become a different girl. She can stay awake longer between naps, and is more alert and smiling. It's amazing."

About Stella, 6th week

What Is Your Baby Looking At? How Can You Help?

Your baby looks longer than before at objects that interest them. The brighter the colors, and the greater the contrast between the colors, the more fascinating they will find them. They also like striped and angular shapes. And your face, of course.

"My son stares right into my face and gazes at me for quite some time. He thinks it's funny when I eat. He looks at my mouth and watches me chew."

About Kevin, 6th week

"My daughter is much more aware of everything she sees now. Her favorites are the bars of her crib, which contrast the white walls; books on the bookshelf; our ceiling, which has long wooden slats with a dark strip in between; and a black-and-white ink drawing on the wall. At night, lights seem to interest her the most."

About Emily, 5th week

"When I move a green-and-yellow ball slowly from left to right, my daughter turns her head to follow it. She seems to think it's great fun, although this proud mom probably enjoys it more than she does."

About Ashley, 5th week

If you walk around with your baby, you'll automatically discover what they like looking at best. Give them enough time to have a good look at things—and don't forget their range of focus is not much more than 8 inches.

What Is Your Baby Listening To? What Can You Do?

Most babies are fascinated by sounds. Buzzing, squeaking, ringing, rustling, or whizzing sounds are all very interesting. Human voices are also extremely captivating, especially high-pitched female voices, although nothing can beat the sound of their mother's voice. Even at five weeks old, you can have cozy little chats with your baby. Pick a comfortable place to sit and put your face close to theirs. Chat with them about everyday events, or whatever comes to mind. Stop talking once in a while to give them a chance to "reply."

"I really think my son is listening to me now. It's remarkable."
About Matt, 5th week

"Sometimes my baby chats back to me when I'm talking to her. She talks for longer now, and sometimes it seems as if she's really trying to tell me something. It's adorable. Yesterday, she chatted to her rabbit in her crib and her rattle in her playpen."
About Hannah, 5th week

"The Language of Sounds":
Let Your Baby Know You Understand Them

Your baby may use a greater range of crying and gurgling sounds than before. They may have different sounds for different situations. Babies will often make a whimpering sound before falling asleep. If your baby is really upset, you will be able to tell by the way they cry, because it's a totally different sound. These sounds help parents understand their babies better. If you understand what your baby is trying to tell you, let them know. Babies adore interaction.

"I know exactly when my baby is gurgling with pleasure or grumbling because she's unhappy. Sometimes she gurgles with pleasure when she sees her mobile, and she loves it when I imitate the sounds she makes."
About Hannah, 6th week

BABY CARE: DON'T OVERDO IT

Let your baby's responses guide you. Stop as soon as you notice something is getting too much for them.

- Your baby has become more sensitive now, so you need to be careful not to overstimulate them. Bear this in mind when you play with them, cuddle them, show them things, or let them listen to things. You have to adapt to them.

- Your baby is still unable to concentrate for a long period of time, so they will need short rest breaks. You may think they have lost interest, but they haven't. Be patient. Usually, they'll soon be raring to go again if you let them rest for a short while.

What Is Your Baby Feeling? How Do You Respond to That?

All babies become more aware of being touched at this age. You might hear your baby laughing out loud for the first time now, perhaps when they are being tickled. Although, generally, babies of this age do not particularly appreciate being tickled, as it's often too much stimulation for them.

> *"My daughter laughed out loud, really roared, when her brother started tickling her. Everyone was startled, and it went dead quiet."*
> **About Emily, 5th week**

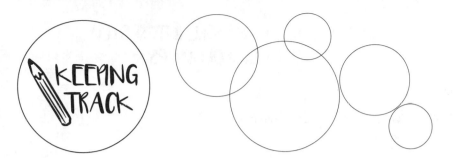

WHAT YOU'VE DISCOVERED: THE WORLD OF SENSATIONS

With every leap, we provide a list with possible changes you may notice in your baby, and things (skills) your baby may suddenly master after making a leap. As your baby goes through more leaps, the greater the range of potential new skills available to them will be. The older your baby gets, the easier it will become to notice the changes in their behaviors and the new skills they have acquired. That makes perfect sense, really, because the older your baby becomes, the more their behavior starts to resemble ours.

As this is the first leap, it may be difficult to notice any new skills. This leap is considerably shorter than other leaps. You may only notice there was a leap once it has passed. Suddenly you realize your baby is "behaving differently" than last week and that actually, the week before was rather difficult in comparison. That "fussiness" was the leap. When you fill in this list of discoveries just before the next leap begins, you will become aware of how many things have actually changed.

Instructions to Fill In This List:

Just before the next leap begins, have a look at this list and check off only the boxes of the things that you clearly recognize. It is absolutely not true that the more boxes you check off, the better it is. Try to find the key to your baby's personality. Stop filling this out once the next fussy phase begins, heralding the next leap.

You made this leap around: _____

On _____, the sun broke through again and now, at the end of the leap, I see you can do these new things.

YOU ARE CLEARLY MORE INTERESTED IN YOUR SURROUNDINGS

Date:

☐ You look at things longer and more often.
  You like looking at:

  _____

  _____

  _____

  _____

☐ You listen to things more often, paying closer attention to:

  _____

  _____

  _____

  _____

  _____

☐ You are clearly more aware of being touched.

☐ You are more aware of different smells.

☐ You smiled for the first time, or more often than before.

☐ You gurgle with pleasure more often, at, for example:

  _____

  _____

☐ You express likes or dislikes more often.

☐ You express anticipation in some way or another more often.

☐ You stay awake longer and are more alert.

PHYSICAL CHANGES

Date:

☐ You breathe more regularly.

☐ You startle less now and your body trembles less often.

☐ You have tears now when you cry.

☐ When nursing, I notice that:

    ☐ You choke less often than before.

    ☐ You vomit less than you did.

    ☐ You burp less often now.

TIP

As you can see, it doesn't take long to complete this list. Try to do it for every leap. When you read the lists again in a few years, you will see their typical personality traits . . . they were there early on!

THE EASY PERIOD: AFTER THE LEAP

At around six weeks, a period of comparative peace dawns. Your baby is more cheerful, more alert, and more preoccupied with looking and listening than before. Many parents claim that their baby's eyes seem brighter. Babies are also capable of expressing their likes and dislikes at this age. In short, life seems a little less complicated than before.

"We communicate more now. Suddenly, the hours that my son is awake seem more interesting."
About Frankie, 6th week

"I feel closer to my baby now. Our bond is stronger."
About Bob, 6th week

Leap 2

The World of Patterns

YOUR BABY FEELS, HEARS, AND SEES THEM . . .
FOR THE FIRST TIME

Sometime between seven and nine weeks, or almost two months, the following developmental leap announces its arrival. Your baby now gets the new ability to recognize simple patterns in the world around them and in their own body. Although it may be hard for us to imagine, this happens with all the senses, not just vision. For example, your baby may discover their hands and feet and spend hours practicing the skill of controlling their arms or legs in certain positions. They may be endlessly fascinated with the way the light displays shadows on their bedroom wall. You might notice they seem enthralled by the array of cans on the grocery store shelf, and fully occupied making short bursts of sounds, such as "ah," "uh," and "ehh."

Just imagine having to adjust to changes like this. Their familiar world is turned upside down. They suddenly see, hear, smell, taste, and feel in a completely new way. As with the previous leap, they may feel puzzled, confused, and bewildered, and need time to adjust. They will want to cling to their daddy or mommy for comfort. This fussy phase could last anywhere from a few days to two weeks.

DO REMEMBER

If you notice your baby is fussier than usual, watch them closely. It's likely that they are attempting to master new skills. Have a look at What You've Discovered: The World of Patterns on page 124 to see what you can watch for.

THE FUSSY PHASE:
THE ANNOUNCEMENT OF THE MAGICAL LEAP

Almost all babies cry more often now, as this is their way of expressing the tension they feel when they make a leap in their development. At this age, crying is still the most effective way to show how they feel. It gets their parents' attention. Colicky babies will sob and scream even more than they did before and drive their mothers and fathers to distraction. Even when parents do everything possible to console these little screamers, they may continue to wail.

In short, your baby is entering a new difficult phase, which is characterized by the three Cs (crying, clinginess, and crankiness), and at least a few other characteristics from a whole list. It is not only difficult for your little one, but also for you, and can result in worries and irritations.

Most babies calm down when they experience close physical contact, although for some babies it can never be close enough. If they had their way, they would want to crawl inside their mother or father. They would like to be totally enveloped in their parents' bodies, arms, and legs. They may demand their parents' undivided attention and will protest as soon as that attention and physical contact wavers.

Because parents feel concerned by this behavior, they tend to watch their baby closely, and then they realize that their baby is actually trying to do many new things.

HOW YOU KNOW YOUR BABY HAS ENTERED THE NEXT FUSSY PHASE

When your baby is in the middle of this leap, you may ask yourself why you haven't noticed it before. There is a good reason that your baby wants to be so close to you now: you are familiar and with you, they feel safe. From that secure base, being with you, they want to discover the world again with the help of their new mental ability. Your baby may demand more attention than before; they may become shy with strangers, lose their appetite, cling to you all the time, or sleep poorly. Some babies show all these characteristics of this leap, and others only a few.

Does Your Baby Demand More Attention Than Before?

Your baby may want you to spend more time amusing them than they did before. They might even want your full attention. At this time, many babies no longer want to lie in their cribs or on a blanket on the floor, even if they had always been happy to do so until now. They might not object to being propped up in a baby chair or even their car seat or stroller, just as long as their parents are close by. They want their parents to look at them, talk to them, and play with them.

"Suddenly, my baby doesn't like going to bed at night. She starts crying and is restless, refusing to settle down. But we need some peace and quiet, too. So we keep her with us on the couch, to hold and cuddle her, and then she's no trouble at all."
About Eve, 8th week

Does Your Baby Become Shy With Strangers?

You might notice that your baby may not smile so easily at people they do not see often, or they may need more time to warm to them than before. Occasionally, some babies will even start crying if other people try to get near them when they are lying contentedly snuggled up to their moms or dads. Some think this is a pity: "They always used to be so cheerful." Others are secretly pleased: "After all, I'm the one who's there for them all the time."

"It seems that my daughter smiles more for us now than anyone else. It takes her longer to loosen up with other people."
About Ashley, 9th week

Does Your Baby Lose Their Appetite?

It may seem that if your baby had their way, they'd be on the breast or bottle all day long. But although they are latched on to the nipple, they seem to hardly take any milk at all. As long as they feel a nipple in or against their mouth, they are content. But as soon as they are taken off the breast or bottle, they start protesting and cry until they feel the nipple again. This generally only occurs in babies who are nursed on demand. Some mothers who breastfeed might start to think that there is something wrong with their milk supply, whereas other mothers question whether the decision to breastfeed was the right one after all. During this fussy phase, the baby is demanding the breast less for nutritional purposes and more as a comfort. This explains why some babies will suck their thumbs or fingers more often during this period.

"Sometimes I feel like a walking milk bottle, on standby 24 hours a day. I wonder if other mothers who breastfeed go through the same thing."
About Matt, 9th week

Does Your Baby Cling to You More Tightly Now?

Your baby might hold on to you even tighter than they did before, when they sense they are about to be set down. Not only will they cling to you with their fingers, they may even use their toes! This show of devotion makes it difficult for parents to put their baby down, both literally and figuratively. Parents may find it touching and heart-wrenching at the same time.

Does Your Baby Sleep Poorly?

In this difficult phase, your baby may not sleep as well as they did before. They might start crying the moment you carry them into the bedroom, which is why parents sometimes think that their baby is afraid of their crib. Various sleeping problems may affect your baby. Some babies have difficulty falling asleep, whereas others are easily disturbed and wake more often. Whatever the case with your baby, the result is the same: they sleep less. Unfortunately, this means your baby is awake for longer periods now, giving them more opportunity to cry.

We are making our way through another #wonderweek. This week she is learning the details of people's faces, observing patterns, and discovering her hands. With all of the new information and sensory overload, the baby is a bit cranky when she's sleepy. Thankfully we are handling it all gracefully!—**Instagram post**

TIP

If you want to know more about sleep and leaps, go to page 59.

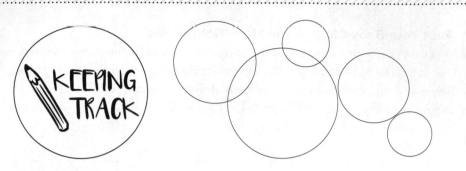

LEAP SIGNS

This is how you let me know the leap has started:

☐ You cry more often than before.

☐ You want to be kept busy, more than usual.

☐ You lose your appetite.

☐ You are shyer with strangers all of a sudden; you only want to be with:

_____

☐ You cling more than usual.

☐ You sleep poorly.

☐ You suck your thumb, or do so more often than before.

☐ Other changes I've noticed:

_____

_____

_____

Do remember: with this list, too, your baby does not necessarily show all these leap characteristics. This list is about which behaviors your baby shows, more than how many of them.

How Are *You* Doing?

As this is only the second leap your baby is taking, you may doubt yourself, or your baby. As time goes on, you will recognize the typical leap behavior, but right now, you are probably more worried than anything else. That is completely normal, and if you are ever in doubt, give your pediatrician a call. You should also try to cultivate a group of friends who can listen and support you. There are lots of Wonder Weeks groups online that have grown organically, and many parents find them very helpful. A leap in development is an overwhelming experience for a baby and therefore also for you. It can be hard to stay patient and keep it together. Add to that the sleepless nights, and you will understand that a leap, worries, and irritations belong together.

You May Be Worried

All parents are concerned when their baby cries often and is clingy, some parents more than others. Only a small number of parents are lucky enough to have no particular worries about their babies at this age. These parents have infants who are easygoing or quiet, who don't cry much more than usual, and who are generally easy to comfort. Temperamental babies are the most difficult to cope with. They will seem to cry 10 times louder and more frequently than other babies, and they will thrash around as if they were in a boxing ring. Their parents often worry the whole family will fall apart during such a fussy phase. Most babies fall somewhere between the two extremes.

When your baby cries more than usual, you might be desperate to figure out why. You may wonder, "Is my milk supply drying up? Are they sick? Am I doing something wrong? When they are on my lap, they're fine—does this mean I'm spoiling them?" After exploring every other avenue, some parents may decide that baby must be upset due to colic. Their baby seems to be writhing around a lot, after all. Some parents are left feeling insecure and may even have a good cry themselves. Occasionally parents will go to see the doctor, or they will call to bring up the issue with the pediatrician.

You May Feel Exasperated and Defensive

When parents can't find any obvious reason that their baby keeps crying and clinging to them, they might feel at the end of their rope. You still have so much to do, and their crying is driving you mad. Plus, you're exhausted. On top of that, "helpful" family or neighbors may seem like they're judging you, and that they see your baby as "difficult" or a "complete nuisance." Trust your instincts and ignore advice to be stern with your baby. Even plagued with doubts about what to do for the best, the urge to go comfort baby usually wins out. And that's the best thing you can do.

"I had to keep my son occupied all day long. Nothing really helped. I tried walking around, stroking him, and singing. At first, I felt completely helpless and depressed, and then suddenly, I felt really frustrated. I sat down and just started sobbing. So I asked the daycare center if they would have him for two afternoons a week, just to give me a few hours to recharge my batteries. His crying sometimes drains me completely. I'm so tired."

About Bob, 9th week

 ANCHOR MOMENTS *

Make sure to never forget what a big task you're doing, bringing up your little one. Allow yourself some great energizing anchor moments, to celebrate you!

In 5 minutes: Stand with your arms up, slightly wider than your shoulders in "I conquered the world" position. Stay here and focus on your breathing. You will feel stronger and better about yourself. Tip: Do this before something you're nervous about doing. The fear will lessen or disappear!

In 10 minutes: Brew a cup of herbal tea. Sit down and sip it slowly. Set a timer and make sure you sit for the full 10 minutes.

More time: Get out and breathe oxygen. Go for a walk in the park or the forest. Don't be in a rush; maybe even take some herbal tea with you . . .

You May Be on the Edge of Really Losing It

Only rarely will a parent admit to having been a bit rougher than necessary when putting their baby down because they were so driven to distraction by the baby's screaming and crying that it happened without their thinking about it. Even thoughts of being rough need to be addressed immediately, because it's an indication that you're overwhelmed and desperate and need to get help right away. There is no excuse for acting on those feelings, however difficult your baby is being. Accept that it can be trying at times and take action before the situation overwhelms you. Talk to someone about how you are feeling.

* For more anchor moments, see page 36.

▬▬▬▬▬▬▬▬ TIP ▬▬▬▬▬▬▬▬

In the "The Top 10 Things You Really Need to Know" chapter on page 195, you will find 10 handy tips that will help you to understand the leaps your baby is going through.

Body Contact: The Best Way to Comfort

Around eight weeks, it is very normal for babies to want to be with their daddy or mommy all day long. It's what all children want, after all. Some children show that desire more than others. At this age, crying and being clingy are the most normal things in the world. It means a baby is making good progress, and that they are taking a leap in their development. They are upset because their world has suddenly changed and the secure base that is their parents helps them feel safe so they can explore their new world.

Imagine you are upset and no one comforts you; you will be more tense and stressed for longer than if someone was there for you. All your energy is swallowed up by the tension and you can't see things clearly. That is how it is for your baby. When they make a leap in their development, it is as if a whole new world opens up for them. It feels like more than they can cope with, so they cry and will continue to cry until someone comforts them. They put all their time and energy into crying, time they could spend discovering their new world.

Their Fussiness Triggers You to Discover Your Baby's New Skills

The difficult first phase of a leap is understandable from a baby's perspective, as explained, but did you know that it has a function for parents as well? As they are paying closer attention because their baby is demanding it, they notice that their baby is in fact trying out new things because the baby has acquired the ability to learn new skills, as outlined in What You've Discovered: The World of Patterns on page 124. When parents realize this, they can help their baby become more independent, and then all the parents' worries and annoyances fade away.

You could say that your baby takes a small step backward (fussy phase) and then, with a bit of help from their parents, they take a giant leap forward in their independence.

Around eight weeks, that new ability is about recognizing and using "patterns." You can compare this new ability with a new world that your baby is discovering for the very first time.

The World of Patterns

Around this age, your baby will start to recognize recurring shapes, patterns, and structures. For instance, your baby might now discover that their hands belong to them. At this age, your baby will look at them in wonder and wave them around. Once they realize that these are their hands, your baby may also try to use them to grab at things. Not only do they begin to see patterns in the world around them, at this time your baby might begin to distinguish patterns in sounds, smells, tastes, and textures, too. In other words, your little one now perceives patterns with all of their senses. This new awareness is not just confined to what is going on outside their body—it also includes an enhanced perception of what is happening inside their body. For instance, now your baby may realize that holding their arm in the air feels different than letting it hang down. At the same time, they might also gain more control from within. Your baby may be able to maintain certain positions, not only with their head, body, arms, and legs, but also with smaller areas of their body. For example, they might start to make all kinds of faces, now that they have more control over their facial muscles. They might make explosive sounds because they can keep their vocal cords in a certain position. They may focus more sharply on an object because they have more control over their eye muscles than before.

Many of the automatic reactions (reflexes) your baby had at birth will start to disappear at this age. They will be replaced by something similar to voluntary movements. They no longer need the gripping reflex, for example, because your baby is now able to learn how to close their hand around a toy or other object. Your baby doesn't use the sucking reflex anymore because they are able to latch on to a nipple in one single movement, instead of finding it by what appears to be sheer coincidence after nuzzling for a while. By now, your infant is no longer completely dependent on reflexes. In general, babies will only resort to their old reflexes if they are hungry or upset. Your baby's first intentional movements are still very different from those of an adult. Their movements will be quite jerky, rigid, and stiff, like those of a puppet, and they will stay like this until the next leap announces itself.

BRAIN CHANGES

At approximately seven to eight weeks, a baby's head circumference dramatically increases. Researchers have recorded changes in the brain waves of babies aged 6 to 7 weeks old. At around 7 weeks, a change takes place in how a baby reaches and grabs at things. Up until now, it was a reflex, but developments in the higher levels of the brain start to take over. This reorganization allows your baby to realize their hands belong to them and they can also try to use them to grab at a toy, for instance.

THE MAGICAL LEAP FORWARD: THE DISCOVERY OF THE NEW WORLD

It is now time for the second part of your "task." The best way to help your baby make this leap is to develop the skills that they find most interesting. Here are a few suggestions of how you can do that.

- Show your baby that you're enthusiastic about every attempt they make to learn something new. If you praise them, you'll make them feel good, and this will encourage them to continue.

- Try to find a balance between providing enough challenges and demanding too much of them. Try to discover what they enjoy doing most.

- Stop as soon as you notice that they have had enough.

HOW TO TELL WHEN YOUR BABY HAS HAD ENOUGH

- Your baby will look away from you.
- If they are physically strong enough, they may turn their body away from you.
- Stop the game or activity as soon as you notice that your baby has had enough. Sometimes they will only want a short break before resuming the game or activity with renewed enthusiasm. They need time to let it all sink in. Always let your baby's responses guide you!

Your baby may want or need to practice some games or activities on their own. As long as you show some enthusiasm, this will be sufficient to reassure them that they are doing well. But there are things you can help them with. If your baby loves to explore the world with their own eyes, you can help them by offering them objects they like looking at. Vary the things around your baby. Help them discover their hands and place an object close to their hands so they can grab at it. The voice is an important tool, so chat with them and give them time to "reply." A pull-up game can be fun if they are ready for it. And keep in mind that playing on their own is also part of growing up!

"The last week and a half has been rough! When you think you know your baby, things change again and again. Micah has definitely showed me this with all the developments and milestones he has achieved the last week. I think I will never forget the day he found his toes or when the streetlight made him turn his head to follow it with intense anticipation. It has however also meant that this overwhelming new world has made him need a lot more comforting and the crying is on a different level. He normally does not even get that upset! Well, during the leap, he definitely does. Apparently my amazing sleeper also want[s] to wake up more during the night and fights naps unless it's in my arms."

About Micah, 9th week

BABIES ARE LIKE THIS

Babies love anything new, and it's important to respond when you notice any new skills or interests. They will enjoy it if you share these new discoveries, and this will accelerate their learning progress.

Show Your Baby "Real Things"

You may have noticed that your baby is more interested in "real things" rather than looking at the object in a picture. At this age, they cannot get close enough to the objects on their own, so they will need your help. They need you to take them to the object or for you to pick it up and show it to them. If you notice that they like looking at "real things," help them do this. Hold up colorful toys at different distances. Make sure you move the object slowly so you can get their attention and keep it for longer. You can also try slowly moving the plaything backward and forward and see to what distance your baby follows it with interest.

> *"My daughter likes looking at everything: paintings, books on the shelf, items in the kitchen cupboard. I have to take her everywhere. I even carry her in my arms when I go outside or when I go shopping."*
> **About Hannah, 11th week**

Variety Is the Spice of Life

After eight weeks, your baby may become bored if they always see, hear, smell, or taste the same old things. Their new awareness of "patterns" means they understand when things are repetitive. For the first time in their life, your baby may get fed up with the same toy, the same view, the same sound, the same feel of an object, and the same taste. They crave variety. If they seem bored, keep them stimulated. Carry them around in your arms or move the position of their baby chair to give them different objects to look at.

> *You stare and stare at patterns—like blankets, rugs, the cracks in logs, rain on windows, the colors on your jammies . . .—***Instagram post**

Help Your Baby Discover Their Hands and Feet

At this age, your baby may notice that familiar objects keep waving across their line of vision. If they investigate, they'll discover their hands or feet. They may gaze at them in wonder and begin to study them in detail. Every baby has their own way of investigating this new phenomenon. Some babies will need a lot of time to complete their explorations, whereas other babies won't. Most babies have a particular fondness for hands. Perhaps this is because their tiny hands pass by more often than other things.

Hands and arms can be placed in a myriad of different postures. Each posture is another pattern to be seen and felt. Allow your baby to study their hands as long as they want and as often as they want to. A baby has to learn what their hands are for before they can learn how to use them properly. Therefore, it is very important for them to get to know all about these "grasping devices."

"Eight week mental development leap—baby finds their hands. Good job, buddy!"
About Mack, 8th week

"My little one studies every detail of how his hands move. He plays quite delicately with his fingers. When he's lying down, he holds his hand in the air, then spreads his fingers. Sometimes he opens and closes his fingers, one at a time. Or he clasps his hands together or lets them touch. It's one continuous flow of gestures."
About Bob, 9th week

Encourage Your Baby to Grab Toys

Have you noticed your baby attempting to use their hands by trying to clasp a rattle, for instance? Holding a plaything involves a "feeling pattern" related to the position of the hand plus the object touching the palm of the hand. A baby's first attempts at grasping an object are generally far from successful. Show them that you are enthusiastic about the effort they are making and encourage each serious attempt. Praise from you will encourage them to continue.

Try to bear in mind that at this age, your baby is definitely not yet able to reach out for something so as to grasp it. They are only capable of closing their hands around an object. Make sure that you always place easy-to-grab toys near their waving hands. Your baby will then get the opportunity to practice the grabbing.

"My son is trying to grab things! His little hand gropes in the direction of his rattle, or he tries to hit it. A moment later he tries to grab the rattle, using a proper clasping motion. He puts a lot of effort into it. When he thinks he's got it, he clenches his fist, but the rattle is still a few inches away. The poor darling realizes his mistake, gets frustrated, and starts to cry."
About Paul, 11th week

Show Your Baby That Their Voice Is Important

A baby's greatest passion is the latest sounds that they make themselves. This is why you should try to respond to every sound your young infant makes. Your baby might be totally enthralled with making explosive sounds, because from this leap onward they can keep their vocal cords in a certain position. Just like a hand position, a vocal cord position is a "feeling pattern." Try to imitate your baby's sounds so that they can hear them from someone else. Respond when they use sounds to attract your attention. These chats will also teach them that their voice is an important tool, just as their hands are.

Encourage Your Baby to Chat

Every parent tries to encourage their baby to "chat." Some mothers and fathers talk to their babies throughout their waking hours as a matter of course, whereas others do this only at certain times, such as when their baby is on their laps. The disadvantage of planned chat times is that the baby may not always be in the right mood to listen and respond. It appears that babies whose parents "plan" chat times do not always understand what is expected of them, and their parents become easily discouraged because they think their babies are not responding properly yet.

Play Pull-Up Games

Many babies like pull-up games. A little one who is able to lift their head on their own may like being pulled up by their arms from a half-sitting position to an upright position or being pulled from a sitting position to standing. Be careful to support their heavy head. If they are very strong, they may even actively participate. This game teaches the baby how different postures feel and how to maintain them. Each of those postures is another pattern that your baby can perceive inside their body. If they cooperate in the pull-up game, they will jerk rather unsteadily from one position to the next, just like Pinocchio. Once they have jerked into a certain position, they will want to retain it for a moment. Although their movements are still far from supple, they will love being in a certain position for a short while. They may even become very upset when you decide it's time to end the game.

Fathers are usually the first to discover that babies enjoy these pull-up games, then mothers will follow, although fathers tend to be slightly more enthusiastic with baby boys than with baby girls.

"Suddenly, my son is jerking all over the place when I pull him onto his feet. He also makes jerky, spastic movements when he's lying naked on his changing mat. I don't know if this is normal."

About Kevin, 11th week

"If my baby had her way, she'd be on her feet all day, listening to me telling her how strong she is. If I don't rush in with compliments, she starts complaining."

About Ashley, 10th week

SOME THINGS TO KEEP IN MIND

- A baby is more eager to learn when they are making a leap in their development. They will learn quickly and easily, and it will be a lot more fun when you give them things that suit their personality and interests.

- Colicky babies automatically get more attention, as their parents strive to keep them amused and satisfied.

- Colicky babies have more chance of becoming the best students of tomorrow if they are given the right help and encouragement in their early years. This is particularly important when you help them learn during a leap in their development.

- Easygoing, quiet babies are easily forgotten, because they don't demand as much attention from their parents. Try to give a quiet baby just that bit more encouragement and stimulation.

Independent Play Is Also Part of Growing Up

You may think that your infant should be able to be a little bit more independent now, because you notice the great pleasure they take in their own hands and feet, their playthings, and their surroundings, and because they enjoy lying flat on their back on the floor. Try putting them on a baby play mat, the kind with soft arches overhead. These usually have appropriate toys hanging within easy reach of your baby's hands, allowing them to swipe at them or watch them swinging backward and forward. Let your baby amuse themselves for as long as possible, presenting them with new playthings when they get bored. With your help, your baby may be able to amuse themselves for about 15 minutes at this age.

"Ella has entered her second leap and has been learning so much! She's discovered her tongue and sticks it out constantly, she's begun to laugh, she pushes toys around and loves staring at Mommy and Daddy. She's also doing this really fun thing where she only sleeps in hour intervals at night!"
About Ella, 8th week

Experience the World Through Your Baby's Eyes

Hold your arms straight out in front of you. How does it feel? Then lie down on your back and turn your head sideways. How does that feel? How does it feel when you sit up and tilt your body forward? All these different postures are different patterns that you feel in your body. Leaning forward in a sitting position is a pleasant physical sensation, which is why your baby enjoys doing it so much when sitting on your lap.

KEEPING TRACK

YOUR FAVORITE GAMES: THE WORLD OF PATTERNS

These are games and activities that your baby may like now and that help them practice their newly developing skills.

Check off your baby's favorite games. After you have filled in What You've Discovered: The World of Patterns later in this chapter, see if there is a link between what interested your baby most and the games they preferred to play. You may have to think about it, but it will give you an insight into your baby's unique personality.

☐ YOUR HANDS OR FEET INTEREST YOU

Give your baby ample opportunity and room to watch their hands and feet. They will need to move freely to be able to take in every detail. The best thing to do is to put them on a large towel or blanket. If it is warm enough, let them play without their clothes on, since they will really enjoy the freedom of their naked body. If you want, you can tie a colorful ribbon around their hand or foot as an added attraction. You could also incorporate a bell in the activity. If you do this, however, be sure it is securely attached and watch the baby closely so that they do not accidentally choke on the ribbon or bell should it come loose.

☐ COZY CHATS

Sit down and make yourself comfortable, making sure that you have enough support in your back. Draw up your knees, and lay your baby on their back on your thighs. They can see you properly from this position, and you'll be able to follow all their reactions. Chat with them about the events of the day, or your plans for later—anything really. The most important things are the rhythm of your voice and your facial expressions. Be sure you give them enough time to respond. Watch your baby's reactions to discover what they find interesting. Remember that a talking mouth, together with a face that shifts from one expression to another, is usually a smash hit! Stop when your baby lets you know they've had enough.

☐ LOOKING AT THINGS TOGETHER

At this age, a baby is still unable to grab objects to take a closer look at them. Until they are able to do this themselves, they will have to rely on you to bring interesting objects to them. Discover things together that baby finds interesting. Explain to them what they are seeing. They will enjoy listening to the intonation of your voice and they will learn a lot from it. Don't forget, let their responses lead you.

☐ THE PULL-UP GAME

You can only play this game if your baby is able to lift their head on their own. Sit down and make yourself comfortable. Make sure that you have enough support in your back. Draw up your knees and put your baby on your legs and tummy so that they are virtually in a half-sitting position. They will feel more comfortable like this. Now, hold their arms and pull them up slowly, until they are sitting upright, giving them words of encouragement at the same time, such as telling them what a clever little baby they are. Watch their reactions carefully, and only continue if you're sure they are cooperating and enjoying themselves.

☐ TAKING A BATH TOGETHER

Babies will particularly enjoy watching water move, and when they feel the waves running over their skin. Place your baby on your stomach and show them drops and little streams of water running off their body. Or lay them on their back on your stomach, and play "Row, Row, Row Your Boat" together: move back and forth slowly to the rhythm of the song, and make small waves.

YOUR FAVORITE TOYS

☐ To look at: playthings that dangle overhead. For example:

_____

_____

☐ To look at: a moving mobile
☐ To look at: a musical box when it's playing

☐ To touch and grab at: playthings you can swipe at or touch. For example:

_____

_____

☐ To talk to or laugh at: a soft toy

☐ Mommy or Daddy is still your favorite toy!

A DEMANDING BABY COULD BE GIFTED

Some babies catch on to new games and toys quickly and are soon growing tired of doing the same things, day in and day out. They want new challenges, continual action, complicated games, and lots of variety. It can be extremely exhausting for parents of these "bubbly" babies, because they run out of imagination, and their infants scream if they are not presented with one new challenge after another.

It is a proven fact that many highly gifted children were whining and demanding babies. They were usually only happy as long as they were being offered new and exciting challenges.

A new ability will offer new opportunities to learn additional skills. Some babies will explore their new world and make discoveries with great enthusiasm, but they demand constant attention and help in doing this. They have an endless thirst for knowledge. They discover their new world with tremendous speed. They try out and acquire almost every skill the new world has to offer, then experiment a little before growing bored again. For parents of babies like this, there is little more they can do than to wait for the next leap.

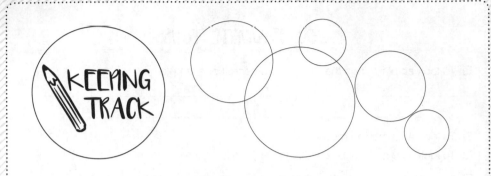

WHAT YOU'VE DISCOVERED: THE WORLD OF PATTERNS

All babies have undergone the same changes and entered the same new world with new discoveries to make and new skills to learn. But every baby decides for themselves what they want to learn, when, and how. They will choose what they consider the most appealing. Some babies will try to learn a variety of new skills, using one or more of their senses. Some will seem particularly interested in exploring this new world with their eyes. Some will prefer to try out their talking and listening skills. Others will try to become more adept with their bodies. This explains why a friend's baby may be doing something that your baby can't, or doesn't enjoy, and vice versa. A baby's likes and dislikes are determined by their unique makeup—their build, weight, temperament, inclination, and interests.

Observe your baby carefully and try to see what they like, what interests them. And do this as objectively as possible. In this list of discoveries, there is space to write down the things your baby has chosen. You can also explore for yourself if there are any skills your baby hasn't thought of trying out yet, but that might interest them.

These are examples of new skills that you may notice in your baby from this age. But it is important to remember that your baby will make choices and will not do everything on the list!

Instructions to Fill In This List:

Just before the next leap starts, check off the boxes in this list of the possible new things (skills) your baby has chosen. Their choices say a lot about their personality. Be critical when you go through the list and try not to make it an "is better than" list. By observing carefully and naturally facilitating your baby, you will see that quality is superior to quantity. The more critical you are, the better you will see the internal motivation behind your baby's character. Check off what your baby does right after the leap. If you would like, for the remaining possible skills, fill in the date later on when your baby has done something for the first time. This could be leaps later! That is normal: personality is not only defined by someone's preferences, but also by the things they are not interested in.

You made this leap on: _____

On _____ the sun broke through again and now, at the end of the leap, I see you can do these new things.

BODY CONTROL

Date:

☐ When you are alert, you can hold your head up by yourself.
To avoid confusion: The earliest possible time that babies are able to do this is with this leap, but it's completely normal for a baby not to do this until they are 6 months old. The average age is 4 months and a week, but this is not about averages but about your baby.

☐ You clearly turn your head toward things.

☐ You turn your head:
   ☐ Toward a sound, for example:

   _____

   _____

   ☐ When you want to see something, for example:

   _____

   _____

   ☐ To something you smelled, for example:

   _____

   _____

   ☐ Other:

   _____

   _____

☐ You "throw" yourself, as it were, from your side onto your stomach or your back.

☐ You roll from your back to your side.
The earliest time that babies are able to do this is with this leap. Some babies don't do it until they are 7 months, and that is normal and fine. The average age is 2½ months.

☐ You kick your legs and wave your arms when you are lying on your back.

☐ You allow yourself to be pulled into a sitting position.

☐ You allow yourself to be pulled into a standing position.
Of course, your baby cannot hold their balance for long and cannot really stand yet. But they can hold their body sturdily enough that they can be pulled into this position for a moment.

☐ You try to lift your head and torso by your arms when lying facedown for the first time/more often/better than before.
Some babies start doing this at 3 weeks but with less strength and stability than after taking this leap. Other babies don't manage until they are 5 months old. On average, most babies do this after making this leap.

☐ You show an increased desire to sit upright when sitting on my lap with your back against me. Of course, you can't sit independently for long and I prevent you from falling forward, but you are enjoying it!
This is the earliest age your baby can start doing this, but some babies don't until they are 6 months old. The average is 3 months and 3 weeks. Remember: any point within this time frame is fine.

☐ You are able to look left and right when lying on your stomach.

☐ You make all sorts of faces, even if unconsciously. You "play" with your face and I enjoy watching it immensely.

GRABBING, TOUCHING, AND FEELING

Date:

☐ You really want to grab that toy that's farther away but, of course, you can't manage it yet.

☐ You "swipe" at toys.
This is a first sign, an announcement that your baby is trying to master grabbing.

☐ You kick in jerky movements against a particular toy.
Jerky movements are typical of how babies move during this leap, as they move abruptly from one posture (perceived as a pattern) to another without any smooth transition.

☐ You close your hand around a toy when it's within easy reach.
It's normal for a baby to learn this between 2 and 7 months old. Anytime within that time frame is fine. The average age is 3 months and 3 weeks.

☐ You grab a toy and move it up and down. The movement is slightly "wooden," just like all movements with this leap.

☐ You feel objects without grabbing them.

LOOKING

Date:

☐ You have discovered your hands! You observe and look at them.

☐ You have discovered your feet! You observe and look at them.

☐ You have discovered your knees!

☐ You like looking at:
    ☐ People moving through the room or while they are busy doing things.
    ☐ Children playing in the room.
    ☐ Images on TV that change rapidly.
    ☐ How the dog/cat does things: for instance, walking, eating, jumping.
    ☐ Waving curtains.
    ☐ Luminous objects, such as a flickering candle.
    ☐ Treetops that you pass by when you are in your sling or on your back in the stroller. You find it particularly interesting to watch how the sunlight shines through and how the wind moves the branches. This is understandable because the sun highlights the patterns of the leaves and creates sharper contrasts, which you also liked at the previous leap.
    ☐ The items on the shelves at the supermarket when you pass by them. All those colorful packages are one big series of patterns. Or at the books on the shelf.
    ☐ Modern art with many shapes (curved lines) and colors. You like looking at it even more if you are being rocked back and forth. It's interesting because

adults concentrate by standing still, while babies observe better when being rocked side to side!

- ☐ Bling bling! You are fascinated by shiny clothing or jewelry. The glistening sparkles are, you guessed it, alternating patterns of shades of light.
- ☐ My mouth while eating or talking.
- ☐ Facial gestures. You study these intently.
- ☐ Other things you like to look at:

_____

_____

LISTENING AND SOUNDS

Date:

- ☐ You enjoy listening to voices, either talking or singing voices. You especially like high-pitched sounds, which is natural, considering you can hear them better than low-pitched sounds.

- ☐ You make short bursts of sounds, such as:
    - ☐ ah
    - ☐ uh
    - ☐ eh
    - ☐ mmm
    - ☐ Other sounds:

    _____

- ☐ You also like listening to yourself. ;-)
  Those "stuttering sounds" are such because your baby's vocal cords are held in a certain "pattern" so air can be pushed through. They are not yet able to make smooth movements with their vocal cords. They will only be able to make smooth sounds with the next leap.

- ☐ You sometimes make a whole series of sounds. You mumble and gurgle, as if you are saying something!

- ☐ If I "entice" you by talking to and encouraging you, you make the same sounds. It's like having a "chat" with us taking turns; you answer, then me, then you again, and so on.

- ☐ You "sing" along in your unique way when I dance and sing with you.

- ☐ You "chat" with and smile at soft toys.

THE EASY PERIOD: AFTER THE LEAP

Around 10 weeks, another period of comparative ease sets in. Most parents seem to put the concerns and anxieties of recent weeks quickly behind them. They sing their baby's praises and talk about their baby as if they had always been easygoing and cheerful.

What changes can you see in your baby at this stage? At approximately 10 weeks, your baby may not require as much attention as they did in the past. They are more independent. They are interested in their surroundings, in people, animals, and objects. It seems as if they suddenly understand and clearly recognize a whole range of new things. Their need to be with you constantly may also diminish at this time. If you pick them up, they may squirm and wriggle in discomfort and attempt to sit up in your arms as much as possible. The only time they might seem to need you now is when you are willing to show them things of interest.

Your baby may have become so cheerful and busy amusing themselves that life is much easier for you now. You may feel a surge of energy. At this age, lots of parents regularly put babies on their play mat, as they feel their children are ready for it now.

"My daughter suddenly seems much brighter. She's lost that newborn dependency. I'm not the only who's noticed. Everyone talks properly to her now, instead of making funny cooing noises."

About Emily, 10th week

"My baby seems 'wise' now. She's become more friendly, happier, and even roars with laughter once in a while. Thank goodness she's stopped that incessant crying. Life has changed drastically, from thinking, 'How can I cope with her screaming?' to enjoying having her around now."

About Jenny, 10th week

"My son no longer seems so vulnerable. I see a definite change in him now. He has progressed from just sitting on my lap to gaining a lot of independence and playing."

About Steven, 10th week

"I think my baby is really starting to develop into a real little person with a life of her own. At first, all she did was eat and sleep. Now she has a good stretch when I take her out of bed, just like grown-ups do."

About Nina, 10th week

"I don't know if there's any connection, but I certainly have noticed that I had a lot more energy this past week, and this coincided with my son's newfound independence. I must say I really enjoy watching the progress he's making. It's fascinating the way he laughs, enjoys himself, and plays. We seem to communicate better now. I can let my imagination run wild with his stuffed toys, sing him songs, and invent different games. Now that I'm getting some feedback from him, he's turning into a little friend. I find this age much easier than when he just nursed, cried, and slept."

About Bob, 10th week

Leap 3

The World of Smooth Transitions

ONE THING CAN FLOW
SMOOTHLY INTO THE NEXT

Around 11 or 12 weeks, or almost three months, your baby will enter yet another new world as they undergo another major developmental leap since their birth. They suddenly see, hear, smell, taste, and feel in a completely new way. You may recall that after the last leap, your baby's movements were jerky and unpolished. At 12 weeks, these jerky actions will start to change and become more fluid, turning a helpless infant into more of an independent little person.

Their world has changed and it will initially make them feel puzzled, confused, and bewildered, and they will need time to adjust. To come to terms with what is happening to them. And the best place to do that is somewhere safe and familiar. They will want to cling to their daddy or mommy for comfort. Fortunately, this fussy phase will not last quite as long as the previous one. Some babies will behave normally again after just a day, whereas others may need a whole week before they feel themselves again.

DO REMEMBER

If you notice your baby is fussier than usual, watch them closely. It's likely that they are attempting to master a new skill. Look at What You've Discovered: The World of Smooth Transitions on page 151 to see what to watch for.

THE FUSSY PHASE:
THE ANNOUNCEMENT OF THE MAGICAL LEAP

All babies will cry more often and for longer periods than before. Some will cry more than others. Some babies will be inconsolable; others may be fretful, cranky, moody, or listless. One baby may be especially difficult at night, whereas another may tend to get upset during the day. Usually, all babies will be a little less tearful if they are carried around or if they are just given extra attention or cuddles. But even under these circumstances, anybody who knows the baby well will suspect that they will cry or fret again at the least opportunity.

In short, your baby is again entering that fussy phase characterized by the three Cs (crying, clinginess, and crankiness) and at least a few other typical characteristics.

This phase is difficult for your baby but also for you, as you're likely stressed and worried. But don't forget that it's also an opportunity to stay close to your baby and discover the many new skills they are acquiring.

HOW YOU KNOW YOUR BABY HAS ENTERED THE NEXT FUSSY PHASE

You will recognize most of the characteristics of this fussy phase from the previous one. During this phase, babies are often shy of strangers, cling tightly to you, lose their appetite, sleep poorly, and suck their thumb more than usual, if they did at all. During the fussy phase of this leap, parents also notice that their baby is quieter or less lively than they normally are.

> *"My son is so terribly dependent on me right now. He is happy only if I hold him close. If he had his way, I think I'd be dancing around with him, too."*
> **About Bob, 12th week**

As well as the three Cs, your baby can also display some of the following characteristics as they enter the next fussy phase.

Does Your Baby Demand More Attention?

Just when you think that your baby has learned to amuse themselves, they don't seem to do so well at it anymore. It may seem as if they want you to play with them more now and keep them entertained all the time. Just sitting with them may not be enough; they might want you to look at them and talk to them, too. This change in their behavior will be all the more obvious if they already showed you that they could be independent after the last leap forward. If anything, you may think that they've suffered a setback.

Does Your Baby Become Shy With Strangers?

One in three babies will be shy with anyone but their parents at this time. If your baby is shy, you will notice that they cling to you whenever you have company. They may start to cry when a stranger talks to them or even looks at them. Sometimes, they may refuse to sit on anyone's lap but yours. If they are safely snuggled up to you, they may give someone else a reluctant smile, but if they are particularly shy, they will quickly bury their head in your shoulder afterward.

Does Your Baby Cling to You More Tightly Now?

Some babies cling to their parents so tightly when you carry them that it seems as if they are afraid of being dropped. Babies who do this may sometimes even pinch their mothers or fathers very hard in the process.

> *Helloooooooo cranky, crying, and clingy Paul-lo! Although these leaps are incredibly tiring, it's magic to see your little human master something new when you surface on other side.* —**Instagram post**

Does Your Baby Lose Their Appetite?

At this time, your baby might drag out each feeding session. Babies who are breast-fed on demand might start behaving as if they want to eat all day long. Bottle-fed babies take longer to finish their bottles, if they manage to get that far. These unruly drinkers spend their time chewing and gnawing at the nipples without actually drinking. They do this as a form of comfort and so they hang on for dear life, afraid to let go. Often, they will drift off to sleep with the nipple still in their mouth. Your baby may try to hold on to your clothing or grab your breast during nursing, even if they are being bottle-fed, as if they are afraid of relinquishing their only source of comfort.

"When I'm bottle-feeding my daughter, she sticks her tiny hand inside my blouse. We call it 'bosoming.'"
About Emily, 12th week

Does Your Baby Sleep Poorly?

Your baby will probably sleep less well now than before. Many babies wake several times a night demanding to be fed. And other babies wake up very early in the morning. Still other babies refuse to take naps during the day. For many families, the normal routine has turned into absolute chaos because the baby's regular feeding and sleeping patterns have changed so drastically.

> ### TIP
> If you want to know more about sleep and leaps, go to page 59.

If you want to know more about sleep and leaps, go to page 59.

LEAP 3

Does Your Baby Suck Their Thumb More Often?

Your baby may discover their thumb for the first time, or they might suck their thumb or pacifier more often or for longer than they did before. Like sucking at the breast or bottle, this is a comfort and can avert another crying session.

Is Your Baby Quieter or Less Lively Now?

Your baby may be quieter or seem less lively than usual. They may also lie still for quite some time, gazing around or just staring in front of them. This is only temporary. Their previous sounds and movements will soon be replaced by new ones.

> *"The only thing my baby likes doing right now is cuddling up close to me in her sling. She's very quiet and no trouble at all—she doesn't do much except sleep. To be honest, though, I'd much rather see her full of life."*
> **About Nina, 12th week**

LEAP SIGNS

This is how you let me know the leap has started:

☐ You cry more often.

☐ You want me to keep you occupied more than before.

☐ You lose your appetite.

☐ You are shyer with strangers than you were.

☐ You cling to me more now.

☐ You want more physical contact during nursing.

☐ You sleep poorly.

☐ You suck your thumb, or do so more often than before.

☐ You are less lively.

☐ You are quieter, less vocal.

☐ And I notice that you:

_____

_____

Do remember that a baby does not have to show all these characteristics! It is about what your baby is doing rather than how many of them they exhibit.

How Are *You* Doing?

Obviously, your baby is not the only one affected by changes occurring within them. The whole family experiences these mood shifts, especially the parents. Now that their baby is three months old, they realize that it can be challenging to stay positive and patient during a developmental leap.

You May Feel Worried

It is normal for parents to feel anxious when they notice their baby is clingier, crying more often, is sleeping poorly, or is not nursing as well as they were. They may be worried because it seems that baby has suffered a setback in producing sounds or movements or seems to have lost the independence they recently acquired. Parents usually expect to see progress, and if this doesn't seem to be happening, even if just for a short while, they get concerned. They feel insecure and they wonder what the matter is. "Is something wrong with the baby? Could they be ill? Could they be abnormal, after all?" are the most common worries. Generally, it is none of the above. On the contrary, your baby is showing signs of progress. A whole new world is there for them to discover, but when this world reveals itself, the baby first has to deal with the upheaval it brings. It's not easy for them and they will need your support. You can do this by showing that you understand they are going through a difficult time.

"When my baby is crying incessantly and wants to be carried around all the time, I feel pressured. I can't seem to accomplish even the simplest things. It makes me feel insecure, and it saps all my energy."
About Juliette, 12th week

"I'm trying to find out why my baby cries so much. I want to know what's troubling her so that I can fix it. Then, I'll have some peace of mind again."
About Laura, 12th week

"I find it really difficult to cope with my son's crying. I just can't take it anymore. I'd even prefer getting out of bed four times a night to deal with a baby who is not crying than twice a night to deal with a tiny screamer."
About Paul, 11th week

"I seem to cope better with my baby's erratic behavior if I don't make plans in advance. In the past, when my plans went completely haywire, I felt irritated. So I've changed my attitude. And would you believe it—I sometimes find I even have a few hours to spare!"
About Laura, 12th week

A study has found that a mom only takes an average of 17 minutes a day for herself. Let's change that . . . take some anchor moments. You deserve them and, nice side effect, it makes you a better parent and partner.

In 5 minutes: Put on your favorite song, sing along, dance along, drum along . . . as long as you enjoy each note of that special-for-you song.

In 10 minutes: Meditate, even if it's just for a couple of minutes. You really don't need to do a daily 30 minutes; anything from 2 to 15 minutes will help.

More time: Plan special you-and-me time. Sometimes relationships get neglected in the effort of looking after a baby. If you don't want or can't find a trusted sitter, just plan a special evening at home. Spending time together, just you and your partner, can be important in keeping the relationship close. And that is good for your baby.

You May Become Exasperated

Parents will need to adjust to their baby's irregular eating and sleeping routines during this time. It will be virtually impossible to plan ahead. The entire schedule is thrown off balance. They often feel under pressure from family or friends, too, because despite their instinct to focus all their attention on their unhappy infant, other people seem to disapprove of too much "babying." The parents may feel trapped in the middle.

"I get irritated every time my son starts fretting, because he can't seem to amuse himself for even just a short while. He wants me to keep him occupied all day long. Of course, everybody loves giving me advice on how to deal with him."
About Kevin, 12th week

After my husband's coworkers told him that he and our son look like two peas in a pod, he stopped criticizing the amount of attention I give Matt when he is crying. In fact, my husband wouldn't have it any other way now, whereas he used to feel I was overreacting and spoiling the baby. Things are running a lot smoother now."
About Matt, 12th week

"I'm doing all I can, but with the deadlines at work, caring for my wife who is still recovering from the birth, not sleeping, and all the changes in our life, it's all becoming a bit too much."
About Timothy, 11th week

* For more anchor moments, see page 36.

If the parents worry a lot about their baby, and they are not given enough support from family and friends, they may become exhausted. Unwelcome advice, on top of exhaustion, could make any parent feel even more irritable and snappish. They feel they have no one to turn to with their problems; they feel alone. However understandable these feelings of frustration may be, one should never act on them. Slapping or hurting a baby in any other way is not acceptable. Seek help if you feel it is all getting too much for you.

SHAKING IS VERY DANGEROUS

Never shake your baby. Shaking a young child can easily cause internal bleeding just below the skull, which can result in brain damage. That may lead to learning difficulties later on, and, in some cases, even death.

The Positive Side of Your Baby's Clinginess—You Notice More!

When a baby is upset, parents will tend to keep an extra close eye on them because they want to know what's wrong. In doing so, they suddenly notice that their baby has actually mastered new skills or is attempting to do so. In fact, you'll discover that your baby is making their next big leap—into the world of smooth transitions.

At approximately 12 weeks, your baby will be able to perceive the subtle ways that things change around them, not abruptly but smoothly and gradually. They will be ready to experiment with making such smooth transitions themselves. Your baby will make many new discoveries in this new world. They will select the things that appeal to them and that they are ready to attempt, physically and mentally. You should, as always, be careful not to push them but do help them with the things they show they are ready to do.

The World of Smooth Transitions

As they enter this new world, for the first time, your baby is able to recognize smooth transitions in sights, sounds, tastes, smells, and touch. For example, they may now notice how a voice shifts from one tone to the next, or how a body shifts from one position to another. With this new ability, not only can they register these smooth transitions when someone else does them, your infant is now able to learn to make them on their own. This new control applies to their body, head, eyes, and even their vocal cords. They can register these smooth transitions in the outside world and in their own body. You can imagine that they are now able to learn a range of new things and they can improve "old" skills.

Your baby learns, for instance, to move smoothly from one position to the next. They can feel how their arm gradually reaches toward a toy; how they gradually stretch their legs and bend them to sit or stand. You will probably notice that your baby's movements are no longer wooden or jerky, as with the previous leap, but that they are now more deliberate and purposeful movements. That is due to the slow, gradual, smooth transitions from one posture to the next.

You will also notice that your baby has better control of their head movements. They can move their head very smoothly from side to side, and they can vary their speed. They are able to follow everything in a more "mature" way now. When your baby was first born, they came equipped with a reflex that moved their gaze in the direction of any new sound. This disappeared somewhere between one and two months after birth, but now they can do the same thing consciously, and the response will be quicker than before.

Furthermore, your baby will now learn to swallow more "deliberately" and smoothly than previously, improving the "wooden" attempts at swallowing that they were first able to do after the previous leap. And that is good progress, of course, because that "wooden" swallowing movement is dangerous. If your baby didn't learn to swallow smoothly, they would choke on solid food.

A baby begins to recognize smooth transitions in pitch and in volume of sounds, and to experiment with their own voice by gurgling and shrieking.

Your baby's sight has improved so much that it is almost like an adult's. They will be able to follow something with their eyes in a controlled, well-coordinated manner. They may even begin to do this without turning their head. They will be able to follow people or objects approaching them or moving away. In fact, they will become capable of surveying the whole room.

After this leap, your baby will only be able to observe or make one smooth transition, such as a simple movement in one direction. When they want to make another movement, there will be a noticeable pause before any change of direction because they don't understand that one movement can flow into the next. They will only learn that with the next leap.

BRAIN CHANGES

Around 10 to 11 weeks, your baby's head circumference drastically increases.

Experience the World Through your Baby's Eyes

Think of five smooth transitions you have perceived during the last 24 hours. You should be able to manage five; in reality you will experience many, many more. But you may find this activity difficult to do, and that is because we witness so many smooth transitions every day that we don't even register them anymore.

To help you on your way, here are a few examples for each sense: you can see the light fading in or fading out; you can feel a smooth transition when stroking your arm tenderly and slowly; you can smell a smooth transition when somebody is cooking in the kitchen and slowly the smell becomes stronger in the living room; you can see and hear a smooth transition when an airplane is making a deep dive, producing a sound that goes down in pitch, followed by a steep rise, producing a sound that goes up in pitch; you can see a ballerina making a smooth movement with her arm and the ballerina can feel and make that smooth transition with the help of the receptors in her tendons, joints, and muscles; you can smell a smooth transition when you place a tiny drop of perfume on the back of your hand and take a deep breath through your nose with your nostrils close to the back of your hand; when a truck passes, you can hear the volume of the sound go up when it approaches and go down when it disappears.

Try to include all the senses. Taste might be a challenge, but you are up for it.

Your baby perceives such smooth transitions every minute of the day. Their entire world is made up of smooth transitions, so many that it is impossible for them to make sense of them all in one go. Or to put it another way: to convert them into skills all at once. That is asking too much of such a little baby, and so your baby always starts by choosing a few of those smooth transitions—the ones that interest them the most. An interactive baby (the kind that generally grows into a chatterbox later on) will choose sounds, but another baby might be more interested in observing the smooth transitions in their surroundings.

THE MAGICAL LEAP FORWARD:
THE DISCOVERY OF THE NEW WORLD

The more your baby plays or experiments with a new skill, the more adept they will become. Although they will play and practice on their own, your participation and encouragement are vital. As well as cheering them on when they do well, you can help when the going gets tough and they feel like giving up. At this point, you can make the task easier for them—usually by rearranging the world so that it is a bit more accommodating. This might mean turning a toy around so that it's easier to grab, propping them up so that they can see the cat through the window, or maybe imitating the sounds they are trying to make.

You can also help by making an activity more complex or vary it a bit so that they stay with it longer and are challenged just a little more. Be careful to watch for signs that your baby has had enough. Remember that they will go at their own pace. Just as all babies are different, so are their parents. Some parents have more imagination than others in certain areas. It may be a particular challenge for you if your baby is the physical type but you prefer talking, singing, and storytelling, and vice versa, but whatever type of baby you have and whatever type of parent you are, your child will always benefit from some help from you.

You can encourage your baby to use their voice by having little "chats" with them, and they will learn when you respond to what they are trying to tell you.

You can help your baby to explore with reaching for and touching objects. Your baby will benefit from spending a little time without any clothes on, so they can experiment with rolling over and pulling themselves up into a sitting or even a "standing" position, if they are physically strong enough. We have listed a few things that you can use to help your baby discover this new world as they try out their new skills. It is much easier for your baby if you help them, and you may even notice that you place less emphasis on your baby "playing on their own" at this point.

Encourage Your Baby to Use Their Voice

If your baby has a special love for sound, encourage them to use their voice. They may now begin to shriek, gurgle, or make vowel-like sounds themselves. These may range from high- to low-pitched sounds and from soft to loud ones. If they also start to blow saliva bubbles, don't discourage them. By doing these things, they are playing with "smooth transitions" and in the process, they are exercising the muscles of their vocal cords, lips, tongue, and palate as well.

Your baby may often practice when they are alone, sounding like somebody who is chattering away just for fun. They do this because the range of notes, with all the high and low vowel sounds and little shrieks in between, sound a lot like talking. Sometimes a baby will even chuckle at their own sounds. Answer your baby's chatter and encourage them to make sounds. By your joining in, they will feel you are listening to them and they will try out even more sounds. You will have the greatest success when you imitate their newest sounds.

Chat With Your Baby

Most babies love to have cozy chats with their parents. Of course, a baby has to be in the mood. The best time to chat is when they attract your attention with their voice. You will probably find yourself speaking in a slightly higher-pitched tone than usual, which is just right for your baby's ear. It is very important that you stick to the rules of conversation—your baby says something, then you say something back. Make sure you let them finish. Because if you don't give them time to reply, they will feel that you aren't listening to them, and they won't learn the rhythm of conversation. The subjects of your conversation don't matter very much at this age, but it is better to stick to familiar territory and shared experiences. Occasionally, try imitating the sounds they are making. Some babies find this so funny they will break into laughter. This is all-important groundwork for later language skills.

It is very important to talk to your baby frequently. Voices on the radio or television, or people talking in the same room, are no substitute for a one-on-one conversation. Your baby is prompted to talk because there is someone who is listening and responding to them. Your enthusiasm will play an important role here.

> *"I always talk back whenever he makes sounds, and if he's in the right mood he'll gurgle back at me again. And sometimes he replies with a smile."*
> **About John, 13th week**

Respond When They "Tell" You How They Are Feeling

Your baby might use one of their latest sounds when they want something. This is often a special "attention!" shriek. If they do this, always answer them. This is important since it will give them the sense that you understand what they are trying to communicate, even if you don't have time to stop and play with them at that moment. They will begin to use their voice to attract your attention. That's a significant step toward language.

When they're happy, a baby will often use a special "cry for joy" sound. They will use it when they see something they find amusing. It's natural to respond to these cries for joy with a kiss, a cuddle, or words of encouragement. The more you are able to do this, the better. It shows your baby that you share their pleasure and that you understand them.

WHEN YOUR BABY LAUGHS, THEY'RE ON TOP OF THE WORLD

When you make your baby laugh, you have struck the right chord with them. You have stimulated them in exactly the right way. Don't overdo it because you may frighten them. On the other hand, half-hearted attempts on your part could lead to boredom on theirs. You must find the comfortable middle ground for your baby.

> *"When my son saw that I was about to feed him, he shrieked with excitement and grabbed my breast, while my blouse was still only half undone."*
> **About Matt, 13th week**

Teach Your Baby to Grab

As your baby now lives in the world of smooth transitions, you may notice that they stretch out toward a toy with a smoother action than before. Help them. They have just entered this new world and reaching is still very difficult. Hold a toy within easy reach of your baby's hands and watch to see if they are able to reach for it. Hold the object right in front of them, keeping in mind that at this age they are only able to make one simple movement with their arm in one direction at a time. Now, pay close attention to what they do. If they are only just starting to master this skill, they will probably react something like this baby.

> *"My son is really starting to reach out to grab things! He reached for a toy dangling in front of him with both hands. He put out his right hand on one side of the toy and his left hand on the other side of the toy. Then, when both hands were just in front of the toy, he clasped them together . . . and missed! He'd tried really hard, so it wasn't at all surprising that he got very upset when he found himself empty-handed."*
> **About Paul, 12th week**

When your child reaches for objects and misses, encourage them to try again, or make the game a little easier for them so that they get a taste of success. At this age, they are not yet able to make an accurate estimate of the distance between their hands and the plaything they are trying to grab. They will not be able to learn this properly until they go through the leap at between 23 and 26 weeks old.

As your baby becomes more adept at grabbing objects, they will want to play the "grabbing game." Because they can turn their head smoothly and look around the room, they can choose what they want from the entire world of things that is now waiting to be grabbed, felt, and touched. After the last developmental leap, most babies spent about one-third of their waking hours playing and experimenting with their hands. After about 12 weeks, this suddenly doubles to two-thirds of their waking hours, and that percentage barely increases after that.

Teach Your Baby to Feel Objects

If you notice that your baby enjoys stroking things with their hands, encourage this activity as much as you can. Not only does the stroking movement involve a "smooth transition," but also the feeling in their hand caused by the moving contact with the object. Carry your baby around the house and garden, letting them feel all kinds of objects and experience their properties—hard, soft, rough, smooth, sticky, firm, flexible, prickly, cold, wet, and warm. Tell them what they feel. Help get your meaning across by using your tone of voice to express the feeling an object or surface arouses. They really will be able to understand more than they are able to tell you.

> *"I washed my baby's hands under running water, which made her laugh out loud. She couldn't get enough of it."*
> **About Jenny, 15th week**

Allow Your Baby to "Examine" You

Many babies like to examine their parents' faces. As your little one runs their hands over your face, they may linger slightly longer by your eyes, nose, and mouth. They might tug on your hair or pull at your nose, simply because they are easy to grasp. Items of clothing are interesting as well. Babies like to stroke and feel fabrics. Watch out for your earrings, too!

Some babies are interested in their parents' hands and they will study, touch, and stroke them. If your baby enjoys playing with your hands, help them with this. Slowly turn your hand over, and show them the palm and then the back of your hand. Let them watch while you move your hand or pick up a toy. Try not to make your movements too fast or to change direction too quickly, or you will lose their attention. Simple movements are all they can cope with in this world. Your baby won't be able to deal with more complicated movements until after another big change in their nervous system, which is the start of the next developmental leap.

Allow Your Baby to Play Without Clothes On

At this age, all babies are getting livelier than before. They are playing with smooth transitions felt inside their bodies, while they kick and wave their arms about. Some babies perform acrobatics; for example, they might stuff their toes in their mouths and almost spin around on their backs in the process. Some babies are not really interested in gymnastic feats, whereas others will get frustrated if their physical strength is not yet up to the task.

Whatever your baby's temperament, they will benefit from a little time spent without their clothes on in a warm environment. You may already have noticed that they are lively when you are changing them, enjoying the opportunity to move freely without being hampered by the diaper and clothes. Success comes more easily without the restriction of clothes. It gives them the chance to practice and, afterward, they will be quicker with their clothes on. A baby will be able to get to know their body better and control it more precisely.

"My son moves his body, arms, and legs around like mad, grunting and groaning in the process. He's obviously trying to do something, but whatever it is he's not succeeding because he usually ends up having an angry screaming fit."
About Frankie, 14th week

Teach Your Baby to Roll

Some babies attempt to roll over at this age, but nearly all of them will need a bit of help with it. If your little squirmer tries to roll over, let them hold on to one of your fingers as they practice. A very persistent baby may manage to roll from their tummy to their back. Some can do it the other way round and go from their back to tummy. Others don't give up even though they can't quite manage it.

Playing On Their Own May Be Less Important Now

Once in a while, parents may attempt to stretch the time their baby plays on their own. If they notice the baby's enthusiasm is waning, they present a new toy, move a plaything around, or make noisy toys squeak. They may try to chat with their baby to keep them entertained. At this age, with a parent's help, some babies can play by themselves for 30 minutes.

Many parents are so proud of all the things their baby is attempting to see, hear, and do that they want to be a part of it all and help their baby. There are so many new things to learn and practice that parents consider it less important for their baby to play on their own at this time.

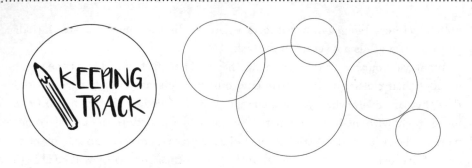

YOUR FAVORITE GAMES: THE WORLD OF SMOOTH TRANSITIONS

At this age, most babies particularly enjoy games when they are "moved around" by their mommy or daddy in slow and even movements. Any game you play should be short; variation is better than repetition at this point.

These are games and activities that your baby may like now and that help them practice their newly developing skills.

Instructions to Fill In This List:

Check off what your baby's favorite games are. When you have filled in the list, take a look at the What You've Discovered: The World of Patterns further on in this chapter. You may see a link between what your baby finds most interesting and the games they played during this leap. It will give you an insight into your baby's unique personality.

☐ PLAYING "AIRPLANE"

Lift your baby up slowly, while making a sound that increases in volume or changes from a low-pitched to a high-pitched sound. They will stretch out their body automatically as you raise them above your head. Then start the descent, making the appropriate airplane sounds. When they are in line with your face, welcome them by burying your face in their neck and giving them a nibble with your lips. You will soon notice that your baby expects you to do this and will open their mouth and nibble back. You will also see your baby opening their mouth again, as if anticipating the nibble, when they want you to repeat this flying game.

☐ PLAYING "SLIDE"

Sit down on a sofa, lean back, and make your legs as straight as possible.
Place your baby as high up on your legs as you can and let them slide gently down to the floor, while you make the appropriate sliding sound. Babies who enjoy water will love this game if you do it in the bath with them.

☐ YOU AS "A PENDULUM OF A CLOCK"

Place your baby on your knees so that they are facing you and slowly sway them from side to side. Try to make all kinds of clock sounds, such as a high-pitched, fast *tick-tock*, or a low-pitched, slow *bing-bong*. Try to make sounds that range from high to low and from fast to slow, or whatever clock sound you notice that your baby enjoys the most. Make sure you hold them firmly and that their head and neck muscles are strong enough to move with the rhythm.

☐ YOUR LAP AS A "ROCKING HORSE"

Place your baby on your knees so that they are facing you and make stepping movements with your legs, so your baby sways up and down as if they were sitting on a horse. You can also make the accompanying *clip-clop* noises or *schlupping* sounds that babies love at this age.

☐ THE NIBBLING GAME

Sit in front of your baby and make sure they are looking at you. Move your face slowly toward their tummy or nose. Meanwhile, make a drawn-out sound increasing in volume, or changing in tone; for instance, *chooooomp* or *aaaaaah-boom* or sounds similar to those the baby makes themselves. Then "play-bite" the tummy or nose.

☐ FEELING FABRICS

Here's a way to play and get chores done! Fold your laundry with your baby nearby, and let them feel different types of fabrics, such as wool, cotton, terry cloth, or nylon. Run their hand over the fabrics to allow them to feel the different textures, too. Babies like touching materials with their fingers and mouths. Try something unusual, such as chamois, leather, or felt.

☐ CLIMBING THE MOUNTAIN

Sit in a slightly reclined position and allow your baby "walk" or "climb" up your body. Make sure you hold on to them. You are actually the one exerting most of the effort and you are simply supporting them as they attempt to walk and climb.

☐ JUMPING AND BOUNCING ON YOUR LAP

A physically active baby loves repeating the same flowing movements over and over again when they are on your lap. Bounce them up and down or make smooth circular movements or move them from left to right. It will probably make them laugh, too, but, again, hold them tightly and watch their head.

YOUR FAVORITE TOYS

☐ Wobbly toys
☐ The clapper inside a bell
☐ A rocking chair
☐ Toys that emit a slow squeak or chime
☐ Rattles
☐ Dolls with realistic faces

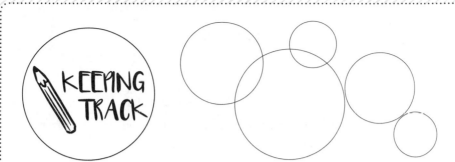

WHAT YOU'VE DISCOVERED:
THE WORLD OF SMOOTH TRANSITIONS

The following is a list of skills that your baby can exhibit at this age. Do remember your baby will not do everything on the list but will choose the skills best suited to them at this time.

Instructions to Fill In This List:

Just as you did with the previous leap, check off the boxes and write down the things you notice when the next leap is about to start. You will notice you can't cross off everything, and that is normal. This list is to give you a picture of your baby's preferences: which of these skills did they "decide" to develop first? By completing the lists, you can unravel a part of their unique personality leap by leap. Even if your baby is not exhibiting these skills now, they will eventually. In the end, all babies will do all the things on the list, but in their own time and way; this says nothing about their intelligence, but everything about their personality. So, as your baby grows, look back through these lists regularly, even if your child is leaps ahead, and, if you would like, fill in the date that you first noticed something. This creates a perfect overview of your baby's interest and preferences (and that they did right away in this leap) and the things that interested them the least (and that they did much later on). If you do this properly, you will see your baby's unique personality emerging as they grow.

You made this leap on: _____

On _____ the sun broke through again and now, at the end of the leap, I see you can do these new things.

BODY CONTROL

Date:

☐ I barely need to support your head, even when you are tired.

☐ You can turn your head in one smooth movement from one side to the next when you want to hear or see something.

☐ You can now follow a toy with a smooth eye movement.

☐ You are generally livelier and more energetic, and you wriggle and twist and turn around more than before.

☐ You make changing your diaper easier: you playfully lift your bottom when I'm doing it.

☐ You roll independently from your stomach to back or vice versa, while holding on to my fingers.

☐ You stick your toes in your mouth and twist yourself around.

☐ You pull yourself up into a sitting position while holding on to my two fingers. Of course, I realize that I am doing most of the work, but your body is strong enough to get to a sitting position with help. I am supporting you the entire time while you are trying to pull yourself up and when you are sitting.

☐ You gradually push off with your feet to the standing position when you are on my lap. I am sitting in a slightly reclined position and you are facing me, and when I then hold your hands and guide you, you pull up to a standing position, even though you are a bit wobbly. You are not yet able to really stand; I am helping you a lot. It will still take a while for you to be able to do this by yourself.

☐ You: use both feet to push off when seated in a bouncing chair or lying on a play mat.

☐ Other things I have noticed:

_____

_____

_____

GRABBING, TOUCHING, AND FEELING

Date:

☐ You grab and hold objects with your two hands.

☐ You deliberately and consciously grab your toy with two hands. I make sure the toy is within grabbing distance and right in front of you, otherwise it is still too difficult for you.

☐ If someone gives you a toy or other object, you deliberately and consciously take it with both hands.

☐ You can shake a rattle, or noisy toy, up and down.

☐ Your favorite toy to shake is:

_____

_____

☐ You study and fiddle with my hands.
At around 4 months, most babies start examining objects with their fingers and eyes instead of simply putting everything into their mouth. Some babies start doing this already at 3 months.

☐ You like studying people's faces, eyes, mouth, hair, etc., and touching them with your hands. It is like you are examining and learning with your hands.

☐ You not only like exploring body parts with your hands, but clothes, too.

☐ You enjoy discovering things with your hands, but you still try to put everything into your mouth. As a baby, you can feel and taste things that I can no longer taste or feel as an adult.

☐ You sometimes stroke your own head, from your neck to your eyes.

☐ You sometimes rub a toy along your head or cheek.

☐ Other things I have noticed:

_____

_____

_____

LISTENING AND TALKING

Date:

☐ Oh, oh . . . all your sounds! You shriek, howl, and can easily shift between loud and soft tones, low notes and high ones.
In short, babies are able to produce smooth transitions with their voice. Not only do they understand the smooth transitions, but they are able to make them with their vocal cords.

☐ You have a whole range of new sounds, and since this leap, they resemble the vowels of real speech. The sounds you make most are:

☐ ee   ☐ ooh
☐ oh   ☐ aah
☐ ehh   ☐ ay
☐ Other:

_____

☐ When lying or sitting down, you sometimes "tell" whole stories.

☐ You have discovered that you can blow saliva bubbles. You often find this very amusing and laugh at yourself doing it.

☐ Other things I have noticed:

_____

_____

LOOKING

Date:

☐ You turn your hands over, observing and studying both sides.

☐ You study your feet moving.

☐ You study faces, eyes, mouths, and hair.

☐ You study people's clothing.

☐ You like studying:

_____

_____

_____

OTHER SKILLS

Date:

☐ You clearly express that you like something by looking at, listening to, and grabbing an object, or by "saying" something and then waiting for the person you "spoke to" to continue with what they were doing.

☐ I notice that you use different "behaviors" with different people. You look, smile, "talk," cry, or move differently depending on who it is.

☐ You clearly show you are bored if you see, hear, taste, feel, or do the same things too often; variety has suddenly become important to you.

☐ Other changes I've noticed:

_____

_____

Experience the World Through Your Baby's Eyes

How does your baby show you what they like? Some babies become more active when they see something they like and they wave their arms and legs around, and even their whole body. That's hard to miss. Parents will be quicker to respond to these active babies and will put the baby in a place where they can see what they want, or parents will put the toy that interests them in their baby's hand.

If your baby is less active and stares at things they like, it is harder to notice what interests them. The quieter and less active your baby is, the easier it is to miss.

By carefully observing your baby, you will notice how they indicate that they like something or want to play with an object. If you respond to your baby, you facilitate their attempts to learn about their surroundings and they will feel that you understand the signals they are giving you, and it will encourage them all the more.

Try to think of five ways your baby lets you know that they want to do, see, or touch something.

THE EASY PERIOD: AFTER THE LEAP

Around 13 weeks, another period of comparative calm sets in. Parents, family, and friends will notice what a cheerful little person your baby has become and admire the wonderful progress they have made.

You may find your baby is much smarter now than before. When they are carried around or sit on your lap, they act like a little person. They immediately turn their head in the direction of something they want to see or hear. They laugh at everyone, and "answer" them when they are talked to. They shift their position to get a better look at things they want to see, and they keep an eye on everything going on around them. They are cheerful and active. It may strike you that other family members now show a lot more interest in them as a person. It appears that they have gained their own place in the family. They belong!

"My daughter is developing an interest in a whole variety of things now. She talks or shrieks at different objects, and when we watch her more closely, we think, 'My goodness, can you do that already?' Or 'Aren't you clever noticing all of those things?'"
About Jenny, 13th week

"My little one is definitely wiser. She's all eyes these days. She likes it when I carry her around and she turns her head left and right to get a good look at things."
About Hannah, 14th week

"My daughter is much more alert now. She responds to everything and immediately turns her little head in response to sounds. She's suddenly gained her own little place in the family."
About Emily, 14th week

"It's wonderful watching my baby enjoying herself so much and chatting affectionately to her cuddly toys and to people."
About Juliette, 14th week

"We have a lot more interaction with our child now because she responds to everything. After I've played a game with her, I can tell when she's waiting for me to play again. She also 'replies' a lot more now."
About Ashley, 13th week

"My son wanted to be close to us all the time; that's the first sign he will be making a leap. He gets bored more easily now, as if he is ready for new things. He doesn't want to nap during the day and he has an insatiable appetite. He seemed to be a lot wiser after the leap."
About Aiden, 15th week

"My daughter used to be so easygoing and quiet, but she's turned into a real little chatterbox now. She laughs and gurgles a lot more often. I really enjoy getting her out of bed to see what she'll do next."
About Eve, 14th week

"My son is much more interesting to watch now because the progress he's made is so obvious. He responds immediately with a smile or a gurgle, and he can turn his head in the right direction, too. I love giving him a good cuddle because he's so soft and chubby now."
About Frankie, 14th week

Leap 4

The World of Events

**THE MOST TROUBLESOME
LEAP OF ALL**

At around 19 weeks (or between 18 and 20 weeks), or 4½ months, your baby will make another leap in their development. You discover that they want and do things that they have never done before. That is because they have gained a new ability that enables them to learn an extensive array of new skills. They will begin to experiment with events. The word "event" has a special meaning here and has nothing to do with special occasions. In fact, here it means a short, familiar sequence of smooth transitions from one pattern to the next. You may be thinking, "Huh?" Let's try to explain what it means.

The realization that our daily experiences are split up into familiar events is something that we as adults take for granted. For example, if we see someone drop a rubber ball, we know that it will bounce back up and will probably continue to bounce several times. If someone jumps up into the air, we know that they will come down. We recognize the initial movements of a golf swing and a tennis serve, and we know what follows. But to your baby, everything is new, and nothing is predictable.

Your baby's awareness of the new changes that accompany this leap in their development actually begins at approximately 15 weeks (or between 14 and 17 weeks).

Their world changes and they don't know how to cope with it all. These changes affect the way they see, hear, smell, taste, and feel. They need time to come to terms with all of these new impressions, preferably in a place where they feel safe and secure. They will once again show a pronounced need to be with their mommy or daddy, to cling to their parents for comfort, and they will grow into their new world at their own pace.

We're sorry to tell you that, from this age on, the fussy periods will last longer than before. This particular one will often last five weeks, although it may be as short as one week or as long as six.

DO REMEMBER

If you notice your baby is fussier than usual, watch them closely. It's likely that they are attempting to master new skills. Look at What You've Discovered: The World of Events on page 187 to see what to look out for.

THE FUSSY PHASE:
THE ANNOUNCEMENT OF THE MAGICAL LEAP

All babies of this age cry more than usual during the fussy phase of the leap. Demanding babies, in particular, will cry, whine, and grumble noticeably more often than they did in the past. They will make no bones about the fact that they want to be with their daddy and mommy. More easygoing babies usually make a bit less fuss, or at least not as often as their more temperamental counterparts. All babies generally cry less when they are with their mommy or daddy, although they may insist you give them your undivided attention. They may not only want to be carried around constantly but also expect to be amused all through their waking hours. If they are not kept busy, they may continue to be extra cranky even when sitting on their mommy's or daddy's lap.

In short, your baby is entering a new difficult phase that is characterized by the three Cs (crying, clinginess, and crankiness) and at least a few others from a whole list of characteristics. This is not only difficult for your baby but also for you, and it can lead to worries and irritations. Fortunately, when this phase passes, your baby will be the sunshine in the house again. Their new skills will emerge and baby will be able to do many new things.

HOW YOU KNOW YOUR BABY HAS
ENTERED THE NEXT FUSSY PHASE

Besides the three Cs, your baby may display some of the following characteristics as they enter this next fussy phase: they may sleep poorly, they may demand more attention, they may always want to be with you, they may lose their appetite, they may be moody, they may be listless, and their head may need support more often now.

Does Your Baby Sleep Poorly?

Your baby may not settle down well at night now. It may be more difficult than before to get them to go to bed in the evenings, or they may lie awake at night. They may want a night feeding again, or they might even demand to be fed several times a night. They might also wake up much earlier in the morning than usual.

TIP

If you want to know more about sleep and leaps, go to page 59.

Does Your Baby Become Shy With Strangers?

Your baby might refuse to sit on anyone else's lap but yours, or they may get upset if a stranger looks at or talks to them. They may even seem frightened of their own father if they are not around him for much of the day. Generally, their shyness will be more apparent with people who look very different from you.

"When my daughter sees my sister, she gets extremely upset and starts screaming at the top of her lungs and buries her face in my clothes, as if she's afraid to even look at my sister. My sister has dark eyes and wears black eye makeup, which tends to give her a rather hard look. I'm blond and wear hardly any makeup at all. Perhaps that has something to do with it."
About Nina, 16th week

"My son won't smile at people who wear glasses anymore. He just stares are them with a stern look on his face and refuses to smile until they have taken their glasses off."
About John, 16th week

Does Your Baby Demand More Attention?

Your baby might want you to amuse them by doing things with them, or at the very least, they may want you to look at them all the time. They may even start to cry the moment you walk away. Some babies can't play on their own for as long as they usually do.

"I have to give my son extra attention between feedings. In the past, he'd lie quietly on his own. Now he wants to be entertained."
About John, 17th week

Does Your Baby Always Want to Be With You?

Your baby may refuse to be set down, although they may agree to sitting in their bouncing chair as long as you stay nearby and touch them frequently.

"My daughter wants to be closer to me, which is unusual for her. If I let go of her for even a second, she starts to cry, but as soon as either my husband or I pick her up, everything's fine again."
About Eve, 14th week

"The app gave me the signal that a leap was on its way, and it was right on time. I noticed that my daughter was demanding my attention more all of a sudden. It got worse by the day. I have ended up carrying her around all day in her sling. It makes life a bit easier for both of us."
About Ellen, 17th week

Does Your Baby's Head Need More Support?

When you carry your fussy baby around, you may notice you have to support their head and body more often now. They may slump down a little in your arms when you hold them, particularly during crying fits. When you carry them, it may strike you that they feel more like the tiny newborn they used to be.

Is Your Baby Moody?

Some babies' moods swing wildly at this time. One day they are all smiles, but the next they do nothing but cry. These mood swings may even occur from one moment to the next. One minute they're shrieking with laughter, and the next, they burst into tears. Sometimes they even start to cry in the middle of laughing. Some parents say that both the laughter and the tears seem to be dramatic and exaggerated, almost unreal.

Jack has gone from tiny little baby to full blown teenager who doesn't know what he wants. Nothing is good enough for him. NOTHING! Lord help me through this fourth leap, please. —**Instagram post**

Does Your Baby Lose Their Appetite?

Both breastfed and bottle-fed babies can temporarily have smaller appetites than usual as they approach this leap. Your baby may be more easily distracted than they used to be by the things they see or hear around them, or they are quick to start playing with the nipple. Occasionally, they may even refuse to drink completely. Nearly all mothers who breastfeed see this refusal as a sign that they should switch to other forms of nourishment. Some mothers feel as if their baby is rejecting them personally. This is not the case at all. Your baby is simply upset.

"Around 15 weeks, my daughter suddenly started nursing less. After five minutes, she would start playing around with my nipple. After that had gone on for two weeks, I decided to start supplementing my milk with formula, but she wouldn't have any of that either. This phase lasted four weeks. During that time, I worried she would suffer from some kind of nutrition deficiency, especially when I saw my milk supply starting to diminish. But now she is drinking like she used to again, and my milk supply is as plentiful as ever. In fact, I seem to have more."
About Hannah, 19th week

Is Your Baby Quieter Than Before?

Your baby may stop making their familiar sounds for a brief period or might occasionally lie motionless, staring into thin air or fidgeting with their ears, for example. It's very common for babies at this age to seem listless and preoccupied. Many parents find their infant's behavior peculiar and alarming. But actually, this apathy is just a lull before the storm. This interlude is a sign that your baby is on the brink of making many discoveries in a new world where they will learn to acquire many new skills.

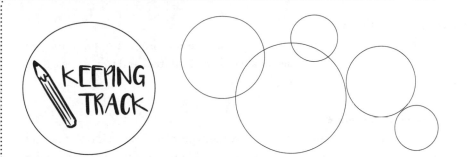

LEAP SIGNS

This is how you let me know the leap has started:

☐ You cry more often.

☐ You are often bad-tempered, cranky, or fretful.

☐ You demand more attention than you did.

☐ You need more support for your head now.

☐ You want more physical contact.

☐ You sleep poorly.

☐ You lose your appetite.

☐ You are quieter, less vocal.

☐ You are less lively.

☐ You have pronounced mood swings.

☐ You want more physical contact during nursing.

☐ You suck your thumb more often, or suck more often than before.

☐ And I notice that you:

_____

_____

As you check off your baby's behaviors on this list, remember that no baby will do everything listed. How much your baby does is not important—your baby will choose the skills best suited to them at this time.

How Are *You* Doing?

As you are aware by now, these fussy phases are not only hard going for your baby but also for you.* You may be exhausted and irritated, and sometimes, it can almost become too much for you . . .

You May Feel Exhausted

During a fussy phase, most mothers and fathers complain increasingly of fatigue, headaches, nausea, backaches, or emotional problems. Some less fortunate parents contend with more than one of these problems at the same time. They blame their symptoms on a lack of sleep, having to constantly carry their little screamers, or worrying about their unhappy infants. The real cause of these symptoms, though, is the stress of constantly coping with a cranky baby. Some parents visit their pediatrician and are prescribed an iron supplement, or go to a physiotherapist for their back troubles, but the real problem is that they are nearing the end of their tether. Especially now, make time for yourself, and give yourself a treat now and then. But remember that your baby will eventually come to your aid by learning the skills they need to deal with their new world, and then the sun will shine again.

You May Be at Your Wits' End

Many mothers and fathers can become annoyed toward the end of a fussy phase. When there seems to be no real reason a baby is upset, it may feel like their baby has no valid reason for making such a fuss, and they are inclined to let them cry a little longer than they used to. Parents may think of comments and helpful advice they've heard from others about "spoiling" their baby. Maybe they *really are* giving in to their whims too much.

We hope you will remember that your baby needs to be comforted. Leaving them to cry will not help them through this fussy phase. When your baby won't stop crying, and you are at your wits' end, get help long before you lose control. Shaking, in particular, can be harmful.

---

* When in doubt, always consult your pediatrician.

"My son refused to continue with his feeding and started having an incredible crying tantrum, while I just kept trying to get his milk down his throat. When the same thing happened with the next bottle, I felt myself becoming terribly angry because none of my little distraction tricks were working. I felt as if I were going around in circles. I put him on the floor where he would be safe and let him scream his lungs out. When he finally stopped, I went back into the room, and he finished his bottle."

About Bob, 19th week

"I started to feel my temper rise every time my daughter launched into one of her crying fits because I'd left her on her own for just a second. I let her get on with it and ignored her."

About Ashley, 17th week

"The last four evenings, my son started screaming at 8 p.m. After consoling him for two nights in a row, I'd had enough. I let him cry until 10:30 p.m. He's certainly persistent, I'll give him that!"

About Kevin, 16th week

ANCHOR MOMENTS *

Yup . . . this might well be the most difficult leap for your baby and therefore for you. Don't forget your three anchors a day, to keep the stress at bay!

In 5 minutes: Massage your hands a bit. Rub from your elbows to the tips of your fingers, then put your hand around each finger and make a twisting movement going toward the fingertips. Pull slightly on the finger at the end. Your hands will feel refreshed and good to go again.

In 10 minutes: Take a moment to look at the things you think you really need to do today. If this feels overwhelming, scratch some of it by realizing the world won't stop turning if, for example, your house isn't as tidy as you would like it to be. Prioritize!

More time: Go out to see something that stimulates your mind and that you truly love to do. Theater, a museum, the new fashion in stores, nature, a car show—it can be anything. Just plan this special outing for yourself and enjoy it!

* For more anchor moments, see page 36.

It Takes Longer for Your Baby to Explore the New World

Because this fussy phase lasts longer than the previous ones, most parents immediately sense that this phase is different. They are concerned about their baby's seemingly slower progress and the fact that their baby seems to have a sudden aversion to the things they liked in the past. But don't worry. From this age on, the new skills are much more complicated to learn. Your little one simply needs more time.

> *"My baby seems to be making such slow progress. Before he was 15 weeks old, he developed much faster. It's almost as if he's come to a standstill these past few weeks. At times, I find this to be very upsetting."*
> **About Matt, 17th week**
>
> *"It's almost as if my son is on the verge of making new discoveries, but something seems to be holding him back. When I play with him, I can sense there's something missing, but I don't know what it is. So I'm playing the waiting game, too."*
> **About Steven, 17th week**

Your Baby's New Ability Is Starting to Bear Fruit

At approximately 19 weeks, you will notice that your baby is once again trying to learn new skills, because this is the age when babies will generally begin to explore the world of events. This world offers them a huge repertoire of event skills. Your baby will choose the skills best suited to them—the ones they want to explore. You can help them with what they are actually ready to do, rather than trying to push them in any and every direction. Remember to look at What You've Discovered: The World of Events on page 187 to see what to look out for.

> *"My daughter has been trying to do lots of new things this week. All of a sudden, it hit me how much she can do at just four months, and to tell you the truth, I feel very proud of her."*
> **About Jenny, 18th week**

The World of Events

After the last leap forward, your baby was able to see, hear, smell, taste, and feel smooth transitions. And they tried them out themselves with their eyes, arms, legs, head, voice, and so on. But they stopped after one "smooth transition." That is all they could understand. Once your baby gets the ability to perceive and experiment with events themselves with this leap, they will be able to see, hear, smell, taste, and feel a short series of smooth transitions and do them themselves. This new ability will affect a baby's entire behavior.

As soon as a baby is able to make several smooth movements in sequence, this will give them more opportunities with objects within their grasp. They might, for instance, be able to repeat the same smooth movement several times in succession. You may now see them trying to shake playthings from side to side or up and down. They may also attempt to press, push, bang, or beat a toy repeatedly. With this new ability, your baby can make one smooth movement flow into the next. For instance, they may grab an object with one hand, then try to pass it to the other hand. Or they may grab a plaything and immediately attempt to put it in their mouth. They are capable of turning a plaything around and looking at it from every possible angle. From now on, they are able to carry out a thorough examination of any object within reach.

In addition, your baby might now learn how to adjust the movements of their body, upper arms, lower arms, hands, and fingers, to reach the exact spot where the plaything is, and they can learn to correct their movements as they go along. For instance, if a toy is farther to the left, their arm will move to the left in one flowing movement. If it is more to the right, their arm will immediately move to the correct spot. The same applies to an object near at hand, one that is farther away, or a toy hanging high up or low down. They will see it, reach for it, grab it, and pull it toward them, all in one smooth movement. As a result, you could say that they can now "really" grab and pick up things. As long as an object is within arm's length, your little one will now actually be able to reach out and grasp the object of their choice.

When a baby is able to make a short series of smooth movements, they can also use them to try out various antics. You may see them twist and turn. They might now learn to roll over or spin on their back easily. They may also make their first attempts at crawling, because they are now capable of pulling their knees up, pushing off, and stretching.

They might also learn to make a short series of sounds now. You can say they have started making movements with their voice, much as they are trying out movements with their body. If they do, they will develop their chatter, which started after the previous leap, to include alternating vowel and consonant sounds. They will gradually use all of these sounds to speak in "sentences." This "abba baba tata" is what adults fondly call babbling. You could say they are now able to become just as flexible with their voice as they are with the rest of their body.

All over the world, babies start playing with these sequences. For example, Russian, Chinese, and American babies all babble the same language initially. Eventually, the babies will start to develop their babble sounds into proper words of their native language, and they will stop using the universal babble sounds. Each baby will then become more proficient at imitating the language they hear being spoken around them, because they will get the most response and praise when they produce something close to home.

Apparently, everyone's ancestors must have felt as if they were being addressed personally when they heard their offspring say "Dada" or "Mammam," because the words for "mommy" and "daddy" are very similar in many different languages. The truth, though, is that the little babbler is carrying out a number of technical experiments with short, familiar sequences of the same sound element: "da" or "ma." But this is also the time at which babies may start recognizing words.

DID YOU KNOW ...?

In an unusual experiment, researchers found that if a part of a minuet by Mozart was played to babies, they showed a definite response if the music was interrupted by random pauses.

Your baby may now begin to recognize a short series of patterns and/or smooth transitions in sounds. They may be fascinated by a series of notes running smoothly up and down a musical scale. They may now respond to all voices that express approval, and they may be startled by voices that scold. It doesn't matter what language is used to express these feelings, since they will be able to perceive the differences in the rise and/or fall of intonation and in the pitch. For the first time, they are now able to pick out one specific voice in the middle of a commotion. Your baby may also start to recognize short, familiar tunes. A good example is the opening tune of the fifth symphony of Beethoven: tatatataaaaa.

Your baby may now learn to see a short, familiar sequence of images. For instance, they may be fascinated by the up-and-down motion of a bouncing ball. There are endless examples to be seen, all disguised as normal, everyday activities or events, such as someone shaking their bottle up and down, stirring a saucepan, hammering a nail, opening and closing a door, slicing bread, filing nails, brushing hair, the dog scratching itself, somebody pacing back and forth in the room, and a whole range of other events and activities.

Two more basic characteristics of the world of events should be mentioned here. First, as adults, we usually experience an event as an inseparable whole. We do not see a falling-rising-falling ball—we see a bouncing ball. Even when the event has only just begun, we already know it's a bouncing ball. As long as it continues, this remains one and the same event—an event for which we have a name. Second, the observer defines most events. For instance, when we speak, we don't separate the words clearly, but run one into the next without a pause. The listener creates the boundaries between words, giving the impression that they are heard one at a time. It is exactly this special type of perception of events that will begin to be available to your baby between 14 and 17 weeks.

Babies love anything new, and it's important to respond when you notice any new skills or interests. They will enjoy it if you share these new discoveries, and this will accelerate their learning progress.

Experience the World Through Your Baby's Eyes

Make a list of 10 events that you see, hear, do, or experience each day. This list will be easier to write than the ones for the previous leaps because we can easily perceive events. The way your baby perceives the world is getting closer to the way we experience it as adults.

1. _____
2. _____
3. _____
4. _____
5. _____
6. _____
7. _____
8. _____
9. _____
10. _____

BRAIN CHANGES

Recordings of babies' brain waves show that dramatic changes occur at approximately four months. Also, a baby's head circumference suddenly increases between 15 and 18 weeks.

THE MAGICAL LEAP FORWARD:
THE DISCOVERY OF THE NEW WORLD

The more your baby comes in contact with events and the more they play with them, the greater their understanding of them will be and the more proficient they will become. It doesn't matter which discoveries they choose to make first in this new world. They may pay close attention to music, sounds, or words. Or they may choose looking and observing, or physical activities. Later on, it will be easy for them to put the knowledge and experience they have gained learning one skill to good use when learning another.

Besides wanting to experiment with the discoveries they make in their world of events, your baby will also become tremendously interested in everything going on around them. This may now occupy most of their waking hours, because they will want to look at and listen to everything they possibly can. Even better (or worse!), every toy, household item, and gardening or kitchen utensil within a small arm's length is theirs for the taking. You are no longer their only toy. They may try to become involved in the world around them by pushing themselves forward with their hands and feet, toward something new, and away from their parents. They may now have less time to spare for their old cuddling games. Some parents feel a little rejected by this.

Even so, they still need your help just as much as ever. Your baby's fascination with the whole world around them is typical at this age. You have probably started to sense these new needs, and your main contribution can be supplying your baby with enough playthings and then waiting to see how they respond. Only give them a hand if you notice they are having real difficulties in fully understanding a toy. You'll also want to keep an eye on your baby to make sure they use their hands, feet, limbs, and body properly when reaching out to grab objects. If you see they have a particular problem, you can help them practice activities like rolling over, turning, and sometimes even crawling, sitting, or standing up.

You can also help your baby by giving them the chance to practice with their hands and fingers; to discover the world, and the smallest details, by allowing them to discover music or by giving them the time to look at things. And speaking of looking at things, from now on your baby will not only watch you while you are eating, they may even try to grab the food out of your mouth. You will notice your baby experimenting with things, and you can help them with that. You can play a "peek-a-boo" game with objects, for example. Or you can help your baby develop their language skills, because at this age they are able to make "babbling sentences" and can understand their first words. It's also a good time to start looking at books, which is enjoyable and educational.

Here are some ways that you can help your baby with all these elements that are part of discovering this new world.

Teach Your Baby to Roll: Turn It Into a Game

Perhaps you have seen your baby spin on their back and squirm in an attempt to roll over from their tummy onto their back. If you did, you saw your little one toying with a short series of smooth movements of several body parts. They can make these now because they are living in the world of events. However, being able to make several smooth movements in succession does not automatically mean they are successful in rolling over or crawling. It usually takes quite some trial and error to get there.

Here's a playful way to help your baby practice rolling from their back onto their tummy. Lay your baby on their back, and hold a colorful plaything next to them. To reach it, they will be forced to reach out and turn so they can't help but roll over. Of course, you have to encourage them in their efforts and praise them for trying.

You can also make a game out of helping them to roll from their tummy onto their back. One way is to lay your baby on their stomach and hold a colorful toy behind them, either to their left or to their right. When they turn to reach for it, move the plaything farther behind their back. At a certain point, they will roll over, simply from turning a little too much when reaching for the toy. Their heavy head will automatically help them in the process.

> She rolls over, hates wearing pants, drools like a St. Bernard and is DEEP into the 4th developmental leap and all that cranky "I-need-mom-ness" that entails.—**Instagram post**

"My son is practicing like crazy to learn to roll over properly. But when he's lying face down, he pulls both arms and legs up at the same time, straining and moaning like mad, and that's as far as he goes."
About John, 21st week

"My daughter keeps trying to roll from her back to her belly. When it doesn't work she gets terribly angry and then there is no pleasing her."
About Ashley, 20th week

> *"I think my baby may want to crawl, but I have the feeling he doesn't know how yet. He squirms and wriggles, but he doesn't move an inch. He gets really upset then."*
> **About Frankie, 20th week**

Teach Your Baby to Crawl: It Sometimes Works

Babies often try to crawl around this age. The problem with crawling is the moving forward part. Most babies would love to move forward, and they do try. Some babies get into the right starting position—they tuck their knees under their bodies, stick their bottoms in the air, and push off—but they don't succeed. Others will sit on their hands and knees and shift their weight forward and backward. There are also little squirmers who slide backward, because they push off with their hands. Others push off with one foot, thus going around in circles. Some lucky babies fumble around for a while and hit on a forward motion seemingly by accident. This is the exception rather than the rule at this age.

Many parents try to help their babies crawl. They carefully push their wriggling infant's bottom forward, or they put all kinds of attractive objects just out of baby's reach in an attempt to coax them forward. Sometimes these maneuvers will do the trick, and the baby somehow manages to move a little. Some babies do this by throwing themselves forward with a thud. Others lie on their tummies and push themselves forward with their legs, while using their arms to steer themselves in the right direction.

If you imitate your baby's attempts, they may find it absolutely hilarious. They may also really enjoy watching you show them how to crawl properly. Nearly every child who is having crawling problems will be fascinated by your attempts. Just try it and see!

LET THEM WRIGGLE AROUND NAKED

Your baby has to practice if they want to learn how to roll over, turn, and crawl properly. It will be a lot more fun, and much easier for them, if they are not wearing their clothes and diaper. Lots of physical exercise will give them the opportunity to get to know their body and help them to increase their control over it.

Give Your Baby the Opportunity to Practice Using Their Hands and Fingers

Many babies like to practice reaching for, grabbing, and pulling a toy toward them in one smooth movement and manipulating it in all sorts of ways, such as shaking, banging, or poking. Let them explore as many objects as they want to. An activity center offers a variety of these hand and finger exercises all on one board. It usually has an element that can be turned and that emits a sound when baby turns it. It may have a knob that also makes a noise when pressed. There could be animals to slide up and down and revolving cylinders and balls to turn, and so on. Each separate activity will emit a different sound when your baby handles it. Lots of babies love their activity centers. But don't expect your little one to understand and use all these features properly at first. They're just a beginner! When you see that your baby is trying to do something without much success, you can help them by holding their hand to show them how to do it properly. Or if your baby has a preference for observing how things are done, let them watch how your hand does it. Either way, you will encourage them to be playful and clever with their little hands.

> Bo is showing Leap 4 who is boss . . . grasping and
> going after toys, everything is hand to mouth these days,
> and he naps on his terms now. —Instagram post

Allow Your Baby to Explore the World

In the world of events, your baby's arms, hands, and fingers are just like the rest of their body—able to make several smooth movements in succession. Thus, they can examine the objects they can lay their hands on. They might turn them around, shake them, bang them, slide them up and down, and stick an interesting part in their mouth to feel and taste it.

If your baby is a keen explorer, you can enrich their environment by offering them playthings and other objects of different shapes, such as round or square things, or made of different materials, such as wood and plastic. Give them fabrics with different textures or soft, rough, and smooth paper to play with. Many babies love empty chip bags, because they slowly change shape and make wonderful crackling sounds when crumpled. Give your baby objects with uneven edges or dents. Most babies have a weakness for weird shapes. The shape of a plastic key, for instance, will challenge them to make a closer inspection. Many babies find the irregular side particularly intriguing and will want to touch it, look at it, and taste it.

MAKE YOUR HOME BABYPROOF

Your baby is now becoming increasingly mobile, so it's time to do a quick safety check.

- Never leave small objects, such as buttons, pins, or coins, near your baby.

- When your baby is on your lap during feeding, make sure they can't suddenly grab a cup or mug containing a hot drink.

- Never leave hot drinks on a table within your baby's reach. Don't even leave them on a high table. If the baby tries to reach it by pulling at the leg of the table—or, even worse, the tablecloth—they could spill the drink over themselves.

- Use a guard or fence around stoves and fireplaces.

- Keep poisonous substances, such as turpentine, bleach, and medicines, out of your baby's reach and in childproof containers when possible.

- Make sure electrical outlets are secured with socket covers and that there are no trailing wires anywhere.

Down to the Smallest Detail

Some babies are drawn to the smallest details. If you have such a tiny researcher, they will probably look at an object from all sides, examining it very carefully. They will really take their time and closely inspect the object. They will fuss with the smallest of protrusions. It may take ages before they've finished stroking, feeling, and rubbing textures, and examining shapes and colors. Nothing seems to escape their inquisitive eyes and probing mind. If they decide to examine you, they will do this meticulously, too. If they study your hand, they will usually begin with one finger, stroke the nail, and then look and feel how it moves before they proceed to the next finger. If they're examining your mouth, they will usually inspect every single tooth. Stimulate their eye for detail by giving them toys and objects that will interest them.

"My daughter is definitely going to be a dentist. I almost choke every time she inspects my mouth. She probes around and she practically shoves her whole fist inside my mouth. She makes it very clear she doesn't appreciate being interrupted while she's working when I try to close my mouth to give her a kiss on the hand."
About Emily, 21st week

Your Baby May Love Music

If your baby is a budding music lover, they may be fascinated by musical tones, and appreciate all kinds of sounds. If so, it's worth stimulating and encouraging this interest. Some babies grab toys and objects primarily to find out if they will make a noise of any kind. They turn around sound-producing objects, not for inspection, but to see if the sound changes when the object is turned quickly or slowly. These babies will squeeze a toy in a variety of ways to see if it produces different sounds. Give them sound-producing objects to play with and help them use them properly.

You Baby May Be a Real "Observer"

The daily routine in every household is full of events that your baby might enjoy watching. Many babies love to watch their parents preparing food, setting the table, getting dressed, or working in the garden. They are now capable of understanding the different actions or events involved in various activities, such as putting plates on the table, slicing bread, making sandwiches, brushing hair, filing nails, and mowing the lawn. If your baby enjoys observing things, let them watch your daily activities. All you have to do is make sure they are in a perfect position to observe what you are doing. It's really no extra trouble for you, but it will be an enjoyable learning experience for them.

> *"My little one smacks her lips, kicks her legs, and reaches out with her hands as soon as she sees me making sandwiches. She's obviously aware of what I'm doing and she's asking to be fed."*
> **About Hannah, 20th week**

Your Baby May Like Eating and Drinking Everything

Does your baby want to grab everything you are eating or drinking? Most babies do. So take care not to drink hot tea or coffee with a wriggly baby on your lap. In an unguarded moment, they may suddenly decide to grab your cup and tip the hot contents all over their hands and face. Most babies still enjoy eating everything at this age.

> *"My son will try to grab my sandwich with his mouth already open in anticipation. Whatever he manages to grab, he swallows immediately. The funny thing is, he seems to enjoy everything."*
> **About Kevin, 19th week**

Help Your Baby Explore Things While Sitting

If your baby gets tired because they have to constantly push themselves up with one hand, support them so they can use their hands freely. For instance, put them on your lap and examine a toy together. They will love being able to play while sitting comfortably. Besides, when they are sitting up, they will be able to look at playthings from a completely different angle. Just watch them to see if they do different things with toys while they are sitting up. Perhaps you may even see new activities.

> *"I put my boy in his high chair for the first time and propped him up with a cushion. He immediately discovered that you can do certain things with toys while sitting up that you can't do on the floor. When I gave him his plastic key ring, he first started banging it on the tabletop, and then he kept throwing it on the floor. He did that about 20 times in a row. He thought it was great fun and couldn't stop laughing."*
> **About Paul, 19th week**

Your Baby Can "Find" Things: Turn It Into a Game

You can start to play the first peek-a-boo and hide-and-seek games at this age. As soon as your baby becomes familiar with the world of events, they can recognize a plaything, even when they can see only part of it. If you see them looking quizzically at a partially hidden toy, or if you want to turn their attempts to retrieve a toy into a game of hide-and-seek, move the object about a bit to make it easier for them to recognize it. At this age, they are still quick to give up. The idea that an object continues to exist all the time, wherever it is, is not yet within their mental grasp.

Your Baby May Make "Babbling Sentences"

Does your baby make "babbling sentences"? Sometimes it may sound as if your little one is really telling you a story. This is because in the world of events your baby becomes just as flexible with their voice as with the rest of their body. They start to repeat whatever syllables they already know and string them together to form a "sentence," such as "dadadada" and "babababababa." They might also experiment with intonation and volume. When they hear themselves making a new sound, they may stop for a while and laugh before resuming the conversation.

It's still important to talk to your baby as often as possible. Try to respond to what they say, imitate their new sounds, and reply when they "ask" or "tell" you something. Your reactions encourage them to practice using their voice.

Your Baby Understands Their First Words

You might notice that your baby understands a word or short sentence, although they cannot say the word or words themselves. Try asking in familiar surroundings, "Where's your teddy?" and you may see they actually look at their teddy bear. Their understanding of speech is therefore more advanced than their own ability to speak.

You will be really enthusiastic and proud when you discover that your baby understands their first short sentence. Initially, you may not believe what has happened. You may keep repeating the sentence until you are convinced it wasn't just a coincidence. Next, you could create a new situation to practice the little sentence your baby already recognizes. For instance, you could put the teddy bear in every conceivable spot in a room to test if your baby knows where it is. You could even show them photographs of their teddy bear to see if they recognize it. Many parents change the way they talk to their babies at this age. They will slow down their sentences when talking to their baby, and often, they will use just single words instead of whole sentences.

> *"In our living room, there's a painting of flowers on one wall and a photo of my son on another. When I ask him, 'Where are the flowers?' or 'Where's Paul?' he always looks at the correct picture. I'm not imagining it, because the pictures are on opposite sides of the room."*
> **About Paul, 23rd week**

Your Baby's First Book

Some babies at this age already enjoy looking at picture books that show events. If your baby enjoys this, they may want to hold the book themselves, using both hands, and gaze at the illustrations in wonder. They may make a real effort to hold the book and concentrate on the pictures, but after a while the book will usually end up in their mouth.

The Virtue of Patience

When your baby is learning new skills, they may exhibit skills that try your patience. Some parents try to discourage their baby from doing these things. Breaking old habits and learning new rules is all part of how each new ability is worked out. You can start demanding the things of your baby that they can now understand for the first time. But no more and no less. Both you and your baby have to adjust to their progress and renegotiate the rules to restore peace and harmony. Remember, from now on your baby will no longer be completely dependent on you for their enjoyment, since they are now in touch with the world around them. They can do and understand a lot more than they did in the past, and, of course, they think they know it all. You may think they are a handful. They think *you* are! If you recognize this behavior, you could say you are experiencing your infant's first struggle for independence. This first display of having their own will is fun and trying at the same time.

Your Baby's Own Will: Fun and Trying

Many babies want to decide for themselves what they want to do, and they are not shy about letting their parents know. They want to sit up, be part of everything and join in when the mood takes them, and, above all, they want to have everything they see. This exhausts many parents and others feel that the baby is still too young to be touching everything in sight. A mother or father may try to distract their infant with cuddling games or a tight embrace as their baby wriggles and squirms in their arms to get at something. But both methods will nearly always have the opposite effect. The baby will squirm and wriggle with even more determination as they struggle to free themselves from their long-suffering parent.

It is much the same with sleeping and eating; a baby decides when they want to go to sleep and when they want to get up. They demand food when they want to eat and decide when they have had enough. You can say this is the first power struggle between the parents and the baby.

> *"My son has become quite the character, with his own will. He lets you know what he does and doesn't want in no uncertain terms."*
> **About Frankie, 21st week**

Grabbing Mania

What irritates many parents more than anything else is a baby's obsession for grabbing everything within reach or anything they see in passing—plants, coffee cups, books, stereo equipment, eyeglasses—nothing is safe from their exploring hands. Parents may get increasingly annoyed with this behavior and they may get accidently hurt. They try to discourage this grabbing mania by firmly saying, "No." This sometimes works.

BITING IS NOT FUNNY

Now that the baby is stronger, they are also capable of causing physical pain. They might bite, chew, and pull at your face, arms, ears, and hair. They may pinch and twist your skin. Sometimes they will do this hard enough that it really hurts. No one finds the biting, pulling, and pinching amusing.

Some parents rebuke their babies if they get too excited. They do this by immediately letting them know that they have gone too far. Usually they do this verbally by saying, "Ouch," loudly and sternly. If they notice that their baby is preparing to launch a new attack, they warn them with "Careful." At this age, babies are perfectly capable of understanding a cautioning voice. If the behavior doesn't stop, parents should walk away and cool down. Letting your baby play in their crib or playpen can provide a needed break during situations like this.

Impatience Is Irritating

Most parents think their babies should learn a little patience at this age. They don't always respond to their babies as quickly as they used to. When the baby wants something, or wants to do something, a mother or father may now make them wait for a few brief moments. Having them wait a few minutes before grabbing food is one way to slow them down.

WHAT MOTIVATES YOUR BABY?

What motivates a baby to do something? Parents enjoy seeing their child trying to sit up, or roll over smoothly, but you are not helping your baby if you only view physical skills as goals in themselves. It is more interesting to understand the "why." Why does your child like rolling over? Why do they want to sit up? Why do they like practicing moving their body? Is it purely a physical desire? Or does your baby want to explore more of the world, and are they driven to put their body in positions to make it easier for them to see more, feel more, etc.? In a way, the gross motor skills are purely a means to an end. They enable a baby to learn and practice other skills from the world of events, such as grabbing, touching, and feeling.

Think about what motivates your baby to do the things with their body that they are attempting to do. Talk about it with your partner, and observe your child closely. And trust your intuition, because no one knows your baby better than you do.

You think your baby is motivated by:

_____

_____

_____

_____

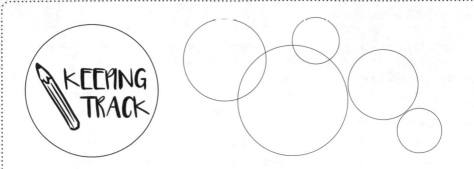

YOUR FAVORITE GAMES: THE WORLD OF EVENTS

These are games and activities that your baby may like now and that help them practice their newly developing skills.

Instructions to Fill In This List:

Check off your baby's favorite games. When you have filled in What You've Discovered: The World of Patterns, see if there is a connection between the things that interested your baby the most and the games they liked playing. You may have to really think about it, but it will give you an insight into your baby's unique personality.

☐ HAPPY TALK

Talk as often as you can to your baby about the things they see, hear, taste, and feel. Talk about the things they do. Keep your sentences short and simple. Emphasize the important words. For instance: "Feel this— grass," "Daddy's coming," "Listen, the doorbell," or "Open your mouth."

☐ WHAT HAPPENS NEXT?

First, you say, "I'm going to [dramatic pause] pinch your nose." Then grab their nose and gently wiggle it about. You can do the same with their ears, hands, and feet. Find out what they enjoy most. If you play this game regularly, they will know exactly what you are going to do next. Then they will watch your hands with increasing excitement and shriek with laughter when you grab their nose. This game will familiarize them with both their body and the words for the body parts as you play together.

☐ LOOKING AT PICTURES

Show your baby a brightly colored picture in a book. They might even want to look at several pictures. Make sure the pictures are bright, clear, and include things they recognize. Talk about the pictures together, and point out the real object if it's in the room.

☐ SINGING SONGS

Many babies really love songs, particularly when they are accompanied by movements, such as "Pat-a-cake, Pat-a-cake, Baker's Man." But they also enjoy being rocked to the rhythm of a song or nursery rhyme. Babies recognize songs by their melody, rhythm, and intonation.

☐ TICKLING GAME

This familiar song encourages tickling, which your baby may love.

This little piggy went to market . . .
And this little piggy stayed at home . . .
This little piggy ate roast beef . . .
And this little piggy had none . . .
This little piggy went . . .
Weeweeweewee all the way home.

While saying this, wiggle each of your baby's toes in turn, before finally running your fingers up their body and tickling their neck.

☐ PEEK-A-BOO

Cover your baby's face with a cloth and ask: "Where's . . .?" Watch them to see if they can remove the cloth from their face on their own. If they can't do this yet, help them by holding their hand and slowly pulling the cloth away with them. Each time that they can see you again, say, "Boo"— this helps mark the event for them. Keep the game simple at this age; otherwise, it will be too difficult for them.

☐ MIRROR GAME

Look in a mirror together. Usually, a baby will prefer looking and smiling at their own reflection first. But then they will look at your reflection, and then back to the real you. This normally bewilders them, and they will usually look back and forth at you and your reflection, as if they can't make up their mind which one is their real parent. If you start talking to them, they will be even more amazed because all of a sudden the noise is coming from the real you. Then they may start laughing before they snuggle up to you.

YOUR FAVORITE TOYS

☐ Bath toys: you can use a variety of household items in the bath, such as measuring cups, plastic colanders, plant spray bottles, watering cans, and soap boxes
☐ Activity centers or soft platforms to play on
☐ Balls with gripping notches or holes, preferably with a bell inside
☐ Plastic or inflatable rattles
☐ A screw-top container with some rice in it
☐ Crackly paper
☐ Mirrors
☐ Photographs or pictures of other babies.
☐ Photographs or pictures of objects or animals they recognize by name
☐ Children's songs
☐ Wheels that really turn, such as those on a toy car

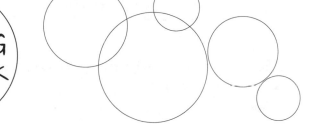

WHAT YOU'VE DISCOVERED: THE WORLD OF EVENTS

All babies acquire the same perceptive ability as they enter the world of events, a world that offers a wide range of new skills to explore. They will choose the things that most suit their inclinations, interests, and physique. There are some babies who specialize in feeling, looking, or gymnastics, and other babies will sample everything, but not elaborate any further. Every baby is unique.

These are examples of skills you could notice from now on, but remember that your baby will not do everything on the list.

Instructions to Fill In This List:

Just before your baby enters the next leap, check off the boxes for things your baby can do, and not the things (skills) they are not yet doing. If you would like, write down the date you notice your baby doing something on the list. It's most likely they will not acquire many of these skills until one, two, or three leaps later. Remember that this is not a reflection of your baby's intelligence. Your baby is not behind other babies, they are simply making choices. This list is longer, as the leap into this world is a pretty big one. They have acquired new individual skills, but due to their new, mental ability, they will also build on old skills from the previous leap. They will be integrated into a more complex whole. It won't come as a surprise to you that this was a big leap; you will have noticed that for yourself, and your baby will have, too. That is why they will be pickier about the things from the list that they do straightaway and the things they leave for later, even if those are unconscious decisions. You will also notice that you will check off fewer things from this list compared to the other leaps. Their personality is unfolding by the day.

You made this leap on: _____

On _____ the sun broke through again and now, at the end of the leap, I see you can do these new things.

BODY CONTROL

Date:

☐ You are suddenly very active. You start moving virtually every part of your body as soon as you are put on the floor.

☐ You roll over from your tummy to your back.

☐ You roll over from your back to your tummy.

☐ You are able to fully stretch your arms when lying on your tummy.

☐ You lift your bottom and attempt to push off, but do not succeed. The fact that you are trying is perhaps more important than whether it works or not.

☐ You raise yourself onto your hands and feet when lying on your tummy, then try to move forward, but do not succeed. It's still a bit too early for that.

☐ You are trying out "creeping" (a precursor to crawling; instead of being on your hands and knees, you push yourself over the floor).

☐ You do manage to move forward or backward a little bit.

☐ When you are sitting in front of me and holding on to my fingers, you can pull yourself up to a sitting position.
The earliest a baby can do this is at 4 months, but a baby may wait until they are 8 months to do this for the first time. The average age is 5 months and 3 weeks.

☐ You sit up straight all by yourself when leaning back against me.

☐ You attempt to sit up straight and you briefly succeed. You lean on your forearms and bring your head forward.
Babies can sit briefly by themselves for the first time between the age of 4 and 8 months when they are put in the position by an adult. The average age is 5 months and a week. But as we have said before, any point in that time period is normal. Earlier is not necessarily better, and averages are just that. Your child is unique.

☐ If I give you two fingers to clamp your fists around, then you pull yourself into standing position.
Babies can do this for the first time between 5 and 12 months, and the average is 8 months. The earliest possible date that some babies will be able to do this is at the end of this leap, just before the next one begins.

☐ You sit steadily in an upright position in the high chair with cushions for support.

☐ You enjoy moving your mouth. For example, you pucker your lips in a variety of ways, or stick your tongue out.

GRABBING, TOUCHING, AND FEELING

Date:

☐ You now succeed in grabbing objects.

☐ You are able to grab an object while it is in contact with you, even if you are not looking at it. You can do this with both hands.

☐ You can grab things, sometimes with your left hand and other times with your right hand. It is not until you get older that I will know whether you are left- or right-handed; you are currently ambidextrous (unlike most adults)!

☐ You are able to pass objects back and forth between your hands.

☐ When holding a toy, you can do the same actions with your right and your left hand.

☐ You like putting someone's hand in your mouth.

☐ You touch someone's mouth when they are talking, or even stick your whole hand in!

☐ You stick toys or objects in your mouth and feel them.

☐ You stick toys or objects in your mouth and bite them.

☐ You are able to pull a cloth from your face by yourself, slowly at first, but quicker the more you do it.

☐ You recognize a toy or other familiar object, even if it is partially covered by something. You try to remove the obstacles, but will soon give up if unsuccessful.

☐ You bang a plaything on a tabletop. This has nothing to do with being aggressive; it's enthusiasm.

☐ You deliberately throw a plaything from a tabletop onto the floor. Not to annoy me or to be naughty, but just to explore what happens. You like the sound as it hits the floor.

☐ You try to grab things that are just out of reach.

☐ You try to play with the activity center.

☐ You understand the purpose of a particular toy; for example, you push buttons on a toy telephone.

☐ You study details. You are especially interested in the minute details of toys, hands, mouths, etc.

WATCHING

Date:

- ☐ You stare in fascination at "events," such as a child jumping up and down, hammering, filing nails, slicing bread, brushing hair, stirring coffee, etc.
- ☐ You stare in fascination at the movements of my lips and tongue when I am talking.
- ☐ You search for me and are able to turn around to do this.
- ☐ You look for a plaything that is partially hidden from sight.
- ☐ You react to your own reflection in a mirror; you are either scared or laugh.
- ☐ You hold a book in your hands and stare at the pictures.

LISTENING

Date:

- ☐ You listen intently to sounds coming from our lips.
- ☐ You respond to your own name.
- ☐ You respond to your own name and also recognize other sounds in the room.
- ☐ You are able to distinguish one particular sound in a medley of different sounds.
- ☐ You genuinely understand one or more words; for example, you look at your teddy bear if I ask, "Where's your teddy bear?" The bear must be in its usual place or you won't respond correctly, because searching for it . . . that is still too difficult for you.
- ☐ You respond appropriately to an approving or scolding voice.
- ☐ You recognize the opening bars of a children's song or tune or your favorite children's TV program.

TALKING

Date:

☐ You make new sounds, using your lips and tongue; you can make the "rrr" known as the "lip r."

☐ The sounds you make most are:

☐ ffft-ffft-ffft   ☐ arrr
☐ vvvvvv   ☐ rrr
☐ zzz   ☐ grrrr
☐ sss   ☐ prrr
☐ brrr

☐ You use consonants: *d, b, l, m.*

☐ You babble and use your first "words": mommom/mammam, baba, abba, hada-hada, dada, tata. Not all babies can do this now, but you are enjoying it a lot.

☐ Your favorite "words" are:

_____

_____

_____

_____

☐ You make noises when yawning and are aware of these noises.

BODY LANGUAGE

Date:

☐ You stretch out your arms when you want to be picked up.

☐ You smack your lips when you are hungry. You sometimes wave your arms and legs about to make it doubly clear you are hungry.

☐ You open your mouth and reach toward your food and drink.

☐ You "spit" when you've had enough to eat.

☐ You push the bottle or breast away when you've had enough.

☐ You turn away from the bottle or breast when you are full.

OTHER SKILLS

Date:

☐ You exaggerate your actions; for example, when I respond to your coughing, you cough again, then laugh.

☐ You get grumpy when becoming impatient.

☐ You scream if you fail to do what you seem to be trying to do.

☐ You now have one favorite soft toy:

    ☐ Cloth   ☐ Other:

    ☐ Slipper

    ☐ Plaything   _____

    ☐ Stuffed animal

TIP

It doesn't take long to complete the list. Remember to do it, as it will give you a wonderful overview of your baby's choices, incentives, and interests during the first 20 months of their life. This is the time when their brain develops all the foundations for the rest of their life. Taking a few minutes per leap to complete the lists will give you an insight into your baby's unique personality that you can treasure forever.

THE EASY PERIOD: AFTER THE LEAP

Around 21 weeks, another period of comparative calm begins. Many parents praise their baby's initiative and love of enterprise.

Babies seem to have boundless energy now. They explore their surroundings with great determination and enjoyment. They grow increasingly impatient with only their mother or father to play with. They want action. They may try to wriggle off your lap at the least opportunity if they spot anything of interest. They are obviously a lot more independent now.

"I put away my son's first baby clothes today and felt a pang of regret. Doesn't time fly? Letting go isn't easy. It's a very painful experience. He suddenly seems so grown up. I have a different kind of relationship with him now. He has become more of his own little person."

About Bob, 23rd week

"My baby drinks her bottle with her back toward me now, sitting up straight, not wanting to miss any of the world around her. She even wants to hold the bottle herself."

About Laura, 22nd week

"When my son is on my lap, he tries to lie almost flat so he doesn't miss anything going on behind him."

About Frankie, 23rd week

"I hardly ever put my baby in the playpen now. I think that he's too restricted in such a small space."

About Bob, 22nd week

"My son is starting to resent being carried around in the sling. At first, I thought he wanted more room because he's so active. But then I put him facing forward, and he's happy now that he's able to see everything."

About Steven, 21st week

Babies who like to be physically active no longer need to be handed the objects they want, because they will twist and turn in every direction to get them themselves.

> *"My daughter rolls from her tummy onto her back and wriggles and squirms all over the place to get to a plaything, or she'll crawl over to it. She's as busy as a bee all day long. She doesn't even have time to cry. I must say she seems happier than ever, and so are we."*
> **About Jenny, 21st week**
>
> *"My baby crawls and rolls in every direction. I can't stop her. She tries getting out of her bouncing chair, and she wants to crawl up onto the sofa. The other day we found her halfway into the dog basket. She's also very busy in the bath. There's hardly any water left in it once she's practically kicked it all out."*
> **About Emily, 22nd week**

During this time, the calm before the next storm, most babies are more cheerful than before. Even colicky babies are happier now at this stage. Perhaps this is because they are able to do more, so they are less bored.

> *"My little one is in such a cheerful mood now. She laughs and 'tells stories.' It's wonderful to watch her."*
> **About Juliette, 23rd week**
>
> *"I'm enjoying every minute I spend with my daughter again. She's such a cutie, really easygoing."*
> **About Ashley, 22nd week**
>
> *"My son is suddenly easier. He's back in a regular routine, and he's sleeping better."*
> **About Frankie, 23rd week**
>
> *"My son is surprisingly sweet and cheerful. He goes to sleep without any complaining, which is an achievement in itself. He sleeps much longer now in the afternoons, compared to these past weeks. He's so different from how he was several months ago when he cried all day. Apart from a few ups and downs now and again, things are steadily improving."*
> **About Paul, 22nd week**

The Top 10 Things You Really Need to Know!

Your baby has now made the first four leaps in their mental development. They have changed so much in such a short time . . . they have really grown! Many parents say that the fourth leap, the entry into the world of events, was very difficult for their baby. And that is not surprising, really, as this leap combines all the abilities from the previous leaps and builds on them. As you noticed already, the older your baby gets, the more intense the changes become. So we have compiled a list of the top 10 things you really need to know to give you a better understanding of what to expect during the following developmental leaps.

WHAT TO EXPECT DURING A LEAP

1. You can anticipate when a leap will happen by age, but your baby's choices make them unique.
2. Take advantage of your baby's fussy phases—they are alerting you to new skills. We'll tell you what to look out for so you don't miss them.
3. It's not a motor skill competition! We help you look at other developments that are just as important.
4. We help you find patterns in your baby's behavior during the fussy phase of a leap by offering checklists to prompt you.
5. You can take an active role during a leap. By helping and guiding your baby, you build a safe and strong bond, which is a gift for life.
6. Skills appear during a range of time! Don't focus on the earliest possible age, as most babies exhibit these skills on the later side of the range.
7. It's your baby's intention that counts, not the perfect end result that parents expect.
8. Keep in mind that circumstances—like a stressful move or job disruption—may prevent you from recognizing a fussy phase. That's okay.
9. A leap equals stress for baby and family, which means low resistance. Take care, as sometimes this might cause the sniffles!
10. A leap means progress, even if it feels like a step back at first.

1. ALL BABIES GO THROUGH LEAPS AT THE SAME AGE

All babies go through a leap in their mental development around the same age, calculated from the due date (see page 22). By saying that, we are not claiming that all children are exactly the same. On the contrary, with each developmental leap that every baby makes around the same age, babies gain the same new ability to perceive aspects of the world that they could never have experienced before. That new ability enables them to master numerous new skills. And we mean numerous. So many, in fact, that it is impossible for a baby to explore them all at once. Your baby therefore chooses what they find interesting and explores that first.

Those choices are instinctual and specific to your baby. They do not consider what skills would be better to develop, or which would be more advantageous in the long run, as adults do. Your baby will focus on what they find most appealing and what interests them. And that is what makes each child unique. All babies "choose" different things to explore first.

It is intriguing to look at your baby's choices because they reflect their personality in its purest form, which is not always easy to spot. That is why we prompt you with the lists of discoveries for each leap. If you complete the lists after the leaps, you will gain insight into what drives and motivates your baby.

Experience the World Through Your Baby's Eyes

With every leap, take 10 minutes to complete the corresponding list about your baby's choices. You will be amazed to discover patterns in what they do and where their preferences lie. When you read these lists and your answers in 10 years, you will see how the personality traits they display at 10 years old have been there all the time. Now is your chance to uncover your baby's unique personality as it develops. It is a wonderful opportunity and the lists should only take you about 10 minutes per leap.

2. PRACTICE MAKES PERFECT

From the list of all possible things that your baby is now able to do, they will choose whatever matches their interests and suits them best at this stage in their development. Do they master all the new skills straightaway? Yes and no. It is typical of a leap that, as a parent, you notice the new things immediately. They seem to have come out of nowhere. Of course, that is not true. It is the new ability that enabled them. You simply notice the end result.

Some skills are harder to master. Your baby may find them interesting and "choose" to work on them after making the leap, but they take time and effort to master. Your baby needs your help to practice the new things they so desperately want to explore. And you can help your baby by enabling them to develop the skills they are most interested in. If you do not help your baby, they may become frustrated and give up. And that would be a shame. Below are some ideas how you can best help your baby.

Facilitating Parenting: The term may sound complicated, but it is quite simple. To enable your child to discover things, you have to manipulate the situation so your child can do something for themselves, and so that they can learn from the experience. If you take it out of their hands and do it for them, they wouldn't learn anything. This is called "facilitating parenting." Take the example of learning to grab something. If you push the toy into your baby's hand each time, they will not learn to grab because you are effectively doing it for them. If a toy is just out of reach and they can't get it, then every attempt at grabbing is doomed to failure and they may give up completely. Facilitating parenting prevents both failures. It is making it easier for your baby to reach their goal with a bit of effort. If they can't reach the toy, you place it closer to them, so they can grab it themselves. Very logical, really. You are giving your baby the opportunity to learn and increase their independence. You are facilitating that—hence the term "facilitating parenting."

Praise Attempts, Not Just Successes: Recent research has shown that children grow from being encouraged and praised for their attempts and the effort they make. It is the same for babies. When a baby is trying things out and learning to do something, it costs them a lot of energy and it is not easy. Babies grow from compliments and encouragement from you: you show them they are doing well by challenging themselves. By your complimenting and praising your baby for their attempts, they learn from an early age that it is good to challenge themselves to achieve something, and that failing is all part of the learning process. You will increase their self-confidence and their independence and they will not give up as easily if they don't succeed straight away. So it is a gift for life.

Prevent Too Much Frustration: No matter how much you facilitate your child's learning and how much encouragement and praise you give them, it is frustrating when something doesn't work. We know that feeling all too well as adults. Babies, like adults, can learn from a bit of frustration; it gives a baby that extra push to try something again and perhaps even to go about it a different way to reach their goal. But beware of too much frustration. Constant failure can lead to so much frustration that they may give up completely, and that is not the intention. As a parent, you know your child better than anyone else, and you will instinctively feel when it is enough or is becoming too much for your baby. And that is where you step in with your facilitating role. Respond to your baby's attempts by making things a little easier for them or help them just enough so that they do succeed.

New ability

↓

Attempts to master a skill

↓

Frustration

Just enough to motivate

↓

Skill is mastered

Too much, close to giving up

↓

Facilitating parenting

3. IT'S NOT A MOTOR SKILL COMPETITION!

Is your child not walking yet? Oh dear! And they are not crawling, either? Such questions drive you mad, and make you insecure. And what is more, even the most self-confident parent hates these remarks (or should we say "mean questions"?).

To relieve some of your doubts and insecurities, remember that humans have seven forms of intelligence, and physical intelligence is only one of them. Society tends to focus on physical ability, not because it is more important than the other forms, but because it is the easiest to observe and compare.

It is a lot harder to see a baby using elementary skills to discover the world through experimenting with feeling and touching. Or, in plain English: to see that baby run their fingers over the edge of something to experience how it feels. But because, as a society, we do not pay attention to these "small" (read: very important) things, we tend to focus on things that are easy to observe and measure: the gross motor skills.

Take it from us: every healthy person learns to walk, and later in life it makes little difference whether your baby walked early on or a bit later. Let's focus on nonphysical skills that could perhaps be even more important in your child's development . . .

4. YOU'LL SEE THE THREE CS BUT MAYBE ONLY A FEW OF THE OTHER CHARACTERISTICS OF THE FUSSY PHASE

Every baby makes a developmental leap around the same age. The changes happen whether your baby wants them to or not, and they can't influence the timing. Compare the leaps to puberty. Every child goes through puberty around the same age. But the way puberty affects a child differs per individual. One teenager may become stubborn and rebellious, whereas another may withdraw more into themselves. Even though puberty differs from the mental development your baby goes through, they are comparable in that all babies go through leaps at the same age, and yet they will respond to the fussy phase in their own way. And, what is more, your baby may find one leap more troublesome than the other. And that's very normal.

If your baby is very outgoing and expressive, it will be relatively easy to recognize that they are making a leap. Your little sir or madam will certainly let you know about it. It's a different ball game with quieter, more easygoing babies, as they may not express it as clearly. In these cases, parents have to be more observant to pick up on the signals for when their baby needs that extra comfort and support. And your baby needs that support from their parents all the more when they are going through a leap.

5. YOU CAN TAKE AN ACTIVE ROLE

You are far from helpless during a leap. If you have calculated the timing of the leaps using the schedule in this book or with our app, then you will know when your baby will be making a leap forward in their mental development. Hopefully that in and of itself will make it easier to cope when the three Cs show up. *The Wonder Weeks* helps support parents, and also provides ideas on how you can best comfort and support your baby during these times. You'll want to help your baby when they are going through a fussy phase by comforting them and making them feel safe and loved.

You can also guide and support them after the difficult phase, as they explore the new world. By reading about the leap, you know what to watch for. You will gain an insight into what is going on inside your baby's head and you can help and guide them through the learning process.

6. WE LIST THE SKILLS AT AS EARLY AN AGE AS POSSIBLE

With each age-linked leap, we include a list of things that a baby could do for the first time at that earliest possible age. The key words are "could do" and "earliest possible." As we have stated before, babies don't do all the skills all at once, hence "could do." The age at which these skills appear for the first time varies greatly, sometimes by many months. Because we explain in each chapter about the age-linked leap and the new ability your baby has gained in that leap, we automatically tell you that earliest possible age at which the associated skills could appear. That is what each leap is about, after all. By knowing about these skills, you can watch for and recognize the signs that your baby is starting to develop them, and you will know what to look out for. To illustrate the large differences in ages when skills appear, we also state for some motor skills the average age and "maximum" age at which children master the skill. And we do that because we notice that parents want to know. But do keep in mind that averages say nothing about your baby.

TIP

With each leap chapter, we provide a list of possible characteristics that your baby may show during the fussy phase of the developmental leap. Check off the things you really notice your baby doing, remembering that every baby doesn't exhibit every item on the list, and that they might even be doing some you *don't* notice! It's fascinating to look back at previous lists, as you may discover a pattern in their behavior and characteristic behavioral changes during the fussy phases of the leaps. These lists will only take a few minutes of your time to complete, but they will provide you with an insight into your baby's personality as it emerges.

As you've figured out by now, *The Wonder Weeks* looks at the leaps every baby makes in their mental development in the first 20 months. After that, you're "on your own." We get notes all the time asking what happens after the 10th leap, but we haven't gathered that data in the same way. However, if you are aware of how your baby reacts to those fussy phases, you will be able to recognize them a lot easier as they grow into toddlers and beyond. That can only help you and your baby.

---

7. IT'S THE INTENTION THAT COUNTS, NOT A PERFECT RESULT

There are people who are shocked when we state the earliest possible age that a baby or toddler can start doing something. For example, drawing a car, brushing their hair, peeling an orange, or getting dressed. Surely those things are impossible for little ones at that age . . . aren't they?

If you demand a perfect result, then yes, they are impossible for a baby or toddler. Even a three-year-old may struggle to draw a nice car, or peel an orange and remove all the white flesh, or to brush their hair neatly and get out all the knots. Even dressing themselves properly can be a challenge.

If you only look at the end result and set the bar high, you are not being fair to your baby or toddler. In the life of a developing child, it is not about perfect end results but about the intention. If a little child scribbles a few lines on a piece of paper and says that it is a horse, then it is a horse. If they peel an orange and remove half of the peel, then we are proud of their achievement. As parents, we simply remove the rest of the peel for them. If, after the leap of sequences, a child grabs a hairbrush and rubs it against their head, they are attempting to brush their hair. If a child has put their pants on back to front and with the pockets sticking out, they deserve praise for that.

The perfect result that some people strive for will come quicker if you take a baby's first attempts seriously and praise them than if you don't. Positive comments and support will encourage a baby or toddler to try again. After all, practice makes perfect.

8. CIRCUMSTANCES MAY PREVENT YOU FROM RECOGNIZING THE FUSSY PHASE

Sometimes it's not easy to know if the fussy phase is due to a leap or to other circumstances. Sometimes you might not notice that a fussy phase has arrived. After all, if your baby is ill and they are clingy, crying, and cranky, is this behavior due to a leap or are these symptoms of the illness? And if something really stressful happens and your whole household is out of balance, it is logical your baby will feel this, too. Again, you might wonder if the fussiness is due to the leap or to the unexpected circumstances you're all experiencing. The good news is: your baby will make this leap, even if you don't clearly notice the fussy phase at the time. Even more important: don't blame yourself. We all have periods in our life when our family is under stress. Consider how you feel when moving to a new house, during a busy period at work, or, even worse, when a family member is sick or dies. The list could go on. When you or your family is dealing with these type of life events, it is harder to notice that a baby is going through a leap.

You cannot avoid all stress. We are human, after all, and we all go through difficult periods in life. But by supporting each other, your baby will know that you are there for them. What is more, you do not have to hide your feelings from your baby. Of course, they would rather see a happy parent, but a baby picks up on your emotions whether you like it or not. So don't try and kid them. Be honest about how you are feeling. But do let them know that they are a source of comfort and joy for you, even when they are going through a fussy phase.

Other major changes that may cause stress can be planned, however, and you might want to consider planning those at moments when your baby isn't under the stress caused by a leap. Perhaps try waiting to stop breastfeeding or going to a babysitter or childcare for the first time until your baby is in between leaps. These events change everything for your baby, and it is stressful adjusting to a new situation. When your baby is making a leap in their development, all manner of things are already changing for them and that is also stressful. Try to plan major changes so that they don't coincide with the timing of a leap. It will make things easier for your baby and easier for you—and it will make it easier to recognize the leap your baby is making.

If you cannot avoid the change, and the added stress, then make sure you pay extra attention to your baby and that you are there for them.

9. A LEAP EQUALS STRESS, WHICH MEANS LOWER RESISTANCE TO INFECTION

As you have just read, a leap is stressful for a baby, and a baby's behavior during the fussy phase has repercussions for the rest of the household. Stress affects a body physically; its natural resistance is weakened. It is therefore no surprise that babies and toddlers fall ill more often after they have entered the fussy phase.

10. A LEAP IS CAUSE FOR CELEBRATION!

It may not always be easy to see a leap as a reason to celebrate, but do remember that the fussy phase soon passes and then you will notice major progress. So, although the first phase of each leap may be difficult for both baby and parent, it is the sign that your baby is going through a healthy mental development and is taking a giant leap forward.

Leap 5

The World of Relationships

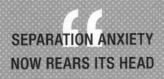

SEPARATION ANXIETY
NOW REARS ITS HEAD

Between 25 and 27 weeks, or 6 months, your baby will start showing the signs of yet another significant leap in their development. Building on their knowledge of events, they are now able to begin understanding the many kinds of "relationships" among the things that make up their world.

One of the most significant relationships your baby can now perceive is the distance between one thing and another. We take this for granted as adults, but for a baby it is an alarming discovery, a very radical change in their world. The world is suddenly a very big place in which they are but a tiny, if very vocal, speck. Something they want can be on a high shelf, and they have no way of getting to it. Their parents can walk away, even if only into the next room, and if they cannot follow, their parents might as well have gone to China as far as they are concerned. Even if they are adept at crawling, they realize that their parents move much faster than they do and can get away from them.

This discovery can be very frightening for a baby, and it may make these few weeks quite taxing for their parents. But when you understand the source of this fear and uneasiness, there are many things you will be able to do to help. Naturally, once your baby learns to control the distance between themselves and the things they want, they will be able to do much more on their own than they used to. But until then, they will need a lot of support from you.

Through all these things, your baby is showing you they are going through a leap in their development. However, they themselves have sensed this leap earlier, at around 23 weeks (between 22 and 26 weeks). That's when your baby usually becomes clingier than they were. They notice their world has changed and that they experience it differently now. They see, hear, smell, taste, and feel things they have never known before. Caught up in a tangle of new impressions, they need to hold on to something old and familiar; to return to their parents, where they feel safest. The familiar feeling of security and warmth the parents provide will help them relax, let the newness sink in, and enable them to grow into the new world at their own pace. This fussy phase often lasts about four weeks, although it may be as short as one week or as long as five.

Since one of the important skills they have to learn during this leap is how to handle the distance between their parents and themselves, your baby may actually become fussy again for a while around 29 weeks, after their new skills have started to take wing.

THE FUSSY PHASE:
THE ANNOUNCEMENT OF THE MAGICAL LEAP

When your baby becomes aware that their world is changing, they will usually cry more easily than before. At this point, many parents might call their babies cranky, bad-tempered, whiny, or discontented. If your baby is already strong-willed, they may come across as being even more restless, impatient, or troublesome than ever. Almost all babies will cry less when they are picked up and cuddled, or when their mother or father are close by while they are playing. Not only do parents notice that their baby clings more, is crankier, and cries more often than they did, but their baby may sleep poorly, become shyer than they were, may want more attention now, and may not want you to break physical contact. They may be listless and lose their appetite. Parents often notice very specific things, such as baby refusing to have their diaper changed or reaching for a cuddly object more often now.

In short, your baby is entering the fussy phase that by now should be familiar. This phase is not only difficult for your baby but also for you, and it can cause worries, irritation, and quarrels. That puts you under strain. But it's not all bad: because parents are concerned, they watch their baby closely and discover that their baby is actually doing many new things.

"My baby is starting to stand up for herself more and more. She makes demands, angrily ordering me to come to her or stay with her. In this way, she makes sure I am there to help reach her toys."
About Hannah, 25th week

"My son seems to be in such a state lately. He doesn't know what he wants. He hurts himself, then he cries, and there is nothing, absolutely nothing, I can do to comfort him. I've never seen him go through such a difficult phase."
About Otis, 24th week

DO REMEMBER

If you notice your baby is fussier than usual, watch them closely. It is likely they are attempting to master new skills. Check out What You Have Discovered: The World of Relationships on page 240 to see what to look out for.

HOW YOU KNOW YOUR BABY HAS
ENTERED THE NEXT FUSSY PHASE

Besides the three Cs (crying, clinginess, and crankiness), here are some of the other signals your baby may give you to let you know they're entering the next fussy phase.

Does Your Baby Sleep Poorly?

Your baby might sleep less than you are used to. Most babies have difficulty falling asleep or wake up sooner compared to before. Some don't want to nap during the day, and others don't want to go to bed at night. There are even those who refuse to do either.

"Bedtime and naptime are accompanied by terrible screaming fits. My son yells furiously and practically climbs the walls. He'll shout at the top of his voice and practically wind himself. I just can't handle it. It seems as if I never see him lying peacefully in his crib anymore. I just pray it doesn't last forever."
About Bob, 26th week

Does Your Baby Have Nightmares?

Some babies sleep uneasily at this time. Sometimes they toss and turn so much during sleep that it looks like they are having a nightmare.

"My daughter is a very restless sleeper. Sometimes, she'll let out a really loud scream with her eyes closed, as if she's having a nightmare. So I'll lift her up for a minute to comfort her. These days, I usually let her play in the bathtub in the evening. I'm hoping it will calm her down and make her sleepier."
About Emily, 23rd week

Does Your Baby Become Shyer With Others,
and Demand More Attention From You?

Many babies do not want other people to look at them, talk to them, or touch them, and they certainly won't want to sit on others' laps. They might even start to want their daddy or mommy in plain sight more often from this age on, even when there aren't any "strangers" around. Almost every parent will notice this now. At this age, shyness is especially obvious, for a very good reason—it has been awakened by the new ability your baby gets with this leap, enabling them to notice and control the distance between you and them.

Many babies want their mommy or daddy to stay with them, and play with them more than before, or just look at them. Your baby may insist on remaining in your arms or on your lap. But some are not completely satisfied sitting on their parent's lap; they want to explore but not leave that cozy lap.

"I can hardly move without my daughter crying out in fear."
About Ashley, 23rd week

"My baby is getting shyer by the day. I need to be where he can see me at all times, and it has to be close to him. If I walk away, he'll try to crawl right after me."
About Matt, 26th week

"My baby doesn't like playing on his play mat for long periods. I really have to keep him occupied on my lap or walk around with him."
About Frankie, 27th week

"My daughter was up to mischief all the time, behaving badly and acting cranky when she wanted attention. I had to play with her or find some way to occupy her all day long. As long as I did that, everything was okay."
About Jenny, 25th week

"My son keeps on bothering me to sit on my lap. But as soon as I take him, there's almost no controlling him. He crawls all over me and gropes around like a monkey for anything he can get his hands on. I try playing games, but it's a waste of time. So he doesn't feel like playing with me, okay, but at least he could stop being so difficult."
About Matt, 27th week

Does Your Baby Lose Their Appetite?

Both babies who are breastfed and those who are bottle-fed sometimes drink less milk at this phase or refuse to drink at all. Other food and drink may be rejected, too. Often, babies also take longer to finish their meals now, and seem to be less interested in eating and drinking.

Does Your Baby Refuse to Have Their Diaper Changed?

Many babies cry when they are set down to be changed or dressed. They just don't want their parents to fiddle with their clothes.

> We're at Leap 5. It's like trying to diaper and dress a cat. Have you ever tried to dress a cat? Please tell me this is temporary.—**Instagram post**

Does Your Baby Reach for the Comfort of a Cuddly Object More Often Now?

Some babies reach for a teddy, slipper, blanket, or cloth more often than before. For most babies, anything soft will do. Sometimes they'll cuddle it while sucking a thumb. It seems to calm them down.

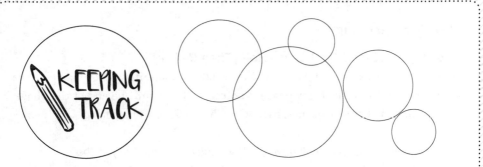

LEAP SIGNS

This is how you let me know the leap has started:

☐ You cry more often than you did.

☐ You are bad-tempered, cranky, or whiny more often than you were.

☐ You want me to keep you occupied.

☐ You want constant physical contact now.

☐ You sleep poorly.

☐ You may have nightmares.

☐ You lose your appetite.

☐ You don't want to be changed/dressed.

☐ You are shyer with strangers than you used to be.

☐ You are quieter, less vocal than you were.

☐ You are less lively than before.

☐ You suck your thumb, or suck it more often than before.

☐ You reach for a soft toy or do so more often than before.

☐ And I've noticed that you:

_____

_____

_____

_____

Do remember that your baby will not necessarily show all these leap characteristics. It's not about how many your baby does, but what they do.

How Are *You* Doing?

You May Be (Even More) Exhausted (Than Before)

Parents may be exhausted. Parents of especially demanding babies may feel like complete wrecks in this fussy phase. And certainly toward the end of the phase. They complain of stomachaches, backaches, headaches, and tension.

> *Whenever I catch myself having a "I wanna chuck my baby in the bin" moment, I always try to look at things differently. For example: I could be super frustrated that Leap 5 has taken my baby who slept and napped perfectly and replaced him with a baby who won't nap unless being held, wakes up hourly at night and is clinging to me like glue. Or I can appreciate that I actually have a baby to go through this with . . . and enjoy all the extra cuddles. Cause one day he's not gonna wanna be with me 24/7 and I'm gonna miss it.*—**Instagram post**

You May Be Concerned About Teething

It's natural for parents to feel troubled when something seems to be the matter, and they can't figure out what it is. At this age, mothers and fathers are quick to embrace the thought that their babies are fussy because they're teething. After all, most babies start cutting their teeth around this age. Still, there is no connection between clinginess due to a leap in the baby's mental development and teething. Just as many babies start teething during fussy periods as in between them. Of course, if your baby starts teething at the same time as they go through a leap, they can become supertroublesome.

Generally speaking, the lower front teeth are cut when the baby reaches six months. By their first birthday, a baby generally has six teeth. At about age 2½, the last molars come through, completing the full set of baby teeth. The toddler then has 20 teeth.

> *"My daughter right now is extremely bad-tempered, only wanting to sit on my lap. Perhaps it's her teeth. They've been bothering her for three weeks now. She seems pretty uncomfortable, but they still haven't come through."*
> **About Jenny, 25th week**
>
> *"My little guy became very weepy. According to the doctor, he has a whole bunch of teeth waiting to come through." (His first tooth didn't emerge until 7 weeks later.)*
> **About Paul, 27th week**

TAKE NOTE!

A high temperature or diarrhea has nothing to do with teething. If your baby shows one of these symptoms, call your pediatrician.

You May Become Exasperated

Parents can become annoyed if they feel they've tried everything and their baby continues to fuss and be difficult. This feeling tends to get stronger toward the end of the fussy phase. Some parents, especially those with very demanding babies, just can't take it anymore.

> *"My son's crying gets on my nerves so much that I'm totally obsessed with 'not crying.' The tension it creates swallows up all my energy."*
> **About Steven, 25th week**
>
> *"One night, I had to keep walking back and forth to put the pacifier in my daughter's mouth. Suddenly, at 12:30 a.m., she was wide awake. She stayed awake until 2:30 a.m. I'd already had a busy day, with a lot of headaches and backaches from walking her up and down. I just collapsed."*
> **About Emily, 27th week**
>
> *"It was a terribly trying week. My son would cry over anything. He demanded attention constantly. He was up until 10 p.m. and agitated. I carried him around an awful lot in the sling. He liked that. But I felt tired, so tired from all that schlepping and continuous crying. Whenever he started throwing one of his temper tantrums in bed at night, it was as if I'd crossed a line. I could feel myself getting really angry. This has happened frequently this past week."*
> **About Bob, 25th week**

Some parents may feel completely fed up with their baby's constant crying and whining. Remember that having feelings of anger and frustration at times is not abnormal or dangerous, but acting on them is. Try to get help long before you lose control.

You May Be At Your Wits' End

Conflicts might develop around mealtimes now. Most parents hate it when their babies won't eat and they continue to try and feed them. They try doing it playfully, or they try to pressure them into eating. Whatever the approach, it's usually to no avail.

At this age, strong-willed babies can be extremely stubborn in their refusal. This sometimes makes parents, who are also being stubborn (but out of concern!) very angry. And so mealtimes can mean war. When this happens to you, try to stay calm. Don't turn it into a fight. You can't force them to eat, anyway. During this fussy phase, many babies are poor eaters. It's a temporary thing. If you make an issue out of it, the chances are your baby will continue to refuse food even after the fussy phase is over. They will have made a habit of it.

At the end of the fussy phase, parents may correctly sense that their baby is capable of a lot more than they thought possible. Parents still need to be available to comfort and care for their child, but you can begin to redirect the baby to a different activity or try to use a stuffed toy to distract from this.

 ANCHOR MOMENTS *

Studies show that parents, mostly moms, can never fully relax, even in quiet moments, if they know that there are jobs that still need to be done. But . . . with a relaxed body and mind, these jobs get done way more easily! It's anchor time.

In 5 minutes: Listen to a classical piece of music, even if classical music isn't your thing. It helps relax the brain.

In 10 minutes: Write a love and appreciation letter to your partner, and ask them to do the same thing for you.

More time: Start exercising, taking your body into account. With modern lifestyles, it is a cliché to say we do not get enough exercise. But many people don't, and it is not only our physical health that suffers. Exercise is now often "prescribed" as a treatment for mild depression and anxiety. For many of us, simply going for a walk can be relaxing; again, we are doing something simple, active, and natural.

* For more anchor moments, see page 36.

Your Baby's New Ability Is Starting to Bear Fruit

At about 26 weeks, you'll discover that your baby is once again trying to learn one or more new skills. The journey of discovery into the world of relationships, which started a few weeks ago, is starting to bear fruit, and your baby starts by choosing the new skills best suited to them. Your baby will make their own choices depending on their own temperament, inclinations, preferences, and physical makeup. And as an adult, you can help them with that.

The World of Relationships

For the first time, your baby can perceive all kinds of relationships and act on them. The whole world is made up of relationships; one thing is always related to another. Something your baby sees can have something to do with something else your baby sees, or hears, feels, tastes, or smells. Your baby will show you endless examples of this. And you will be able to recognize these things, when you know what to look out for. Here are a few examples to help you.

LEAP 5

Your baby can now discover that there is always a physical distance between two objects or two people. And, of course, their distance from you is one of the first things they will notice and react to. While observing this phenomenon, they discover that you can increase the distance too much for their liking, and it dawns on them that they can't do anything about it. Now that they know they have lost control over that distance, they will start to cry.

Your baby now understands that something can be *inside, outside, on top, above, next to, underneath,* or *in between* something else. They will love to toy with these notions.

> "All day long, my son takes toys out of his toy box and puts them back in again. Sometimes he'll toss everything over the side of the playpen. Another time, he'll carefully fit each item through the bars. He clears cupboards and shelves and is thrilled by emptying water from bottles and containers into the tub. But the best thing yet was while I was feeding him. He let go of my nipple, studied it with a serious look on his face, shook my breast up and down, sucked once, took another look, and continued this way for a while. He's never done this before. It's as if he was trying to figure out how anything could come from there."
>
> **About Matt, 30th week**

Your baby can begin to understand that they can cause certain things to happen. For example, they can push a button that causes music to play. They want to explore this, and become attracted to objects such as stereo equipment, television sets, light switches, and toy pianos. They can now start to comprehend that people, objects, sounds, or situations can be related to each other. Or that a sound is related to an object or a particular situation. They know, for example, that bustling in the kitchen means that someone is preparing their dinner, the key in the front door means their daddy (or mommy) is home, the dog has its own food and toys, and that they and their parents belong together. This new skill can make your baby feel wary and uneasy.

Your baby can now begin to understand that animals and people coordinate their movements. Even if two people are walking separately, your baby still notices that they are taking each other's movements into consideration. That is a "relationship" as well. They can also tell when something goes wrong. If their mommy drops something, lets out a yell, and bends down quickly to catch it, if two people accidentally bump into each other, or if the dog falls off the couch, they understand that these things are out of the ordinary. Some babies find this highly amusing; others are scared out of their wits. And others become curious or take things very seriously. After all, they are seeing something that is not meant to happen.

"I've noticed my son is scared of the slicing machine at the bakery. As soon as the bread goes into it, he glances at me as if to ask, 'Are you sure that it's okay?' When I smile at him, he eventually calms down, but not right away. First, he looks frightened, then he looks at me, then frightened again, then at me again."
About Paul, 29th week

Your baby may also begin to discover that they can coordinate the movements of their body, limbs, and hands, and that they work together as one. Once they understand this, they can do more things with their toys. They can learn to crawl more efficiently. Or they may try to sit up by themselves or pull themselves up to stand and sit down again. Some babies now take their first steps with a little help. And the exceptional baby will even do it without help, just before the next leap begins.

Learning to master these physical skills can be frightening to a baby. They may pull themselves up to stand and realize they are not sure how to sit down again without falling. Then, they may cry and need help. They are fully aware when they lose control of their body. They still need to learn how to keep their balance. And keeping one's balance has a lot to do with being able to see distances. Once your baby masters that, they can also learn to keep their balance. Below, in the Magical Leap Forward: The Discovery of the New World section, we pay special attention to how you can help your baby with all skills listed here.

When your baby perceives "relationships" and starts "playing" with them in their unique way, they will use the abilities they have acquired from previous leaps in their mental development. They perceive "relationships" between "sensations," "patterns," "smooth transitions," and "events."

This ability to "see" and play with "relationships" changes your baby's behavior. It affects everything they do. And your baby now sees that the world is full of relationships. They perceive them between people, between things, between people and things, between themselves and other people and things, and between their own limbs.

You can imagine that your baby will be upset when all this dawns on them! For adults, these "relationships" are normal; we have learned to live with them. Your baby hasn't yet.

BRAIN CHANGES

Between 22 and 26 weeks, there is an increase in activity in your baby's brain waves.

LEAP 5

Experience the World Through Your Baby's Eyes

In order to be able to understand the issues your baby is struggling with, you have to be able to imagine them. Imagine you live in a world in which you are fully dependent on one specific person. And, for the first time, you grasp the fact that that person can walk away and you can do nothing about it. You can't go after them because you are unable to move. You can imagine how frightening that would be.

Look around you and take an imaginary photograph of something. What do you see? And what do you "know" but can't actually see? Think about a very simple thing. For example, the floor continues under the desk, cables are connected behind your computer screen. They are still there even though you can't see them. Or look at yourself. Your legs are under the desk, out of sight, but you know they are there. So there are numerous things that you can't see, but your brain fills them in for you.

Think about how many things you see or put *inside*, *on*, *under*, or *behind* something else. Consider the number of relationships that you observe, maintain, or change every day. Your baby is being confronted with these relationships for the first time. Once you realize this, you will understand why this is such a major leap in your baby's development.

THE MAGICAL LEAP FORWARD:
THE DISCOVERY OF THE NEW WORLD

Every baby needs time (sometimes weeks), and lots of help to practice and experiment with their new ability to develop and master a number of new skills. As a parent, you can help them with that. You can give them opportunities to play with relationships. You can encourage them and comfort them when things don't work out. You can offer them new ideas.

Give your baby every opportunity to come into contact with relationships. Let them share your experience of sights, sounds, touch, smells, and tastes whenever they want to. The more they come into contact with these things, the better their understanding of them will be.

It really doesn't matter whether your baby learns about relationships from watching, manipulating toys, language, sounds, music, or physical areas. Later on, they will quickly and easily be able to put this understanding to use in other domains. They simply can't do everything all at once.

Your Baby May Like "Moving" Toys

Allow your baby to put their toys *on*, *in*, *beside*, or *under* something. Let them throw toys *out* or *over* something. Or to pull toys *through* something. To the outsider, it may seem as if they are flying like a whirlwind from one object to the next, but this frenzied activity is providing precisely the input their brain needs to understand this new world of relationships.

> *"My baby will lay her blocks, her pacifier, and her bear in a basket. When she's standing, she'll pick up toys from the floor and toss them on the chair. She also pushes things into her crib through the bars. If she's actually in the crib, she'll throw everything out over the top. She likes to watch what she's done."*
> **About Jenny, 30th week**

Give your baby a shelf or cupboard of their own, which they can empty *out* and you can easily tidy up again. Give them a box they can put their things *in*. Turn a box upside down, so they can put things *on top of* it. Allow them to push things *out of* the crib *through* the bars, or throw them out *over* the top. This is an ideal way for babies who aren't yet interested in crawling to explore relationships, such as *on top of*, *inside*, *outside*, and *underneath*.

Your Baby May Like Knocking Things Over

Another way your baby can toy with relationships is by overturning and dropping objects. It is one way of seeing and hearing what happens. Maybe they want to find out just how a particular object breaks into several pieces. You can watch them enjoy knocking over towers of blocks, which you have to keep building up again. But they will gain just as much pleasure from tipping over the wastepaper basket, or overturning the cat's water and food bowls.

"My daughter loves experimenting with the way things fall. She's been trying it with all kinds of things—her pacifier, her blocks, and her cup. Then I gave her a feather from Big Bird, the parakeet. This took her by surprise. She prefers things that make a lot of noise."
About Nina, 28th week

"Boy, did my son laugh when I dropped a plate, and it shattered into a million pieces. I've never seen him laugh so hard."
About John, 30th week

If your baby tries to make an object roll, such as a ball or a square block with a bell inside, turn it into a game and roll it back to them.

"My daughter has a ball that is not so heavy and she likes to throw it in the air a little or roll it over the floor. When I roll it back to her, she grabs it."
About Ashley, 27th week

"I held a toy bear upside down so that it growled. Then I put the bear on the floor, and my son crawled right over and rolled it around, until it made that sound. He was so fascinated that he kept turning the bear over and over."
About Paul, 33rd week

Your Baby May Be Interested in Things Inside Other Things

Your baby may intrigued by toys "containing something," such as a ball containing a duck swimming in water, a soft toy that makes a sound when manipulated, or a toy piano. But also in things that are not toys but that have something inside.

I love this 5th leap! I'm really noticing A. trying to figure things out and make more meaningful movements. This morning he realized there are things inside this bag and spent 10 minutes trying to get in it!—**Instagram post**

Your Baby May Be Trying to Take Toys Apart

In the world of relationships, your baby may discover that things can be taken apart. They will probably discover that their toys offer this possibility. They will want to take toys apart, such as nesting cups, Lego toys, beads that can be clicked together, or shoelaces. They will pick at and tug on anything attached to objects and toys, such as labels; tags; stickers; the eyes and noses of stuffed animals; and wheels, latches, and doors of toy cars. Buttons on clothes, buttons and wires trailing from electrical equipment, and bottle caps are just as liable to be taken apart whenever possible. In short, they wreck things as they experiment.

"My son keeps pulling his socks off."
About Frankie, 31st week

Your Baby May Like Watching Things Disappear Into Something Else

Sometimes babies like putting one thing inside another. But this only happens by coincidence. They will only be able to distinguish between different shapes and sizes after the next developmental leap.

Babies also like to see how an object disappears *into* something else.

"My girl tries fitting all kinds of things together. A lot of the time, the size is right, but the shape never is. Also, she isn't accurate enough. But if it doesn't work, she gets mad."
About Jenny, 29th week

"My daughter likes to watch the dog emptying his bowl. It seems pretty dangerous to me, because with all that attention, the dog gulps it down faster and faster. On the other hand, the dog suddenly seems to be paying more attention to my daughter as well when she's eating. It turned out she was dropping little pieces of bread and watching him wolf them down."
About Laura, 31st week

MAKE YOUR HOME BABYPROOF

Remember that your baby can be fascinated by things that are harmful to them. They can stick a finger or tongue into anything with holes or slots, including things such as electrical outlets, electronic equipment, drains, and the dog's mouth. Always stay near your baby whenever you let them explore the house freely.

Your Baby May Be Able to Understand Short Sentences and Gestures

Your baby can now start to grasp the relationship between short sentences and their meaning or particular gestures and their meaning. They can also see the relationship between a word and a gesture that goes with it. But you will still find that these babies can only understand these things when they are in their own surroundings and as a part of a familiar routine. If you were to say the same thing in a strange place, they likely wouldn't have the same recognition. That skill doesn't develop until much later.

And yet, even with their still limited skill, they can already learn many new things. If your baby likes playing with words and gestures, then respond to their interest. Help your baby understand what you're saying. Use short sentences with clear and obvious gestures. Explain the things you are doing. Let them see, feel, smell, and taste the things you are talking about. They understand more than you think.

"I get the feeling that my son knows what I mean when I explain something or make a suggestion, such as, 'Shall we go for a nice little walk?' or 'I think it's bedtime!' It's so cute—he doesn't like hearing the word 'bed'!"
About Bob, 30th week

"When we say, 'Clap your hands,' my daughter does. And when we say, 'Jump up and down,' she bends her knees and bounces up and down, but her feet don't leave the ground."
About Jenny, 32nd week

"When I said, 'Bye, say bye-bye,' while waving at her daddy who was leaving, my daughter waved while keeping a steady eye on my waving hand. She now clearly knows she is waving at her dad."
About Emily, 32nd week

Your Baby May Start Using Words and Gestures

Your baby can now start to understand the relationship between a sound, or word, and an event. For example, a "bang" belongs to something falling on the floor. They can also learn the relationship between a gesture and an event. But they can do more. They can start to use words and gestures for themselves. If your baby attempts to "say" or "ask" something with a sound or gestures, make sure you let them know that you are thrilled with their potential. Talk and signal back to them. The best way to teach your baby to talk is by talking to them a lot yourself. Call everyday items by their names. Ask questions, such as, "Would you like a sandwich?" when you put their plate down. Let them hear nursery rhymes, and play singing games with them. In short, make speech appealing.

"Whenever my son wants to do something, he'll put his hand on it and look at me. It's as if he's trying to ask, 'May I?' He also understands 'No.' Of course, it doesn't stop him from trying, but he knows what it means."
About Bob, 32nd week

"Last week, my daughter said 'Oops' for the first time when she fell, and clearly said 'aah' when she petted the cat or us. We also noticed that she was starting to form so-called words with sounds. For instance, 'dadda' for Daddy, 'Po' for Poppy the dog, 'Be' for Bert from Sesame Street."
About Jenny, 29th week

"My daughter is a real chatterbox. She's especially talkative while crawling, when she recognizes someone or something. She talks to her stuffed toys and to us when she's on our laps. It's as if she's telling entire stories. She uses all kinds of vowels and consonants. The variations seem endless."
About Hannah, 29th week

"My son shakes his head 'No' and makes a certain sound. When I imitate him, he starts giggling uncontrollably."
About Paul, 28th week

THEIR FIRST WORD

Once your baby has gained the ability to perceive and experiment with relationships, they may discover they can say their first word. It doesn't mean that they will, though. The age at which babies begin to use words differs greatly. So don't worry if they put it off for a few more months.

Your Baby May Like Looking at Books

If your baby likes chatting, they will usually like looking at pictures in books, too. If this is the case, respond to that. Allow your baby to pick out a book; they will often have a favorite one. Some babies like looking at books purely to practice opening and closing the pages; others like looking at the pictures.

"My son often grabs a plastic picture book. He keeps opening and closing the pages and stares intently at the pictures."
About Paul, 29th week

"My little one really enjoys it when I make the sounds that belong to the animal she is looking at."
About Nina, 30th week

Your Baby May Be Singing and Dancing

If your baby loves music, make sure you do a lot of singing, dancing, and clapping songs with them. This way, your baby can practice using words and gestures. If you don't know many children's songs, YouTube is your best friend!

"When we were singing at the baby swimming class, my baby suddenly started singing along."
About Emily, 30th week

"Whenever my daughter hears music or I start to sing, she immediately starts kicking her legs and wiggling her tummy."
About Eve, 32nd week

Your Baby May Be Starting to Sit: What's Their Balance Like?

In your baby's body, there are numerous relationships between the various parts of the skeleton. Without the efforts of all the muscles, we would lose the relationships that exist between the various parts of the body, and we would collapse like a sack of bones. About this time, your baby may start to try to sit up by themselves.

She is still super fussy at night (really she hates sleep)! But she can now wave when you say hi and she seems to be MUCH more mobile and enjoys sitting up and playing on the floor with her toys a lot more!—**Instagram post**

If your baby is not sitting steadily enough to feel confident on their own, help them. See if you can help them gain confidence by playfully showing them how they can sit most steadily and by playing balancing games in which they have to regain their balance every time the wobble sets in.

> "My son's learned to sit up now. He started out by balancing on one buttock with both hands flat on the floor. Then he lifted one hand. Now he can sit without using his hands at all."
> **About Matt, 25th week**
>
> "Now my baby sits alone without any fear of losing her balance. She couldn't do that last week. She sometimes takes things, holds them over her head with both hands, and then throws them away."
> **About Jenny, 28th week**
>
> "When my son sits up, he often rolls over or back. He also topples forward or backward. Whenever that happens, I'm quick to laugh. Then he'll often start laughing, too."
> **About Bob, 26th week**

Your Baby May Be Starting to Stand: What Is Their Balance Like?

Help your baby when they're not standing firmly, or if they're afraid of tumbling down. Play balancing games with them—these will make them familiar with being in a vertical position. You will find popular balancing games you can play with your baby in the list of Your Favorite Games: The world of Relationships."

> "My baby kept trying to pull herself up this week, and at a certain point she succeeded. She had pulled herself up in bed, stood up right away, and stayed standing up, too. Now she can really do it. She pulls herself up using the bed, playpen, table, chair, or someone's legs. She also stands by the playpen and takes toys from it with one hand."
> **About Jenny, 28th week**

Your Baby May Be Walking With Help: What Is Their Balance Like?

If you notice that your baby wants to walk, give them a hand. Hold on to them tightly, because their balance is usually unstable. Play games with them that will familiarize them with keeping their balance, especially when they shift their weight from one leg to the other. Never go on hour-long walks with them. They really won't learn any faster that way. Your baby won't start walking until they are ready to.

ONLY WITH THE RIGHT PHYSIQUE CAN YOUR BABY LEARN TO WALK

Once your baby has acquired the ability of perceiving and experimenting with relationships, they can understand what walking is. But understanding doesn't mean they will actually do it. They might not succeed because their body is not ready. Your baby won't learn how to walk at this age unless the proportions between the weight of their bones, the mass of their muscles, and the length of their limbs compared to their torso meet perfect specifications. And perfect doesn't necessarily mean "beautiful."

Your Baby May Be Playing With "Relationships" Between Body Parts

Your baby can use two fingers in a concerted action; for instance, their thumb and forefinger. If it interests them, they will be able to pluck extremely small objects, such as threads, from the carpet. They can learn to pick blades of grass, or they may take pleasure in touching and stroking all kinds of surfaces with their index finger. And they may have great fun examining every detail of very small objects, as they can now grab them between their fingers instead of only with their whole hand.

Your baby can now also begin to understand the connection between what their left hand is doing and what their right hand is doing. They have better control over the movements both make. This way, they can start to use them simultaneously. If you see your baby trying to use both hands at the same time, get them to hold a toy in either hand and clash them together. Or help them make this clashing movement without toys, so that they clap their hands. Give it a go. Let them knock toys against the floor or the wall. Encourage them to pass toys from one hand to the other. And see if they can put two toys down at the same time, and pick them up again.

> *"My daughter has the hitting syndrome. She beats anything she can lay her hands on."*
> **About Jenny, 29th week**

Allow Them to Crawl "On," "In," and "Under"

If your baby can crawl, allow them to roam freely around a room where they can do no harm. When they enter the world of relationships, they begin to understand that they can crawl *into*, *out of*, *under*, *over*, *in between*, *on top of*, and *through* something. They will love to toy with these various relationships between themselves and the objects in their surroundings. See if they also do the following.

> *"I like to watch my son play in the living room. He crawls up to the couch, looks under it, sits down, quickly crawls over to the closet, crawls into it, rushes off again, crawls to the rug, lifts it up, looks under it, heads toward a chair that he crawls under, whoosh, he's off to another cupboard, crawls into that one, gets stuck, cries a little, figures out how to get out and closes the door."*
> **About Steven, 30th week**

If your baby takes pleasure in doing these things, leave some objects around that will encourage them to continue their explorations. For instance, you can make hills for them to crawl *over* using rolled up blankets, quilts, or pillows. Of course, you should adjust this soft play circuit to suit what your baby can do. You could place a big box on the floor and cut out a hole so they can easily crawl *into* it. You can also build a tunnel from boxes or chairs that they can crawl *through*. You can make a tent out of a sheet, which they can crawl *into*, *out of*, and *under*. Many babies enjoy opening and closing doors. If your baby likes this, too, you can include a door or two. If you crawl along with them, it will double the fun. Try adding some variety with peek-a-boo and hide-and-seek games, too.

Show Your Baby That You Are Not Deserting Them

When they are in the world of relationships, almost every baby begins to realize that their parents can increase the distance between them and can walk away and leave them. Previously, their eyes could see it, but they didn't fully grasp what leaving means. Now that they do, it poses a problem. They get frightened when it hits them that their parents are unpredictable, that they can leave them behind at any time and even if they're already crawling, their mommy and daddy can easily outdistance them. They feel they have no control over the distance between themselves and their daddy or mommy. Your baby has to learn how to deal with this "development." It takes understanding, compassion, practice, and above all, time.

Not all babies want to keep you close to them. Generally, babies panic the most around 29 weeks. Then, it improves somewhat, until the next leap begins.

Respond to your baby's needs. Give them the opportunity to grow accustomed to the new situation at their own pace. Then, they will feel you are there if they really need you. You can help them by carrying them more often or staying a bit closer to them than usual. Give them some warning before you walk away, and keep talking to them as you walk away and when you're in the other room. This way, they will learn that you are still there, even if they can't see you.

You can also practice "leaving" by playing peek-a-boo games. For example, you can hide behind a newspaper while sitting next to your baby, then you can hide behind the couch close to your baby, then behind the cupboard a little farther away, and finally behind the door.

"Everything's fine as long as my daughter can see me. If not, she starts crying."
About Eve, 29th week

"My son has his moods when he screams until he's picked up. When I do, he'll laugh, utterly pleased with himself."
About Frankie, 31st week

"My little girl had been with the babysitter, as is usual. She wouldn't eat, wouldn't sleep, wouldn't do anything. She just cried and cried. I've never seen anything like it with her. I feel guilty leaving her behind like that. I'm considering working shorter hours, but I don't know how to arrange it."
About Laura, 28th week

"My daughter has days when if she even suspects I'll be setting her down on the floor to play, she starts whining and clinging with intense passion. So now I carry her around on my hip all day long. She has also stopped smiling the way she used to. Just last week, she had a smile for everyone. Now it's definitely less. She's been through this once before, but in the past, she'd always end up with a tiny grin on her face. Now, it's out of the question."
About Nina, 29th week

Allow Them to Follow You

If your baby is already somewhat mobile, you can reassure them with their feeling of desertion by helping them to follow you. First try telling them you are leaving—this way, your baby will learn they do not have to keep an eye on you and that they can continue to play at ease. Then slowly walk away, so that they can follow you. Always adjust your pace to your baby's. Soon, your baby will learn they can control the distance between the two of you. They will also come to trust that you will not completely disappear, and they won't bother you as much.

> "At first, my son used to cling to my leg like a monkey and ride on my shoe when I walked. I had to drag this 'ball and chain' around everywhere. After a few days, he started keeping a slight distance. I could take a few steps to the side before he'd crawl up to me. Now, I can go into the kitchen while he's crawling around. He won't actually come looking for me unless I stay there for a while. He now crawls perfectly on his hands and knees and can reach quite a speed."
> **About Bob, 31st week**

Often, the desire to be near you is so strong that even the inexperienced crawler is willing to put in some extra effort, and ends up improving their crawling. The desire to keep up with their mommy and daddy, along with the coordination they're able to utilize at this age, might provide just the extra incentive they need.

Promoting Progress by Raising Expectations

Breaking old habits and setting new rules are also part of developing new skills. You can demand the things of your baby that they now understand. But no more, or no less. When your baby is busy observing and playing with relationships, they may also exhibit behavior you find irritating. This is because old ways of doing things and established rules of behavior may no longer suit the baby's current progress. Both parents and baby have to renegotiate new rules to restore peace and harmony.

At first parents worry when their baby enters a new fussy phase. They get annoyed when they discover that nothing is wrong with their baby and, to the contrary, they are in fact ready to do more. It is then that they start demanding that their baby do the things they feel their baby is able to do. As a consequence, they promote progress.

CONSTANT CLINGING

Over the weeks, parents can grow more and more irritated if they don't get the opportunity to continue their everyday activities. Once their baby has reached 29 weeks, most parents try to slowly gain more independence by distracting their baby, allowing them to cry for a while, or by putting baby to bed. Whatever you decide to do, consider how much your baby can handle.

Dinnertime Blues

At this age, many babies come to realize that certain foods taste better than others. So why not pick the tastier one?

Many mothers and fathers think it's funny at first. Soon, however, almost every parent becomes worried at first, then sometimes annoyed when their baby gets picky about their food. They wonder whether the baby is getting enough nutrition. They try to distract the fussy eater so they can stick the spoon in their mouth at an unsuspected moment. Or they run after them with food the whole day. Don't do these things. Strong-willed babies will resist something that is being forced upon them even more. And a worried parent will in turn react to that. This makes meals a battleground.

Stop fighting it. You can't force a baby to swallow, so don't even try to. If you do, you might only increase their dislike of anything that has to do with food. Resort to different tactics and make use of other new skills your baby is able to learn now. At this stage, they can try holding something between their thumb and forefinger, but they will still need a lot of practice, and feeding themselves is good for their coordination. A baby at this age also loves to make their own decisions, and the freedom to eat by themselves will make eating more enjoyable. Use these new skills to their advantage. Allowing them to finger-feed themselves could put them in a better mood so they let you feed them as well. It can be messy, but encourage them anyway. Keep putting two pieces of food on their plate, so that they are kept occupied. Generally, it will be easy to feed them in between. You can also

make eating more pleasurable for your baby by feeding them in front of a mirror. This way, they can watch as you put a spoonful of food in their mouth or in your own. Don't worry if it doesn't work first time. Many babies go through eating problems, and they also get over them.

Touching Everything and Not Listening May Be Normal, but It's Still Annoying!

Now that their baby is in the middle of learning new skills, many mothers and fathers constantly find themselves having to forbid things. A crawling baby is especially liable to inspect all your possessions. You may be tempted to snatch something back, but be careful not to lash out.

Let's be clear: your baby does not learn anything from a "correcting" slap on the hand. And more important, hitting a baby is never acceptable, even if it is "only" a slap on the hand. It's better to remove your baby from things they are not allowed to touch. And to clearly say "no" when they are doing something that is against your rules.

Babies Are Impatient Little People!

Babies can be impatient for all sorts of reasons. For instance, they don't want to wait for their food. They get mad if they fail to accomplish something, if something is not allowed, or if they aren't paid attention to quickly enough.

> *"My daughter's becoming very impatient. She wants to have it all, and she gets furious if she can't reach something and I tell her 'No.' Then she'll really start screaming. It irritates me and makes me think she's only doing it because I work. She's much sweeter with the babysitter."*
> **About Laura, 31st week**
>
> *"My baby was carrying on something awful and screaming during supper. She feels it isn't going fast enough, so she starts yelling, twisting, and wriggling after every bite."*
> **About Ashley, 28th week**

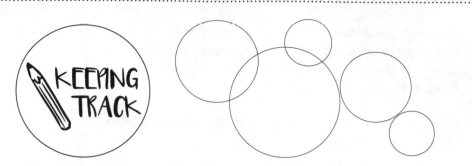

YOUR FAVORITE GAMES: THE WORLD OF RELATIONSHIPS

These are games and activities that your baby may like now and that help them practice their newly developing skills.

Instructions to Fill In This List:

Check off your baby's favorite games. When you have completed the list, go to What You've Discovered: The World of Relationships to see if there is a link between the things that interested them most during this leap and the games they liked playing. You may have to think about it for a while, but it will give you an insight into your baby's unique personality.

PEEK-A-BOO AND HIDE-AND-SEEK GAMES

Your baby now really loves peek-a-boo. The variations are endless.

☐ PEEK-A-BOO WITH A CLOTH

Put a cloth over your head and see whether your baby will pull it away. Ask: "Where's Mommy?" or "Where's Daddy?" Your baby will know you're still there, because they can hear you. If they don't make any attempts to pull away the cloth, take their hand and pull it away together. Say "peek-a-boo" when you reappear.

☐ VARIATIONS ON PEEK-A-BOO

Cover your face with your hands and then take them away, or pop up from behind a newspaper or book held between you and the baby. Babies also like it when you appear from behind a plant or under a table. After all, they can still see parts of you.

☐ HIDE YOURSELF COMPLETELY

You can also hide in a conspicuous place, such as behind a curtain. This way, your baby can follow the movements of the curtain. Make sure your baby sees you disappear. For example, announce that you're going to hide (for noncrawlers), or that they have to come look for you (for crawlers). If they didn't watch you or were distracted for a moment by something else, call their name. Give it a try in the door opening, too. This will teach them that leaving is followed by returning. Reward them every time they manage to find you. Lift them up in the air or cuddle them—whatever they like best.

☐ WHERE ARE YOU?

A lot of babies discover they can hide themselves behind or under something. They usually start with a cloth or an item of clothing while being changed. Take advantage of any opportunity to develop a game that the baby has started. This way, they'll learn that they can play an active part in the game.

☐ HIDING TOYS

Try hiding toys under a handkerchief. Make sure you use something your baby likes or that they're attached to. Show them how and where you hide it. Make it easy for them the first time around. Make sure they can still see a tiny part of the toy.

☐ HIDING TOYS IN THE BATHTUB

Put bath foam in the bathtub and allow your baby to play with it. Try hiding toys under the foam sometime and invite them to look for them. If they can blow, try blowing at the foam. Or give them a straw and encourage them to blow through it.

ENCOURAGING TALKING

You can make talking appealing by talking to your baby frequently, by listening to them, by "reading" books together, and by playing whispering, singing, and word games.

☐ LOOK AT PICTURE BOOKS TOGETHER

Take your baby on your lap—they usually like that best. Let them choose a book to look at together. Whatever your baby looks at, call it by its name. If it's a book with animals in it, mimic the sounds the animals make. Babies generally love hearing their father or mother making sounds like barking, mooing, and quacking. They are also sounds babies can mimic, and then they can really join in. Let them turn the pages by themselves, if they want to.

☐ WHISPERING GAME

Most babies love it when sounds or words are whispered in their ears. Making little puffs of air that tickle their ear is interesting, too, perhaps because a baby can now understand what blowing is.

☐ SONG AND MOVEMENT GAMES

These games can be used to encourage both singing and talking. They also exercise the baby's sense of balance. On the Internet, you can find many clips showing you the right gestures and words. Why not try "Giddy-up, Giddy-up, Little Rocking Horse," "This Is the Way the Lady Rides," or "The Wheels on the Bus."

BALANCING GAMES

A lot of singing games are also balancing games. You can also do balancing games without music.

☐ SITTING GAME

Sit down comfortably. Take your baby on your knees. Hold their hands, and move them gently from left to right, so that they shift their weight from buttock to buttock. Also try making them lean forward or backward carefully. Babies find the latter the most exciting. You can also move them in small or large circles, to the left, backward, to the right, and forward. Adjust yourself to what your baby is doing. The movement has to challenge them just enough. You can try doing a seated version of the "Hokey Pokey," or let them swing like a pendulum of a clock while you say "tick-tock, tick-tock" in time with the movement.

☐ STANDING GAME

Kneel comfortably on the floor and have your baby stand in front of you while you hold their hips or hands and move them gently from left to right, so that they transfer their weight from one leg to the other. Do the same thing in a different plane so that their body weight shifts from back to front. Adjust yourself to what your baby is doing. It has to challenge them just enough to make them want to find their balance themselves.

☐ FLYING

Grasp your baby firmly, lift them, and "fly" them through the room, making them rise and descend. Turn left and right. Fly in small circles, in a straight line, and backward. Vary the movement and speed as much as possible. If your baby enjoys this, then try making them land carefully upside down, headfirst. Naturally, you'll accompany the entire flight with different zooming, humming, or screeching sounds.

☐ STANDING ON THEIR HEAD

Most physically active babies love horsing around and being stood on their heads. However, others find standing on their heads frightening or overexciting. Only play this game if your baby likes playing rough. It's a healthy exercise for them.

GAMES WITH TOYS AND HOUSEHOLD OBJECTS

For now, the best games are emptying cupboards and shelves, dropping toys, and throwing toys away.

☐ BABY'S OWN CUPBOARD

Organize a cupboard for your baby and fill it with things that they really like. Usually this will include empty boxes, empty egg cartons, empty toilet paper rolls, plastic plates, and lidded plastic bottles filled with something that rattles. But also include things they can make a lot of noise with, such as pans, wooden spoons, and old sets of keys.

☐ DROPPING WITH A BANG

Some babies like hearing a lot of noise when they drop something. If your baby does, you could make a game of "dropping" things by putting them in their high chair and placing a metal serving tray on the floor. Hand them blocks, and show them how to let them go so that they fall on the tray.

☐ DROPPING AND PICKING UP

Sit your baby in their high chair. Tie a short string to some of their playthings. When they throw them onto the floor, teach them how to pull them back up again.

OTHER ACTIVITIES

☐ SWIMMING FOR BABIES

Many babies love playing in the water. Some swimming pools have specially heated pools for small children and special hours when a group of babies can play games with parents in the water. Always be careful with a baby in water, and never leave them unattended.

☐ VISIT A PETTING ZOO

A visit to a petting zoo, deer camp, or duck pond can be extremely exciting for your baby. They can see the animals from their picture books. They'll enjoy looking at their wobbly, pattering, or leaping motions. And they'll particularly like feeding the animals and watching them eat.

YOUR FAVORITE TOYS

- ☐ Your very own cupboard or shelf
- ☐ Doors
- ☐ Cardboard boxes in different sizes; also, empty egg cartons
- ☐ Wooden spoons
- ☐ (Round) stacking cups
- ☐ Wooden blocks
- ☐ Large building bricks or blocks
- ☐ Balls (light enough to roll)
- ☐ Picture books
- ☐ Photo books
- ☐ Children's songs
- ☐ Bath toys: things to fill and empty out, such as plastic bottles, plastic cups, plastic colanders, funnels
- ☐ Toy cars with rotating wheels and doors that can be opened
- ☐ Soft toys that make noise when turned upside down
- ☐ Squeaky toys
- ☐ Drums
- ☐ (Toy) pianos
- ☐ (Toy) telephones

DO REMEMBER

Your child will choose the things that most suit their own inclinations, interests, physique, and weight. You therefore cannot compare babies; each baby is unique.

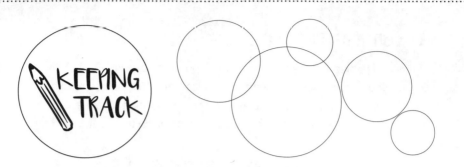

WHAT YOU'VE DISCOVERED:
THE WORLD OF RELATIONSHIPS

These are examples of skills you could notice from now on, but remember that your baby will not do everything on the list.

Instructions to Fill In This List:

Just as with the other leaps, complete this right before the next leap starts. Look critically at what your baby has started doing and what they are not doing, because, here too, what they don't do says as much about their interests as what they do. Life is made up of choices, and choices say a lot about a person. You will notice it is getting more difficult to complete the list, as the examples are becoming more diverse and you often have to focus on the intention and effort rather than the end result. It requires you to look at things in a different way than how we as adults are used to doing. For example, if your baby likes continually closing cupboard doors, are they doing that because they like the sound it makes, because they like swiping at the door, or because the door is then back "inside" the cupboard? In short: observe your baby and try to discover what they are interested in and what drives them to do what they are doing. This list will guide you and show you the things to look out for.

You made this leap on: _____

On _____ the sun broke through again and now, at the end of the leap, I see you can do these new things.

LOOKING

Date:

☐ You look from one toy, object, or food to another when you are holding something different in each hand.

☐ You look from one picture book to the other showing the same animal.

☐ You look from one photograph to another showing the same person.

☐ You observe the movements of an animal or person. You really like it if the movements are unusual.

☐ Movements you like to watch are:
    ☐ Someone singing
    ☐ Someone dancing
    ☐ Someone clapping
    ☐ Someone standing on their head
    ☐ A dog pattering across a wooden floor
    ☐ Other:

_____

_____

_____

☐ You explore your own body—particularly your penis/vagina.

☐ You pay a lot of attention to smaller details or parts of toys and other objects. You examined:
    ☐ Labels
    ☐ Tags
    ☐ Stickers on toys
    ☐ Other:

_____

_____

_____

☐ You select books yourself.

☐ You select toys yourself.

MANIPULATING OBJECTS

Date:

☐ You lift the rug to look underneath it.

☐ You hold a stuffed animal upside down to hear the sound inside.

☐ You roll a little ball across the floor.

☐ You invariably grab a ball rolled toward you.

☐ You knock things over, such as the wastepaper basket to empty out its contents.

☐ You throw things away.

☐ You are busy putting your toys down in all sorts of ways. For example, you put toys *in* and *next to* a basket, *in* and *out of* a box, or *under* and *on* a chair, or push them *out of* the crib. You are playing with the relationships between objects. Aren't you clever?

☐ You try to fit one toy inside another.

☐ You take playthings, such as stacking cups, apart.

☐ You try prying something out of a toy that's inside, such as a bell.

☐ You pull your own socks off. Not because I ask you to, but because you simply like doing it.

☐ You pry your shoelaces loose.

☐ If I leave you to it, you empty cupboards and shelves.

☐ You drop objects to test how something falls. You are not throwing things on the floor because you like it and want to break objects—you are experimenting.

☐ You put food in my mouth, or in the mouth of

_____

☐ You push doors closed. Perhaps this is because you like the notions of "in" and "out" now or maybe you just like closing doors, I don't know. But you do it with a lot of enthusiasm.

☐ You like rubbing your hand or a cloth over surfaces. If I didn't know better, I'd think you were polishing. But of course, you are not busy cleaning, you simply like the movement and imitating adults.

LISTENING

Date:

☐ You really have started to understand more and make connections between words, or short sentences, and the accompanying actions. For example, I've noticed that you comprehend the meaning of:
    ☐ No, don't do that
    ☐ Come on, let's go
    ☐ Clap your hands
    ☐ Other:

_____

_____

☐ You listen to explanations intently and sometimes seem to understand.

☐ You like to hear animal sounds when looking at animal pictures.

☐ You are very interested in my cell phone. You listen intently to voices you hear coming out of the telephone when I am on the phone.

☐ You pay attention to sounds that are related to a certain activity. These are often sounds I usually take little notice of but, by observing you, I have become more aware of them. These are all kinds of sounds, such as:
    ☐ Washing windows
    ☐ Squeaking of the windshield wipers
    ☐ Sound of my telephone vibrating
    ☐ Ticking the keys on a keyboard
    ☐ Other:

_____

_____

☐ You listen to sounds you make yourself, such as:
    ☐ When you draw your nails across the wallpaper
    ☐ When you slide across the floor on your bare bottom
    ☐ Other:

_____

_____

TALKING

Date:

☐ You understand the link between words and actions or motions. For instance, I have noticed that you have made these connections:

WORD	ACTION/MOTION
☐ "oo" (oops)	When you fall
☐ "aah"	When you pet an animal or person
☐ "a-choo"	When someone sneezes
☐ Other:	

_____

_____

_____

PARENT-BABY DISTANCE

Date:

☐ You protest when I walk away.

☐ You try to crawl after me.

☐ You repeatedly make contact with me when you are playing, to make sure I am still there.

MIMICKING GESTURES

Date:

☐ You wave goodbye.

☐ You clap your hands.

☐ You mimic clicking with your tongue.

☐ You mimic shaking and nodding your head, although I notice you often only nod with your eyes!

MAINTAINING BALANCE

Date:

☐ **You sit up by yourself from lying down.**
Babies aged between 6 and 11 months (average is 8 months and a week) can pull themselves into a sitting position using a piece of furniture, for instance. Remember that any time during this period is fine; early is not better and later is not worse.

☐ **You stand by yourself by pulling yourself up.**
Between 6 and 11 months, babies learn to pull themselves up to a standing position, often using furniture. The average age babies learn this is 8½ months.

☐ **While standing up and holding on to something, you sit down again by yourself. You sometimes land harder on your bottom than you wanted to.**

☐ **While standing up and holding on to something, you sometimes let go! It's only briefly, but you do it!**

☐ **You can walk a few steps with support.**
It's still too early to walk independently. Babies take their first steps between 7 (at the end of this leap) and 12 months, on average at 9½ months. Don't be too concerned with the ages; every healthy and functioning body will walk when the time is right, and no one has ever won an award for walking. In short: all the things in this list are at least as important as learning to walk.

☐ **At the very end of this leap, you walked around the edge of something you could hold on to, such as the crib, table, etc.**
All babies are mentally capable of this now, but most babies are still physically unable to do it. They are not interested, are busy with other skills, or are simply not yet strong enough.

☐ **You sometimes lunge from the table to the chair, while holding on, and you take a step.**
Although all babies have the mental capacity to do this, few do.

☐ **You make a jumping movement, but without leaving the ground.**

☐ **You grab a toy from an overhead shelf or table.**

☐ **You dance to the sound of music: you sway your tummy back and forth . . . it's lovely to watch!**

BODY CONTROL

Date:

☐ Most babies don't crawl yet, but you are a real physical explorer and like crawling *into* (such as the closet or a big box) and *under* (such as a chair or the stairs)
things.
There is a huge difference in the age babies start crawling; it can be anywhere
between 5 and 11 months. On average, babies crawl at 7 months.

☐ You crawl back and forth *over* slight elevations in height.

☐ You crawl *in* and *out* of rooms.

☐ You crawl *around* the table.

☐ You bend over or lie flat on your stomach to get something from *under* the couch.

☐ You increasingly oppose your thumb and index finger to feel or grasp things. Very
few people will comment on this; the general focus is on crawling and walking. But
fine motor skills are just as important, if not more so!
Babies start using this combination of thumb and index finger between 6 and 10 months.
The average age is 7 months and 2 weeks.

☐ You like playing with two things in your two hands. For example, to bash two toys
against each other.
Babies do this for the first time between 6 and 10 months. The average age is 8½ months.

THE EASY PERIOD: AFTER THE LEAP

Around 31 weeks, another comparatively easy period begins. For anywhere from one to three weeks, a baby is admired for their cheerfulness, independence, and progress.

"Frankie was extremely cheerful, so it wasn't hard to have fun with him. It also pleases me to see him a little more active and livelier in the physical sense. But he's at his best when he can observe people. He's very talkative, too—a great kid."

About Frankie, 30th week

"My daughter's obviously gotten bigger and older. She reacts to everything we do. She watches everything. And she wants to have whatever we have. I'd almost say that she wants to be a part of it."

About Ashley, 34th week

"Finally, some rest after a long period of constant changes. A wonderful week. He's gone through another change. He cries less, sleeps more. I can see a certain pattern starting to develop again, for the umpteenth time. I talk to him much more. I've noticed myself explaining everything I do. When I go to prepare his bottle, I tell him. When it's time for him to go to bed, I tell him that it's time to sleep and I will be in the other room and will get him out later. I explain why he has to take a nap. And these talks seem to do me good. The daycare center is going well now, too."

About Bob, 30th week

"We seem to have a different kind of contact now. It's as if the umbilical cord has finally been cut. The feeling of complete dependency is also gone. I'm quicker to rely on a babysitter. I also notice that I've been giving my son a lot more freedom. I don't have to be on top of him all the time."

About Bob, 31st week

Leap 6

The World of Categories

DIVIDING THE WORLD INTO GROUPS

At around 37 weeks (or between 36 and 40), or 8½ months, you may notice your baby has a new ability. You discover that they are doing or wanting to do things that are new to them. You can therefore see that they are making a leap in their development. At this age, a baby's explorations can often seem very methodical. For example, you may notice your little one picking up specks from the floor and examining them studiously between their thumb and forefinger. Or a budding little chef may explore the food on their plate by testing the way a banana squashes or spinach squishes through their tiny fingers. They will assume the most serious, absorbed expression while carrying out these investigations. In fact, that is just what they are—investigations that will help the little researcher begin to categorize their world.

Your baby has felt this leap coming before now. Around 34 weeks (between 32 and 37 weeks), you can expect your baby to be fussier than they have been these past one to three weeks. Babies' brain waves show drastic changes again around this time. In addition, the baby's head circumference increases dramatically, and the glucose metabolism in the brain changes at this age. These changes will begin to alter the way your baby perceives their world. They will notice that they can see, hear, smell, taste, and feel things that are unknown to them, which will be disturbing to them at first, and they will want to cling on to something safe and familiar: Mommy or Daddy. This fussy phase will often last for four weeks, but it may last anywhere from three to six weeks.

THE FUSSY PHASE:
THE ANNOUNCEMENT OF THE MAGICAL LEAP

All babies cry more easily now than they did during the past few weeks. They may seem cranky, whiny, fidgety, grumpy, bad-tempered, discontented, unmanageable, restless, or impatient. All of this is very understandable.

Babies are now under extra pressure because from their last leap, they know that their parents can go away from them whenever they please and leave them behind. At first, most babies were temporarily distressed by this discovery, but over the past few weeks, they have learned to deal with it in their own way. It all seemed to be going much more smoothly than it was—and then the next leap came along and ruined everything. Now your baby wants to stay with their mommy and daddy again, as they realize perfectly well that their parents can walk away whenever they choose. This makes the baby feel even more insecure and increases their tension.

DO REMEMBER

If you notice your baby is fussier than usual, watch them closely. It's likely that they are attempting to master new skills. Have a look at What You've Discovered: The World of Categories on page 276 to see what you can expect.

During this leap, as in the previous one, you may notice that your baby is very fidgety, restless, and ready to make trouble. They also may seem shyer, want to stay close to you, and want you to keep them occupied more than usual. Do remember that this is a difficult time for your baby most of all. They may sleep poorly and even have nightmares. During the day, they may be quieter than usual or act unusually sweet. And once again, during this leap your baby may refuse to have their diaper changed or wiggle around so much that it is almost impossible. And let's not forget eating . . . that can become a battlefield.

> "These past few days, my daughter insists on sitting on my lap constantly. For no apparent reason, I might add. When I don't carry her around, she screams. When I take her for walks in her stroller, the moment she even thinks I've stopped, she demands to be lifted out and held."
> **About Ashley, 34th week**
>
> "My baby acts cranky and seems to be bored. She picks up everything and just tosses it away again."
> **About Laura, 35th week**

Babies will usually cry less when they are with their mother or father, especially when all the attention is on them and they have their parents all for themselves.

HOW YOU KNOW YOUR BABY HAS ENTERED THE NEXT FUSSY PHASE

Besides the three Cs, your baby can show some of the following characteristics when they are entering the next fussy phase.

Is Your Baby Clinging to You, or Doing So More Often Than Before?

Noncrawlers who become anxious when their parents walk around can do nothing but cry. For some, every step their parents take is reason for genuine panic. They sometimes cling so tightly to their daddy or mommy that they can hardly move. They may get furious if you dare to put them down unexpectedly.

> "It was another difficult week with a lot of crying. My son literally clings to me. When I leave the room, he starts crying and crawling after me. When I'm cooking, he'll crawl behind me, grab hold of my legs, and hold on in such a way that I can't move. Putting him to bed is a struggle all over again. He falls asleep very late. He'll only play if I play with him."
> **About Bob, 38th week**
>
> "I call my baby my little leech. She persists in holding on to my trousers all day like a leech. Once again, she wants to be around, with, and on me constantly."
> **About Emily, 36th week**
>
> "My son wants to be carried all of the time, and he clings to my neck or hair really tightly in the process."
> **About Matt, 36th week**
>
> "It's almost as if there's something about my baby's bed. I'll take her upstairs, sound asleep, and as soon as she feels the mattress, her eyes pop open. And boy, does she start screaming!"
> **About Laura, 33rd week**

Is Your Baby Shy?

The desire for your baby to be close to their mommy or daddy may become even more apparent in the presence of other people—sometimes even when that other person is a brother or sister. Often, their mommy or daddy is the only one allowed to look at them and talk to them. And they are almost always the only ones allowed to touch them.

> *"When strangers talk to my son or pick him up, he starts crying immediately."*
> **About Paul, 34th week**
>
> *"When visitors arrive, my son will race to me, climb on my lap, tummy to tummy, cling to me, and only then look to see who's here."*
> **About Kevin, 34th week**

Does Your Baby Demand (More) Attention (Than They Did)?

Most babies start asking for more attention at this stage, and even easy ones are not always content at being left alone. Some babies are not satisfied until their parents' attention is focused entirely on them. They want their parents completely for themselves and for them to watch as their baby plays. They may do naughty things to get attention as soon as their mother or father dares to shift their focus to someone or something else.

> *"When I'm talking to other people, my son always starts screaming really loudly for attention."*
> **About Paul, 36th week**
>
> *"My son doesn't like playing alone on his play mat anymore. He demands attention and is only happy if there is someone around him all the time."*
> **About Frankie, 34th week**

Does Your Baby Sleep Poorly?

Most babies start sleeping less than before. They may refuse to go to bed, don't fall asleep as easily, and wake up sooner than usual. Some are especially hard to get to sleep during the day; others, at night. And some stay up longer now both during the day and at night.

TIP

If you want to know more about sleep and leaps, go to page 59.

Does Your Baby Have Nightmares?

Some babies sleep uneasily at this time. Sometimes they toss and turn so much during sleep that it looks like they are having a nightmare.

So far each leap has been a little worse than the last. Tonight was by far the worst night of sleep yet. She tossed and turned most of the night. She had two nightmares with periods of crying and whimpering in her sleep that lasted up to 15 mins before she cried herself awake. She's clingy. She is super distractible. And I've been up since 2 a.m. tonight and can't get back to sleep myself.

Here's the thing, though. As parents we complain about how hard these developmental phases are for us, having to function on little to no sleep with a baby who isn't quite their normal self. But imagine how hard it is for the wee babe. The changes and growth they experience in that first year are enormous, and probably very scary. So if they need constant reassurance and comfort . . .
*isn't that what we are there for?—***Instagram post**

Does Your Baby Act Unusually Sweet?

At this age, your baby may employ entirely new tactics to stay close to their mommy or daddy. Instead of whining and complaining, they may opt for something entirely different and kiss and cuddle up to you. Often, they will switch back and forth between troublesome and sweet behavior, trying out what works best to get the most attention. Parents of an independent baby are often pleasantly surprised when their baby finally starts cuddling up to them!

"Sometimes my baby didn't want anything. At other times, she became very cuddly."
About Ashley, 36th week

"My son is more affectionate than he's ever been. Whenever I get near him, he grabs and hugs me tightly. My neck is full of red blotches from nuzzling and snuggling. He's also not as quick to push me away anymore. Sometimes he'll sit still so I can read a book with him. I love it! He finally wants to play with me, too."
About Matt, 35th week

"My baby expresses his clinginess by acting sweeter and more affectionate, coming to lie down with me and snuggling up against me."
About Steven, 36th week

Is Your Baby "Quieter"?

Your baby may become quieter for a while. You may hear them babbling less often, or you may see them moving around and playing less than before. At other times, they might briefly stop doing anything and just lie there, gazing into the distance.

"My son's quieter and often lies there staring into nothingness. I wonder if something's bothering him or he's starting to get sick."
About Steven, 36th week

Does Your Baby Refuse to Have Their Diaper Changed?

Most babies protest, scream, wriggle, act impatiently, and are unmanageable when you set them down to be dressed, undressed, or changed.

"Dressing, undressing, and changing diapers is a nightmare. My baby screams the moment I put her down. It drives me crazy."
About Juliette, 35th week

Does Your Baby Seem More Babyish Now?

For the first time, some parents will notice the recurrence of infantile behavior that they thought had been left behind. They have probably experienced setbacks before, but the older the baby gets, the more obvious they become. Parents dislike seeing setbacks. It makes them feel insecure, but setbacks really are perfectly normal. Brief setbacks happen during every fussy phase.

> *"My baby has difficulty falling asleep. She starts crying the same sort of cries as she did when she'd just been born."*
> **About Juliette, 32nd week**
>
> *"I have to rock and sing my son to sleep again every night, just like I used to."*
> **About Steven, 35th week**

Does Your Baby Lose Their Appetite?

Many babies seem less interested in food and drink at this time. Some seem to have no appetite and may dig in their heels and refuse some meals altogether. Others will only eat what they put into their mouths themselves. Others still are picky, spill things, and spit things out. Because of this, mealtimes may take longer than they used to. Your baby may also be unmanageable during meals, not wanting to eat when they are given food and wanting it as soon as it has been taken away. Or they may demand a lot of food one day and refuse to eat the next. Every variety of behavior is possible.

> *"My son refused my breast for three days. It was terrible. I felt like I was going to explode. Then, just when I decided it might be time to start cutting down on breastfeeding because it was getting to be that T-shirt time of year again, he decided he wanted to nurse all day long. So then I was afraid I might not have enough because he wasn't eating anything else anymore. But it seems to be working out okay. So far, I haven't heard him complain."*
> **About Matt, 34th week**

> *Leap 6 . . . basically my baby is acting like a psycho drunk person. That's all.* —**Instagram post**

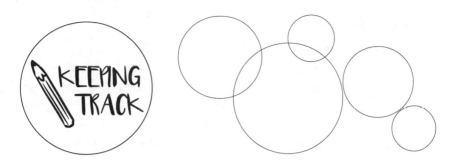

KEEPING TRACK

LEAP SIGNS

This is how you let me know the leap has started:

☐ You cry more often than usual.

☐ You are frequently bad-tempered or cranky.

☐ You demand more attention than you did.

☐ You are cheerful one moment and cry the next.

☐ You want to be kept busy more often now.

☐ You cling to me, or do so more often than before.

☐ You act unusually sweet.

☐ You throw temper tantrums, or do so more often than before.

☐ You are shyer, or shyer than you were.

☐ You protest more or more often than usual when I stop holding you.

☐ You sleep poorly.

☐ You seem to have nightmares more frequently than before.

☐ You lose your appetite.

☐ You babble less than usual.

☐ You are less lively than you were.

☐ You sometimes just sit there, quietly daydreaming.

☐ You refuse to have your diaper changed or to be dressed.

☐ You suck your thumb, or do so more often than before.

☐ You reach for a soft toy, or do so more often than before.

☐ You are more babyish than you were.

☐ And I've noticed that you:

_____

_____

Remember that babies do not have to show all these characteristics of a leap. It is about what your baby does and not how many things they do.

How Are *You* Doing?

You May Feel Insecure

A fussy baby usually makes parents worry. They want to understand what is making their baby behave this way, and when they believe they have found a good explanation, it puts their minds at ease. At this age, as in the previous leap, many parents decide it must be teething pain. There is no correlation between the timing of the leaps and teething, but your baby may be dealing with both!

> *"She was so upset, I thought she was cutting teeth, but they never came. I realized she was going through another fussy phase!"*
> **About Sara, 34th week**
>
> *"He is easily startled, and wakes up crying in the middle of the night. Sometimes three times a night, and the only way to comfort him is to bring him to our bed."*
> **About Steven, 33rd week**

You May Be Exhausted and Aggravated

Parents of demanding babies who sleep little may feel extremely tired, especially toward the end of the fussy phase, and they may think they can't go on much longer. Some parents also complain of headaches, backaches, and nausea.

Almost all parents become increasingly worn out by their baby's behavior during fussy phases. They become tired of the bad tempers, impatience, crying, whining, and constant demands for physical contact or attention.

⚓ ANCHOR MOMENTS *

Inspiring, energizing anchor moments for awesome you:

In 5 minutes: Take 10 Breath-FS exercises. To release the most tension possible through breathing, say FFFFFF while breathing out. When you have almost completely exhaled, say SSSSS. You will exhale deeper than you usually do.

In 10 minutes: Take a contrast shower: hot-cold-hot-cold. It might not seem as relaxing while being under the cold water, but your body will feel reborn and energized afterward!

More time: Let a trusted family member or sitter stay with baby for a few hours. Treat yourself to a glass of wine with your partner or friend. Enjoy talking about anything but parenthood for an hour or two. It will be difficult, but you'll come back refreshed.

* For more anchor moments, see page 36.

Quarrels

Toward the end of every fussy phase, most breastfeeding mothers consider stopping. The baby's fickle behavior, sometimes wanting to nurse, sometimes not, irritates them. And the demanding fashion in which a baby continuously tries to get their way is another reason mothers think seriously about giving up breastfeeding.

> "My son wants my breast whenever it suits him. And he wants it immediately. If it happens to be in some way inconvenient for me, he'll throw a raging temper tantrum. I'm afraid those tantrums are starting to turn into a habit and that pretty soon he'll try getting his way every single time by kicking and screaming."
> **About Steven, 36th week**

Quarrels can also develop when parents and babies fail to negotiate the amount of physical contact and attention their baby wants and their mommy and daddy are willing to give.

> "I keep getting more and more annoyed by my baby's clinging and whining. When we go to visit friends, he'll hardly let go of me. It makes me feel like just pushing him away from me, and sometimes I do. But that only makes him angrier at me."
> **About Kevin, 37th week**

Your Baby's New Ability Is Starting to Bear Fruit

When your baby is approximately 37 weeks, you will notice them calming down. If you watch closely, you may see them trying or doing new things. For example, you may see them handling their toys in a different way, enjoying new things, or behaving in a more concentrated and inquisitive manner. They are beginning to explore the world of categories that started a few weeks ago, and that is now starting to bear fruit. Your baby will start choosing the new skills that best suit them. They will choose whatever matches their predisposition, preferences, and temperament. And, as an adult, you can help them with this.

> "I feel at a deadlock again. My son's toys are lying somewhere in a corner. They have been for some weeks now. I think that I need to supply him with more stimulating toys that will challenge him. But outside, he's very lively because there's plenty to see. He is bored indoors."
> **About Bob, 36th week**

The World of Categories

After the last leap, your baby started to understand relationships between different things they saw, heard, smelled, tasted, and felt, both in the outside world and inside and with their own body. They became more familiar with every aspect of their world. They discovered that they are the same kind of being as their mommy and daddy are, and that they could move in exactly the same way they do, and vice versa. They learned that some other things can move as well, but that they move in very different ways than human beings, and that some other things can't move on their own at all, and so on.

Once your baby acquires the ability to perceive and experiment with categories, they begin to understand that they can classify their world into groups. It will dawn on them that certain things are very much alike, that they look similar, or they make similar sounds, or they taste, smell, or feel the same. In short, they discover that different things can share the same traits.

For instance, they can now discover the meaning of the word "horse." They can learn that every horse falls into this category, whether it is brown, white, or spotted; whether the horse is out in a field, in a stable, in a photograph, in a painting, or in a picture book; whether it is a clay horse or a live horse. It's still a horse.

Naturally, this new understanding of categorizing the world will not happen overnight. They must first get to know people, animals, and objects well. They have to realize that things must possess certain similarities in order to belong to a specific category. Therefore, they have to be able to spot these similarities, and this takes practice and time. When your baby acquires the ability to perceive categories, they will start experimenting with them. They will start to study people, animals, and objects in a particular way. They will observe, compare, and arrange them according to similarities, and then place them in specific categories. Your baby's comprehension of a category is the result of a lot of research that they conduct much as a real researcher would. They observe, listen to, feel, taste, and experiment with both similarities and differences. Your baby works hard at this.

Later on, when your child starts talking, you will see that they have already discovered many of the categories we use and sometimes will have made up their own names for them. For instance: they may call a garage a "car house," an apartment building a "block house," or a fern a "feather plant." The names they use refer directly to whatever trait they found most characteristic.

As soon as your baby acquires the ability to divide their world into categories, they can start doing just that. They not only examine what makes something a *horse*, *dog*, or *bear*, but also what makes something *big*, *small*, *heavy*, *light*, *round*, *soft*, or *sticky*, as well as what makes something *sad*, *happy*, *sweet*, or *naughty*.

Games played during research with babies clearly show that from this age on, babies' reactions take on a different quality. Some researchers believe that intelligence makes its first appearance at this age. At first look, it might seem that way, but it does not mean that babies didn't have any thoughts prior to this age. In fact, they have had their own ways of thinking that were perfectly suited to each stage of their development. Unfortunately, these ways are lost to adults, and we can only imagine what they might be like. When the baby begins to classify the world in groups as we do, though, their way of thinking becomes more like an adult's does. Because they start to think in a way that is closer to ours, we are able to understand them better than before.

When your baby perceives categories, they do so in the way a 37-week-old baby does. They use the abilities they gained during the previous developmental leaps. They cannot use abilities they won't gain until a later age. Therefore, at around 37 weeks, your baby can learn to categorize "sensations," "patterns," "smooth transitions," "events" and/or "relationships."

This ability to perceive and experiment with categories affects a baby's behavior and everything a baby does. Their whole perceptive world has changed. They notice that people, animals, things, and feelings can be divided into groups that have common characteristics. And that they have one name.

You can imagine that your baby is upset when this dawns on them. To us, as adults, "categories" are normal and our thoughts and language are filled with them. We are actually dependent on them. Your baby is realizing this for the first time.

BRAIN CHANGES

Your baby's brain waves will show dramatic changes again at approximately eight months. In addition, the baby's head circumference increases drastically, and the glucose metabolism in the brain changes at this age. Laboratory research has confirmed that nine-month-old babies (so after this leap) are able to make categories after watching a series of pen drawings of real animals, such as different species of birds or horses.

Experience the World Through Your Baby's Eyes

By doing this activity, you will come to understand how difficult it is to divide the world into categories. It is something we can all do and we do it every day, but we can't always put into words how we do it. Our brain is busy doing something we can't explain.

Imagine that you still had to learn about categories and that you had to recategorize everything in the room you are currently in. Try and purposely make five "wrong" categories; for example, the category "wall hangings" containing paintings, posters, and mirrors. It is not important what categories you make. This is about becoming aware of the process of dividing things up into them. This is what your baby is doing all day long. Growing up is hard work!

THE MAGICAL LEAP FORWARD: THE DISCOVERY OF THE NEW WORLD

Every baby needs time and help to enable them to understand why something does or does not fall into a certain category. You can help them with this by giving them the opportunity and the time to experiment and play in such a way that they will learn why something belongs to a certain category. You can encourage and console them when necessary and present them with new ideas. Give your baby the opportunity to expand their understanding of categories. It makes no difference which categories they explore first.

Once they get the idea about one or two categories, it will become easier for them to apply this understanding to other categories later on. Some babies will prefer to start out with recognizing objects, whereas others will begin with recognizing people. Let your baby be your guide. After all, it is impossible for them to learn everything at once. You can help them with this leap by encouraging them and by giving them the opportunity and the time to explore and play in such a way that they will learn to discover categories.

BABIES ARE LIKE THIS

Babies love anything new, and it's important to respond when you notice any new skills or interests. They will enjoy it if you share these new discoveries, and this will accelerate their learning progress.

Allow Your Baby to Discover Categories

When your baby starts to experiment with their ability to perceive and make categories, you will notice that they are actually busy examining an entire range of characteristics and comparing them. They are using relationships to work out what categories are about. By doing this, they will learn the most important characteristics of whatever they are examining. They will find out whether or not something bounces back, whether it's light or heavy, how it feels to the touch, and so on. They will examine something from all sides, hold it upside down, cock their head, move the object around quickly and slowly. This is the only way for them to find out: "This is a ball, that isn't" or "This block is round, the other one isn't." Have you ever noticed how your baby looks at things that are at a distance and attract their attention? They usually do this while moving their head from left to right. They do this to learn that even when they move around, things stay the same size and shape. They are exploring. Find out what your baby likes and how they want to do it. Offer them the opportunities they need.

> "My son tries to catch the running water in the tub when the tap is on. He'll close his hand around the water, and then when he opens it there's nothing in it. He finds this most peculiar. But he can keep it up for some time."
> **About Paul, 43rd week**
>
> "She examines things all day long: corners, holes, all kinds of fabrics, anything she can get her hands on. I've not seen her do this before."
> **About Alice, 43rd week**

Allow Your Baby to Explore the Notions "One" and "More Than One"

Stack some blocks for your baby so they can remove them one by one. You can do the same with doughnut rings of different sizes that stack on a rod. Also try giving them a pile of magazines, which they can move one by one. See what other games your baby makes up with "one" and "more than one."

> "My little guy first puts a bead in a transparent pot and then shakes it. Then he adds more beads and shakes it again. He listens so intently and is having a lot of fun."
> **About John, 41st week**

Allow Your Baby to Explore the Notions "Roughly" and "Carefully"

Some babies like to experiment with handling people, animals, and objects *roughly* and *carefully*. If you see yours being rough, let them know that certain things hurt and objects can break. They know perfectly well what they are doing.

> "My son often bites me and sometimes handles his toys and other things very roughly. And yet, at times he can also be careful in an exaggerated way. He'll stroke flowers and ants with one little finger, only to squash them seconds later. Then, when I say, 'Shh, careful,' he'll start touching with one little finger again."
> **About Bob, 40th week**

> "First, my baby examines my eyes, ears, and nose with her little index finger. Then she tickles them. Then, as she gets more and more excited, she gets rougher, pushing and poking at my eyes, pulling at my ears and nose, and sticking a finger up my nostril."
> **About Nina, 39th week**

Allow Your Baby to Explore Different Shapes

Some babies are particularly interested in different shapes, such as round, square, and notched shapes. They look at the shape and trace its perimeter with one little finger. Then they do the same with a different shape. They are comparing shapes, so to speak. With blocks, they usually pick out round ones first, which shows they are able to recognize them. If your baby seems fascinated by shapes, give them a set of blocks with all sorts of different shapes. You will also see that your baby can find more than enough things in the house with shapes that interest them.

Allow Your Baby to Examine the Components of Things

Many babies like to examine the different parts of things. If your baby is one of them, they may suck successively on different sides of an object, for instance, or press on the top, in the middle, and on the bottom of something. Their explorations can have surprising side effects.

"My son likes to fiddle with locks on cabinets and doors. Even if the key's been turned a quarter of the way, he still manages to get it out."
About John, 37th week

"My baby's crazy about knobs. This week, he explored every nook and cranny on the vacuum cleaner. He touched the knobs as well. Accidentally, he pushed the right button and whoosh, the vacuum switched on. It scared the living daylights out of him."
About Bob, 38th week

Allow Your Baby to Explore How Materials Feel

Some babies love touching things with their hands to find out how they feel. This way they test for categories, such as *firmness, stickiness, roughness, warmth, slipperiness,* and so on. Allow your baby to explore. There are wonderful board books that feature different textures and that can entertain babies for hours.

"My son's playing is much more concentrated now. Sometimes he'll even examine two things at the same time. For instance, he will take his time to mash a piece of banana with one hand, and crush a piece of apple with the other. Meanwhile, he'll look from one hand to the other."
About Frankie, 42nd week

"My baby examines sand, water, pebbles, and sugar by putting some in his fist and feeling it for a very long time. Then he'll put it in his mouth."
About Bob, 40th week

Sometimes, a baby loves rubbing other parts of their body against objects, or they will pick something up and run it past their body. They want to know how something feels with all parts of their body. This way, the baby will become even more familiar with whatever they are examining, so give them this opportunity.

> *"I put a swing up for my son in a doorway. There's a knot under the seat, and that's his favorite part. He'll sit under the swing and hold on to the doorpost, so that he can raise himself a little when the knot swings past his head and touches his hair. He'll just sit there, experiencing the feeling of it."*
> **About Bob, 39th week**

Allow Your Baby to Explore the Notions "Heavy" and "Light"

Does your baby compare the weights of playthings and other objects? Give them the opportunity to do so, if your house is set up in such a way that it is safe.

> *"My baby lifts up for a moment everything that she walks past."*
> **About Jenny, 41st week**

Allow Your Baby to Explore the Notions "High" and "Low," "Little" and "Large"

Usually, your baby studies the concepts *high* and *low*, *little* and *large* through their body by crawling, climbing, standing, or walking. They will climb *onto*, *over*, and *under* everything. They will do this sedately, in a controlled manner, almost as if they are planning how to do things.

> *"My son tries to crawl under and through everything. He looks for a while, then off he goes. Yesterday, he got stuck under the bottom step of the stairs. We all panicked!"*
> **About John, 40th week**

Give Your Baby the Room to Investigate

From this age on, it usually becomes more and more important to give your baby enough room in order to provide them ample opportunity to investigate all sorts of categories. With you standing by for assistance, you can encourage them to crawl through your home, climb onto things, and hoist themselves up on the most impossible ledges. Secure the safety gates by the stairs on the second or third step, and allow them to practice going up and down stairs, with you on hand.

Your baby can learn a lot outside as well. Give them room there, too. For instance, walk with them in the woods, on the beach, at a lake, in a sandbox, and in the park. Just as long as you do not lose sight of them.

PAY ATTENTION

Make sure the space your baby is exploring is safe. But nevertheless, do not take your eyes off them for a single second. They will always manage to find something that can be dangerous that you might not have thought of.

Give Your Baby the Opportunity to "Playact"

If your baby is very socially aware, from this point on they will be able to pretend they are sad, sweet, or distressed. Such emotional states are categories, too. This means that they can start manipulating or taking advantage of you. Usually, mothers and fathers fall for this at first. Some simply refuse to believe that their children, still only babies, could be capable of doing anything like this deliberately. Others are secretly a little proud. If you see your little one is putting on an act, allow them to have a taste of success, if possible. But at the same time, let them know that you know what they are doing. This will teach them that using emotions is important, but that they can't use them to manipulate you.

"During the day, my girl is very troublesome, really pesky, but when it's time for her to go to bed in the evening, she plays like a little angel. It's as if she thinks, 'As long as I behave myself, I don't have to go to bed.' It's useless, anyway, trying to put her to bed when she isn't tired yet, because she'll refuse to stay lying down. Last Friday she went to bed at 10:30 p.m."
About Jenny, 37th week

"If I'm talking to someone, my son will suddenly need instant help, or he'll pretend that he injured himself on something."
About Matt, 39th week

"My son reacts differently when he sees himself in the mirror and when he sees someone else in it. He loves watching himself. He studies how his body moves and how he makes sounds as he 'chatters' away to himself. When he sees another child in the mirror, he gets really enthusiastic and starts waving his arms and legs about and calling out, 'Yoo-hoo,' to them."
About Thomas, 40th week

DO REMEMBER

Breaking old habits and setting new rules are also part of learning to use the new ability. You can only demand of your baby that they follow the new rules they understand—no more, but also no less.

A baby can now take up a role they have seen their parents or an older child perform. This is possible now because they know that they are a person, the same way other people are. In other words, both they and other people belong to the same category. As a result, they are able to do the same things that other people can do. They can hide, just as their mother and father used to, and make their parents the seeker. They can go and get their own toys when they feel like playing with them. Always respond to this behavior, even if only for a short while. This will teach them that they are making themselves understood and that they are important.

"This week, another child a little older than my son visited our home. My son and the other little girl each had a bottle. At a certain point, the little girl stuck her bottle in my baby's mouth and started feeding him. She kept holding the bottle herself. The next day, I had him on my lap and was giving him a bottle (it's the only time I can keep him on my lap) and then suddenly, he took the bottle and stuck it in my mouth, then started laughing, drank some himself, then stuck it back in my mouth. I was amazed. He'd never done anything like that before."
About Paul, 41st week

Some babies love to play the role of giver. It doesn't matter what they are giving, just as long as they can keep giving and receiving—preferably the latter. If your baby gives you anything at all, it goes without saying that they expect to get it back immediately. They will often understand the words "Can I have . . . ," as well as "Please." So you can combine the giving and receiving game with speech, which will greatly improve their understanding of things.

"My daughter likes to show everyone her biscuit with a big smile on her face. Of course, you are not expected to take the biscuit. She quickly retreats her hand when she thinks this might happen. The other day, she proudly reached out to show Granddad's dog her cookie, but he wolfed it away in a flash. Flabbergasted, she looked at her empty hand and then she cried in anger."
About Victoria, 41st week

Show Understanding for "Irrational" Fears
When your baby is exploring their new ability, they may also discover things or situations they don't understand. And some babies can become scared. They may discover a new danger and develop fear. One of those is the fear of heights. When your baby suddenly acts scared, sympathize with them.

"My baby always used to like walking when I would practice with her. Now, suddenly, she's stopped. She seems scared. If she even suspects I might let go of one hand, she'll sit down right away."
About Ashley, 46th week

"My son can't stand being confined now. When he's strapped into a car seat, he becomes absolutely hysterical."
About Paul, 40th week

THE IMPORTANCE OF CONSISTENCY

Parents are always proud of their baby's progress and accomplishments when they see them for the first time. And they automatically react with excitement and surprise. Something "mischievous" is usually "progress" or amusing when it first happens. And, of course, their daddy or mommy react with surprise, but for a baby that seems as though their parent is applauding them. They think they are being funny and will repeat the behavior time after time, even when their mother or father tells them, "No." You will now need to be more consistent with your baby. They need it. When you disallow something once, it is better not to condone it the next time. Your baby loves putting you to the test.

"My baby's getting funnier and funnier because she's starting to become mischievous. She says 'brrr' when she's got a mouth full of porridge, covering me with the stuff. She opens cupboards she's not allowed to touch and throws the cat's water all over the kitchen and things like that."
About Laura, 38th week

"My daughter won't listen to me. When I tell her, 'No,' she laughs, even if I'm really angry with her. But when her babysitter says, 'No,' she cries. I wonder if this is because I work. Perhaps I give in too much when I'm home, out of guilt."
About Laura, 39th week

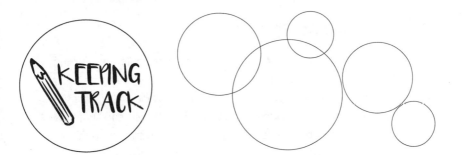

YOUR FAVORITE GAMES: THE WORLD OF CATEGORIES

These are games and activities that your baby may like now and that help them practice their newly developing skills.

Instructions to Fill In This List:

Check off your baby's favorite games. When you have completed What You've Discovered: The World of Categories, see if there is a relationship between the things that interested them the most and the games they preferred playing. By taking a little time to fill in the list, you will get a unique insight into your baby's personality.

EXPLORING TOGETHER

Some things will seem absolutely fascinating to your baby, but because it is impossible for them to explore everything on their own, you help them do that.

☐ BELLS AND LIGHT SWITCHES

Allow your baby to ring the doorbell. They will be able to hear right away what they are doing. You could let them press a button on the elevator as well. Then, they will feel what they are doing. Allow them to turn on the light when it is very dark, so that they can see what the effect is. Let them push the button in the bus sometimes, or at a pedestrian crossing, and explain to them what is happening so they know what to look for. This will teach them something about the relationship between what they are doing and what happens next.

☐ GETTING OUTSIDE TOGETHER

At this age, most babies can't get enough of being outdoors. Taking your baby outdoors will teach them a lot as well. They will see many new things, and can see things that are at a greater distance now. Use the jogging stroller to run around the neighborhood, and be sure to stop now and then to allow your baby to look closer at, listen to, and touch things.

☐ SHOW THEM HOW YOU DRESS AND UNDRESS THEM

Many babies seem to have no time for dressing and grooming. They are far too busy with other things. But they love to look at themselves and are even more interested when something is being done to them. Use this to its advantage. Towel off your baby, dress, and undress them in front of a mirror so they can play a sort of peek-a-boo game with themselves at the same time.

LANGUAGE GAMES

Your baby often understands a lot more than you think, and they love being able to demonstrate this. They will now start to enjoy expanding the range of words and phrases they understand.

☐ NAMING THINGS

Name the things your baby looks at or listens to. When your baby uses gestures to express what they want, translate their question for them by putting it into words. This will teach them that they can use words to express themselves.

☐ NAMING THINGS IN BOOKS

Take your baby on your lap or seat them snuggled up to you. Let them choose a book and give it to them. This way they can turn the pages by themselves. Point to the picture they are looking at and name the object. You can also make the appropriate sounds for the particular animal or object you are pointing to. Encourage your baby to make that word or sound as well. Don't try to continue if your baby loses interest. Some babies need a momentary cuddle or tickle after each page to keep their attention focused.

☐ PLAYING WITH SMALL, SIMPLE TASKS

Ask your baby if they will give you whatever they are holding by saying, for instance, "Give it to Mommy, please." Or ask them to give it to someone else who is in the room. You can also ask them to get something for you—for instance, "Get your toothbrush, please" and "Look for your ball." Also try calling them when you are out of sight: "Where are you?" and get them to answer. Or ask them to come to you: "Could you please come over here?" Praise them if they participate, and continue for as long as your baby enjoys it.

COPYCAT GAMES

Your baby studies other people with great interest and loves imitating what they see other people do.

☐ DOING AND COPYING

First, challenge your baby to imitate whatever you are doing, then imitate them again. Often, they will be able to go on forever, taking turns doing the same thing over and over. Try alternating your gestures as well, making them a little faster or slower. Try making them with the other hand, or with two hands. Try making them with sound or without, and so on. Try doing this game in front of a mirror as well. Some babies love repeating gestures in front of a mirror while watching themselves to see how everything is done.

☐ TALKING IN THE MIRROR

If your baby is interested in the positions of the mouth, try practicing with them in front of a mirror. Turn it into a game. Sit down in front of the mirror together and play with vowels, consonants, or words, whatever your baby likes best. Give them time to watch and copy. Many babies love watching themselves imitating gestures as well, such as movements of the hands and head. Try this, too. If your baby can see themselves while they are imitating you, they will immediately be able to see whether they are doing it in the same way you are.

☐ JOINING IN WITH SONGS AND MOVEMENT GAMES

Sing "Pat-a-cake, Pat-a-cake, Baker's Man," and let your baby feel every movement that goes with the song. In order to do this, take their hands in yours and make the movements together. Sometimes babies will imitate the clapping of their own accord, or they will raise their hands. They are still unable to imitate all the movements in sequence at this age, but they are able to enjoy them.

ROLE-SWITCHING GAMES

Encourage your baby to take up all kinds of roles. They will learn a lot from it.

☐ CHASE

You can consider this the first game of tag. It can be played crawling or walking. Try turning the game around sometimes as well—crawl or walk away, and clearly indicate that you expect them to come after you. Try to escape if your baby makes attempts at catching you. If your baby does catch you, or you have caught them, cuddle them or raise them up high in the air.

☐ WHERE IS . . . ?

Hide yourself in such a way that your baby sees you disappear, then let them look for you. Also try pretending sometime that you have lost them and are looking for them. Sometimes babies are quick to hide and will stay behind their beds or hide in corners very quietly. Usually, they will pick the spot you were just hiding in or one that was a smash hit the day before. React with enthusiasm when you have found each other.

YOUR FAVORITE TOYS

☐ Anything that opens and closes, such as doors, latches, and drawers

☐ Pans with lids

☐ Doorbells, pushbuttons in the bus, elevator pushbuttons, pushbuttons at the pedestrian crossing, or bicycle bells

☐ Alarm clocks

☐ Pegs

☐ Magazines and newspapers to tear

☐ Plates and cutlery

☐ Things that are larger than yourself, such as boxes or buckets

☐ Pillows to sit on and play with

☐ Containers, especially round ones; pots; and bottles

☐ Anything you are able to move, such as handles, locks, or knobs

☐ Anything that moves by itself, such as shadows, moving branches, flickering lights, or laundry flapping in the wind

☐ Balls of all sizes, from Ping-Pong balls to large beach balls

☐ Spinning tops

☐ Dolls with distinct faces

☐ Blocks in all shapes, the larger the better

☐ Paddling pool

☐ Sand, water, pebbles, and spade

☐ Swings

☐ Picture books with one or two large distinct pictures per page

☐ Posters with several distinct pictures

☐ Toy cars

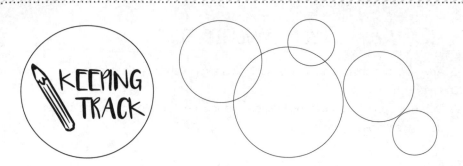

WHAT YOU'VE DISCOVERED: THE WORLD OF CATEGORIES

These are examples of skills your baby can exhibit from this age. And for clarity: your baby will not do everything on the list!

Instructions to Fill In This List:

Complete this list right before the next leap, just as you have done with previous leaps. But this time, it will help if you read through these pages regularly during this leap so you know what to look out for. With this leap, the new skills are not easily perceivable; dividing the world into categories is somewhat abstract. And although all babies are working on this at this age, they will all do it in their own way. What categories is your baby making? It's not easy to see and understand from your perspective as a parent. It would be easier to sit down and have a nice chat with your child to figure it all out, but of course that's not an option. You therefore have to rely on your instincts and observations.

If you read through these pages regularly, you will know what to look out for. The list has been compiled from the things other parents have noticed their babies doing, so there is a good chance you will also see your baby exhibit some of these new skills. At least, you will know what to expect. We provide space so that you can write down the way your baby explores the world of categories, because your baby will choose the things that interest them. And as we have said before, the way your baby does this, the things that interest them, and how they handle things makes your baby unique. Keep filling in the lists and you will create a unique record of your baby's unique personality as it emerges.

You made this leap on: _____

On _____ the sun broke through again and now, at the end of the leap, I see you can do these new things.

RECOGNIZING ANIMALS AND OBJECTS

Date:

☐ You can recognize some things very well, whether in a picture, film, photographs, or real life.

☐ I notice that you really recognize the following things:

☐ Airplanes	☐ Birds
☐ Cars	☐ Horses
☐ Fish	☐ Other:
☐ Ducks	_____
☐ Cats	_____
☐ Dogs	_____

☐ You show that you can distinguish shapes; for example, "round," because you keep picking up the round shape from a pile of objects.
Your baby could, of course, show a preference for another shape.

☐ You show that you think something is dirty; for example, by wrinkling up your nose.

☐ You show that you think something is fun or tasty by making a characteristic sound or movement, or by _____

☐ You understand names of animals or objects, such as "toothbrush," "lamb," "cat," "duck," or "mobile." When I ask, "Where is _____?" you look at it.

☐ When I say: "Get your _____" then you get it.

☐ You repeat words.

☐ You like looking at things through something else. For instance, through a sieve in the sandbox, the mesh of a screen door, or through glass.

RECOGNIZING PEOPLE AS PEOPLE

Date:

☐ You clearly relate to other people with sounds and gestures.

☐ You imitate people a lot of the time; you copy what they do. Things you have mimicked other people doing are:

_____

_____

_____

☐ You clearly want to play with other people more often than before.

☐ You "call" people you know well. Each member of our family has their own sound; that sound is the "name" you are calling.

RECOGNIZING PEOPLE IN DIFFERENT CIRCUMSTANCES

Date:

☐ You recognize people when you see them in unrelated situations.

☐ You recognize people in the mirror. For instance, you look in the mirror to find the person in the room.

☐ You show that you recognize yourself in a photograph or in the mirror.
For example:

    ☐ You pull silly faces at your mirror image.

    ☐ You stick out your tongue and laugh at your mirror image.

    ☐ Other:

    _____

    _____

    _____

RECOGNIZING EMOTIONS

Date:

☐ You understand when I am being nice to another child and . . . you have become jealous for the first time when I give attention to another child. You would not be jealous if I were annoyed with another child.

☐ You comfort a soft toy when it falls to the floor, or when you have thrown it to the ground on purpose. It's a brief moment of comfort, almost too quick to notice, but you do it.

☐ You act extra sweet when you want something done.

☐ You exaggerate your mood, playing a role to let every-one clearly know how you are feeling.

☐ You are more aware of other people's moods. For instance, you start to cry when another child is crying.

PLAYING MOMMY'S ROLE

Date:

☐ You can turn the roles around and initiate a game by yourself.

☐ You play peek-a-boo with a younger baby.

☐ You use the bottle to feed me, or _____

☐ You "ask" me to sing a song, for instance by:
    ☐ Clapping your hands
    ☐ Rubbing your hands together
    ☐ Other:

_____

☐ You "ask" to play hide-and-seek by crawling behind something, or by putting a cloth on your head.

☐ You "ask" to build blocks together by handing me your blocks.

☐ Other games you initiate, and how you do that:

_____

_____

The type of categories your baby explores tells you a lot about their personality. Which categories do they choose? Are they more motoric, verbal, or emotional, and so on?

DO REMEMBER

All babies have gained the ability to observe and form "categories." A new world full of possibilities is open to your baby. Your baby will show you what they prefer in this world and therefore what makes them special. They will choose whatever suits them best at this stage in their development and matches their interests, physique, and weight. Do not compare your baby to other babies; every baby is unique. Watch your baby closely and see what interests them. In What You've Discovered: The World of Categories, there is space for you to write down what your baby chooses between the ages of 37 and 42 weeks. As you look through it, you may see things on the list that you think your baby may also like.

Help, My Baby Can't Do Everything!
No, Of Course Not; That's Impossible!

The first phase (clinginess) of this leap is age-linked and predictable, emerging at about 34 weeks. Most babies start the second phase of this leap 37 weeks after the due date. The initial perception of the world of categories sets in motion the development of a whole range of global concepts, such as "animal" or "car," for instance. However, the first categories are acquired through experiences, by comparing things, and through experimentation. The difference between the mental capacity (ability) and the actual act of doing (skill) depends on your baby's preferences. Consequently, there may be a difference of many weeks or even months between two babies' mastering certain categories. The skills and activities listed in *The Wonder Weeks* are stated at the earliest possible age the ability could appear (but they do not necessarily appear at that time), so you can watch out for and recognize them (they may be rudimentary at first). This enables you to respond to and facilitate your baby's development. All babies gain the same ability at the same age, but they differ in what they do with it and when. That makes every baby unique.

THE EASY PERIOD: AFTER THE LEAP

At around 39 weeks, another relatively easy period sets in. For the following one to three weeks, many babies are admired for their progress, independence, and cheerfulness. They find a wide range of things interesting now, from people on horseback to flowers, leaves, ants, and mosquitoes. Many children want to spend more time outdoors now. Other people suddenly start to play an increasingly important part in their lives, as well. They make contact with them much more often and are more willing to play games with them than they were before. In short, babies' horizons are broader than ever.

"At the moment, my boy's a doll. He laughs all day long. Sometimes, he'll play by himself sweetly for an hour. He seems like a completely different child this past week. He doesn't look as bloated anymore, and he feels very lithe. He was always a little unwieldy, but now he seems to have loosened up a lot more. He's now much livelier, more energetic, and adventurous."
About Frankie, 42nd week

"My son understands much more and has a different 'place' in the family. He is more part of it all now. I need to be able to talk to him easily, so he has a seat at the table at talking distance, for instance. That's important now. He's focusing on other people much more outside of the house as well. He makes contact with them right away by blowing bubbles, making certain calling sounds, or by tilting his head questioningly."
About Bob, 40th week

Leap 7

The World of Sequences

DOING TWO THINGS CONSECUTIVELY

Babies are natural mess-makers, and during the previous leap in your baby's mental development, this talent revealed itself in full force. You may have wondered in despair where your baby's knack for destruction came from as they disassembled, tossed around, and squished everything in their path. You'll be relieved to know that during Leap 7, at around 46 weeks (44 to 48 weeks), or almost 11 months, this will change. You may suddenly notice them doing things that are quite the opposite. They will begin, for the first time, to try to put things together. And by doing so, they are showing you that they are making a leap in their development.

Your baby now has the ability to perceive and play with "sequences." From this age on, they have the ability to realize that to reach many of their goals, they have to do things in a certain order.

As in the other leaps, this one is announced by the fussy phase. At around 42 weeks (or between 40 and 44 weeks), your baby will have noticed that their world suddenly changed and they are experiencing it in a new way. They may see, hear, smell, taste, and feel things previously unknown to them, and that can be upsetting. So upsetting, in fact, that they grab on to the most familiar thing they know: you. This fussy phase will often last for five weeks, but it may last anywhere from three to seven weeks.

THE FUSSY PHASE:
THE ANNOUNCEMENT OF THE MAGICAL LEAP

Parents may say their baby is fussy, cranky, whiny, weepy, grumpy, bad-tempered, unmanageable, and restless during this time. Baby will do whatever they can to be able to be with you. Some are preoccupied by this all day long, others less time. Some little clingers get more frantic at the prospect of separation than others. They will use every possible means they can think of to be able to stay with their parents. As with previous leaps, you will probably notice that they are shyer, want to cling to you, and want more physical contact with you now. Many babies become jealous and have mood swings. Nighttime is also troublesome, as they may sleep poorly or have more nightmares than they did before. During the day, they may be quieter than usual; they may squirm around when you are trying to change their diaper or refuse to let you to change or dress them. Other babies may be unusually sweet to get their own way and others particularly mischievous. Some babies exhibit all these characteristics, and others only a few.

In short, your baby is entering the fussy phase characterized by the three Cs (crying, clinginess, and crankiness) and at least a few other typical characteristics.

This period is difficult for your baby but also for you, and it can cause worries and exasperation and quarrels and put you under strain. On the other hand, when you're watching your baby so closely, you may see how many new things are happening. Staying close to them, especially if you can give them undivided attention, may mean your baby will cry less. Of course, that can be difficult to maintain and perhaps not desirable.

"Whenever my baby's brother comes anywhere near him or touches him, he'll start to cry immediately because he knows it will get a reaction out of me."
About Kevin, 41st week

"I do my housekeeping carrying my baby on my hip or my arm because otherwise I can't move an inch with her clinging to my leg. I explain to her what I'm doing, for example, how I'm making tea or folding towels. We also usually go to the bathroom together. When I do go on my own, I leave the door open. I do this firstly so that I can see if she's doing anything dangerous, but also because then she can see me and follow me to her heart's content. And she always does. This way of going about things is the only way either of us will get any peace of mind."
About Emily, 43rd week

DO REMEMBER

If you notice your baby is fussier than usual, watch them closely. It's likely that they are attempting to master new skills. Have a look at What You've Discovered: The World of Sequences on page 307 to see what you can expect.

HOW YOU KNOW YOUR BABY HAS ENTERED THE NEXT FUSSY PHASE

Besides the three Cs, here are some of the signals that your baby may give you to let you know they're entering the next difficult phase.

Does Your Baby Cling to You More Now?

Some babies go to great lengths to stay as close to you as possible. They may literally wrap themselves around you, even when there are no strangers present. Some babies don't necessarily cling to their parents, but do want to stay extremely close to them so that they can keep an eye on them at all times. And there are those who keep checking back in with their parents, as reassurance before they leave them again.

"My son wants to sit on my lap, ride on my arm, crawl all over me, sit on top of me, or cling to my legs all day long, like a parasite clings to a fish. When I put him down, he bursts into tears."
About Bob, 41st week

"At the moment, my daughter tends to stay near, but she still does her own thing. It's almost as if she's circling around me like a satellite orbits the earth. If I'm in the living room, she'll be doing something next to me, and when I go to the kitchen, she'll be emptying a cupboard next to me there."
About Jenny, 47th week

Is Your Baby Shy With Strangers?

When there are strangers near them, looking at them, talking to them, or, worse still, reaching a hand out toward them, your baby may become even clingier with you than they already are.

"I noticed this week that my baby was really starting to cling to me a lot. Now, whenever a stranger reaches out to embrace her, she'll grab me. But if people give her some time, she often ends up going to them by herself in the end. They just have to make sure that they don't pick her up too soon."
About Ashley, 47th week

"My son is a little shy. When he sees new people, or if someone suddenly enters the room, he'll bury himself in my neck. It doesn't last long, though. He just needs to get used to them."
About Matt, 42nd week

Does Your Baby Not Want to Break Physical Contact With You?

Some babies hold on to their mothers and fathers as tightly as they can once they have a hold on them or when they are sitting on their parents' laps, as if they don't want to give their parents the chance to let go. Other babies get furious when they are set down or when their parents walk across the room to get or do something.

> *"If we're apart for even a moment, my daughter cries with rage. When I return, she'll always hit, claw, pinch, and push me for a moment first. If the dog's around, she'll immediately go for him. Once I came back to find her with a whisker in her hand."*
> **About Emily, 43rd week**

Does Your Baby Want More Attention and Seem Jealous If They Don't Get It?

A demanding baby would, if they could have their way, be entertained by you night and day. They want their parent to have eyes only for them and can be extra cranky and naughty when you pay attention to someone or something else. Or they might act overly sweet to win your attention back. This change in behavior usually makes a parent wonder if their baby might be jealous. This discovery usually comes as a surprise.

> *"When my son is nursing, he wails if I do anything or talk to anyone. I have to look at him, fiddle around with him, or stroke him. As soon as I stop for a second, he'll wriggle uncontrollably and kick furiously, as if to say: 'I am here.'"*
> **About Matt, 43rd week**
>
> *"I babysit a four-month-old baby. My son always finds it very interesting when I give her a bottle. But this week, he was impossible. He kept doing things he normally never does. He was really causing trouble, being obnoxious. I think he was a bit jealous."*
> **About John, 44th week**

Does Your Baby Act Unusually Sweet?

A fussy baby can now also find nicer ways of asking for more physical contact or attention. This happens more and more often and in increasingly sophisticated ways. They may bring their parents books or toys "asking" that they play with them. They may charm you into playing games with them with a variety of ploys, such as laying their little hand on your lap, snuggling up to you, or resting their head against you. Often, they may alternate between being troublesome and sweet, using whichever works best at the time, to get the desired touch or attention. Parents of independent babies who don't usually seek much physical contact are overjoyed at the prospect of finally being able to give them a cuddle again.

> *"My daughter would come up to me now and again for a cuddle. She was extremely charming this week."*
> **About Ashley, 46th week**
>
> *"My son was very cuddly and kept clinging to me this week."*
> **About Matt, 42nd week**
>
> *"When my son is in the bicycle seat or stroller, he keeps looking back to check if I'm still there, and then he'll give me his tiny hand."*
> **About Paul, 44th week**

Is Your Baby Notably Mischievous?

Some parents notice that their babies are naughtier than they used to be. It may seem your baby does everything they are not allowed to. Or they may be especially mischievous at times when their daddy or mommy is rushing to finish something and is very busy.

> *"We're not allowed to attend to our own business. If we do, then everything we told our daughter not to touch suddenly becomes extremely interesting, such as the telephone and the knobs on the stereo. We have to watch her every second of the day."*
> **About Jenny, 47th week**
>
> *"My daughter keeps crawling after me. I think that's adorable. But if she doesn't do that, she makes a mess of things. She'll pull the books off their shelves and scoop the dirt out of the flower pot."*
> **About Ashley, 43rd week**

Is Your Baby Moody?

Your baby might be cheerful one day and the total opposite the next. Their mood can also change suddenly. One moment, they may be busy and happy doing something; the next, they could start whining and complaining. The mood swings come out of the blue for no apparent reason as far as their parents can tell, which can be confusing.

> *"My baby would cling and cry her eyes out one moment and seem to be having the greatest fun the next—as if she could turn it on and off at the flick of a switch. I just don't know what to do. I wonder if something could suddenly be hurting her."*
> **About Nina, 43rd week**

Does Your Baby Sleep Poorly?

Most babies sleep less well now than they did before. They either refuse to go to bed, have more difficulty falling asleep, or wake up earlier than usual. Some are particularly troublesome sleepers during the day. Others are worse at night, and still others are reluctant to go to bed at any time.

"My baby wakes up two or three times a night and doesn't sleep well in the afternoon, either. Sometimes it takes me three hours to get her to go to sleep."
About Jenny, 48th week

"My son is more restless now. When it's time for bed, I have to force him to calm down. Then he wakes up a few times during the night."
About Frankie, 45th week

Does Your Baby Have Nightmares?

Some babies sleep uneasily at this time. Sometimes they toss and turn so much during sleep that it looks like they are having a nightmare.

"Thomas had his first real nightmare. He was crying for ages in his sleep—well, it felt like it went on for ages. He has never done that before. Since then he has let out an occasional scream at night."
About Thomas, 43rd week

Is Your Baby "Quieter"?

Your baby may temporarily be a little apathetic; some babies are. They are less active or babble a little less than before. They may even stop all activity for a while and simply lie down and stare ahead. Parents don't like seeing this happen. They think it's abnormal, and they may try to get the little daydreamer moving again.

"My daughter is not as active anymore. Often, she just sits there, wide-eyed, looking around."
About Hannah, 45th week

"My son is more passive, quieter. Sometimes he'll sit there, staring off into the distance for a few moments. I don't like it one bit. It's as if he's not normal."
About Bob, 41st week

Does Your Baby Refuse to Have Their Diaper Changed?

Many babies become more impatient and unmanageable now when they are being dressed, undressed, or changed. They may whine, scream, and writhe as soon as you touch them. Sometimes parents become aggravated with or concerned about a troublesome squirmer.

"Dressing, undressing, and changing are a nightmare. This happened a while ago as well. Back then, I thought the lower part of her back might be troubling her. I started to worry more and more. So I took her to the pediatrician, but he said that her back was perfectly fine. He had no idea what could be causing it, either. But then it cleared up by itself."
About Juliette, 46th week

Does Your Baby Lose Their Appetite?

Many babies seem less interested in food and drink at this time. Or they may be very choosy, eating something only if, and when, they feel like it. Parents are usually worried and aggravated by poor appetites and fussy eating.

"My son is not eating well. But all of a sudden, he does want to be breastfed in the middle of the day, and he'll start whining and pulling at my blouse to get what he wants. He wakes up a lot during the night as well, wanting to breastfeed."
About Matt, 43rd week

Does Your Baby Behave More Babyish Again?

Sometimes a babyish behavior that you thought was long gone suddenly reappears. Parents don't appreciate such revivals. They see them as backward steps and would put a stop to them if they could. Yet it's perfectly normal to have relapses during fussy phases. It means that another huge leap forward is about to happen.

"My daughter relapsed into crawling this week, instead of walking"
About Jenny, 44th week

"My son doesn't want to hold his bottle himself anymore but prefers to lie back in my arms and be fed like a tiny baby. A while ago, however, he insisted on holding the bottle himself. His relapse is actually bothering me quite a bit. I kept thinking, 'Cut it out, son, I know you can do it yourself.' A few times I put his hands on the bottle, but he wouldn't budge."
About Bob, 41st week

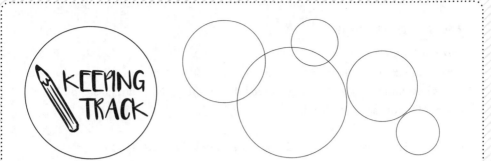

LEAP SIGNS

This is how you let me know the leap has started:

☐ You cry more often than before.

☐ You are bad-tempered or cranky more than usual.

☐ You are cheerful one moment and cry the next.

☐ You want to be kept busy more often than before.

☐ You cling to me and want to be around me more than you did before.

☐ You act unusually sweet.

☐ You are notably mischievous.

☐ You throw temper tantrums, or throw them more often than before.

☐ You are jealous, or more often jealous than you were.

☐ You are shyer with strangers than before.

☐ You get upset if I break physical contact.

☐ You sleep poorly.

☐ You have nightmares, or have them more often than before.

☐ You lose your appetite.

☐ You "talk" less than usual.

☐ You are less active than you were.

☐ You sometimes just sit there, quietly daydreaming.

☐ You refuse to have your diaper changed or to be dressed.

☐ You suck your thumb, or do so more often than before.

☐ You grab your soft toys, or do so more often than before.

☐ You seem more babyish again.

☐ And I've noticed that you: _____

Do remember that a baby does not necessarily show all these characteristics of a leap. This is more about which things you see and not how many.

How Are *You* Doing?

You Feel Insecure

Parents are concerned when their baby is upset. They try to find a cause for their baby's now more frequent crying. Could it be teething? Not enough sleep? A pesky sibling? Or perhaps it's a leap!

You May Be Exhausted and Grow Annoyed With Your Baby

Parents are usually thoroughly exhausted toward the end of a fussy phase. They are tired of being at the whim of their baby's demands, especially since, by this time, their baby can do more independently.

> *Reasons why Karl was crying like this yesterday: I took the toilet paper away from him, he was playing with his favorite toy, I changed his very wet diaper, I set him down so I could use the restroom (for 5 seconds), he hit his head on the door, I put him in the car seat, the dog walked away from him, I wouldn't let him bite me, and lastly, FOR ABSOLUTELY, NO REASON AT ALL. Leap 7 is really hitting this guy hard and we still have 23 days till it's over.* —**Instagram post**

Battles of Will

During a fussy phase, breastfeeding babies often want to nurse more. It may seem as if they're nursing all day long. This is why many breastfeeding mothers think about stopping during this phase, or at least refusing the breast sometimes. The little one, however, finds this unacceptable, and before you know it, begins screaming.

> *"I keep getting more and more annoyed because I have to lull my son to sleep at my breast. I had to start doing it again when he was having so much trouble falling asleep. Now it's starting to become a habit again. Besides, he wants to nurse an awful lot and starts screaming when he doesn't get his way. I just don't feel like doing it anymore."*
> **About Matt, 47th week**

The good news for mothers who do persist with breastfeeding is that the normal feeding pattern will restore itself as soon as the fussy phase is over. Once everything has settled down again, mothers seem to forget their irritations.

Another battleground is the familiar territory of negotiating deals between the parent and child about the amount of physical contact and attention. You may feel angry, but while these feelings are not abnormal or dangerous, acting on them is. Hurting your baby, or child, is never a way to teach them the rules.

 ## ANCHOR MOMENTS *

We hope you are incorporating your daily anchor moments. Even if it's for less than five minutes. As long as you take some time for yourself.

In 5 minutes: Stare at something you like, even if it's a plant or the sky, and focus on that for a couple of minutes. Know it's okay to do so. These minutes are all about you and that special one thing you like so much.

In 10 minutes: Allow yourself 10 minutes a day to read a book or a magazine. Do this every day, at least until you finish your book or magazine and . . . maybe you want to continue on to the sequel or the following issue?

More time: Make and plan the time to watch your favorite soap or TV program undisturbed.

Your Baby's New Ability Is Starting to Bear Fruit

At about 46 weeks, you will see your baby calming down and attempting to do things that are brand new to them. You will see them handling their toys in different ways and enjoying new activities. Their actions will be more precise than ever before, and they will pay even greater attention to detail now. Your baby's voyage of discovery into the world of sequences, which started a few weeks ago, is now starting to bear fruit, and your baby is beginning to choose the new skills that suit them best. Your baby will make their own selection based on their inclinations, preference, and temperament. And as an adult, you can help them with that. Regularly look at What You've Discovered: The World of Sequences on page 307 to see what to look out for.

LEAP 7

* For more anchor moments, see page 36.

The World of Sequences

Since the last leap forward, your baby has realized that certain things have so much in common that they belong to one group or category. In order to categorize things, they would often examine them by breaking them down and taking them apart. For instance, they might have taken a tower of blocks apart one by one, removed a key from a lock, or loosened a handle on a chest of drawers.

When the ability to observe and implement "sequences" takes wing, your little one concerns themselves with constructing, putting things together, and linking things. For instance, they may now take a key off a table and try putting it in a lock of a cabinet. They can learn to dig up sand with a spade and then put it in a bucket. They can learn to run after a ball, with or without your help, and aim and kick the ball. While singing a song, such as "Pat-a-cake, Pat-a-cake, Baker's Man," they can begin to make different gestures successively, without your having to set the example. They can learn to scoop up food with a spoon and then put it in their mouth for the first time. Your baby may try putting on their shoes by getting them out, but then sit down and rub them against their feet trying to put them on. They may pick up the sweater you have just taken off and dropped on the floor and then put it in the laundry basket (where it belongs).

Your baby is beginning to be aware that they will always need to do actions in a specific order to succeed at what they are attempting to do. You now see that your baby first looks to see what things fit together and how before they try to put them in or on each other. For instance, when trying to put one block on top of another, they will first aim. Before putting a shape in a hole, they will compare the shape of the block they have chosen with the shape of the hole. You will see that there is more "purpose" in their actions than ever before, that they now know what they are doing.

You can also tell by your baby's reactions that they are beginning to realize how certain events usually follow one another in the normal course of events and that they now know what the next step is in any particular sequence.

> "When a song is finished, my son now looks up at my phone (where the music is coming from) and not at the speaker. He now knows that I have to do something on my phone if he is to hear more music."
>
> **About Bob, 48th week**

Your baby can now also start pointing out and naming different people, animals, and objects in a sequence. When they do this on their own, they may often still say "da" instead of using the proper word. When they do this together with you, they may point out things and want you to name them, or have you make the appropriate sound. They might like to play the game the other way around, having you point while they tell you what they call the object. When you are carrying them around, you may also start to notice that your baby will point in the direction that they want you to go.

> "Adam's favorite activity at the moment is pointing at everything that makes a noise. It's become such a daily activity that I make sounds wherever we go so he can point to where it comes from. You should have heard the teenagers at the bus stop when I suddenly mooed like a cow . . . Hahaha."
> **About Adam, 47th week**

The very act of naming is a way of relating a spoken word or sound to a person, animal, or object. Pointing or looking followed by a word is a sequence as well.

Now that your baby can observe and make a sequence themselves, they can also choose not to make that choice. One baby decided to use the word "yuck" not only for something dirty but also for everything he had to be careful with.

Experience the World Through Your Baby's Eyes

Try to observe all the things that are made up of a sequence of actions during a day. You will see quite a few. Your baby is now learning this for the first time. So, during your daily activities, say out loud what you are doing. For example, say that you are picking something up and what you are going to do with it. Explain all the things that you do while you perform a sequence of actions. Speak in simple language that is easy enough for your baby to understand.

BRAIN CHANGES

Between 40 and 44 weeks, the area of your baby's brain that perceives and remembers the order in which events occur begins to mature. This ability is necessary to discover the world of sequences. A fascinating experiment shows how this works: a baby is seated on their parent's lap at a testing table with two embedded wells, A and B. An experimenter sits across the table, facing the parent and baby. While the baby is watching, the experimenter holds up a favorite toy and slowly hides it in one of the wells, then covers both wells with a cloth. The baby is then distracted for 10 seconds, not looking at the table, then encouraged to search for the toy. After the distraction, babies up to and including the age of nine months (39 to 43 weeks) don't remember where the toy is, while older babies do. By 12 months of age, they all remembered correctly. It was shown that maturation of a part of the brain called the dorsolateral pre-frontal cortex makes this task achievable. This ability relates to your baby's everyday sequences, too, such as scooping up food with a spoon and putting it in their mouth, or getting their own basket filled with their doll's laundry and putting it in the washing machine.

THE MAGICAL LEAP FORWARD: THE DISCOVERY OF THE NEW WORLD

Every baby needs time and help to learn to turn the new ability into skills they can actually master in the end. As a parent, you can help your baby by giving them the opportunity and time to toy with sequences. You can encourage them when they succeed and console them when they don't. You can present new ideas. Give your baby plenty of opportunities to come into contact with sequences themselves. Allow them to see, hear, feel, smell, and taste and indulge in whatever they like best. The more they encounter and play with sequences, the better they will learn to understand them. It doesn't matter whether they prefer learning about sequences through observing, handling toys, speech, sounds, music, or locomotion. Soon they will be able to put the expertise they have gained in one domain into practice in other domains with no trouble at all. They can't do everything at once.

You will notice that your baby wants to experiment themselves and do as much by themselves as they can. They may get frustrated if they don't succeed. Others look for interaction, and they challenge you. It is your task to tell them what they are doing "wrong" and what they are doing "right." You can now also distract them by doing something you know they like. You will notice your baby "telling" you things. In short, your baby will be doing all kinds of new things after making this leap. And with every leap, so this one, too, remember not to force your baby to do something. Your baby will choose what interests them and what best suits their stage of development.

Your Baby May Be Experimenting With Doing Things Their Way

When your baby enters the world of sequences, it dawns upon them for the first time that they have to do things in a certain order, if they want to succeed. They have observed how adults perform a particular sequence, but they have to master it themselves through trial and error. Often their "solutions" are peculiar. And that's putting it mildly.

Your baby may be experimenting to see if things can be done differently. They may try out different ways of going up or down the stairs or attempt to copy with their left hand what they can do with their right. They may go around putting things in places they know they don't belong. If your baby is doing these things, they are experimenting and seeing what happens when you vary the "sequence." They know that dirty clothes go into a container. So why only in the laundry basket and not in the trash bin or the toilet as well? They fit in there, after all. Always keep an eye on your baby to keep them safe during these experiments.

"My son pulls plugs from their outlets and then tries putting them into the wall. He also tries sticking other objects with two protrusions in the outlets. I have to watch him even closer now."
About Bob, 48th week

"When he's in his high chair, my son throws everything onto the floor and watches to see if and how I pick it up. He does the same with my shopping list when we are in the supermarket. I say to him, 'Please hold on tight to my shopping list,' but Thomas throws it on the floor and watches me while I pick it up. He'll do it about 10 times in a row."
About Thomas, 42nd week

"When my daughter wants to climb onto our bed, she opens a drawer of our nightstand, stands on it, and then climbs onto the bed. If she opens the drawer too far, the whole night-stand starts swaying back and forth."
About Jenny, 49th week

Your baby knows how you walk up the stairs, but the steps are too high for them, so they have to crawl from one step to the next. However, they stand up on every step.

Your Baby May Want to Do Everything Themselves

Many babies refuse to be helped and resist any form of interference by others. These babies want to do everything they can, or think they can, by themselves. Does your baby want that, too? Your baby may want to feed themselves, brush their own hair, wash themselves, or even try to walk on their own or to climb up or down the stairs without the support of your hand. Try to have as much consideration for their feelings as possible. This is just the age when many little ones like to start asserting their independence.

"My son always liked practicing walking together. But if I hold his hands now, he'll immediately sit down. Then, when I leave, he'll give it another try. At every successful attempt, no matter how slight, he'll look at me triumphantly."
About Paul, 46th week

"My son keeps trying to scribble something on paper with a pencil, just as his older brother does. But whenever his brother tries to guide his hand to show him how it's supposed to work, he'll pull his hand away."
About Kevin, 48th week

"My son will eat only if he can put the food in his mouth himself. When I do it, he'll take it out again."
About Thomas, 42nd week

Show Some Understanding for Frustrations

Your baby simply wants to do things by themselves. They are becoming aware of what belongs together and the order in which things need to be done. They aren't rejecting your help, they are just convinced they know it all and are capable of doing anything. They no longer want you to interfere or to tell them how things should be done. They want to make their own decisions. But, as their parent, you are not really used to this. You naturally help them as you always have. You know perfectly well that your baby is still unable to properly carry out the things they want to do. And you know that they will inevitably make a mess of things if they try.

The interests of baby and parents are therefore at odds here, with all the consequences that entails. You may see your baby as being difficult, and your baby feels that you are causing all the trouble. We all know that adolescents can go through difficult phases, but babies and toddlers run a close second.

If your baby is frustrated by things they are not able or allowed to do, you can still quite easily distract them with a favorite toy or game. This is of course, different for every baby.

Your Baby May Be Testing You; Correct Them When Necessary

During this time, many parents spend huge amounts of time taking things away from their children and correcting them. It's important to consider that your baby isn't necessarily being disobedient. They just want to do things by themselves and they may feel you are standing in their way because they are not able to or are not allowed to do something. If you make it clear to them when they are doing something wrong and just why it's bad or dangerous, they can learn a lot from it.

> *"We're stuck in one of those 'No, don't touch that' and 'No, don't do that' phases now. But my son knows exactly what he wants, and he can get very angry when he doesn't agree with something. Recently, he got so upset that he didn't even notice he was standing by himself."*
> **About Frankie, 49th week**

DO REMEMBER

Breaking old habits and setting new rules are also part of working out each new ability. You can only demand of your baby that they follow the new rules they understand—no more, but also no less.

Praise Them for Good Behavior and Self-Correction

Let your baby know what they're doing "right" by praising them. They will equate feeling good with whatever action is happening. Most babies ask for praise themselves, anyway. When they do something right, especially a behavior that you may have corrected in the past, they look at you and laugh, full of pride, or call for attention. Of course, they may do it time and again, asking for reassurance each time.

"Every time my daughter puts a ring around the cone, she'll look at me, grinning like mad and clapping."
About Eve, 49th week

"This week, my son loved playing football. He'd kick the ball really hard and then we'd run after it really quickly while I held his hands. It made him laugh so hard sometimes he had to lie down on the ground for a moment to stop laughing."
About Paul, 48th week

"My son keeps wanting to help out. He thinks that's the best thing ever and starts beaming. I do have to take my time with him, though. It takes me 10 times longer to put a pile of diapers away in the cupboard with his help. He'll hand me each diaper separately, but before he lets me have each one, he'll put it on his shoulder and rub the side of his chin against it."
About Matt, 48th week

Your Baby May Be Playing With Words

A chatty baby entering the world of sequences may start pointing out and naming different people, animals, and objects. Pointing or looking, followed by a spoken word, is a sequence. If you notice your baby doing this, respond to them, listen to them, and tell them that you think they are wonderful and that you understand them. Do not try to correct their pronunciation. Instead, make sure to enunciate your words properly. This way, your baby will automatically learn the right pronunciation in due time.

"My daughter is starting to use words and point at whatever she's talking about. At the moment, she's in love with horses. When she sees a horse, she points to it and says, 'Hoss.' Yesterday at the park, a large Afghan dog ran past her. She called that a 'hoss,' as well."
About Hannah, 48th week

"My son suddenly said 'Nana' to a toy cat. We have never used that word. He has a lot of toy animals. When I asked, 'Where's Nana?' he kept pointing to the cat."
About Paul, 48th week

Your Baby May Be Trying to Tell You Something

Some babies can use body language and sounds to tell you that they remember certain situations or that they have seen certain people before. If you notice your baby doing this, talk to them a lot, explain to them what you are seeing, and react to what they tell you about it later on.

> "We go swimming every week. Usually, we see the same people there. One day, we saw one of the mothers on the street. Immediately, my son called out, 'Oh oh.' and pointed to her as if he recognized her. Then he saw a girl in the swimming pool who lives near us and whom he's seen only a couple of times, and he reacted the same way."
> **About Paul, 49th week**

> "My son asks me if he can watch a children's program. He looks at the TV, then at me, then at the remote control and then back at the TV. He adds grunting sounds to make it clear. He started 'asking' for things a few days ago, but it was never such a complete sequence."
> **About Thomas, 42nd week**

Let Your Baby Steer the Conversation and Activity

When you see that your baby is not interested in some activity you're trying to engage them in, stop. They may be busy with other things. Things that fascinate them more at that moment.

> "I'm very busy practicing saying 'Daddy' with my boy and playing games like 'Where's your nose?' But so far, we've had little result. He just laughs, jumps around, and would rather bite my nose or pull my hair. But I'm happy enough that he's become such a lively little fellow."
> **About Frankie, 49th week**

> "I try to sing songs with my son, but I don't feel as if they are doing much good. He doesn't seem particularly interested. He seems to be preoccupied by his surroundings."
> **About John, 47th week**

Show Understanding for "Irrational" Fears

When your baby is working out their new ability, they may also encounter things that they don't yet fully understand. In a way, they discover new dangers—dangers that up until now they didn't realize existed. When they understand these dangers better, their fears will pass. So show them a little understanding.

> "My daughter keeps wanting to sit on her potty. Even if she hasn't done anything, she'll take the potty into the bathroom to empty it and flush the toilet. But while she seems fascinated by flushing, at the same time she's also scared of it. She doesn't get as frightened when she flushes the toilet herself, only when someone else does. Then, she doesn't like it at all."
> **About Jenny, 50th week**

> "My daughter is fascinated by airplanes. She recognizes them everywhere: in the air, in pictures, and in magazines. This week, she suddenly became frightened by the sound."
> **About Laura, 46th week**

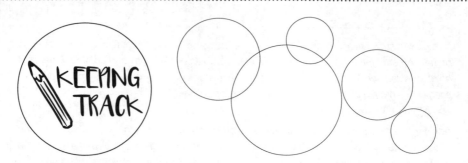

YOUR FAVORITE GAMES: THE WORLD OF SEQUENCES

These are games and activities that your baby may like now and that help them practice their newly developing skills.

Instructions to Fill In This List:

Check off your baby's favorite games. See if you can find a link between your baby's interests during this leap and the games they liked best.

HELPING

Your baby likes to feel needed. Welcome help from them. It may not amount to much, but it helps them understand the actions involved in many common activities (sequences). Plus, it is a good way of preparing them for the next leap.

☐ HELPING WITH HOUSEWORK

Show your baby how you cook, polish, and clear up. Explain what you are doing, and ask them to pass you things. Give them one of your dusters. This will be much more interesting than using their own cloth. When you are baking a cake, give them their own plastic mixing bowl and spoon.

☐ HELPING OUT WITH GETTING DRESSED

This is the most fun in front of a mirror. Try undressing your baby, toweling them down, and dressing them while they watch themselves. Name the parts you are drying. When you notice they are starting to cooperate, ask them to help out. Ask them to raise an arm or stretch their leg when you are about to put a shirt or sock on them. Praise them when they do it.

☐ GROOMING THEMSELVES

Let your baby do something for themselves from time to time. This is most fun in front of a mirror. They will then see for themselves what they are doing. They will learn faster and enjoy it more. Brush their hair in front of the mirror and let them try it for themselves. You can do the same with brushing their teeth. You can also see if they will wash themselves. Give them a washcloth when they are in the bath, and say something such as, "Go on, wash your face." Respond with enthusiasm at every attempt. You will see how proud this makes them.

☐ FEEDING THEMSELVES WITH A SPOON

Allow your baby to eat by themselves with a spoon. Or give them a baby fork to eat cubes of bread or pieces of fruit. Place a large sheet of plastic under their chair so that afterward you will easily be able to clean up the mess they make.

POINTING AND NAMING GAMES

Your baby often understands a lot more than you think, and they love being allowed to prove it.

☐ THIS IS YOUR NOSE

Touching and naming parts of their anatomy will help your baby to discover their own body. You can play this game while dressing or undressing them or when you are sitting together. Also, see if they know where your nose is.

☐ POINTING AND NAMING

For many babies, pointing out and naming things, or making the appropriate sounds, is a fun game. You can play this anywhere: outside, in a store, on the changing mat, or with a book. Enjoy your baby's misnomers as well.

SONG AND MOVEMENT GAMES

Now your baby may enjoy and want to actively participate in songs and the gestures that go with them. They may start to make one or two movements that go with them by themselves, as well. Children's songs are good for the brain. First, music has a positive effect on brain development and, second, your baby also learns various combinations of words and gestures when they watch films of other people singing and making the gestures. They will gradually copy the gestures themselves. You may also notice that your baby asks you to repeat these songs. They can do so very subtly, by looking at you and clapping their hands together, for instance. That might mean they are in the mood for "Pat-a-cake, Pat-a-cake, Baker's Man." And remember: you can find numerous songs and corresponding films with gestures on YouTube. You can watch the clips together and join in.

HIDE-AND-SEEK GAMES

Many babies like uncovering playthings that you have made disappear completely.

☐ UNWRAPPING A PARCEL

Wrap a plaything in a piece of paper or crackly chip bag while your baby watches. Then give them the parcel and let them retrieve the plaything. It appears as if by magic. Encourage them with each attempt they make.

☐ WHICH CUP IS IT UNDER?

Put a plaything in front of your baby and place a cup over it. Then put an identical cup next to the first one and ask your baby where the plaything is. Praise them every time they look for the hidden plaything, even if they do not find it immediately. If this game is still a bit too complicated, try playing it with a cloth instead of a cup. They will be able to see the contour of the plaything through the cloth. Play this game the other way around, too—let your baby hide something that you have to find.

YOUR FAVORITE TOYS

☐ Wooden trains with blocks
☐ Toy cars
☐ Dolls with toy bottles
☐ Drum, pots, and pans to beat on
☐ Books with pictures of animals
☐ Sandbox with a bucket and spade
☐ Balls: of all sizes, from Ping-Pong balls to large beach balls; a fairly soft, medium-size ball is a favorite among soccer fans
☐ Large plastic beads
☐ Clothes pins
☐ Stuffed animals that make music when you squeeze them
☐ Children's songs
☐ Jigsaw box with holes for various shaped blocks
☐ Bicycles, cars, or tractors that they can sit on
☐ Large, clickable, plastic building blocks or wooden building blocks
☐ Small plastic figures
☐ Mirror

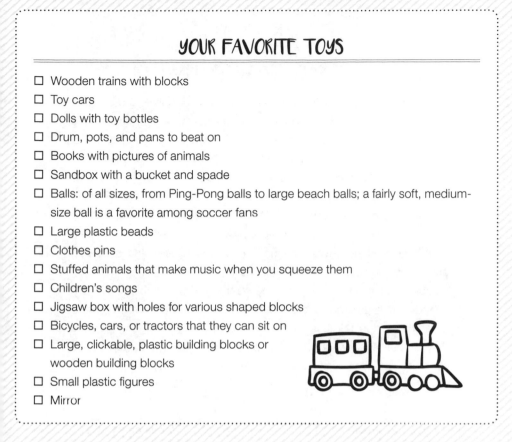

Your Baby's Choices: A Key to Their Personality

All babies now have the ability to perceive and play with sequences. This new world of sequences opens a new world of possibilities, and your baby will make their own choices. They will select what suits their preferences and that is what

makes them special. Between 46 and 51 weeks, they will select the things they like best from this world of sequences. In that period, they will make choices according to their inclinations, interests, build, and weight. You may find it irresistible to make comparisons with other babies, but remember that every baby is unique. Watch your baby closely and you will see what they are interested in. In What You've Discovered: The World of Sequences, there is space for you to write down what your baby chooses between 46 and 51 weeks. You can also look around and see if there are things you can think of that your baby will enjoy.

THE RACE TO WALK FIRST

We would like to stress here once again that your baby's gross motor skills are not the only thing to look out for as they grow. From this age, a baby could possibly walk (no joke, the earliest walkers can take their first steps at the end of this leap and all babies have the mental capacity to walk). But most babies don't because they are busy exploring other skills or their bodies aren't yet strong enough. Most babies will not take their first steps for another few months. That is absolutely normal and, remember, just because a baby starts walking now doesn't mean they are ahead in the game. All healthy babies learn to walk eventually, and observing and learning to communicate are just as important.

Babies learn to walk without help between 9 and 17 months. As you can see that is a large window; there is a difference of eight months between the earliest and latest ages. And some babies wait even longer before they start taking those first steps, and there is nothing wrong with that. In short: let your baby decide when they are ready. It's not a race.

*Trying not to stress that Isaac isn't walking yet and focus on what is he doing—recognizing common sequences of events, connecting individual elements, and knowing what to expect to come next. Like when I get the diaper bag out of the closet, Isaac crawls to the door and sits next to it so I can open it—knowing that me holding the diaper bag meant we were headed out! When I started preparing his meal on his plates, he crawls to his high chair and tries to climb in. He understands that first we get the diaper bag, then we leave the house; first we prepare the food, then we sit down and eat. Look at how he's growing cognitively!—*Instagram post

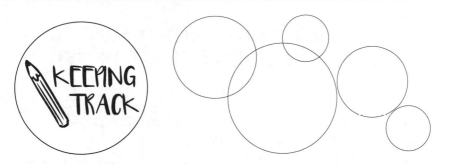

WHAT YOU'VE DISCOVERED: THE WORLD OF SEQUENCES

These are examples of skills you could notice your baby exhibiting from this point on. And for clarity: your baby will not do everything on this list.

Instructions to Fill In This List:

As you will notice, the number of new skills after making this leap is even longer than after the previous leap. The older your baby gets, the easier it becomes to see what they are and are not interested in. With every choice your baby makes, they reveal a little more of their personality. They are instinctually drawn to whatever appeals most to them at that time. Look through the lists regularly to get an idea of what to watch for as your baby makes this leap in their development. When you know what to expect, you will all of a sudden notice all the new things your baby can do. Before the next leap starts, check off the changes you have noticed. Later on, if you would like, put the dates next to the skills they are only beginning to display then—it could be one, two, or even three leaps later.

You made this leap on: _____

On _____ the sun broke through again and now, at the end of the leap, I see you can do these new things.

POINTING AND LINKING A WORD OR SOUND TO A PERSON, ANIMAL, OBJECT, OR PART THEREOF

Date:

☐ You point successively to a person, animal, or object that I have just named, whether in a big picture, poster, or in real life.

☐ You challenge me by pointing out something in a book, on a poster, or in real life, and then you want me to name it.

☐ You point out objects, animals, or people while "naming" them (with the sound you make to indicate that object, animal, or person).

☐ You look through a book, making different sounds to go with the pictures.

☐ When I ask: "Where is your . . . ?" you point to it.
    ☐ Nose
    ☐ Mouth
    ☐ Other:

_____

☐ You turn the game around and point, for instance, to your nose or my nose, wanting me to name it.

☐ You imitate the sound of an animal when I name it. For instance, when I ask, "What does the _____ say?" Then you say, "_____"

☐ When I ask, "How tall are you going to be?" you raise your arms.
    ☐ Other: _____
    ☐ When I ask, "_____?" Then you "_____"

☐ You say "yum" when you want the next bite.

☐ You say "no, no" when you don't want to do something.

☐ You use a word in various situations, because the word has a certain meaning to you. For instance, you say "yuck" for something dirty but also when you have to be careful of something, because to you, "yuck" has come to mean "don't touch."

KNOWING WHAT GOES TOGETHER AND WHAT MUST BE DONE IN SUCCESSION

Date:

☐ You know that you can push a round peg through a round hole; for example, you choose the round peg from a pile of pegs and try to push it through the round hole of a peg board.

☐ You can put together three pieces of a simple puzzle.

☐ You can push coins through a slot.

☐ You try to put differently sized square containers inside each other.

☐ You take a key from somewhere else and insert it in the keyhole of a cupboard.

☐ You look at the lamp and reach for it when you flick the light switch.

☐ You know talking goes with my telephone.

☐ You put blocks in a box, close the lid, open it again, take out the blocks, then start all over again.

☐ You put "doughnut" rings on a ring pyramid.

☐ You push cars around, making a "vrrrmm" sound.

☐ You scoop up sand with a spade and then empty it into a bucket.

☐ You fill a watering can with water when you are in the bath and then empty it again.

☐ You examine two clickable building blocks and then try fitting them together.

☐ You try scrawling on a piece of paper with a pencil.

TOOL USE

Date:

☐ You find an object to push to help yourself learn to walk.

☐ You open a drawer and use it as a step to climb on a cupboard or table.

☐ You often point in the direction you want to go when I am carrying you in my arms. You want me to go to where you are pointing.

MOTOR SKILLS

Date:

☐ You clamber down the stairs, or off a chair or couch, backward. In the beginning, you sometimes even started crawling backward out of the room before going on your explorations.

☐ You stand on your head and want me to help you do a somersault.

☐ You bend your knees, then stretch your legs powerfully so that you jump off the ground with both feet.

☐ You run (with or without help) after a ball, and "aim" before kicking it away.

☐ You first look to see whether you can reach another supporting object within the number of steps you can take by yourself.

INVITATIONS TO PLAY

Date:

☐ You really play with me now. You clearly express which games you want to play by starting them and then looking at me expectantly.

☐ You repeat a game.

☐ You entice me to help you by pretending you need my help with something even when I know you can do it yourself.

HIDING AND SEEKING

Date:

☐ You search for something that I have hidden, completely concealing it with something else. I often do this as a game, but not always, as sometimes I do not want you to get hold of something. But you find it, anyway!

☐ You hide things that belong to someone else; you wait and watch, then laugh when the other person finds the item.

COPYING A SERIES OF GESTURES

Date:

☐ You imitate two or more gestures in sequence.

☐ You study the way the same sequence of gestures looks in reality, and in the mirror.

☐ You copy various movements while I am singing a song with you.

☐ You copy the gestures with these songs:

_____

_____

_____

HELPING OUT WITH THE HOUSEKEEPING

Date:

☐ You sometimes help me by handing me things I want to put away in a cupboard; for instance, your diapers. You like giving them to me one by one!

☐ You go and get simple objects, if I ask you to.

☐ For example:

    ☐ You get the hairbrush if I ask you to when I am doing my hair

    ☐ Other:

    _____

    _____

☐ You pick up the sweater I have just taken off and try to put it in the laundry basket.

☐ You get your own bucket with doll's laundry, and put it in the washing machine (with my help).

☐ You get out a broom or vacuum cleaner and "sweep" the floor with it.

☐ You get a cloth out and "dust."

☐ You "stir" in a bowl when I am baking a cake.

DRESSING AND GROOMING YOURSELF

Date:

☐ You try to undress yourself; for instance, you try to take a sock off but pull at your toes.

☐ You try to take your shirt off. It doesn't work because you don't understand that it needs to go over your head and it won't work by pulling hard on the front of it.

☐ You try putting on your shoe or sock by yourself. For instance, you hold on to your shoe and foot and rub them together.

☐ You help me when I am dressing you. I can feel you lean toward me when I pull a sweater on or off. You stick out your arm for the sleeve, and stick out your foot a little bit when the sock or shoe is coming.

☐ You "brush" your hair. You don't brush out all the knots, far from it, but when you see the brush, you grab it and push it against your head. That's what you understand to be "brushing hair."

☐ You "brush" your teeth by putting the brush against your mouth. It doesn't matter; to you it's brushing your teeth and I am proud of you.

☐ You sometimes (and then only sometimes, but you are making a start) use a potty.

EATING BY YOURSELF AND FEEDING OTHERS

Date:

☐ You sometimes offer others a bite or sip while eating and drinking.

☐ You blow on your food before taking a bite. Of course, that little "blow" doesn't really cool it down, but you are trying and understand the idea, and that's great.

☐ You can stick a piece of food on a baby fork and eat it.

☐ You can scoop up food with a spoon and put it in your mouth. It doesn't always hit the target and it sometimes lands against your mouth or close to it.

Help, My Baby Can't Do Everything!
No, Of Course Not; That's Impossible!

The first phase (clinginess) of this leap is age-linked and predictable, emerging between 40 and 44 weeks. Most babies start the second phase 46 weeks after the due date. The ability your baby gains around 40 weeks through the leap of sequences sets in motion the development of a whole range of skills and activities. However, the age at which these skills and activities appear for the first time varies greatly per child. For example, the ability to perceive sequences is a necessary precondition for being able to pull on a string in order to reach a toy ring attached to that string, but this skill normally appears anywhere from approximately 46 weeks to many weeks or even months later. The difference in age between the emergence of the mental ability (i.e., to perceive sequences) and the actual appearance of one of the many skills produced with the help of that ability depends on your baby's preferences, experimentation, and physical development. The skills and activities in *The Wonder Weeks* are presented at the earliest possible age they could appear, so you can watch out for and recognize them. They may be rudimentary at first. In this way you will be able to respond to your baby's development and help them with it. All babies gain the same ability at around the same age, but they differ in what they do with it and when. That is what makes every baby unique.

THE EASY PERIOD: AFTER THE LEAP

Around 49 weeks, another period of comparative ease sets in. For one to three weeks, you may be amazed by your baby's cheerfulness and independence. Parents notice their baby pays much better attention when they talk now. They may seem calmer and more controlled when they are at play, and they may play well on their own again. And finally, they may look remarkably older and wiser.

"My daughter has become a real playmate for her older sister. She responds exactly as you'd expect her to. They do a lot more things together. They take their bath together as well. Both of them enjoy each other tremendously."
About Hannah, 47th week

"These were lovely weeks. My son is more of a buddy again. The daycare center is working out fine. He always enjoys seeing the other children and comes home in a good mood. He sleeps better at night. He understands a lot more and seems fascinated by the toys he plays with. He crawls into another room on his own, and laughs a lot. I'm enjoying every minute with him."
About Bob, 51st week

Leap 8

The World of Programs

THE PARTS BELONG TOGETHER

Every child's first birthday is a significant occasion. For many parents, the end of the first year means the beginning of the end of babyhood. Your little cherub is about to be promoted to toddler. In many ways, of course, they are still a baby. They still have so much to learn about their world—which has become such an interesting place to explore. They can get around so much better now and they have become adept at getting into everything that interests them.

Take a moment and reflect again on the Top 10 list we provided for you after Leap 4. For the full explanations, see page 195.

REMEMBER

1. You can anticipate when a leap will happen by age, but your baby's choices make them unique.

2. Take advantage of your baby's fussy phases—they are alerting you to new skills. We'll tell you what to look out for so you don't miss them.

3. It's not a motor skill competition! We help you look at other developments that are just as important.

4. We help you find patterns in your baby's behavior during the fussy phase of a leap by offering checklists to prompt you.

5. You can take an active role during a leap. By helping and guiding your baby, you build a safe and strong bond, which is a gift for life.

6. Skills appear during a range of time! Don't focus on the earliest possible age, as most babies exhibit these skills at the later side of the range.

7. It's your baby's intention that counts, not the perfect end result that parents expect.

8. Keep in mind that circumstances—like a stressful move or job disruption—may prevent you from recognizing a fussy phase. That's okay.

9. A leap equals stress for baby and family, which means low resistance. Take care, as sometimes this might cause the sniffles!

10. A leap means progress, even if it feels like a step back at first.

Shortly after their first birthday, at around 55 weeks (give or take two weeks), you will notice that your little one will have gained a new ability. They have entered the world of programs. This will make them seem even wiser than before. A watchful parent will begin to see the blossoming of a new understanding in their baby's way of thinking.

The word "programs" is very abstract. Here's what it means in this context. In the past leap in development, your baby learned to deal with the notion of sequences—the fact that events follow one after another or objects fit together in a particular way. A program is a degree more complicated than a sequence since it allows the end result to be reached in any number of ways. Once your child becomes capable of perceiving programs, they can begin to understand what it means to do the laundry, set the table, eat lunch, tidy up, get dressed, build a tower, make a phone call, and the millions of other things that make up everyday life. These are all programs.

Before this happens, though, the cranky period will appear. At around 51 weeks (plus or minus two weeks), your child once again starts becoming clingier than they have been for the past one to three weeks. Once again, their world is changing. They see, hear, smell, taste, and feel unfamiliar things. They get upset and cling on to the safest thing they know: you. This fussy phase can be as short as three weeks or as long as six weeks.

DO REMEMBER

If you notice your baby is fussier than usual, watch them closely. It's likely that they're attempting to master new skills. Look at What You've Discovered: The World of Programs on page 343 to see what to look out for.

Look at What You've Discovered: The World of Programs on page 343 to see what to look out for.

THE FUSSY PHASE:
THE ANNOUNCEMENT OF THE MAGICAL LEAP

The previous few weeks may have been calmer, without tears. But as if to announce the leap, there is more crying, and it comes upon your baby much more quickly. They want to be on, or near, their mothers and fathers. They seem clingy, cranky, whiny, impatient, and temperamental. Many parents also notice that their baby displays many of the same characteristics as they did during the fussy phase of the previous leap. Babies may become shyer with strangers than they were, want to be as close to you as they can, and want you to entertain them; they may be more jealous than usual, be very moody, sleep poorly, and have (more) nightmares (than they did). Babies may become quieter during the day, lose their appetite, and be babyish again. Other babies may be unusually sweet or more mischievous; some have temper tantrums, and they reach for a soft toy for comfort more often than before.

In short, the three Cs (crying, clinginess, and crankiness) and at least a few other typical characteristics are back.

This period is difficult for your baby but also for you, as you are both worried and exasperated. It's a stressful phase. But remember that this vigilance in observing your baby can help you see how many new things your baby is actually doing.

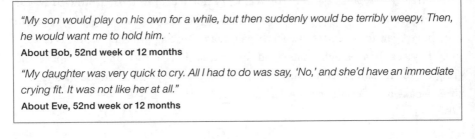

"My son would play on his own for a while, but then suddenly would be terribly weepy. Then, he would want me to hold him.
About Bob, 52nd week or 12 months

"My daughter was very quick to cry. All I had to do was say, 'No,' and she'd have an immediate crying fit. It was not like her at all."
About Eve, 52nd week or 12 months

Children usually cry less when they are with you or when you are occupied with them in some way, playing with them, or watching them.

"While my little girl is doing things, I'm supposed to stay sitting on the sofa, preferably not doing anything myself. I long for the day when I'll be able to knit something quietly while I'm sitting there."
About Emily, 53rd week or 12 months

"Whenever I'm busy doing something, my son wants to be picked up. But once he's on my lap, he wants to get off quickly again, and he expects me to follow him around. He's absolutely impossible."
About Frankie, 52nd week or 12 months

HOW YOU KNOW YOUR BABY HAS ENTERED THE NEXT FUSSY PHASE

Besides the three Cs, your baby can display some of the following characteristics as they enter the next fussy phase.

Does Your Baby Cling to You More Often Than They Did?

Some children start clinging more to their parents again. They may cling to your legs or want to be carried around. Others don't necessarily need physical contact, but they may keep coming back to be near you for only brief moments to "check in."

Some children don't want to be put down. There are also babies who don't mind being put down, as long as their daddy or mommy doesn't walk away. The only one who's allowed to leave is the baby themselves.

"My daughter stays around me more, plays for a moment, and then comes back."
About Hannah, 54th week or 12 months

"One evening, I had to go away. When I set my son down to put on my coat, he started crying, grabbed me, and tugged at my hand, as if he didn't want me to leave."
About Paul, 52nd week or 12 months

Is Your Baby Reacting Differently to People Than Before?

When there are strangers near, many babies cling to their parents even more fanatically than they already did. Once more, many children suddenly want to have less to do with strangers now. They also might choose to favor one parent over the other.

"This week, my daughter would suddenly become extremely upset, and she'd want only to be with me. If I put her down or gave her to my husband, she'd panic."
About Jenny, 56th week or 12 months

"My daughter was completely crazy about her father for two days. She didn't want to have anything to do with me then, even though I hadn't done her any wrong. If he didn't pick her up right away, she'd start crying."
About Juliette, 53rd week or 12 months

Does Your Baby Demand Your Attention More Than Usual and Act Jealous If It Wanders?

Most babies start asking for more attention at this point. They become cranky, mischievous, or bad-tempered when their parents pay attention to someone or something else.

"My son gets jealous when I give something to the tiny baby I look after."
About Matt, 53rd week or 12 months

"My friend came over with her baby. Every time I said something to her baby, mine would step in between us with this big grin on her face."
About Jenny, 54th week or 12 months

"If I don't respond immediately when my daughter wants attention, she gets furious. She'll pinch the skin right off my arm, nastily, quickly, and violently."
About Emily, 53rd week or 12 months

Is Your Baby Moody?

Your little one may be happily occupied one moment, then become sad, angry, or infuriated the next. You may not be able to pinpoint a particular cause.

"Sometimes my son will sit and play with his blocks like a little angel, but then suddenly he'll become furious. He shrieks and slams his blocks together or throws them across the room."
About Steven, 52nd week or 12 months

Does Your Baby Sleep Poorly?

Most children sleep less now. They resist going to bed, have difficulty falling asleep, and wake up sooner than you are used to. Some sleep less well during the day, others are restless at night, and still others simply refuse to go to bed quietly at any time.

"This week, I noticed for the first time that my toddler often lies awake for a while at night. Sometimes she'll cry a little. If I pick her up, she goes back to sleep in seconds."
About Ashley, 54th week or 12 months

"We'd really like our daughter to make less of a fuss about going to sleep. Right now, it involves a lot of screaming and crying, sometimes almost hysterics, even when she's exhausted."
About Jenny, 52nd week or 12 months

"My son is sleeping well again. It's often the case just before a leap comes. It's like a warning bell that Thomas is going to be fussy again."
About Thomas, 49th week or 11 months

TIP

If you want to know more about sleep and leaps, go to page 59.

Does Your Baby Have Nightmares?

Some babies sleep uneasily at this time. Sometimes they toss and turn so much during sleep that it looks like they are having a nightmare.

"My son is awake a lot during the night, terribly distressed. He really panics. Sometimes it's hard to get him to calm down again."
About Bob, 52nd week or 12 months

Does Your Baby Sit Quietly Daydreaming?

Occasionally, some children may just sit, staring out into nothingness, as if they are in their own little worlds. Parents don't like this dreaming one bit, and they will often try to break these reveries.

"Sometimes my daughter will sit, slouching and rocking back and forth, gazing into thin air. I always drop whatever I'm doing to shake her and wake her up again. I'm terrified there might be something wrong with her."
About Juliette, 54th week or 12 months

Does Your Baby Lose Their Appetite?

Many babies seem to lose interest in eating and drinking. Their parents almost always find this troubling and irritating. A child who is still being breastfed usually wants to suckle but doesn't actually eat. They want to stay close to their mother.

> *"My daughter is suddenly less interested in food. Previously, she would finish everything within 15 minutes. She was like a bottomless pit. Now it sometimes takes me half an hour to feed her."*
> **About Ashley, 53rd week or 12 months**
>
> *"My son sprays his lunch around with his mouth. He dirties everything. The first few days, I thought it was quite funny. Not anymore, I should add."*
> **About Bob, 53rd week or 12 months**

Is Your Baby More Babyish Again?

Sometimes the babyish behavior that supposedly vanished will resurface. Parents don't like seeing this happen—they expect steady progress. Yet, during fussy phases, relapses such as these are perfectly normal. It tells you that progress is on its way.

> *"My daughter crawled again a couple of times, but she probably just did it to get attention."*
> **About Jenny, 55th week or 12 months**
>
> *"My daughter is putting things in her mouth a little more often again, just like she used to."*
> **About Hannah, 51st week or 12 months**
>
> *"My son wants me to feed him again. When I don't do this, he pushes his food away."*
> **About Kevin, 53rd week or 12 months**
>
> *"My son wants me to put him on my lap and give him his bottle of fruit juice again. If he even suspects it might not happen quickly enough, he'll toss his bottle across the room and start screaming, yelling, and kicking to get me to take it back to him."*
> **About Matt, 52nd week or 12 months**

Does Your Baby Act Unusually Sweet?

Some children suddenly come up to their mothers or fathers for a few moments just to cuddle with them, then they are off again. Others act sweet and cuddly in an exaggerated way in order to get their father's or mother's attention.

> *"Sometimes my son comes crawling up to me just to be a real sweetie for a moment. He'll lay his little head very softly on my knees really affectionately."*
> **About Bob, 51st week or 12 months**
>
> *"My daughter often comes up for a quick cuddle. She says, 'Kiss,' and then gives me a kiss."*
> **About Ashley, 53rd week or 12 months**

Is Your Baby Mischievous?

Many babies try to get their parents' attention by being mischievous, especially when you are busy and really have no time for them.

> *"I have to keep telling my daughter 'no' because she seems to do things just to get my attention. If I don't react, she will eventually stop. But I can't always do that because sometimes there's a chance she might break whatever it is she's taking apart."*
> **About Jenny, 53rd week or 12 months**
>
> *"My son is being a handful at the moment. He touches everything and refuses to listen. I can't really get anything done until he's in bed."*
> **About Frankie, 55th week or 12 months**
>
> *"Sometimes I suspect that my son doesn't listen on purpose."*
> **About Steven, 51st week or 12 months**

Does Your Baby Have Many Temper Tantrums?

Sometimes a child may go berserk as soon as they fail to get their own way. You may even see a tantrum that comes out of nowhere, perhaps because they are anticipating that you may not allow them to do or have what's on their mind.

> *Cross your fingers that I get through these next two weeks of this leap and don't go insane. He went from being the best age: learning new things, giving kisses, cuddling, exploring . . . to slapping me in the face, throwing things at me, screaming constantly—full on toddler tantrums.*—**Instagram post**

Does Your Baby Reach for a Cuddly Object More Often Now?

Many children cuddle a favorite object with a bit more passion than before, especially when they are tired or when their mothers or fathers are busy. They cuddle soft toys, cloths, slippers, or even dirty laundry. Anything soft that they can lay their little hands on will do. They kiss and pet their cuddly things as well.

LEAP 8

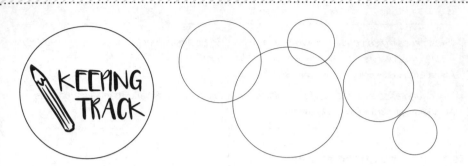

LEAP SIGNS

This is how you let me know the leap has started:

☐ You cry more often than before.

☐ You are cranky, whiny, or fretful more often than before.

☐ You are cheerful one moment and cry the next.

☐ You want to be kept busy, or express this more often than before.

☐ You cling to me more often than you did and want to be near me all the time.

☐ You act unusually sweet.

☐ You are mischievous.

☐ You throw temper tantrums more often than before.

☐ You are jealous.

☐ You are shyer with strangers more often than before.

☐ You protest if I break off physical contact with you.

☐ You sleep poorly.

☐ You have nightmares, or have them more often than before.

☐ You lose your appetite.

☐ You just sit there, quietly daydreaming, more often than you did.

☐ You suck your thumb, or do so more often than before.

☐ You reach for a soft toy, or do so more often than you did.

☐ You are more babyish than you were.

☐ And I notice that you:

_____

Do remember that no baby will do everything listed. How much your baby does is not important—it's about what your baby does.

How Are *You* Doing?

As a parent, you want nothing more than for your child to be happy or at least seem contented. And if that is not the case, you may become anxious.

You May Feel Insecure

A fussy baby is hard to ignore. Parents are concerned and want to understand what is wrong. If they can't find a source of the problem, concern can change to annoyance. And then, concerned about physical progress, they start thinking about how other babies may already be walking and wonder if there is something physically wrong with their child.

> *"I'm amazed that my daughter can't walk on her own yet. She's been walking while holding my hand for so long now that I feel she should have been walking long ago. Besides, I think one of her feet is pointing inward, so she keeps tripping over it. I showed them at the daycare center. They told me that I wasn't the only mother worried about a foot pointing inward at this age. Still, I'll be happier when she's walking."*
> **About Emily, 53rd week or 12 months**

You May Become Irritated and Quarrelsome

Now that baby is a year old, they seem capable of being "good." When your baby seems to be mischievous on purpose and throws temper tantrums, it can be hard to stay calm and clear-headed.

But a "good smack on the bottom" does not solve anything. It hurts your baby unnecessarily and only serves to damage the trust your baby has in you.

Along those same lines, giving up breastfeeding now, since the baby keeps wanting the breast in fits and starts, and their demands are accompanied by temper tantrums, may not result in a change in behavior.

⚓ ANCHOR MOMENTS *

One year of being a parent! Congratulations! Celebrate you and don't forget your well-deserved anchor moments.

In 5 minutes: Charge yourself with superpowers—the green kind, that is! Make a juice or smoothie. You deserve this extra vitamin health shot!

In 10 minutes: Sit down for a (healthy) lovely snack you bought or made just for you. Enjoy it to the max. Nobody deserves it more than you do.

More time: Duo-reflection: sit down together with your partner and reflect on all the beautiful things you've experienced these last weeks. Really take a moment to realize what great things came your way. Tell each other what you each did that made you feel appreciated or good about yourself or your family.

Your Baby's New Ability Is Starting to Bear Fruit

Around 55 weeks, you will notice that your little one is less fussy than before. At the same time, you should notice that they are attempting and achieving entirely new things again, that they deal with people, toys, and other objects in a more mature way, and that they like different things now. The exploration of the world of programs that began a few weeks ago is now starting to bear fruit, and your baby will choose the new skills best suited to them at this time based on their inclinations, preferences, and temperament. And as an adult, you can help them with that. Look at the What You've Discovered: The World of Programs on page 343 every so often to see what to watch out for.

BABIES ARE LIKE THIS

Babies love anything new, and it's important to respond when you notice any new skills or interests. They will enjoy it if you share these new discoveries, and this will accelerate their learning progress.

---

* For more anchor moments, see page 36.

The World of Programs

When your baby can perceive and play with "programs," they understand the meaning of doing the laundry, washing the dishes, setting the table, eating, dusting, tidying up, getting dressed, drinking coffee, building towers, making a telephone call, and so on. These are all programs. A program is characterized by not having a prescribed order; it is flexible. You do not necessarily have to "dust" in the same way each time. You can vary it by first dusting the table leg and then the top or vice versa. You could also dust the four legs first, or start with the chair and then move on to the table or the other way around. You can choose which sequence of actions to follow on that particular day, for that room, for that chair. Whichever sequence you choose, you are doing the "dusting" program. A "program" is therefore a network of possible sequences that are not fixed and you can reach the end result in any number of ways.

When your baby is exploring a program, they can decide which direction to take within it. They will keep encountering a point when they have to decide what to do next. During lunch, after every bite they will have to decide whether they would rather take another bite of the food, or have a sip of their drink, or perhaps even three sips. They can decide whether to take the next bite with their fingers or use a spoon. Whatever they opt for, it will still be the "eating" program.

Your baby will "play" with the different choices they can make at every juncture—they may just want to try everything out. They need to learn what the possible consequences are of the decisions they make at different points—so they could decide to empty the next spoonful on the floor instead of in their mouth. Your baby will undoubtedly think up a whole range of possible and impossible choices.

They can also "plan" for themselves to begin a certain program. For example, they can get the broom out of the closet because they want to sweep the floor. They can get their coat because they want to go outside, or go shopping. Unfortunately, misunderstandings are quick to occur. After all, they can't yet explain what they want yet, and their parents can easily interpret them wrongly. This is very frustrating for a baby, and a temperamental child might even throw a tantrum. Even if a parent does understand their child correctly, they may simply not want to do whatever their child wants at that very moment. This, too, can frustrate a baby quite quickly, as they can't understand the idea of "waiting" at this age.

Besides being able to carry out a program themselves, your baby can now perceive what program someone else is involved in. So they can begin to understand that if you are making coffee, then a coffee break will follow—with a cookie, or not. Now that your baby can learn to perceive and explore programs, they also understand that they have the choice of refusing a program. If they don't agree with what you are doing, they may feel frustrated and sometimes even have a temper tantrum. To you, it seems like it has come from nowhere.

Experience the World Through Your Baby's Eyes

We have already mentioned a few, but numerous programs play out every day in each household; there can be dozens of them, if not hundreds. Try to think of 10 programs we haven't mentioned. The more you think about it, the better you will understand what your baby is occupied with at the moment.

For example, think aboiut how you dress yourself. Picture it.

Then, think about it: do you really get dressed following the steps you pictured? Do you always put your socks on first before your shirt? Or do you sometimes vary the order of the steps in this program? Also think about which steps you absolutely have to do first, and for which parts you can vary the order.

You will probably notice that you carry out programs with a set routine in a way that suits you. The routine you generally use is the one your baby learns and they think that is how a program should be carried out, in that order and in that particular way. When your baby goes through their next set of changes, they will learn that they can vary certain programs and adapt what they do to the situation.

BRAIN CHANGES

At approximately 12 months, there is a sudden change in the glucose metabolism in the brain. In addition, babies' brains start responding quicker to stimulation, meaning the nervous system reacts to touch, sound, or visual cues more quickly.

THE MAGICAL LEAP FORWARD:
THE DISCOVERY OF THE NEW WORLD

Give your baby the opportunity to play with programs. Let them watch you as you carry out a program. Offer them opportunities to help you and also to explore programs on their own. Allow them to do things by themselves, such as feeding themselves (with your help). Replay certain basic parts of programs using toys. Let them experiment with "real things," or do more "let's pretend" games with them. Stories are also programs, so you can play with stories, too. You may also notice that conversations have moved on to a new level, and you will probably see confirmation that songs are still a favorite pastime during this leap, mainly because songs are programs, too. Your baby may want to help out more and explore their social skills. Encourage them. In this phase, baby can also learn to consider you (and others). Allow them to find their own solutions and experiment; it's the only way they can really come to grips with the concept of programs. Here are some ideas on how to help them.

Playing With Dressing and Grooming

If your child is interested in dressing, undressing, and grooming themselves, then show them how you do these things. Explain to them what you are doing as well as why you are doing it. They will be able to understand more than they are able to tell you. Also give them the opportunity to wash, dry, and dress themselves, or someone else. Although they won't do these things flawlessly, they know what they are supposed to do. And help them if you see they would enjoy that.

"My daughter tries pulling her trousers up by herself or putting her own slippers on, but she can't do it yet. Then, suddenly, I found her walking around in my slippers."
About Jenny, 55th week or 12 months

"As soon as my daughter is dressed, she crawls over to my dressing table and tries to spray herself with perfume."
About Laura, 57th week or 13 months

"This past week, my son kept putting all sorts of things on his head: dishcloths, towels, and, a few times, someone's underpants. He'd walk around the house impervious to his surroundings while his brother and sister were on the floor laughing."
About Frankie, 59th week or 13 months

Frankie is a perfect example of playing with the program of "getting dressed." His father saw what his son was attempting to do: put on a hat. Some parents may dismiss this as "It's not getting dressed, because it's a cloth and not clothing." They are of course partly right; it isn't really a cap, or hat, but it is to Frankie. He is getting dressed. Compliments to Frankie for playing and experimenting with programs; it's the only way babies can learn. And compliments to Frankie's father for realizing what Frankie was trying to do and not dismissing it as silly. A baby's actions may sometimes seem silly and "wrong," but usually it's simply because adults don't understand what their baby is doing.

Attempting to Feed Themselves

If your baby wants to eat on their own, let them try it. Keep in mind that they are creative enough to want to test different methods of eating—and all of them will probably be messy. You can make cleaning up easier for yourself by placing a large sheet of plastic on the floor under their chair. You won't mind the mess so much then.

"Since my son has learned how to eat food by himself with a spoon, he insists on doing it completely on his own. Otherwise, he won't eat. He also insists on sitting in his chair at the table when he's eating."
About Kevin, 57th week or 13 months

"My son loves eating raisins from a packet by himself."
About Matt, 57th week or 13 months

"Thomas was insisting on feeding himself and wouldn't accept any help. But it's hard work for him. If he is trying to feed himself with the spoon and it doesn't work quickly enough, he puts his mouth to the plate and tries to suck the food off it, like he's drinking. Other times, he uses his other hand to scoop the food in his mouth."
About Thomas, 56th week or 12 months

Playing With Toys

Many babies now become interested in more complex playthings that allow them to imitate programs, such as garages with cars, trains with tracks, farmhouses with animals, dolls with diapers or clothes, tea sets with pots and pans, or play shops with packages and boxes. If your little one shows an interest in such toys, offer them opportunities to play with them. Help them once in a while. It's still a very complicated world for them.

> *"When I sit next to my son on the floor and encourage him, he'll sometimes build towers as high as eight blocks."*
> **About Matt, 57th week or 13 months**
>
> *"My son is getting much better at playing by himself. Now he is seeing new possibilities in old playthings. His cuddly toys, trains, and cars are starting to come alive."*
> **About Bob, 55th week or 12 months**
>
> *"He really loves it when we play with his cars with him, driving them over the roads on his play mat. Thomas really laughs when we go round the corners and parallel park."*
> **About Thomas, 56th week or 12 months**
>
> *"My little girl 'feeds' her dolls, gives them a bath, and puts them to bed. And if she has to use the potty, her doll is put on it, too."*
> **About Jenny, 56th week or 12 months**

Let your child see "real things," too. For example, if your baby is interested in garages, take them to a garage. If they are interested in horses, tour a riding school. And if their tractor, crane, or boat is their favorite toy, they will certainly want to see a real one working.

Playing With Real Things

Bags, purses with money inside, the television set, the radio, cleaning utensils, makeup—many little ones want to use everything the same way their daddy or mommy does. Some children now leave their own toys lying somewhere in a corner. Try to work out what your little one is trying to do, even if they do not always make life easy for you.

> *"I saw my son pushing phone buttons for the first time today, putting the receiver to his ear, and babbling busily. A few times he said 'Dada' before hanging up."*
> **About Frankie, 56th week or 12 months**
>
> *"My son loves the toilet. He throws all sorts of things in it, and cleans it with the brush every two minutes, drenching the bathroom floor at the same time."*
> **About Adam, 56th week or 12 months**
>
> *"My son brings me newspapers, empty bottles, and shoes. He wants me to tidy up and put them away."*
> **About Frankie, 56th week or 12 months**

"Let's Pretend" Games

Your baby may also like acting out stories, especially those relating to themselves. When they use their imagination they can experiment and pretend that they are doing "real things."

"My little boy plays 'baby' with me. We are both babies and we talk in babyish voices. Adam really enjoys it, especially when I pretend I can't do something like open the safety gate. He plays along for a while, but when he's had enough he reverts to his normal voice and lets me know the game is over and that I am more than capable of opening the gate by myself."
About Adam, 57th week or 13 months

Playing With Stories

When they leap into the world of programs, your child becomes fascinated by stories. You can enable them to hear and see them. You could let them watch stories on television, you could let them listen to a story on YouTube, or best of all, you could tell them a story yourself, with or without a picture book. Just make sure that the stories correspond with whatever your child is experiencing themselves or with their interests. For some children, this will be cars, for others it will be flowers, animals, water, or soft toys. Keep in mind that most little ones of this age can only concentrate on a story for about three minutes, so each story must be short and simple.

"My son can really become absorbed in a toddler show on television. It's very funny. Previously, he just wasn't interested."
About Kevin, 58th week or 13 months

Also offer your baby the opportunity to tell their own story when you are looking at a picture book together.

"My daughter can understand a picture in a book. She'll tell me what she sees. For instance, if she sees a kid in a picture giving a treat to another kid, she'll say, 'Yum.'"
About Hannah, 57th week or 13 months

They will love acting out stories, especially if the story is about them.

> *"Thomas understands everything. I was talking to my mom on the telephone, telling her about all the new things he can do, and he was acting them all out in the room. He mimicked words, pretended to make a phone call, showed me how big he was, how nice he was, etc. It had been a few months since his grandma had heard him play so quietly in the background and we were chatting on the telephone for quite a while. I realized that Thomas was listening in and knew it was about him so he was showing off all the things he could do. He chatted to Grandma at the end and kissed the telephone during their chat."*
> **About Thomas, 56th week or 12 months**

Playing With "Conversations"

Many little children are eager chatterboxes. They will tell you entire "stories," complete with questions, exclamations, and pauses. And they expect a response. If your child is a storyteller, try to take their stories seriously, even if you are still unable to understand what they are saying. If you listen closely, you may sometimes be able to make out a real word.

> *"My son talks until your ears feel like they're about to drop off. He really holds a conversation. Sometimes he'll do it in the questioning mode. It sounds really cute. I would love to know what he's trying to tell me."*
> **About Frankie, 58th week or 13 months**

> *"My son chatters away like crazy. Sometimes he'll stop and look at me until I say something back, and then he'll continue his story. This past week, it sounded like he was saying 'Kiss,' and then he actually gave me a kiss. Now I pay 10 times more attention; it's so lovely."*
> **About Adam, 59th week or 13 months**

Playing With Music

Many babies love listening to children's songs as long as they are simple and short, preferably under three minutes. Such songs are programs as well. If your child likes music, they may now want to learn how to make all the appropriate gestures, too.

"'Itsy-Bitsy Spider' is by far her favorite song. She has trouble getting her fingers in the right position for the first gesture so I wasn't quite sure what she was trying to do to start with. But now I know, we sing it all day long and she joins in with her own little gestures."
About Jasmine, 58th week or 13 months

"My daughter plays 'Pat-a-cake, Pat-a-cake, Baker's Man' all by herself, complete with incomprehensible singing."
About Jenny, 57th week or 13 months

Some babies also have a lot of fun playing their own piece of music. Drums, pianos, keyboards, and flutes seem to be their particular favorites. Naturally, most babies will prefer grown-up instruments, but they will be able to do less harm with a toy instrument.

"My daughter loves her toy piano. Usually, she plays with one finger and listens to what she's doing. She also likes to watch her father play his piano. Then she'll walk over to her piano and bang on it with both hands."
About Hannah, 58th week or 13 months

Be Happy With Your Baby's Help

When you notice your child is trying to lend you a hand, then let them. They are beginning to understand what you are doing and are learning to do their own share.

> *"My daughter wants to help with everything. She wants to carry the groceries, hang the dish-cloth back in place when I'm done, carry the place mats and silverware to the table when I'm setting the table, and so on."*
> **About Emily, 62nd week or 14 months**
>
> *"My daughter knows that apple juice and milk belong in the fridge and runs to the door to open it. For cookies, she goes straight to the cupboard and gets out the tin."*
> **About Jenny, 57th week or 13 months**
>
> *"Thomas starts his own 'programs.' Just recently he has started picking up the remote control and aiming it at the TV—stretching out his arm toward the TV. Another example is when his daddy is downstairs in his study and Thomas wants to go on the computer, he rattles the safety gate. He also picks out a computer game and knows how his father starts it up. But if his daddy checks his mail first, Thomas gets angry because he is interrupting his 'computer game program.'"*
> **About Thomas, 58th week or 13 months**

Teach Them to Be Considerate of You

Many babies can now understand that you can also be in the middle of a program, such as when you are busy washing the dishes or tidying up. When you notice your baby is starting to comprehend these things, you can also start asking them to have consideration for you so that you can finish what you are doing. At this age, however, you can't expect them to wait too long.

Allow Your Baby to Find Creative Solutions

Let your baby play with various behaviors within one and the same program. A baby may know how something should be done, but some children are exceptionally creative when it comes to inventing and trying out different ways to attain the same final goal. They continually try to see if things can be done some other way. Whenever they fail or are forbidden to do something, they always look for another way around the problem or prohibition. They are not discouraged but become highly inventive.

"When my son is doing something, for instance building, he suddenly shakes his head, says, 'No,' and starts to do it in a different way."
About Kevin, 55th week or 12 months

"My daughter gets out her little locomotive to stand on when she wants to get her things from the closet. She used to always use her chair."
About Jenny, 56th week or 12 months

"When I ask my daughter if she needs the potty, she does if she really needs to. She pees, carries the potty to the toilet, and flushes. At other times, she sits, stands up, and pees next to the potty."
About Jenny, 54th week or 12 months

"When my son wants to get his own way, he'll lie down on the floor just out of my arm's reach. That way I have to come to him."
About Matt, 56th week or 12 months

DO REMEMBER

Breaking old habits and setting new rules are also part of working out each new ability. You can only demand of your baby that they follow the new rules they understand—no more, but also no less.

Let Your Baby Experiment

Some babies experiment endlessly. You could see them performing the following program or experiment: How do these toys land, roll over, and bounce? Your little Einstein can go on experimenting with these things for what seems like forever. For instance, they might pick up different toy figures and drop them on the table 25 times and then repeat this up to 60 times with all sorts of building blocks. If you see your child doing this, then just let them carry on. This is their way of experimenting with the objects' characteristics in a very systematic way. They are looking at how these things land, roll, and bounce. They will be able to put this information to good use later on when they have to decide in the middle of a program whether to do something this way or that. Babies are not simply playing—they are working hard, often putting in long hours, to discover how the world works.

"Dan can pile up two blocks, perhaps even more. He could probably build a whole tower but he's not interested. Instead, he puts one block on another one and studies how they individually twist and turn. I watched him to see if I could figure out what Dan was doing and it seems he is playing with suction. He holds a block in each hand, slides them over each other, and then pulls them apart; he keeps repeating it. He has discovered that there is no suction when the blocks are too far apart.

About Dan, 56th week or 12 months

"He is not at all interested in sorting shapes (in a box)—that is, unless he can see the purpose and has a goal in mind. For instance, he put pieces of paper, bits of food, and small thin bags through the long slit under the fridge for days on end until I discovered his secret hiding place."

About Jim, 56th week or 12 months

"Luke can spend the whole day watching other people doing things, especially his father. He watches him walk, turn around, touch things, etc. He particularly likes watching how his dad plays with his toy cars. Luke then often mimics the action with his hand and then grabs the object and tries to do the same himself. He studies how things work. He is very calm, cautious, and seems totally absorbed in what he is doing, so much so that he doesn't hear you when you talk to him."

About Luke, 56th week or 12 months

BE PREPARED FOR THE UNEXPECTED

Some children are exceptionally creative when it comes to inventing and trying out different ways to attain the same final goal. This can be particularly exhausting for parents.

- They continually try to see if things can be done some other way.

- Whenever they fail or are forbidden to do something, they always look for another way around the problem or prohibition.

- It seems like a challenge to them never to do something the same way twice. They find simply repeating things boring.

Show Understanding for "Irrational" Fears

When your little one is busy exploring their new world, they will run into things or situations that they don't fully understand. Along the way, they discover new dangers, ones that they never imagined existed. They are still unable to talk about them, so show them a little understanding. Their fear will only disappear when they start to understand everything better. So be sympathetic.

"All of a sudden, my son was frightened of our ship's lamp when it was on, probably because it shines so brightly."
About Paul, 57th week or 13 months

"My daughter is a little scared of the dark. Not once she is in the dark, but to walk from a lit room into a dark room."
About Jenny, 58th week or 13 months

"My son gets frightened when I inflate a balloon. He doesn't get it."
About Matt, 58th week or 13 months

"My daughter was frightened by a ball that was deflating."
About Eve, 59th week or 13 months

"My son gets terribly frightened by loud noises, like jet airplanes, telephones, and the doorbell ringing."
About Bob, 55th week or 12 months

"My daughter is scared of everything that draws near quickly. Like the parakeet, fluttering around her head; her brother trying to catch her; and a remote-control car belonging to her brother's friend. It was just too fast for her."
About Emily, 56th week or 12 months

"My son refuses to go in the big bath. But he will sit in the baby bath in the big bath."
About Frankie, 59th week or 13 months

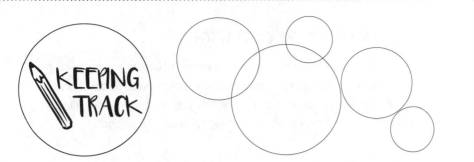

YOUR FAVORITE GAMES: THE WORLD OF PROGRAMS

These are games and activities that your toddler may like now and that help them practice their newly developing skills.

Instructions to Fill In This List:

Check off your toddler's favorite games and compare them to the discovery list. Is there a link between them?

DOING A JOB BY THEMSELVES

Many toddlers love being allowed to do something by themselves that only adults are allowed to do. Making a mess with water is the most popular job. Most children calm down when they play with water, especially more active children. Give it a go, but remember never to leave your toddler alone with water.

☐ GIVING THE DOLL A BATH

Fill a baby bath or a dishpan with lukewarm water. Give your child a washcloth and a bar of soap, and let them lather up their doll or plastic toy. Washing hair is usually a very popular part of this game. Only give them the towel when they are finished or it will end up in the water, too.

☐ CLEANING THE CAR OR TRACTOR

Put your toddler's bicycle or ride-on toy outside where they can play with water. Give them a bucket of warm water with soapy bubbles and a brush or cloth, and let them clean their bicycle. You can also give them a garden hose with a small trickle of water so they can wash off the soap.

☐ DOING DISHES

Tie an apron on your child, and put them on a chair in front of the sink. Fill the sink with lukewarm water, and give them your dish sponge and an assortment of baby-friendly items to be washed, such as plastic plates, cups, egg cups, wooden spoons, and all sorts of strainers and funnels. A nice topping of bubbles will make them even more eager to get to work. Make sure the chair they are standing on does not become slippery when wet, causing the busy one to lose their footing in their enthusiasm. Then stand back and let the fun begin.

HELPING OUT WITH IMPORTANT CHORES

Your toddler cannot do most chores on their own yet, but they can help you. They will like nothing better. They can help prepare dinner, set the table, and shop for groceries. It will take you longer than usual with their help, and they may make more mess and work for you when they are trying "something new," but they will learn a lot by doing it. And when they help you with important chores, they will feel grown-up and content.

☐ UNPACKING AND PUTTING AWAY GROCERIES

Put fragile and dangerous things away first, then let your little assistant help you unpack. You can have them hand you or bring you the groceries one by one, as they choose. Or you can ask them, "Could you give me the . . . please, and now the . . ."

You can also ask them where they would put things. And finally, they can close the cupboard doors when you are finished. Encourage and thank them. Many toddlers like to have a tasty snack and a drink after all the "work."

HIDE-AND-SEEK GAMES

Now you can make these games more complicated than before. When your child is in the right mood, they will usually enjoy displaying their talents. Adjust the pace to your child. Make the game neither impossibly difficult nor too easy for them.

☐ DOUBLE HIDING GAME

Place two cups in front of your child and put a plaything under one of them. Then switch the cups around by sliding them across the table. This way, cup A will be where cup B was, and vice versa. Make sure that your child is watching closely when you move the cups and encourage them to find the toy. Give them plenty of praise for each attempt to find the toy. This is really very complicated for them.

☐ WHERE IS THE SOUND COMING FROM?

Many toddlers love looking for sounds. Take your child on your lap and let them see and hear an object that can make a sound—for instance, a music box. Cover their eyes and have someone else hide the object while it is playing. Make sure that your little one cannot see where it is being hidden. When it has vanished from sight, encourage them to look for it.

YOUR FAVORITE TOYS

☐ Dolls (especially those that can go in water), doll strollers, and doll beds
☐ Farmhouses, farm animals, and fences
☐ Garages and cars
☐ Trains with tracks and tunnels
☐ Unbreakable tea sets
☐ Pots, pans, and wooden spoons
☐ Telephones
☐ Clickable building blocks or large building blocks
☐ Bicycles, cars, toy horses, or engines they can sit on themselves
☐ Push-along wagons that they can use to transport all sorts of things

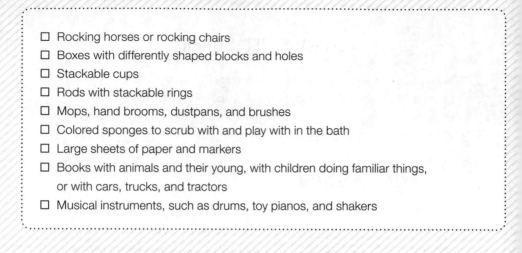

☐ Rocking horses or rocking chairs
☐ Boxes with differently shaped blocks and holes
☐ Stackable cups
☐ Rods with stackable rings
☐ Mops, hand brooms, dustpans, and brushes
☐ Colored sponges to scrub with and play with in the bath
☐ Large sheets of paper and markers
☐ Books with animals and their young, with children doing familiar things, or with cars, trucks, and tractors
☐ Musical instruments, such as drums, toy pianos, and shakers

What Does Your Toddler Choose From the World of Programs?

All toddlers have now gained the ability to perceive and play with programs, opening a wide range of new skills to master. Your child will choose the things that interest them and they prefer the most. Between 54 and 60 weeks, they will choose whatever most suits their own inclinations, interests, physique, and weight. Do not compare your child to others, because every child is unique.

Watch your toddler carefully to determine where their interests lie. In the What You've Discovered: The World of Programs, there is space for you to write down other interests. You can also look around and see if there are other things that you think your toddler will like.

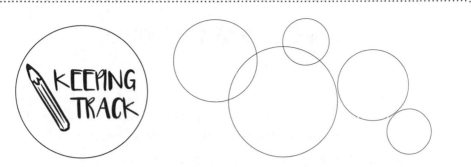

WHAT YOU'VE DISCOVERED: THE WORLD OF PROGRAMS

These are examples of skills your toddler could show from this age. Do remember: your toddler will not do everything on the list!

You may be surprised by some of the things on this list and say to yourself: "Isn't that a bit early?" Yes, you are correct if you are thinking in terms of a perfectly performed skill. But the thing is that they are often performed so rudimentarily, you could easily miss your toddler doing them. It would be a shame to miss them doing these things. For instance, it only takes a few seconds to deliberately push a cloth across the floor; it's such a small movement. But in your child's mind, they are helping you clean the floor. When you are going through the list, keep your toddler's intentions in mind. If they think they are cleaning, well then, that's what they are doing. It is not about actually scrubbing the floor but what they are attempting to do while practicing programs. So look at their intention rather than the final result.

Instructions to Fill In This List:

Now that your baby is growing into a toddler, you may find it increasingly difficult to complete these lists. There are hundreds if not thousands of programs, and we can only name a small number of the most common ones. It is therefore important that you understand what a program is before going through this list. It will help you to recognize various patterns and variations in them. Regularly consult this list and remember: you are not necessarily looking for exactly these skills—although these examples occur often—but also for similar actions your toddler performs.

You made this leap on: _____

On _____ the sun broke through again and now, at the end of the leap, I see you can do these new things.

LEAP 8

STARTING A PROGRAM THEMSELVES

Date:

☐ You get out a broom or duster and try sweeping or dusting. It's simply an action—nothing really gets cleaned—but you are trying and the intention is there. You often grab any cloth within reach whether it's meant for cleaning or not.

☐ You bring all kinds of things to me that you want to be put away.

☐ You get the cookie jar and expect a tea or coffee break.

☐ If they are within reach, you come to me with your shoes and a bag and that means you want to go shopping.

☐ You get out your bucket and shovel, which means you want to go to the sandbox.

☐ You get the dog leash for a dog walk.

☐ You get out your clothes and attempt to put them on. You don't manage yet and you only get clothes that are within reach.

☐ Other programs you started, how you did them, and when:

_____

_____

_____

_____

_____

JOINING IN WITH A PROGRAM

Date:

☐ You throw the cushions from the chair in advance to help when I am cleaning.

☐ You try to hang the tea towel back in place when I am finished.

☐ You put some objects or food items away in the right cupboard.

☐ You bring your own plate, cutlery, and place mat when I am setting the table.

☐ You clearly tell me that it's time for dessert when you have finished eating your main meal. You say "ice"—for ice cream—for instance.

☐ You put spoons in cups and start stirring.

- ☐ You grab an item I have just bought and want to carry it yourself.
- ☐ You try to put an item of clothing on by yourself while I am dressing you. You try to put your foot in a slipper or to pull up your pants when I have put your legs in.
- ☐ You pick out your favorite app on my telephone.
- ☐ You know which button to press to turn the TV on.
- ☐ Other programs you joined in with, how you did them, and with whom:

_____

_____

_____

_____

_____

_____

_____

EXECUTING A PROGRAM UNDER SUPERVISION

Date:

- ☐ You put different shaped blocks through the correct holes in a box when I help by pointing out what goes where.
- ☐ You use the potty when I ask you to or when you need to. You then carry the potty to the bathroom yourself or help me carry it and you flush the toilet.
- ☐ You get out pens and paper and "draw" when I give you instructions.
- ☐ These are examples of other programs you did under supervision:

_____

_____

_____

_____

_____

_____

_____

EXECUTING A PROGRAM INDEPENDENTLY

Date:

☐ You try to feed dolls or soft toys; you are copying my program of feeding you.

☐ You try giving a doll a bath by copying my program of bathing you.

☐ You try putting your doll on the potty sometimes after sitting on it yourself (and sometimes after having used it).

☐ You eat everything on your plate without (much) help; you prefer to do this while sitting politely at the table like the grown-ups.

☐ You eat raisins/_____ from a packet by yourself.

☐ You build a tower of at least three blocks.

☐ You find my telephone very interesting. Sometimes you press spots on the screen, start talking, and then say, "Bye," and put down the phone at the end of the "conversation."

☐ You crawl through the room following "paths" of your own choice. You often indicate which direction you intend to go first before changing direction. You choose "paths" and crawl under chairs and tables, and through small tunnels.

☐ You crawl through the room with a toy car or train saying, "Vroom vroom." You follow all sorts of different routes—under chairs and tables, or between the couch and the wall.

☐ You are now capable of finding something I hid and that you cannot see.

WATCHING OTHERS CARRYING OUT PROGRAMS

Date:

☐ You watch toddler shows on the television, computer, or laptop, and you can concentrate on them for about three minutes.

☐ You listen to short, simple stories, suitable for your age. The story must not last longer than three minutes.

☐ You express an understanding of what is happening in pictures. For example, you say "yum" when the child or animal in the picture is eating or being offered something to eat.

- [ ] You look and listen when I play with your dolls or soft toys. For instance, if I give them a bath, feed them, dress them, or talk to them and have them "answer" me.

- [ ] You study older children when they are carrying out a program with a toy; for instance, with a:

  - [ ] Tea set
  - [ ] Garage with cars
  - [ ] Doll and doll bed

  - [ ] Other:
  _____
  _____

- [ ] You study me when I am carrying out a program. For instance:

  - [ ] Getting dressed
  - [ ] Eating
  - [ ] Cooking
  - [ ] Crafting
  - [ ] Hammering

  - [ ] Telephoning
  - [ ] Other:
  _____
  _____

Help, My Toddler Can't Do Everything!
No, Of Course Not; That's Impossible!

The first phase (clinginess) of this leap is age-linked and predictable, emerging between 49 and 53 weeks. Most toddlers start the second phase of this leap 55 weeks after the due date. The ability your toddler gains with the leap into the world of programs sets in motion the development of a whole range of skills and activities. However, the age at which these skills and activities appear for the first time varies greatly per child. For example, the ability to perceive programs is a necessary precondition for "washing dishes" or "vacuuming," but these skills normally appear anywhere from 55 weeks to many months later. The difference in age between the mental capacity (ability) emerging and actually doing something (skill) for the first time depends on your toddler's preferences, their desire to experiment, and their physical development. The skills and activities in *The Wonder Weeks* are presented at the earliest possible age they could appear so you can watch for and recognize them (they may be rudimentary at first). This way, you can respond to and facilitate your toddler's development. All toddlers gain the same ability at the same age, but they differ in what they do with it and when. That makes every child unique.

THE EASY PERIOD: AFTER THE LEAP

Around 58 weeks, most toddlers become a little less troublesome than they were. Some are particularly admired for their friendly talkativeness and others for their cute eagerness to help out with the housekeeping. Most are now beginning to rely less on temper tantrums to get their own way. In short, their independence and cheerfulness assert themselves once again. With their new liveliness and mobility, however, many parents may still consider their little ones to be a bit of a handful.

"My daughter is painstakingly precise. Everything has its own little place. If I make changes, she'll notice and put things back. She also doesn't hold on to anything anymore when she's walking. She will happily walk right across the room. To think I've been so worried over this."
About Emily, 60th week or 13 months

"Now that my son runs like the wind and wanders through the entire apartment, he also does a lot of things he shouldn't. He keeps putting away cups, beer bottles, and shoes, and he can be extremely imaginative. If I take my eye off him for a moment, those things end up in the trash can or the toilet. Then, when I scold him, he gets very sad."
About Frankie, 59th week or 13 months

"My daughter doesn't play with toys anymore; she won't even look at them. Watching, imitating, and joining in with us is much more fascinating to her now. She's enterprising as well. She gets her coat and her bag when she wants to go out and the broom when something needs cleaning. She's so big all of a sudden."
About Nina, 58th week or 14 months

"My son is perfectly happy in the playpen again. Sometimes he doesn't want to be taken out. I don't have to play along with him anymore, either. He keeps himself occupied, especially with his toy cars and puzzles. He's much more cheerful now."
About Paul, 60th week or 15 months

"My daughter is such a lovely little girl, the way she plays, chitchatting away. She's often so full of joy. Those temper tantrums seem like a thing of the past. But perhaps I'd better knock on wood."
About Ashley, 59th week or 14 months

AROUND 64 WEEKS

Leap 9

The World of Principles

LEARNING THE RULES

By now, your little one understands the concept of a "program." Your daily programs of eating, shopping, taking a stroll, playing, and washing the dishes seem normal to them at this stage. Sometimes they follow your lead, but they might instead grab the opportunity to show you what they can do. As mentioned in the previous chapter, your little helper may have a slightly different approach to household chores than you. They use a piece of string to "vacuum" and a rag to "mop," perhaps wetting it in their mouth. And they may banish anything and everything around them to a special out-of-the-way spot: the toilet bowl, the trash can, or the laundry basket. They come back to you proudly, with no more mess. Your little helper is still bound by certain strict routines, which tend to be a tad mechanical in nature. They are just a beginner in the complex world of programs, not yet able to adapt the program they are carrying out to different circumstances. It will require several years of experience before they become proficient in such matters.

As adults, we have the benefit of experience. We are able to adapt to change. We can vary the order in which we do things. While grocery shopping, we opt for the short line at the butcher instead of joining a long line at the deli counter. You make choices depending on the circumstances. We also adjust to those around us. If anyone asks your opinion, you consider the person asking the question before you respond. You are also able to adapt yourself to your mood or, at least, the direction you want your moods to go. You prepare a meal and set the table in different ways depending on whether you are going to have a dinner party or whether you have to rush off to an important meeting. You anticipate everything happening around you that concerns you. At the simplest level, you know what you want and how best to get it. You make sure that you achieve your goals. It's because of this that your programs appear to be so flexible and natural.

Your little angel will start to pick up on how they can better deal with certain situations as soon as they take their next leap, Leap 9. They will land in the world of principles. Around 64 weeks—approaching 15 months—you will notice them stepping up to try new things.

Around 61 weeks (59 to 63 weeks)—14 months—your little one starts noticing that their world is changing. A maze of new impressions is turning their reality on its head. Initially, it's quite a task for them to deal with the changes. First, they will have to create some order in this newfound chaos. They return to familiar surroundings and once more look to you for reassurance.

THE FUSSY PHASE:
THE ANNOUNCEMENT OF THE MAGICAL LEAP

Many parents complain that they rarely hear their toddler laugh anymore right around this time. They see their toddler being "earnest" or "sad." The moments of sadness are unexpected, and are usually short-lived with no clear cause. Your little one could also be irritable, impatient, frustrated, or angry; for instance, if they even think that their mommy or daddy is not standing by at their beck and call, or does not understand what they want or say, or corrects them or tells them "NO!" This can even happen if their latest building project topples or if a chair refuses to move or if they run into a table.

In short, you'll be welcoming back that fussy phase characterized by the three Cs (crying, clinginess, and crankiness) and at least a few other typical characteristics.

This period is difficult for your toddler but also for you, and it can cause worries and irritation and put you under strain.

Fortunately, this fussy phase won't last long and your toddler will soon be the sunshine in the house again. Their new ability will break through and you will see your toddler doing all kinds of new things.

"This week he cried a lot. Why? I don't know. He burst out in tears at unexpected moments."
About Gregory, 64th week or 14 months

"If she does not receive my direct attention, she sprawls out on the ground bawling."
About Josie, 62nd week or 14 months

"He is really struggling. If he is unable to do something right the first time, he throws a tantrum or throws things around the room."
About Gregory, 66th week or 15 months

DO REMEMBER

If you notice your toddler is fussier than usual, watch them closely. It's likely that they are attempting to master new skills. For what to expect, see What You've Discovered: The World of Principles on page 388.

HOW YOU KNOW YOUR TODDLER HAS ENTERED THE NEXT FUSSY PHASE

Besides the three Cs, here are some of the signals that your toddler may give you to let you know they're entering the next fussy phase.

Does Your Toddler Cling to You More Often Now?

Most toddlers do whatever is necessary to be *closer* to their mommy and daddy most of the time. (That motivates the behavior of babies and toddlers for quite some time to come.) As babies grow older, this closeness to the parents may change shape: instead of physical contact, they may be content with contact at a distance. They make it into a game of "making eye contact at a distance every so often." That is a considerable step toward independence, much in the same way that young adults going through a crisis may be content with a phone call with their parents at the other end of the country. However, more often than not, your toddler still behaves like a small baby during this phase.

"He followed me constantly, dragging his toy. If I stood still or sat down, he would play at my feet or even under them. It began to wear me down."
About Kevin, 62nd week or 14 months

"He loves to get my attention from a short distance, just glancing at each other. He glows from our mutual relationship."
About Luke, 63rd week or 14 months

"This week he clung to me, literally. He climbed up my back, hung in my hair, crawled up against me. He sat between my legs and clamped on so that I was unable to take a step. All the while making a game of it, and making it difficult to become impatient. And, in the meantime, he had it his way."
About Matt, 65th week or 15 months

Is Your Toddler Shy?

Most children don't stray from your side when in the company of strangers. Some seem to try to climb back into you. They certainly don't want to be picked up by another person. Their daddy or mommy is the only one allowed to touch them, sometimes the only one who can talk to them, and on occasion even their father may be too much. Mostly, they seem frightened. You think sometimes that they are becoming shy.

> *"He cries if I walk out of a room and leave him with other people. If I go to the kitchen, so does he. Especially today, he never left my side, and this while his grandmother was in the room. He knows his grandmother well and sees her every day."*
>
> **About Frankie, 63rd week or 14 months**
>
> *"Even if her father wants her attention, she turns her head away. And when he puts her in her bath, she starts to scream. She only wants to be with me."*
>
> **About Josie, 64th week or 14 months**

Does Your Toddler Not Want You to Break Physical Contact?

Often a small child does not want the distance between them and their mother or father to increase. If anyone is going to go anywhere, then the toddler wants to be the one. Their mommy or daddy must remain exactly where they are and not move one bit.

> *"He gets angry when I drop him at daycare and he lets me know when I pick him up. He ignores me for a while, as if I don't exist. However, when he is done with ignoring me, he is really sweet and snuggles up by putting his head on my shoulder."*
>
> **About Mark, 66th week or 15 months**

Does Your Toddler Want to Be Entertained More Often Than Before?

Most toddlers don't like to play alone. They want their mommy or daddy to play along, and if they don't, the toddler will follow them if they walk away. With this behavior, what they are really saying is: "If you don't feel like playing with me, then I'll just tag along with you." And because your tasks are usually domestic, household tasks are very popular, although not for every child. Now and then, some clever little one thinks up a new strategy with a playful trick or antic to lure you to play. Such an enterprise is difficult to resist. Even though you may be held up with your work, you are willing to overlook it. Your toddler is already getting big.

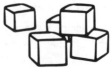

"She hardly plays anymore; she follows me around constantly. Just wants to see what I'm doing around the house and put her nose in the middle of it."
About Jenny, 64th week or 14 months

"He almost never wanted to play by himself. The whole day long, it was horse riding and Mommy was the horse. He kept me occupied with cute little ploys, all the while thinking that I wasn't onto his little game."
About Matt, 65th week or 15 months

Is Your Toddler Jealous?

Sometimes toddlers want extra attention from their parents when they are in the company of others—especially when around other children; otherwise, they become insecure. They want their mommy or daddy for themselves; they must be the center of their mother's or father's attention.

"He particularly wants my attention when I'm around others, especially if the others are children. Then he gets jealous. He does listen, though, if I tell him that it's time to go and play by himself, but he stays around me."
About Thomas, 61st week or 14 months

Is Your Toddler Moody?

Some parents notice that their little one's mood can completely change very quickly. One moment, the little chameleon is grumpy; the next, they are all smiles. One minute, they are very cuddly; the next, so angry that they sweep their cup clean off the table, then they can become sad with gushing tears, and so on. You could say that your toddler is practicing for puberty. Little ones at this age are capable of many forms of behavior to express their feelings. And a child who is at odds with themselves tries them all.

"She went back and forth from sulky to cheerful, clingy to independent, earnest to silly, unruly to compliant. And all these different moods took turns as if everything was completely normal. It was quite a chore."
About Juliette, 62nd week or 14 months

"One moment, he is into mischief; the next, he's an example of obedience. One moment, he is hitting me; the next, he is kissing me. One moment, he insists on doing everything himself,. and the next, he's pitiful and needs my help."
About Mark, 65th week or 15 months

Does Your Toddler Sleep Poorly?

Many little ones sleep less well at this point. They don't want to go to bed and they cry when it's time, even during the day. Some parents say their child's entire sleeping pattern seems to have changed. They suspect that their child is on the verge of moving from two naps a day to one. Although the children do fall asleep, many parents don't get any rest. The poor sleepers cry in their sleep, or they regularly wake up seeming helpless. They are clearly afraid of something. Sometimes they fall back asleep if comforted. But some only want to continue sleeping if their mommy stays with them or if they can occupy the precious spot between their mommy and daddy in the big bed.

> *"If she wakes up during the night, she clamps herself onto me. As if she were afraid."*
> **About Jenny, 62nd week or 14 months**
>
> *"She gets very busy and bothersome, and tries to bite when bedtime comes. It seems like she doesn't want to sleep by herself. It takes some doing. After crying a while, she does finally fall asleep, but after that I'm mentally drained. Last night, she slept in between us. She spreads out with an arm and a leg on Daddy and an arm and a leg on Mommy."*
> **About Emily, 64th week or 14 months**

Does Your Toddler Have "Nightmares"?

Many toddlers have nightmares more often than before. Sometimes they wake up sad, sometimes afraid or in a panic. And other times, very frustrated, angry, or hot-tempered.

> *"Twice this week he woke up screeching, covered in sweat, and completely in a panic. It took him half an hour to stop crying. He was practically inconsolable. This has never happened before. I also noticed that it took him a while before being at ease again."*
> **About Gregory, 62nd week or 14 months**

TIP

If you want to know more about sleep and leaps, go to page 59.

LEAP 9

Does Your Toddler Daydream?

Sometimes little ones sit staring off into the distance. It's a time of self-reflection.

"I noticed that he was rather quiet. He sat there staring. He'd never done that before."
About Thomas, 63rd week or 14 months

Does Your Toddler Lose Their Appetite?

Many toddlers are fussy eaters. Sometimes they simply skip a meal. Parents find it difficult if their child does not eat well, and this gives the little one the attention they need. Breastfeeding toddlers, however, do seem to want to feed more often. But as soon as they have sucked a little, they let go of the nipple and look around, or they just hold the nipple in their mouth without drinking. After all, they are where they want to be: with their mom.

"He wakes up often during the night again and wants the breast. Is it habit or does he really need it? I wonder because he wants to feed so often. I also wonder if I'm not making him too reliant on me."
About Bob, 63rd week or 14 months

Is Your Toddler More Babyish Again?

It could seem like your toddler is a baby again. That's not really the case. Regression during a clingy phase means that progress is coming. And because children at this age are capable of so much more, a regression is more evident.

"He's crawling more often again."
About Luke, 63rd week or 14 months

"If we timed it right and asked if she needed to pee, she would generally go to her potty, but now she is back to solely using diapers. As if she has completely forgotten how."
About Jenny, 62nd week or 14 months

Does Your Toddler Act Unusually Sweet?

Some parents succumb to a generous hug, kiss, or barrage of petting from their children. The little ones have certainly noticed that displays of affection work better than the whining, clinging, and being a nuisance.

Does Your Toddler Reach for a Soft Toy More Often?

Sometimes toddlers use cloths, soft toys, and all things soft to snuggle. They especially do this if their mother or father is busy.

Is Your Toddler Mischievous?

Many toddlers are naughty on purpose. Being naughty is the perfect way to get attention. If something breaks, is dirty or dangerous, or if the house gets turned upside down, their mommy and daddy will have to go to them and address this misbehavior. This is a covert way of getting a "mommy or daddy refill."

Does Your Toddler Have Many Temper Tantrums?

Many toddlers get more irritable, angry, and out of sorts quicker than parents are used to from them. These little ones roll kicking and screaming on the ground if they don't get their way, if they can't manage something first time, if they are not understood directly, or even without any clear reason at all.

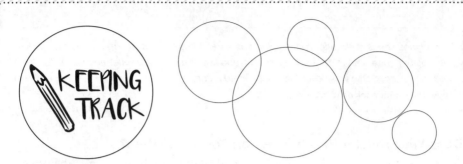

LEAP SIGNS

This is how you let me know the leap has started:

☐ You cry more often than before.

☐ You are cranky more often than before.

☐ You are fretful more often than usual.

☐ You are cheerful one moment and cry the next.

☐ You want to be entertained more often than usual.

☐ You cling to me—all day, if you could.

☐ You want to be closer to me now.

☐ You act unusually sweet.

☐ You are sometimes notably mischievous.

☐ You throw temper tantrums, or throw them more often than before.

☐ You are jealous.

☐ You are shyer with strangers than I am used to seeing.

☐ You clearly let me know that you don't like my breaking physical contact with you.

☐ You sleep poorly.

☐ You have nightmares more often than before.

☐ You lose your appetite.

☐ You just sit there, quietly daydreaming, more often than before.

☐ You reach for a soft toy, or do so more often than before.

☐ You are more babyish than you were.

☐ You resist getting dressed.

☐ And I notice that you: _____

As you check off your toddler's leap characteristics on the lists, remember that no toddler shows all of them. It is more about which things your toddler does and not how many.

How Are *You* Doing?

Many parents have less patience with clinging, whining, and provocation from a child of this age. Six months earlier, such behavior may have made them worry. Now it annoys them. Even though it isn't easy having a persistent, whining, and exasperating toddler around, don't forget that this leap is even tougher for your toddler than for you.

The moment parents get annoyed, they will show it. At this age, a persistent toddler will hear when their parents disapprove of their behavior. Using words the toddler understands, their mommy and daddy explain what they don't like. Language starts to play a greater role in this. And a whining toddler is quicker to land in a timeout than when they were younger. They find out that unreasonable demands for attention may lead to their being ignored.

"Sometimes he wants to be picked up at the very moment I am busy with something and that bothers me. I try to explain in simple terms why I can't pick him up. And explaining helps!"
About Gregory, 65th week or 15 months

"I can get rather perturbed when he pretends not to hear what I say. I turn him to face me, so that he has to look at me and listen when I say something."
About Taylor, 65th week or 15 months

Don't Let Quarrels Escalate

Your toddler is getting bigger. More and more often, you may not see eye-to-eye. If they are not allowed to interrupt, to cling, or to be unruly, they rebel fiercely, and this can result in real quarrels. Such an eruption is most likely at the end of the fussy phase. That's when both the parents and child are most short-tempered. No matter how bad the outbursts or quarrels are, stay calm and consistent. Screaming is never a good example; even a small smack on their bottom or hand will work against you in the end. Physical violence can never be justified.

*Things Ruth hates today: being asleep, being awake, cows—especially cows—all humans, diaper changes, having a wet diaper, eating, not having food in her mouth, clothes, blankets, being cold, someone else holding her, me holding her, being more than 2 inches away from me, being near me, being in the carrier, being in the stroller, being put down to walk, playing. So yep, it's pretty much just an awesome and SUPER productive day here today.—***Instagram post**

ANCHOR MOMENTS *

It's easy to forget about yourself during the big job of raising a toddler. These are some examples of special anchor moments that benefit you.

In 5 minutes: Look in the mirror and smile. Even if it's a "fake" smile, each smile releases dopamines, making you feel happier and less stressed. Make this your smiling day: smile to others, to yourself. Let your smile take the stress away. Want to go for a real laugh? Sit down and watch a video that makes you laugh and enjoy the full dopamine effect!

In 10 minutes: Sit down and give yourself some good advice and reassuring words. What would your 80-year-old self tell you now?

More time: Make an appointment for a good massage or ask your partner to give you a good massage. Not as a form of sexual intimacy, but just as a means of your relaxing your body.

Your Toddler's New Ability Is Starting to Bear Fruit

Around 64 weeks—almost 15 months—you will notice that much of the clinginess starts to disappear. Your toddler is a bit more enterprising again. Perhaps you already see that they are different, and act differently. They are getting much more willful. They think differently. They handle their toys differently. Their sense of humor has changed. You see these changes because at this age, your toddler's ability to observe and implement "principles," which emerged a few weeks ago, is starting to bear fruit, and they will start choosing the skills that suit them best. Find out where they are going and help them with it.

"My son doesn't want to sit on my lap as much, he's active again."
About Thomas, 67th week or 15 months

"All listlessness and bad moods have passed. She even was happy to go to daycare. The difficult phase has passed."
About Josie, 66th week or 15 months

* For more anchor moments, see page 36.

Compared to before, they play longer by themselves and are calmer, more focused, more solemn, enterprising, testing, observant, and independent in the sense that they do things by themselves. They are less interested in toys now. Their interests are more toward the domestic. Furthermore, they really like being outside, just wandering and exploring. They do need you to be around, though.

The World of Principles

In general, you could say that when pursuing a certain goal or carrying out a program, a principle is a common strategy that we use without having to go through all the specifics one by one. Once your toddler takes their first steps into the world of principles, you will notice that they complete various "programs" more smoothly, and naturally than before. You can now understand better what they are doing and what they want. This is because your child is able to have more complex thoughts, more like an adult. Principles will influence their thought process. Your toddler is no longer "caught up" in a program, but rather, they can "create" or change a program and even consider the value of it. And as they already think about each move when executing programs in order to decide if they will do it this way or that, your little one starts thinking about thinking in the world of principles. They are busier in their heads. And they feel that.

> "He's feeling his way with his head. Literally. Several things he touches with his forehead: the ground, the table leg, a book, his plate, and so forth. He calls to show me. I can't follow him. Certain times, I think he wants to say that you can bump into these things. Other times, it seems to be the start of a new way of thinking, as if he feels that he can mentally comprehend the world."
>
> **About Luke, 67th week or 15 months**

In the world of principles, your little one will think ahead, contemplate, consider the consequences of their actions, and make plans and evaluate them. They will come up with strategies: "Should I ask Dad or Grandma to get the candy?" "How can I create a subtle delay?" Naturally, your toddler is not yet devising plans as easily and routinely and in such complex ways as we do. As adults, it has taken us years to master this. Through practice, every one of us has learned certain principles by executing programs and checking the end results in thousands of different situations. Your little rookie can't fully comprehend the meaning of so many new things. As an "Alice in Wonderland," they wander the complicated world of principles. It begins to sink in that from morning till night, they will have to make choices. They notice that it's unavoidable: they must choose, choose, and choose again. Perhaps you have noticed your little one endlessly hesitating over what they should do. Thinking is a full-time job.

> *"He now realizes that he has to make all kinds of choices the whole day through. He chooses very consciously and takes his time. He hesitates endlessly if he should turn on the TV, or perhaps not. If he should throw something off the balcony, or better not. If he will sleep in the big bed or the little one, and if he will sit with his father or with me. And so on."*
> **About Luke, 67th week or 15 months**

In the world of principles, your child not only has to choose what they will do, but while they are doing it, they must continually make choices: "Should I wreck my tower, just leave it, or build it higher?" And if they choose the last option, they must choose how to do it: "Should I put another block on my tower or a doll this time?" With everything they do, they will have to choose time and again: "Should I go about it thoroughly, sloppily, recklessly, quickly, wildly, dangerously, or carefully?" If their mother or father thinks that it is bedtime, they will have to choose whether to go along quietly or whether to try to delay it. Again, they must choose: "Which is the best strategy for keeping me out of bed the longest? Just scampering away as fast as I can? Pull a plant out of its pot? Or pull some other stunt?" And if they know full well that something is not allowed, they must choose whether or not to just go for it or whether to wait until the coast is clear. They contemplate, choose, test, and make their parents desperate.

With all these choices, it dawns on your toddler that they, too, can manage things, just like their mommy, daddy, and everyone else. They become possessive as well. They don't readily share their toys, especially not with other children. They now count as a person. Their own will is on overtime. One moment, they decide to place a full cup on the table carefully and the next they let the cup fall down and spill the contents over the table. One moment, they try to get a cookie from you with kisses and caresses. The next moment, they opt for a tantrum, and you have no idea that they are after a cookie!

Your toddler is full of surprises. By using their whole arsenal and by studying your and others' reactions, they discover that the various strategies they employ give different results. So your toddler discovers when they can best be friendly, helpful, aggressive, assertive, careful, polite, and so on. Your child thinks up some of the strategies by themselves; others, they imitate: "Oh, that kid hit their mother, should I try that?" Your toddler wanders around in the world of principles and really needs their parents and others in their learning process.

We adults already have years of experience in the world of principles. We have become skilled in this world through trial and error. We know, for example, what justice, kindness, humanity, helpfulness, ingenuity, moderation, thriftiness, trust, frugality, caution, cooperation, care, empowerment, assertiveness, patience, and caring mean to us. We know what it means to be considerate of others, to be efficient, to cooperate, to be loving and respectful, and we know how to put others at ease. Yet we don't all interpret these principles in the same way. We know, for instance, that it is polite to shake hands when we introduce ourselves—that is, in the Dutch culture. In England, however, people do not expect a handshake; there, a nod and a greeting are sufficient. And in Tanzania, people expect both hands; one hand is just a half-offering and is considered rude because you keep one hand ready to pull the other hand back with. We fulfill our principles according to our personality, family, and the culture in which we have grown up.

The previous examples are mainly moral principles, which deal with standards and values. But there are other types of principles that concern the way we do things. For example, there are the strategies you use when playing a game of chess to keep "control over the middle" of the board. You keep open the option of moving your pieces to the middle of the board. This allows for many more follow-up moves than from the sides of the board. Another example is the principle of making long journeys more comfortable by planning a schedule in which you get enough hours of sleep. Yet another principle is that when writing an article, you must take your intended audience into account. Or the principle of keeping dual accounting, or developing a musical "theme." Then there are the laws of nature that dictate how things move, chemical equations describing how complex matter is built up by simple elements, or the geology that describes the consequences of the movements of the earth's crust. All these belong to what we call the world of principles.

A toddler is naturally nowhere near being ready for such adult applications of principles, such as strategy in chess, laws of nature, or adult standards or norms. Those are all very big words that we don't usually associate with toddlers. But in their own rudimentary way, your child gets started in the world of principles. They have already devised strategies to get to stay up longer (social strategy)! And some toddlers spend all day playing with toy cars, watching them descend an incline (a basic principle of physics).

There can be stark differences between ways in which an adult handles a principle in practice. We constantly ready ourselves for the changing conditions that present themselves. Suppose your spouse and your toddler both give you a drawing of an apple and look at you full of expectation. You will most likely be more honest with your spouse. Even if it does resemble a piece of fruit, you'll be more critical and less likely to praise them. But you will praise your toddler regardless of the outcome. Even if you can't tell what it is, you say that this is the most charming apple you've ever seen. You'll hang it on the fridge and admire it. You automatically take into account the fact that your toddler and your spouse would react differently to your comments, and that negativity might cause significant distress. You might have permanently destroyed their will to draw.

At this age, your toddler can't yet react to all the changing circumstances. They have yet to acquire the subtleness. They are still stuck in the first strategies they came up with. This is because they have just gotten their first whiff of principles, and they are only able to apply them in set ways. It's only after they have made their next leap that you will notice your child beginning to become more adaptable to their surroundings. They will adapt their strategy. Just like your toddler was able to grasp the programs after making their leap into the world of principles, it is only after the next leap that your toddler will grasp that they can vary and choose what they want to be: honest, friendly, helpful, careful, patient, resourceful, efficient, just, caring, or frugal. And that they can choose to be none or all of those things. They begin to understand that they can pay attention to Grandpa, or that they don't have to, that they can comfort a friend, or choose not to. Or that they can treat the dog gently, or they can be rough, that they can be polite to the neighbor and cooperate with their mother and father, or not . . .

BRAIN CHANGES

From US research on 408 identical twins, it was concluded that around 14 months of age, there was clear hereditary influence upon mental development. The development concerned both nonverbal skills as well as speech comprehension.

THE MAGICAL LEAP FORWARD:
THE DISCOVERY OF THE NEW WORLD

In the world of principles, your toddler will discover that there are several ways to accomplish a goal. These are all strategies they can utilize: "Should I do it carefully, recklessly, pushily or sweetly? Or should I try a prank?" Your toddler is becoming more resourceful. They owe this to the fact that they are growing sharper in all domains. They begin walking more adeptly and are able to get around quickly. They understand you better now and can sometimes answer back. They practice playing with their emotions, and not always around you. They can think ahead and know that they count as a person, too. They are better at eating and drinking, cleaning up, building towers, and putting things together. Their throwing aim has improved, as have other things.

Everything will come more naturally to them in the coming weeks. And again and again, they will use every newly acquired strategy to achieve their objectives. Of course, not every one will achieve the desired effect. That requires time and practice, but by trying things out, your toddler realizes that various strategies bring different results. Some are a smashing success; others, the opposite; and most are just so-so.

Give your child the opportunity to experiment with all sorts of strategies, to test them out and reflect on them. The only way they will learn how to behave in certain situations is by being resourceful, by gauging your reaction, and through lots of practice.

You will notice that all these ways of experimenting with and learning about principles can be categorized as: becoming skillful, nagging and trying to get their own way, and being nice and placating. Some toddlers suddenly develop "irrational" fears, and for all toddlers, the time has come to learn the ground rules.

TODDLERS ARE LIKE THIS

Toddlers love anything new, and it's important to respond when you notice any new skills or interests. They will enjoy it if you share these new discoveries, and this will accelerate their learning progress.

Skillfulness

When your toddler is trying to make their way in the world of principles, they will also want to know what their little body is capable of—in other words, how to use their body when they want to be quick, slow, careful, funny, or clever. They also want to get acquainted with the outside world, become more skillful with things (which they are very creative with!) and with language, will imitate others and replay their actions, will practice with emotions, and will start thinking ahead. You will also notice that they will enjoy endlessly repeating things while they experiment to find out the best way to do something.

Physical Antics

Your little one will test their body's capabilities. "Can I fit between there?" "How do I climb the stairs and how do I go down again?" "How do I go down the slide?" "Can I lie comfortably on all these household goods and toys?" "What is not nice to lie on and what things do I not fit in?" "How strong am I?" In short, your toddler is becoming resourceful with their body. They sometimes appear reckless, which frightens their mother and father.

"She goes up and down a step upright. She practices that the whole day through. Now I keep my eyes open for other objects of different heights, so she can develop this skill."
About Hannah, 67th week or 15 months

"Every day he discovers new games. He has found a small tunnel behind his bed and chest of drawers and loves going back and forth behind them. He slides under the couch and sees how far he can go before he gets stuck. And he gets a kick sliding around the room on his knees instead of using his feet."
About Matt, 70th week or 16 months

"She practices different ways of walking. Walking backward, turning circles, walking fast, walking slowly. She is very studious about all these tricks."
About Eve, 64th week or 14 months

"She lies in and on everything: in the doll's bath, in the doll's bed, and on the cushions spread on the floor."
About Ashley, 64th week or 14 months

"We put a mattress on the ground so that she can jump around on it. She loves galloping over it; she dives on the mattress and tries a somersault. She keeps testing how far she can go on the soft surface."
About Josie, 66th week or 15 months

Getting Acquainted With the Outdoors

Many toddlers enjoy browsing around in nature. They look like they're just fumbling about, but in fact they are surveying the area. This is not to say that they don't need you: they do! Many question everything endlessly: What is this and what is that called? And all children absorb what you say and what they see with the utmost concentration.

"She was startled when she walked through a puddle and got wet. She walked back to look at and investigate the puddle."
About Ashley, 64th week or 14 months

"She stood eye-to-eye with a real live cow and was really at a loss. This was at the children's zoo. She wasn't ready to pet the animal yet. Even when she was in her daddy's arms. On the way home, she was quiet as she mulled it over. She was very impressed by the living version of the cow from the book."
About Victoria, 61st week or 14 months

Getting Skillful With Things

Your child will become ever more resourceful with games and objects in the world of principles. They will only eat properly if they can feed themselves. Helping them when it's not wanted could result in everything ending down on the floor. They manage quite well building things or playing with their game of rings and puzzles. But beware! They try to turn on the faucet and open bottles and jars with twist-off lids on a regular basis. That's because your toddler is, above all, interested in what strategies work best for what results. They contemplate and experiment. "What will happen if I drop the key chain behind the cabinet? What if I put it under the bed? And what will happen to the key chain if I let it slide down between the couch and the wall? And how will I make it reappear? And if I am unable to reach it, can I get to it with a broom handle?" In short, they are learning how to hide something, put something away, and recover it. Later, if they are skillful enough or think themselves to be, they will, perhaps, use their tricks to amuse you with a prank. They could also hide a toy if, for instance, they don't want one of their friends to play with it. Do watch what they are up to. Put dangerous items out of reach and keep an eye on your little explorer.

> *"We do puzzles together. Now he likes it and participates gladly. Not that it always goes well, but it's a start."*
> **About Kevin, 65th week or 15 months**
>
> *"She throws things on the floor when you are least expecting it. She studies the effect her throwing has on the object."*
> **About Josie, 64th week or 14 months**
>
> *"When she is vacuuming with her battery-powered vacuum, she prefers to go for the most impossible spots. She does those spots as if her life depended on it: under the cabinet, between the chairs and table legs, in open cupboards. She skips the easy, large, open spaces."*
> **About Victoria, 61st week or 14 months**

Becoming Skillful With Language

In the world of principles, your toddler is continuously getting a better grasp of what the grown-ups around them are saying to each other and to them. They are also getting better at understanding brief instructions and often carry them out with great enthusiasm. They feel like they count for something. They also have fun pointing to parts of the body when you name them. The same goes for various things in the home, whether they are on the floor, the walls, or the ceiling.

Get your child to play a game of pointing and naming with you. You name something and let your child point to it, whether it's a toy, a body part, or whatever. And try to see what your child thinks of a game of calling to each other. It's best if they start by calling you. Call their name to get them to call your name. Call out their name again. For many children, it gives them a sense of pride and importance that their egos require.

GOOD TO KNOW

Many parents think that their little one should be talking more, given that they already know so much. But that is not the case. It is only after the next leap that your toddler's speech really takes off. Your child is 21 months by then. In the world of principles, most children are content with pronouncing single words, imitating animal sounds, and reproducing all sorts of other noises

"He understands more and more. Unbelievable how quickly a child picks up new words. Yet he picks out only a few to use in his speech. He prefers words that begin with 'b' like his favorite things: ball and boy. He pronounces the words well and completely. It seems like he knows how to pronounce the words but he doesn't have the coordination."
About Harry, 69th week or 16 months

"She cried, 'Daddy,' when I was busy in the kitchen. The calling out automatically evolved into a language game. Taking turns, we called out each other's name: 'Anna . . . ,' 'Daddy . . . ,' 'Anna . . . ,' 'Daddy.' Endlessly. Now it happens all the time if we are out of each other's sight."
About Anna, 70th week or 16 months

Imitating Others

In the world of principles, your toddler will observe how adults or other children do things and what effect their actions have. "How do they do that so skillfully?" "That kid gets immediate attention from everyone if they bite Grandma." "Mom and Dad regularly sit on the toilet. That must be a part of being 'big.'" These are just for starters. They copy, imitate, and try out what they see. The people around them are their role models. The behavior they see in books and on TV also gives them an inexhaustible source of ideas.

Respond to your child's behavior. Let them know what you think of their behavior. This is the only way they will learn what's right and wrong, and if they can do things better, quicker, more efficiently, or in a nicer way than they are doing.

"Imitating is now his main occupation. He imitates every behavior he sees: someone stamps her feet, he stamps his feet; someone hits, he hits; someone falls, he falls; someone throws, he throws; someone bites, he bites."
About Thomas, 63rd week or 14 months

"She wants to brush her teeth by herself. She slides the brush up and down once and knocks it on the edge of the sink—knock, knock, knock—slides the toothbrush up and down in her mouth again and knocks again—knock, knock, knock. And on she brushes. The funny thing is that she is imitating me. I knock the toothbrush on the edge of the sink, but only after I am completely finished and have rinsed my brush. I do it to shake the water off my brush."
About Victoria, 61st week or 14 months

"Initially she would turn her vacuum on with her fingers. Then she saw that I use my foot to turn mine on. Since now she uses her foot to start hers, too."
About Victoria, 61st week or 14 months

Replaying

In the world of principles, your child replays daily domestic activities and many more besides. They "cook," "shop," "take walks," "say goodbye," and "take care of their doll children." Naturally, they do all of this in their toddler way. Yet you are getting better at recognizing what they are up to. Above all, you see whether they do their best to be careful or helpful or if they are just being bossy, or if they're sweetly sucking up. They may do these things simply because they think it's part of their role or because they are imitating the people around them.

Give your child the opportunity to settle into their role. Play along with them once in a while. Your toddler then feels like they count and that what they do is important. Many toddlers at this age are very keen for signs of appreciation. They really want to be understood.

"He bakes mud pies: scoops and scoops buckets full to dump them out again. He finds it all very interesting."
About Thomas, 66th week or 15 months

"For the past few days, he has been pouring water from one bucket into the other. It's keeping him busy. Now and again I get a request to fill up a bucket. Otherwise, he seems to have forgotten me and is consumed with his special brew."
About Steven, 63rd week or 14 months

> *"My little man shops all day . . . he grabs a bag or box and looks around the room for things he wants to 'buy.' When he's done shopping, he gives me the bag or box. He's so proud of himself!"*
> **About Ethan, 65th week or 15 months**
>
> *"He often snuggles, kisses, comforts, and caresses his dolls and bears. He also puts them to bed. Really loving."*
> **About Luke, 66th week or 15 months**

Sometimes a child imitates being a father or mother. They study how it is to be their daddy or mommy. When a little girl wants to be her mom, her real mother is actually in the way. They then seem to be competing. Naturally, the same happens if their father is home and they want to walk in their dad's shoes. And if a little boy is playing dad, he wants to know how his mom reacts to this new dad.

Try and understand what your child is doing. Give them the opportunity to play their role and play along. Your little one learns a lot from this. They feel the need to express themselves in this way and to experience how it is to be their mom or dad.

> *"He goes and spreads out on his father's bed and looks around as if it is his. Also, just like his father, he goes and sits in his chair to read the paper. It is important to him to do as his dad does. He wants my reaction to it all as well."*
> **About Jim, 66th week or 15 months**
>
> *"As soon as I take off my shoes, she's in them. And then she follows up by taking a walk around in my shoes. She also regularly wants to sit in my chair. I have to vacate it for her. She starts pulling and yanking me and if I don't concede, she throws a tantrum."*
> **About Nina, 69th week or 16 months**

Practicing With Emotions

In the world of the principles, many toddlers experiment with their emotions. How does it feel if I am happy, sad, shy, angry, funny, or emotional? And when I greet someone, what does my face do then? What does my body do? And how can I use those emotions if I want others to know how I feel? And how should I act if I badly want to have or do something?

"He walks around laughing very artificially like he is experimenting with how it feels to laugh. He does the same with crying."

About Bob, 63rd week or 14 months

"She wanted to read a certain book again for the eighth time and noticed that I had had enough of it. She sat there a bit with her head facing downward. Very quietly, she practiced a pout. When she thought she had the right expression, she looked at me with a perfectly pouting lip and passed the book back to me."

About Josie, 65th week or 15 months

Thinking Ahead Has Begun

In the world of principles, your toddler can think ahead, contemplate, and make plans. They now understand that their mother and father can and do that, too. They realize what the consequences are for something that you do or want them to do. And all of a sudden, they express their opinion of something that they used to find quite normal or even liked. Remember, though, that they are not unruly. Their development has just made a leap. It is progress!

"Now she has a hard time when I leave for work. Up until recently, she ran to the front door to give me a send-off. Now she protests and holds me back. I think this is because she now understands the effects. Sending someone off can be fun, but when Mom leaves, she is gone for at least a few hours. And that's not so nice."

About Eve, 67th week or 15 months

"Thinking ahead has started! I brush her teeth after she has had a go. That always leads to terrible shouting matches. Up until recently, when she heard 'Time to brush our teeth,' she came running. Now she throws the toothbrush in the corner when I hand it to her, because she knows what follows after the fun of doing it herself."

About Laura, 67th week or 15 months

"Now he remembers where he has hidden or left his things, even from yesterday."

About Luke, 63rd week or 14 months

"This was the first time that I was able to see that she had a clear expectation. We had finger-painted and she had decorated the mirror. While she was bathing, I snuck off to clean the mirror. I shouldn't have done that. When she got out of the bath, she walked right to the mirror looking for her decoration. Very sad."

About Josie, 65th week or 15 months

Nagging and Getting Their Own Way

Whether you like it or not, nagging and trying to get their own way are normal at this age. In fact, your toddler learns from such behavior. Help them discover that there are other and better strategies they can use when they want to get something done, other "principles" that are more successful and better received. In the time ahead, you will experience drama games, them wanting to have their say, even aggression, and your toddler will experiment with the concepts of *mine* and *yours*.

> *Today's mood: Anya spilled a large juice all over the floor in the store. Screamed while in the trolley. Screamed while in the carrier. Gave in and gave her my phone to watch something. Of course, the connection wouldn't work. Threw phone at my face, threw phone at the floor. Seriously. Leaving the shop, she pulled strawberries out of the bag and dropped them all over the parking lot. Napped for 40 minutes. Cried when eating lunch, cried not when eating lunch. What else can we fit in today?*—**Instagram post**

The Drama Class

Does your little one try to get their own way by screeching, rolling, stamping, and throwing things? Do they lose their temper for the slightest reason? For example, if they don't get attention immediately, if they're not allowed to do something, if their play is interrupted for dinner, if their building topples over, or just out of the blue without your detecting that anything is wrong? Why does a toddler put on such an act? It's because you and the toys aren't reacting the way the toddler thinks they should be reacting. They are frustrated and need to express it. They do this using the most obvious strategies: getting as angry and making the biggest fuss possible.

They have yet to discover and practice more successful, quicker, sweeter strategies in order to persuade you to do what they want, or to build a better tower. Your nagging toddler is only able to make their wishes known by acting like they do.

Understand your toddler's frustration. Let them blow off some steam if they need to. And help them discover that there are other and better strategies they can use when they want to get something done, ways that are more successful and better received. Also let your child know that you will take them into consideration, if they are clear about what they want.

"She throws an increasing number of temper tantrums. Yesterday, I got her out of bed and for no reason she threw a temper tantrum. This one lasted quite a long time, complete with rolling on the floor, banging her head, kicking and pushing me away, and screeching the whole time. Nothing I tried helped, not cuddling, not distracting her or stern words. After a while, I went and sat perplexed on the couch, leaned back, and watched while she rolled around on the floor. Then I went into the kitchen for an apple. She slowly calmed down, came to the kitchen, and stood next to me."

About Julia, 65th week or 15 months

"He's thrown a number of temper tantrums this week. One was so bad that he went completely limp. If he doesn't get his way, he gets really angry and then it's a real battle. He is really in his own world! At the moment, he doesn't listen well at all."

About James, 67th week or 15 months

They Want Their Say

In the world of principles, your little one discovers that they have their own will, too, just like all the grown-ups. They begin to speak up for themselves. But sometimes it goes too far: their will is law and they will not be swayed. This happens because it is becoming ever clearer to them that they can impose their will. They count, too! They realize that just like their mom or dad, they can decide if, when, or where they want to do something; how they will do it, and when they will finish. On top of that, they want to put in their "two cents, worth" if their mom or dad wants to do something. They want to help decide how it is done. And if they don't get their way or if it doesn't go according to plan, they become angry, disappointed, or sad. Show them understanding. They still have to learn that they can't always do what they want to do right away, and that they also have to consider the wishes of others, even though they want to stand up for and assert themselves.

Aggression

Many parents say that their sweet toddler sometimes turns into an aggressive tiger, and this makes them uneasy. Yet it is an understandable change. In the world of principles, your child tries all types of social behavior. Being aggressive is one of those. Your toddler studies how their parents, other adults, and children react if they hit, bite, push, or kick, or if they deliberately break something. Show your child what you think of their behavior. This is the only way that they will learn that being aggressive isn't sweet, interesting, or funny. This way they learn that it's hurtful and that adults are not amused by aggressive or destructive behavior.

LEAP 9

ADVICE ABOUT AGGRESSION

Research has shown that shortly after the first birthday, parents report the first physical aggression. At 17 months, 90 percent of parents report that their child is sometimes aggressive. Physical aggression peaks just before the second birthday. Thereafter, this type of behavior recedes. By the time children have reached school age, under normal circumstances, it will have mostly disappeared. Of course, some children are more prone to aggressive behavior than others. Yet a child's surroundings are also very important. They help determine how long a child remains aggressive. If little children live with adults and children who are aggressive, then they will assume that "being aggressive" is normal social behavior. However, children also live in environments where aggression is not tolerated and where sweet and friendly behavior is rewarded. The result is that the child will not start hitting and kicking when they are frustrated, want something, or are corrected. They will use more acceptable ways of expressing themselves.

Mine and Yours

In the world of principles, your little one discovers that some toys in the house are theirs and only theirs. Just like grown-ups, they are suddenly the proud owner of their own stuff. This is quite a discovery for a toddler. They also need time to grasp what *mine* and *yours* mean. Things aren't easy for them while they are figuring this out. Some toddlers find it disturbing if another child grabs something out of their hands for no reason without recognizing them as owner. Such lack of understanding starts them crying. Others become very wary and protect their territory as best they can. They come up with all sorts of strategies to prevent others from getting close to their things or, even worse, touching them. They especially don't trust children. Your toddler still has to learn to lend, share, and play with others.

> *"She is developing a certain urge to own. When we have guests, she comes and proudly shows her possessions. If we go over to play at a friend's house, she grabs her things and gives them to me for safekeeping. She hopes that by doing so, she can prevent her friend from playing with them."*
> **About Eve, 64th week or 14 months**
>
> *"Every time his little friend snatches one of his toys, my son bursts out in tears."*
> **About Robin, 68th week or 15 months**
>
> *"Kevin doesn't let anyone take anything from him. You can't even tempt him with a 'good trade,' either. If he's got ahold of it, he's keeping it. He's keen, though, to snatch things from others. In that, he has no scruples at all."*
> **About Kevin, 65th week or 15 months**

Being Nice and Placating

A developing sense that they have their own will, wanting to get their own way, nagging, and tantrums are all part of growing up. But your toddler is also smart enough to know that they can use other strategies to get what they want, strategies that people easily fall for, whether consciously or unconsciously. They now understand they can be overly nice, play tricks and jokes, ask for help, cooperate, be helpful, or be very neat and careful to achieve their goal. They can use positive emotions as a means to an end. Aren't they clever?!

The Joke Strategy

In the world of principles, tricks and antics play an ever-increasing role in your little one's life. Your toddler may start making their first jokes, and they themselves will get the biggest kick out of these jokes. You might notice that they appreciate others' jokes as well; many toddlers do. They enjoy gags, and when people or animals do something out of the ordinary, whether in real life or on TV, it makes them laugh. They find it exciting. Some children pull pranks to try getting around the rules.

You may notice that "being funny" is being used as a strategy to get away with doing something that would otherwise be frowned upon. Something pleasant and unexpected becomes increasingly more successful for getting on Mom or Dad's good side than a temper tantrum is. Give your child the opportunity to be creative while making fun and pulling pranks. Be very clear when they overstep the bounds. It is only with your help that they will learn the difference between what is and isn't acceptable.

> "He is constantly kidding around and has a great time doing it. He and his friends have a barrel of laughs acting silly. He really cracks up if he sees an animal do something silly or unexpected."
> **About Robin, 68th week or 15 months**

> "He loves just being silly. He giggles, and if his sister joins in, he really bursts out laughing."
> **About James, 69th week or 16 months**

> "He loves me to chase after him saying, 'I'm gonna get you.' However, when I want to put on his jacket, he runs away squawking and making a game of it."
> **About James, 70th week or 16 months**

> "She loves playing pranks. When we get to the front door, she doesn't wait for me to put the key in the lock; she just continues walking to the next door. She really thinks she's funny."
> **About Ashley, 70th week or 16 months**

Negotiating and Bargaining

It used to be that parents laid down the law and children had to obey. Adults didn't take kindly to backtalk. But everything changes, fortunately. Nowadays it is generally assumed that children who have learned to negotiate grow up better able to think for themselves. When your toddler lands in the world of principles, you could see a budding negotiator.

> "My daughter knows she is not allowed to take nuts straight from the bowl on the table. So she has figured out her own way to get what she wants and still follow the rules. She gets her own plate and spoon and spoons nuts onto her plate, then she eats them with the spoon. In her mind, she is allowed to eat them that way."
> **About Ashley, 68th week or 15 months**

Experimenting With "Yes" and "No"

Does your toddler experiment with the words "yes" and "no?" They sometimes do so when nodding or shaking their heads, occasionally pronouncing the actual words out loud. They also try nodding while saying no and shaking their head while saying yes, which is very funny to them. Their stuffed animals have mandatory "yes" and "no" lessons. Other times, they practice on their own while building something or wandering through the house just looking for mischief to get into, but mostly they practice their yes and no routine with their parents. You are also good for trying out their jokes on.

Give your child the opportunity to be inventive with the concepts of yes and no. This type of practice allows them to learn how a yes or a no should sound to reach their goal. And to learn how you do it. They can find the yes and no strategy that fits best in various situations. They discover which strategy is best suited to meet their needs.

> *"He is able to answer all sorts of questions with just a 'yes' or 'no.' He sometimes makes a mistake. He says 'yes' when he means 'no' and if I act upon his answer, he smiles and quickly changes to a 'no,' in a tone of 'not really.'"*
> **About Luke, 65th week or 15 months**
>
> *"She tests the words 'yes' and 'no' on me continuously: Is her 'yes' a real yes and will her 'no' remain a no? Perhaps I can find a way to cheat? She tests me to see how far she can go."*
> **About Nina, 70th week or 16 months**
>
> *"He knows what he wants and is getting better at answering with a definite 'yes' or 'no.' He also has different yeses and noes. Some indicate very clearly where his boundaries lay. When he reaches his limit, I know that he is dead set. His other yeses and noes lack finality. I then know that I can press him for a better deal."*
> **About Paul, 71st week or 16 months**

Asking for Help

Your toddler can be inventive in trying to put someone on the spot. They can use clever, sneaky, or sweet ways. They still require some practice in learning the tricks of the trade. Just watch your little one go to work on you or someone else when they need to get something done. Tell them what you think of it. Your child is still researching in the world of principles. They learn from your feedback.

> *"When he asks me to get something for him and I ask where I should put it, he walks to a spot and points where I should put it down. Then he is very friendly and easygoing."*
> **About Steven, 65th week or 15 months**
>
> *"She is getting better at expressing her wishes. She takes my hand and leads me off if she needs a new diaper. She grabs my finger if she needs me to do something for her with my finger, like pressing a button. She also leads me to where she doesn't want to go alone. It doesn't matter if I'm in the middle of something or not. She wants things done right away."*
> **About Josie, 67th week or 15 months**

"He points at things more and more. He also points to the things he wants you to get for him. This week, he lured his grandmother to the kitchen, walked to the cabinet where the cookies are, and pointed to the top shelf."
About Frankie, 63rd week or 14 months

"These past weeks, he has been commanding like a general. He cries out loudly and force-fully: 'Mom! Mom!' when he wants something. When I look at him, he sits there with his arm outstretched, pointing at the toy of his choosing. He wants them brought to him, and when he gets his request, he pulls his arm back and carries on playing. Giving orders has become second nature to him. This week was the first time I really noticed it."
About Matt, 68th week or 15 months

Cooperation

In the world of principles, your child has choices: "Am I going with the flow or against it?" "Do I care what Mom or Dad says or not?" In addition to that, your toddler is growing ever more outspoken and more capable. Small assignments are getting easier for them, like: "Get your shoes, please" "Go get your bottle, please" "Throw that in the trash, please" "Give it to Daddy, please" "Put it in the hall, please" or "Put it in the hamper, please." You might have already noticed that sometimes you don't have to say what to do. Your little toddler already grasps what you want and is working along. It is increasingly easier to lay down certain ground rules.

Try involving your child in day-to-day business and getting involved in their day-to-day, too. It makes them feel understood, appreciated, and important. Their ego is growing. Praise them, too, if they are thinking ahead for you. They are demonstrating that they know what is about to happen.

"Every time before we go somewhere, she gets her own jacket."
About Josie, 65th week or 15 months

"He now understands that he needs to stay with me when we're on the sidewalk."
About Luke, 66th week or 15 months

"When she needs changing, she walks with me to her dresser. She lies still and practically helps me."
About Laura, 63rd week or 14 months

Being Helpful

When toddlers land in the world of principles, most of them are particularly interested in all the goings-on about the house, although there is a big chance that your little one is no longer content just watching you do things. They want to help. They want to lighten your load. Let your child do their part. They really want to believe that they are a big help and that, without them, things would be a huge mess or that dinner wouldn't be any good. Be sure they receive a well-deserved compliment. They are, of course, still too young to set the table, wipe it down, or clean up. But in their own way, they are trying to do their bit to help, and they are experiencing what it is like to clean up, set the table, or help you with other tasks. Their intention is right, and the result is less important. It encourages a child when you acknowledge what they have tried to do: they helped set the table and clean the table, and helped with other tasks.

> "He constantly wants to help me. Whether it is straightening up, cleaning, going to bed or somewhere else, it doesn't matter. He very much wants to take part in the day-to-day routine of his own accord. When he is taken seriously, it gives him profound contentment. Understanding one another is central these days."
> **About Jim, 64th week or 14 months**
>
> "My daughter gladly helps making drinks. Sometimes I let her make her own drink. She uses all kinds of ingredients. When she drinks it, she goes around murmuring, 'Yum, yum, yum.'"
> **About Juliette, 68th week or 15 months**
>
> "As soon as I grab the vacuum cleaner, she grabs her toy one. She wants to help oh so badly. So what happens is that she wants to use my vacuum because it's better. Therefore, I begin with hers and when she takes it back, I can peacefully go on with the real one."
> **About Victoria, 61st week or 14 months**

Being Careful

Does your toddler experiment with being rash or careful? "Should I fling my cup on the ground or should I place it carefully on the table?" Reckless behavior seems to be very popular. Running, climbing, wild horseplay, and treating objects recklessly are the favorite pastimes. But do realize that by experimenting and getting your reaction to such behavior, your little one learns what it means to be reckless or to be careful.

"When you're least expecting it, she throws her bottle away—for instance, when we are cycling—and then she studies our reaction to her behavior out of the corner of her eye."
About Hannah, 64th week or 14 months

"He climbs like a monkey. He climbs on everything. He climbs on chairs a lot. I also constantly find him on the dining room table, claiming that he can't get down! He is careful. He is aware of the danger, but sometimes he falls pretty hard."
About Frankie, 66th week or 15 months

"Wrestling with his brother is now the top draw. Sometimes they get really rough."
About Kevin, 69th week or 16 months

"She spilled a few drops of her drink on the floor. I grabbed an old sock that was lying around and mopped up. She looked at me shocked and amazed, went purposefully to the baby wipes, took one out of the box, and mopped all over again. When she had finished, she looked at me as if she wanted to say, 'That's how it should be done.' I was taken aback at the level of cleanliness, and I praised her for it."
About Victoria, 61st week or 14 months

"She is very capable of expressing that something is dirty. She repeatedly says, 'Poo,' to the slightest smudge in bed."
About Josie, 64th week or 14 months

"When her brother was looking through her dolls in search of a special robot, he swept all her dolls onto the floor. Even Elisabeth's baby doll. She immediately ran to her fallen child and picked her up, hurried to me, and thrust the doll to my breast. She then gave her brother a dirty look."
About Elisabeth, 63rd week or 14 months

Show Understanding for "Irrational" Fears

When your toddler is busy becoming more comfortable in the world of principles, they will encounter things and situations that are new and foreign to them. They will experience their world in new ways, some that feel dangerous. They can't articulate these fears to their parents, and only when they are better able to understand what is happening will they be less fearful. Keep this in mind if you're feeling that they are irrationally scared of something, and show sympathy.

> "James is scared of his sister's ducky. He walks around it if it's in the way. When he grabs it, he drops it immediately."
> **About James, 66th week or 15 months**
>
> "She is afraid to sit in the bathtub by herself; she yells and screeches. We don't know the reason. She wants to get in, provided one of us joins her."
> **About Josie, 67th week or 15 months**

Learning the Rules

Whining to get one's way, childish behavior like constantly needing to be entertained or asking for a pacifier, being messy without any cause, not being careful and intentionally hurting others, going out of their way to be naughty—your little one is really pushing your buttons. You may wonder if you're the only one that is having such behavioral troubles. Rest assured that you are not. That said, your toddler is no longer a baby, and it's a reasonable time to lay down some ground rules. Your toddler is ready for you to start asking and expecting more from them. What's more: they are searching for these boundaries.

Now that they have entered the world of principles, they yearn for rules. They are looking for your guidance on what is acceptable and what is not. Give them a chance to familiarize themselves with rules. Social rules are particularly important, as they will not be able to figure out how to behave in these situations, with other people, unless you show them. There is no harm in laying down the law. On the contrary, you owe it to them, and who better to do it than someone who loves them?

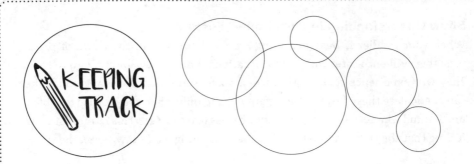

YOUR FAVORITE GAMES: THE WORLD OF PRINCIPLES

These are games and activities that your toddler may like now and that help them practice their newly developing skills.

Instructions to Fill In This List:

Check off your toddler's favorite games. After filling in the What You've Discovered: The World of Principles, see if there is a link between the things that most interested your child during this leap and the games they liked best. You may have to think about it, but you will gain a unique insight into your toddler's personality.

SKILLFULNESS

In the world of principles, toddlers thoroughly enjoy endlessly practicing variations and experimenting with programs. By doing so, they become skillful and discover how and when they can best get things done. They are also keen observers.

☐ You like physical games, such as:
- ☐ Running
- ☐ Climbing
- ☐ Chasing other children
- ☐ Walking over a mattress/waterbed/other soft surfaces, and then letting yourself fall down
- ☐ Doing somersaults
- ☐ Rolling on the floor
- ☐ Play-wrestling with other children
- ☐ Playing "I'll get you"

- ☐ Walking and balancing on ledges
- ☐ Jumping off something
- ☐ Other:

  _____

  _____

☐ Exploring the outdoors
  - ☐ Roaming around and scouting about
  - ☐ Inspecting and experimenting with anything you find outdoors
  - ☐ The zoo, especially a petting zoo
  - ☐ The playground
  - ☐ Looking around while being carried on my back or when on the bike

☐ Pointing games/Where is . . . ? games. For example:

  Body parts: _____

  Toys: _____

  People: _____

  Animals: _____

☐ Games using hands and feet with singing and rhyming. Your favorite songs with gestures are:

  _____

  _____

  _____

  _____

☐ Calling games

  You call out to me, I call out to you. You feel proud hearing your name and it makes you feel like you count.

KIDDING AROUND

In the world of principles, kidding around and joking will start to play a more important role in daily life. By now, your toddler has figured out how things work to some degree. So when things get out of whack, they really get a kick out of it, whether it's someone acting in a silly or unexpected way or bending the rules.

☐ Being silly, and watching others being silly
You cracked up when:

_____

_____

_____

☐ Watching children's TV programs or looking at books where the characters do something silly, or when something unexpected happens

HOUSEHOLD GAMES

In the world of principles, your child reenacts the daily business in the family and beyond. Give them the opportunity to do this and play along with them sometimes. It makes your toddler feel they are part of the club. Sometimes they may surprise you by actually helping!

☐ Cooking
When I give you some small bowls, a bowl of water, and a few little pieces of real food, you mush it up and feed me or your doll, for instance.

☐ Vacuuming
Vacuuming back and forth with a real vacuum or toy one.

☐ Doing the dishes
Perhaps the plate won't be clean enough to eat from, but you enjoy playing with the water and soap, and giving everything a good stir with the brush.

GAMES WITH EMOTIONS

Your toddler will be experimenting with emotions, such as varying their expressions when they greet people or when they want something. Play along—for instance, by taking time for the greeting. Or you can imitate their emotions and play at being excited or pitiful. It will probably make them laugh.

☐ Pulling silly faces to display emotions
☐ Imitating emoticons

HIDE-AND-SEEK

☐ Yourselves
☐ Things

YOUR FAVORITE TOYS

☐ Jungle gyms, slides with steps
☐ Balls
☐ Books
☐ Sandbox
☐ Tea sets with water or cold tea in cups and mugs

☐ Puzzles
☐ Plastic bottles
☐ Household utensils
☐ Toy vacuum
☐ Toy on a string
☐ Cartoons

Experience the World Through Your Baby's Eyes

We grown-ups often take the little things for granted. Try to rediscover the little joys that are great joys for your little one now. Let yourself fall on a mattress; walk on little walls, practicing your balance . . . love life and all that it has to give!

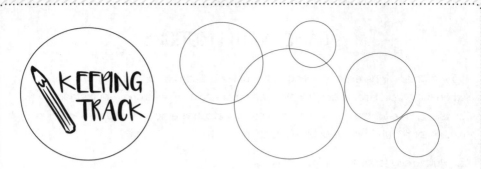

WHAT YOU'VE DISCOVERED: THE WORLD OF PRINCIPLES

This is a list of skills that your toddler can display from this age. For clarity: your toddler will not do everything listed.

Instructions to Fill In This List:

Every parent with a child making this leap will notice a lot of changes. This is a large and intense leap. Remember, we have only described some examples and your child may do other, similar skills. Take the time to observe your child carefully and write down the choices they make.

You made this leap on: _____

On _____ the sun broke through again and now, at the end of the leap, I see you can do these new things.

YOU CAN DO THIS NOW, OR BETTER THAN BEFORE

Date:

☐ You are getting better at eating and drinking by yourself. It's a lot better all of a sudden.

☐ You walk more adeptly and get around quickly.

☐ You build more stable, higher block towers than before.

☐ You can now put things together, such as:

_____

_____

- ☐ You throw with greater accuracy now.
- ☐ Even though it looks like you are just scouting around outside, you are clearly exploring everything.

THINKING UP AND CARRYING OUT PHYSICAL STRATEGIES

Date:

- ☐ You are trying out strategies with your body. You use your body to show something or to experiment.
    - ☐ You use body language to show you are clever/quick/funny.
    - ☐ You seem more reckless and take more risks than you did.
    - ☐ Other:

    _____

    _____

- ☐ You experiment with ramps and slopes. For example, you run your finger over them or let a toy slide off them.
- ☐ I can see you wondering: shall I do it carefully or recklessly? For instance, one moment you decide to place a cup on the table carefully, and the next, you throw it down on the table or floor. It is not so much about the cup, but about the different ways of doing things with your body and the effect your actions have.
- ☐ You experiment with stashing and recovering objects.
- ☐ You experiment with crawling in or behind something and getting out again.
- ☐ You like endlessly repeating things, and sometimes you practice variations to experiment with physical strategies, such as:

    _____

    _____

    _____

LEAP 9

MAKING UP SOCIAL STRATEGIES

Date:

☐ You choose consciously.

☐ You take initiatives.

☐ You think ahead. I notice that through:

_____

_____

_____

☐ You like observing grown-ups.

☐ You like observing children.

☐ You experiment with the meaning and use of "yes" and "no."

☐ You like playing tricks on me. For instance, you pretend you are being disobedient.

☐ You play jokes to get others to do something.

☐ You are or try to be helpful more often.

☐ More often than before, you accept that you are still small, require help, and therefore must listen to me. You grasp, for instance, that streets are dangerous and therefore we must walk hand in hand.

☐ You make use of others to get something done that you are otherwise unable to do yourself and that I wouldn't do for you. For instance, you get someone to give you a forbidden cookie from a high shelf.

☐ You are or do your best to be obedient more often now.

☐ You are extra sweet to get your way more often than before.

☐ These are four examples of how I see you choosing a strategy to get what you want:

Your goal:	Your strategy:	Date:

☐ I have given you these opportunities to experiment with strategies:

_____

_____

_____

_____

☐ You like endless repetition and sometimes you vary things to experiment with social strategies, such as:

_____

_____

_____

_____

IF YOUR STRATEGY DOESN'T WORK ... TANTRUMS

Date:

☐ More often than before, you try to get your way by having a tantrum.

☐ More often than before, you show your feelings through having a tantrum.

☐ When I showed you that a certain strategy doesn't work, or it caused the opposite effect, you responded and changed your strategy.

Your old strategy: How I corrected you: You used this new strategy:

☐ Anger
☐ Nagging
☐ Whining
☐ Other:

_____

_____

MAKING CHOICES: WHAT DO I WANT, AND HOW AM I GOING TO PHYSICALLY DO THAT?

Date:

☐ You experiment with things: what you can do with them and how you do that.

☐ You are or try to be cautious and careful more often than before.

☐ You experiment with your body. When you are doing something, I can see you thinking how you are going to do it. I can see you thinking: "How do I go down the stairs? "How do I get off the couch?" "What ways can I use to climb on something else?"

☐ You copy fine motor skills you see others doing, like holding a pencil.

☐ You imitate things that surprise you, like someone on a pogo stick.

☐ You try out what ways you can do all kinds of physical antics.

☐ You like gross motoric actions, like somersaults or climbing

MAKING SOCIAL CHOICES: WHAT AND HOW?

Date:

☐ You are busy making choices all day long.

☐ When you want to reach a goal, you can be:
    ☐ Careful
    ☐ Reckless
    ☐ Pushy
    ☐ Angry
    ☐ Extra sweet, giving kisses
    ☐ Very helpful
    ☐ Pitiful, hoping for sympathy
    ☐ Other:

_____

_____

☐ These are examples of how I saw you applying "what do I want, how do I get it?"

What you wanted: How you wanted to achieve that:

_____

_____

_____

☐ You imitate sweet/aggressive/_____ /_____

/_____ behavior

☐ You imitate what you have seen on TV or in a book.

☐ You sometimes play with emotions. You are teaching yourself to act!

OWN WILL

Date:

☐ You want a say in what others are doing.

☐ You have a strong desire to belong, to be accepted.

☐ You are possessive with toys.

☐ You want a say, even if not in words, when we are going to do something. You want to show us that you also have an opinion and count.

☐ You do what you feel like; you go your own way more often than before.

FEARS

Date:

☐ You suddenly have an "irrational" fear of:

_____

_____

_____

LANGUAGE

Date:

☐ You understand adults talking to each other better than before.

☐ You understand what we are saying to you better than before.

☐ You understand brief instructions better and follow them enthusiastically.

☐ When I ask you: "Where is your . . . ?" you point to the object.

☐ You can still only say single words (not sentences).

☐ You imitate animal sounds.

☐ You copy a variety of other sounds, better and more often than before.

☐ You understand what I am saying better now and can even answer sometimes:

I said: _____

You answered: _____

I said: _____

You answered: _____

I said: _____

You answered: _____

THE "TEENAGE TODDLER" PHASE

The degree to which you understand the "negative" strategies your toddler uses, the way you react to them, and the opportunities you give your child to experiment with a variety of strategies will greatly affect the time ahead. This so-called teenage toddler phase—also called the phase of nagging and more nagging—doesn't have to be so terrible if you start guiding your child in time and show them the right way. So take the time to observe your child, correct them, and give them room to find the right, positive strategies that do produce the desired effect. By filling in What You've Discovered: The World of Principles (page 388), you will learn more about your toddler's personality, but you will also gain insight into your role as a parent.

THE EASY PERIOD: AFTER THE LEAP

Around 66 weeks, or just over 15 months, most toddlers become a little less troublesome than they were. They are bigger and have grown wiser and are joining in with the daily activities. You sometimes forget that they are still very young.

"He looks slimmer, less stocky, his face thinner; he is growing up. I sometimes see him sitting calmly, focused on his food. He seems rather mature then."
About Luke, 66th week or 15 months

"Everything comes easier to her now, from feeding herself to cleaning up. She is really just like the rest of us. I keep forgetting that she is still a very small child."
About Eve, 67th week or 15 months

LEAP 9

Leap 10

The World of Systems

THE CONSCIENCE EMERGES

Since the previous leap, your toddler has started to understand what "principles" are. They rose above the previous confines of "programs," and they shed their mechanical character. For the first time, they were able to evaluate existing programs and even to change them. You could see them constantly changing programs, then studying the effects. You could also see them performing physical antics, exploring the great outdoors, getting skillful with objects and language, imitating others, replaying the day-to-day, trying out emotions, beginning to think ahead, staging their own dramas, insisting on having their say, using aggression, learning what's theirs and what's not, using pranks as a strategy to an end, experimenting with "yes" and "no," being resourceful by putting people on the spot, learning to cooperate, wanting to help out around the house, and experimenting with being reckless and being careful.

Just as the toddler's programs were mechanical before they rose to new heights, their principles were also lacking a certain flexibility. They were only able to apply them in set ways, always the same, regardless of the situation.

We adults are capable of adjusting our principles to fit different circumstances. We are able to see a bigger picture. We see how certain principles are linked and form an entire system. The concept "system" encompasses our idea of an organized unit. We use the term "system" if the parts it comprises are interdependent and function as a whole. There are tangible examples, such as a grandfather clock that needs winding, an electrical network, or the human muscle system. These systems form a coherent set of principles of gear ratios, electric amps and volts, and balanced muscle tensions, respectively.

There are examples that are less tangible. Take human organizations: they are arranged on the basis of principles that you cannot always put your finger on. There are rules (or agreements) for duties assigned to certain positions, rules for social behavior like being on time, and rules for learning the goals imposed by your boss. To name just a few examples of human organizations, take the bakery, the hairdresser, Scouts, families, drama clubs, police stations, the church, our society, our culture, and the law.

When your toddler makes their next leap, they will land in the world of systems. For the first time in their life they will perceive "systems." Of course, it's all new to them. They will need a number of years before they fully understand what our society, our culture, or the law really entail. They start with the basics and stay close to home. They develop the idea of themselves as a system, and that together with Mom and Dad they form a family. And their family is not the same as their little friend's, nor is their house the same as their neighbor's house.

Just as your child learned to be more flexible with programs after they made the leap into the world of principles, after leaping into the world of systems they start being more flexible in how they apply principles. Now they begin to understand that they can choose what they want to be: honest, helpful, careful, patient, and so forth. To be or not to be: that is the question. They apply principles less rigidly and start to learn how they can refine their approach to all sorts of different circumstances.

Around 75 weeks, or 17 months and a week, you usually notice that your little one starts trying new things. However, they already felt the leap into the world of systems coming at an earlier age. From week 71, or just over 16 months onward, your toddler notices their world is changing. A maze of new impressions turns their familiar reality on its head. They cannot process the novelty all at once. First, they will have to create order out of the chaos. They return to a familiar and safe base. They exhibit crying, clinginess, and crankiness. They need a good dose of "mommy or daddy time" to create order in this 10th new world that opens up when they take this leap.

DO REMEMBER

If you notice your toddler is fussier than usual, watch them closely. It's likely that they're attempting to master new skills. Have a look at What You've Discovered: The World of Systems on page 473 to see what to expect.

THE FUSSY PHASE:
THE ANNOUNCEMENT OF THE MAGICAL LEAP

In this chapter, we are no longer going to describe in detail the clues that tell you that your toddler is about to make a developmental leap. These will be familiar to you by now. For this reason, we are only repeating the following list as a memory aid. Remember that your toddler is only after being near you and having your undivided attention. They are also much bigger and smarter now and more capable of finding new ways to achieve these same goals.

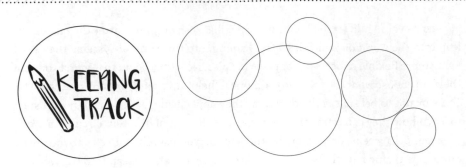

LEAP SIGNS

This is how you let me know the leap has started:

☐ You cry more often.

☐ You are more often cranky, grumpy, or whiny than before.

☐ You are cheerful one moment and cry the next.

☐ You want to be kept occupied more often than usual.

☐ You want to be near me all the time.

☐ You protest immediately if I break physical contact.

☐ You act unusually sweet.

☐ You are mischievous.

☐ You throw temper tantrums, or throw them more often than before.

☐ You are newly jealous, or act jealous more often than before.

☐ You are shy with strangers more than I am used to seeing.

☐ You sleep poorly.

☐ You sit there, quietly daydreaming, more often than before.

☐ You reach for a soft toy, or do so more often than before.

☐ You are more babyish again.

☐ And I notice that you: _____

Do remember that your toddler may exhibit only a few of the characteristics listed. How many your toddler displays is not important; it's about which ones you see.

How Are *You* Doing?

Initially, when your baby became clingy, cranky, and cried more often than usual, your sole concern was that something was wrong with them. By the time they were six months old, you began to become increasingly annoyed when it became clear that nothing was wrong, but generally, you let it pass. After all, they were so tiny then. After their first birthday, you started to take action if you were annoyed and that sometimes resulted in quarrels with your toddler. You were able to enjoy the true pleasures of parenthood! With this leap, all parents report that they quarrel with their "teenage" toddler. Teens have been known to have the ability to make life rotten for their parents. Toddlers can do it, too. It gives you a preview of what is to come 10 years down the line. It's part of the bargain.

> *This too shall pass: one of my least favorite phrases.*
>
> *I know it's well meaning, but when you're in the thick of it, it can feel minimizing. My littlest is currently in a huge leap (last and final Leap 10), and it's a real doozy. And yes, I know this will pass, it always does, but right now it's hard. Only wanting mommy, clinging to me all day, screaming if others attempt to hold her, waking up and screaming during the night. It's exhausting!*
>
> *I'm not looking for pity, mom-life is hard and exhausting and rewarding and I get all of that. But sometimes it is just really hard. And yes, it will pass, but right now I need empathic listening. Validation. And maybe a hot meal, cuz let's be real, cooking with a crying clinging toddler is no picnic.*—**Instagram post**

LEAP 10

ANCHOR MOMENTS *

We hope you made a habit of allowing yourself to have some anchor moments. If not . . . it's never too late!

In 5 minutes: Do a small warm-up of your body, even if you're not going to exercise. Stand in a comfortable and stable position, and do some dynamic or static stretches. Make sure to activate—stretch—each part of your body.

In 10 minutes: Journal reflecting. Sit down and write down five things that make you happy, four things you are grateful for, three things that make you laugh, two things you are proud of, and one thing you are allowing or giving to yourself today because you are such an awesome person.

More time: Try not to spend your free time planning the next day or your next tasks. Spend your free time reading a book, doing arts and crafts, writing in a journal. Be consciously aware of the fact that this is an anchor moment for you and that making a plan is not part of an anchor moment.

Your Toddler's New Ability Is Starting to Bear Fruit

Around 75 weeks, or 17 months, you will notice that most of the clinginess disappears. The temper tantrums and quarreling with your "teenage" toddler subside. They're back to their enterprising selves. You may notice that they've changed, that their behavior is different, that they are becoming very aware of themselves as a person, that they think differently, and that they have a better sense of time than ever before. They play with their toys differently and their use of fantasy takes off. Their humor has changed. This change is evident because at this age your toddler's ability to perceive systems and to apply the concept of systems is emerging, and your toddler is starting to choose the new skills that best suit them at this time. Your toddler, with their talents, preferences, and temperament, chooses where they will start exploring. Try to understand what they are doing and help them. But watch out! They want to do it all by themselves.

* For more anchor moments, see page 36.

> *"When we spend dad and son time together, I notice I have more patience."*
> **About Gregory, 74th week or 17 months**

> *"Things went much easier with her, although she is very stubborn and needs a lot of attention."*
> **About Juliette, 75th week or 17 months**

The World of Systems

When your child enters the world of systems, they are mastering their own ability to adjust principles to changing circumstances. They no longer apply principles as rigidly as before; they apply them with flexibility. For instance, they are now able to choose to apply a moral principle, or not. From this age, you can see that they develop the earliest beginnings of a conscience, of systematically applying values and norms.

> *"She jumps when we catch her doing something she's not allowed. Then she blurts out, 'No.'"*
> **About Jenny, 73rd week or 16 months**

The system your child lives with day in and day out is the one they themselves know best—themselves. They are their own person. When the world of systems opens up to them, they start to develop their notion of self, and self-consciousness. This has several consequences. Your child now discovers that they own and control their own body. They also discover that they can orchestrate things, that they can do things by themselves, that they can control things around themselves, and that they can make decisions, all things that stem from their growing concept of self.

> *"Now he expressly does things differently than is expected or asked of him. For instance, if you ask him: 'Give Mom a kiss?' he gives everyone a kiss, walks to me, and says: 'Hahahahaha' and doesn't give me a kiss. It seems to me that he wants to show that he's his own person. That he's no longer one with me, but a separate person. That's all."*
> **About Thomas, 80th week or 18 months**

Your toddler begins to understand that their parents are separate people. They start using terms such as "you" and "me" and are also very interested in the body of the person or people they see the most. A boy discovers that he has a penis just like his father. They size up all the similarities and differences. For the first time in their life, your toddler can put themselves in someone else's place, now they realize that they are an individual, and that the other person is, too. For the first time, they see that not everyone likes the same things as they do. That would have never occurred to them when they were younger. We can sum this up with one elegant word: they have become less "egocentric." That has all sorts of consequences. They are now able to comfort someone. They are at their high point in mimicry; they copy anything and everything around them. Their imagination comes to life.

Your explorer is also fascinated by other living creatures: ants, dogs, and so forth. They are all systems, too.

Your "teenage" toddler starts realizing that they are part of a family, and that their family is different from their little friend's family, whom they visit twice a week. After all, their family is the first human organization they get to know from the inside, and they will definitely notice that their little friend's family doesn't necessarily have to eat a savory sandwich before starting on the sweet stuff. In their family, they have a different set of rules.

Just as your toddler recognizes their family as a system, they begin to distinguish their family from other families. They already do the same with their friends, house, and neighborhood. They are getting better at finding their way around in the familiar surroundings outside their house.

They start paying great attention to their clothes. They can be quite vain and are very possessive of their toys.

Your little artist starts to create art with a capital *A*. They no longer scribble; now they draw "horses," "boats," and "themselves." They can also begin to appreciate music—that, too, is a system.

Your toddler starts to develop a sense of time. They are now better able to recall past experiences and have a better understanding of what the future will bring.

They will now begin forming their first sentences. Not every toddler does this, though. Just as with other skills, the age at which children start with a certain skill differs greatly from one child to the next. All toddlers now understand much of what you say to them, but some only say a few words. Others use many words and constantly mime, but don't produce sentences yet. A few, though, do speak in sentences. Whether your toddler does partly depends on how you interact with them.

To clarify what we mean by a system, a few examples from the adult world will help.

Take, for instance, practicing mathematics. On the level of programs, we think, use logic, and handle mathematical symbols. On the level of principles, we think about thinking and therefore we think about how we use mathematics. On the systems level, we look at mathematics as a whole, as an intellectual system.

In a similar way, the science of physics is a large system consisting of carefully discovered principles. This also applies to the science of biology and the theory of evolution and the accompanying principles of natural selection. This applies to other sciences as well.

Worldviews or outlooks on life are also systems. Our everyday lives offer examples of systems. Our approach to diet leads us to formulate principles regarding food, which in turn determines our eating programs. The same applies to our beliefs about the function of sleep, and our opinions on how our society is functioning economically. Another example of a system is democracy. Just as with other human organizations, some aspects are tangible and demonstrable, whereas others are very transient. By the time someone else is able to see something the same way you do, the situation could have changed completely. We can point to government buildings, to the annual budget being presented, or employee hiring practices. What we are unable to do is point to authority, cooperation, backroom politics, compromises, or organization in general. You can point to what you think is evidence of the existence of these, but you can't demonstrate them as easily as you can something simple and tangible, such as a rock.

Other examples of human organizations as systems are families, schools, churches, banks, factories, armies, governments, soccer clubs, and bridge clubs. Such social institutions have the important task of encouraging their members to familiarize themselves with their goals, norms, and values. Some institutions insist on it. In the family, it's called socialization. In the family unit, learning values, norms, and other principles is practically automatic because toddlers imitate anything and everything they see. There are also countless learning opportunities, where such things are often not emphasized, but acted out as a matter of course.

This may seem different from a system like physics or mathematics. "That's far too advanced for such a little guy," most people will say. "They won't learn that until high school." But when you observe your toddler playing, when you see how they hold a ball underwater again and again to see it fly up out of the water, when you watch them endlessly rolling things down an incline or running up and down an incline again and again, you can't ignore that they are experimenting with the fundamental principles of physics to establish systems of their own in their mind, which puts them in good company. It was Newton himself who once experimented with something as simple as a falling apple. Perhaps it wouldn't be a bad idea for physics teachers to seek advice from toddlers at play to come up with a few good demonstrations for their classes.

This applies to other systems as well as those of physics and math. A toddler is also interested in basic architecture. They can watch builders for hours or imitate one of their parents making cement. They mix water and sand the whole day long and then they start "plastering walls." Their constructions have also become more complex. For instance, they can lay down train tracks and run their trains along them.

BRAIN CHANGES

Between 16 and 24 months, the number of synapses in the cerebrum vastly increases, both within the various subareas of the cerebrum and in between those subareas. In the second half of the second year, a part of the cerebrum behind the forehead matures (the orbitofrontal lobe), and a cascade of new skills emerge. The right half of the brain develops in leaps and bounds in the first year and a half. Then development in the left half of the brain, where the language centers reside, takes over. As far as the comprehension of single words is concerned, at 20 months, a confinement takes place from the whole cerebrum to a few small areas in the left half.

TODDLERS ARE LIKE THIS

Toddlers love anything new, and it's important to respond when you notice any new skills or interests. They will enjoy it if you share these new discoveries, and this will accelerate their learning progress.

Experience the World Through Your Toddler's Eyes

You could say that we are actually quite boring. We don't even notice many of the amazing and amusing things that surround us anymore; we take a lot for granted. And that's a shame. When you take the time to look around you, you will understand how wonderful your child's world is, what fascinates them, and what they enjoy. So it is time to rediscover the child within you. Try the following things; they are a lot of fun to do. There is actually an Einstein in all of us.

- Stand on a threshold and rock back and forth. Feel the difference in height.

- Put your finger slowly into a cup of water and see how the water rises. Take your finger out and see how the water goes back down.

- Put some soap in water, take a straw, and blow soapy bubbles.

- Place your arm on a table, pull it back slowly, and feel how your arm slides off the table. Make circles with your head and feel how it is first slow and then speeds up when your head falls forward. Feel the extra effort it takes to heave your head up the "slope" of your shoulders and how easy your head goes down the "slope."

THE MAGICAL LEAP FORWARD: THE DISCOVERY OF THE NEW WORLD

In the world of systems, your toddler will discover that they can choose their principles. They will discover themselves, their family, their friends, their house, their neighborhood, their art, and more. Give your toddler the opportunity to experience all sorts of systems. They learn how the world of systems is made up through their ingenuity, from seeing your reactions, and through much practice.

A WORD ABOUT SYSTEMS

When reading the short description of this leap, you may have had to reread a few of the sentences to really grasp what a "system" is. Imagine then how difficult it is for a toddler to perceive and understand systems. It is almost impossible to explain, but it is easier if you have a few concrete examples. Therefore, we have included lots of examples in this chapter in the form of quotes from parents talking about their toddlers. They will give you an idea of how broad and diverse the new perceptual world of systems is. We could have included hundreds more examples, but by reading these parents' experiences, you will get an idea of what to look out for. And you will soon realize that toddlers can do more than we think.

Me and My Conscience

The conscience is a system of moral principles, of norms and rules. The development of a conscience is not to be taken for granted. Your toddler has to construct their conscience using examples they encounter and the feedback you give them. You must demonstrate right and wrong. It takes time, a lot of time, before your toddler has seen enough examples from which to draw conclusions. Hopefully, your actions have been consistent. If you say one thing one time and something else another, it will take your toddler much longer. The same applies if you give them confusing signals. They will not be able to figure it all out. From this age on, your little control freak tries to discover a system in everything, especially in norms and rules. They crave rules and test the boundaries. Just as they are entitled to their daily meals, likewise they are entitled to their daily portion of rules.

"She knows that the things on the top shelf of the closet are her brother's. Now she climbs in the closet to grab and sneak something out. If she's seen, she drops it and looks at you with a look of 'How did that get there?'"
About Victoria, 76th week or 17 months

"He imitates everything he sees on TV. For instance, he falls to the floor on purpose, and in one film, he saw children fighting. He observed this and hit himself."
About Thomas, 80th week or 18 months

"I also noticed that he wouldn't listen and he's behaving badly. I've never seen him like this. He hit someone on the head for no reason and threw another to the ground by his T-shirt. It's very irritating and a couple of times I have gotten really angry. I keep explaining that it hurts if he does that. Maybe I talk to him too much, so that he only listens when he wants. It has no effect on him if I tell him he can't do something or I ask him to help with something. I figured out that I just need to go over to him, then say that we need to do the chore together. Like putting a bottle back where it belongs instead of just throwing it."

About Jim, 81st week or 18 months

"I noticed if Taylor falls down, he doesn't cry too quickly and takes his bumps well. But if he thinks that he's corrected unfairly, he's very hurt and confused. For instance, he bawled because he wasn't allowed on the bed with his boots. I said it was fine because they were clean, but our sitter Ellen didn't know and didn't understand. I could tell from the way he cried that it really upset and hurt him, even though it wasn't that big of a deal. I rarely hear him like that. I do hear the same cry after he has been staying with his father, who tells him yes where I say no."

About Taylor, 81st week or 18 months

"He is now able to 'lie.' For instance, when eating a cookie at a party and his mouth is covered in chocolate and someone hands out more tasty treats, he quickly hides the cookie in his hand behind his back and says that he hasn't gotten one yet. If he is allowed to take another one, he laughs and then shows the one he already had in his hand."

About Thomas, 87th week or 20 months

Me and My Notion of Self

The system your toddler comes into contact with the most is themselves. That is the system they get to know first, and it has all sorts of consequences. Your toddler discovers that they own their body and that they have control over their own body. They also discover that they can make things happen, that they have their own will and can make their own decisions, and that they have power to influence. They think in terms of me, me, me.

Below you can read about other parents' experiences divided up into the categories: "Me and my body," "I have control over my body," "I can do it myself," "I have my own will," "I can decide for myself," and "I want power." One by one, they will help you understand your toddler better and see how they deal with their new ability to perceive systems.

Me and My Body

When toddlers make this leap, it is like they are discovering their body and their body parts all over again. They experiment with how their body feels and what they can do with it. This is clear from the following experiences shared by other parents.

"He is very interested in his 'weenie.' He plucks at it and rubs it whenever he can. I often let him walk around naked."
About Mark, 72nd week or 16 months

"It seems as if she has rediscovered her toes. She studies them bit by bit, for minutes at a time."
About Victoria, 73rd week or 16 months

"She calls herself Mita. She gave herself that name."
About Victoria, 75th week or 17 months

"Often he hits his head hard against the wall. It makes me feel ill. I'd like him to stop. I think he does it to experience his notion of self."
About Kevin, 76th week or around 17 months

"No one is allowed to touch him. Not the doctor while weighing and measuring him, nor the hairdresser, even though she was a friend. Not even his grandma while getting dressed."
About Matt, 82nd week or 18 months

"She also says: 'Is me.' "
About Hannah, 83rd week or 19 months

"If anyone says to him: 'Nice curls,' he runs his hands through his hair like the star in the movie Grease."
About Thomas, 86th week or 20 months

I Have Control Over My Body

With this new ability to perceive systems, your toddler will be eager to try out new ways of using their body for antics, feats, and acrobatics. It can be unsettling for parents. Not only is your toddler exercising their little body, they are busy experimenting with these movements as systems and observing their effect. These antics are both a physical and mental exercise. The following examples from parents give you an idea of what you can expect.

"He goes up the stairs with a straight body, taking big steps. That means: right foot on one step and the left foot on the next, and so on."
About Bob, 72nd week or 16 months

"I already got angry once this week. She climbed up a dangerous flight of stairs after I'd already forbidden it."
About Eve, 74th week or 17 months

"She finds all kinds of ways to get to where she's not allowed. I have put certain things away and protected others. That's no use anymore. She finds a way to get to them. Even if she needs to drag over a chair or get a ladder."
About Victoria, 76th week or 17 months

"She learned to somersault, slide down the slide by herself, and climb back up by herself. She now gets in and out of bed by herself."
About Nora, 81st to 83rd weeks or 18 to 19 months

"He keeps jumping from high places. It makes him feel good if he thinks he can do it. When he can't, he says, 'Scary,' and sticks his arms out, which says: 'It's too high for me, can we do it together?' He also likes to walk along little walls, practicing his balance. He enjoys it if the wall is about four feet tall. I act calm, but inside it scares me."
About Luke, 83rd to 86th weeks or 19 to 20 months

I Can Do It Myself

Prepare yourself, toddlers are all about "Me do it," and that is actually a positive and natural development. But for parents, it can be a scary time. Where are the limits? How much do you allow them to do and what should you do for them? The golden rule is: if it is dangerous, you do it. If something is simply frustrating for your toddler because they are not (yet) able to do it or they have to put in some effort to do it, then let them do it for themselves. They learn from that frustration and effort. More than that, frustration and effort are essential to teach your toddler that in life you need to try and do your best to achieve something. However, having said that, too much frustration can hurt your child's self-confidence. So help them along by making things easier but allow them to do the rest themselves. This is about "facilitating parenting," remember?

Mind you, a toddler will need longer to work things out than you do, and that is normal. Give your child time, be patient, and don't try to rush them or do it yourself to speed things along. If you do that, you are basically telling them they aren't good enough and you can do it better.

The following are numerous examples from parents that may inspire you to observe your child carefully during this leap and see how they handle this new ability.

"She peels and eats an orange by herself, opens doors, and can say her own name. She winds up her toy radio herself and walks around with it against her ear."
About Juliette, 72nd week or 16 months

"She doesn't want to sit in her high chair much anymore. She wants to sit in a normal chair at the dinner table. Also, she doesn't want to wear a bib and she wants to feed herself."
About Julia, 73rd to 75th weeks or 17 months

"This week he walked around with napkins. He used them as a bib or towel, but particularly as an oven glove. I mean, when he goes to pick up something, he puts the napkin on top and then picks the thing up. He mainly did this in the kitchen with the grips on the drawers."
About Paul, 74th week or 17 months

"Now it's not about me showing him what we are eating and telling him what it's called. He looks and identifies it himself. Playing with the bucket with the shape-sorting lid has taken on a new twist. It's now about him putting the pieces in as he wants. He purposefully tries to ram the shapes through the wrong holes. If he accidentallly puts one in the proper hole, he quickly pulls it out. He wants to put the pieces in as he sees fit, not according to the rules of the game."
About Frankie, 76th week or 17 months

"If I ask, 'Do you want Mom to do it?' she says: 'No, Anna.' Even if she has broken something and we ask who has done it, she says: 'Anna.' She is very conscious of herself. She laughs if she drops something or throws something on the ground."
About Anna, 77th week or 17 months

"He can now function as an 'errand boy.' He gets whatever is asked of him. He gets the remote control, the newspaper, socks. He gets the shoes. Gets the cleaning products. And if he and Dad are playing the flight simulator on the computer, he follows his commands: 'Gas!'—'Landing gear!'—'Eject!' I am proud of my big little boy. He really gives it his all and does everything asked of him right away."
About Thomas, 80th week or 18 months

"She is able to arrange the colors. She saw that one of the markers had the wrong color top on it."
About Victoria, 84th week or 19 months

"He can blow his nose. Now he tries to blow his nose into everything, even the coasters."
About Gregory, 88th week or 20 months

Me and My Toilet Training

Many toddlers are now occupied with their body in the form of toilet training. Make it as easy as possible for them to use the potty. Place potties all over the house (in set places) and let them walk around without any clothes on as often as you can. When they feel the need to use the potty, they have to be able to get there fast. Be patient and don't force anything.

"She gets onto the potty herself if she's already naked. If she's wearing pants, she does it in her pants, but tells us right away."
About Hannah, 87th week or 20 months

"Now and again, she wants to use her potty. She sits down for a second and goes to wiping furiously, but has yet to do anything on the potty."
About Eve, 85th week or 19 months

"Our daughter grasps that she can use her potty to do her business. Twice she went and sat down with a diaper on and relieved herself."
About Josie, 73rd week or 17 months

"This week he came walking up proudly with a full potty. I was just as proud as he was. If he goes around without a diaper, he's indicating that he wants to use his potty or he sits on it before I even know about it. He waits to pee until he has the potty. He uses all his might to do a number two and every little bit must be flushed down the toilet. Endearing. Then he says, 'More.' That means he wants to use it again. When he's all done, he says, 'Finished.' "
About Mark, 78th to 79th weeks or 18 months

"He likes to walk around naked after his bath. Then he crouches down and strains to go pee. Once, he peed in his closet."
About Robin, 82nd week or 19 months

I Have My Own Will

"Teenage" toddlers are known for their nagging, moodiness, and "I want." You probably don't need us to tell you that this phase is now in full swing. The pushiness and "I want" often arise from frustrations when toddlers explore the world of systems. Here you can read a few quotes from parents as their toddlers go through the changes with this leap of systems.

"The last few months he's been naughty and has been testing the waters to see what's allowed and what's not, as well as the consequences. At the moment, he knows full well what's allowed. Now he's just naughty to show: 'I do what I want. So what are you going to do about it?'"

About Harry, 76th week or 17 months

"He doesn't listen to warnings anymore. It looks as if he's proclaiming that he knows what he's doing. Experimenting has taken priority: falling down, heat, strong spices, etc. He decides what he eats, when, and how."

About Matt, 76th week or 17 months

"He gets into everything, but I have to keep a close watch on him because what he's doing is too dangerous or because he's testing the boundaries of what is and is not allowed. He tried to light the stove with a hot pan on it. It really made me jump. He certainly got a real, physical warning. I hope it's sunk in that he's not allowed to touch the gas. It's really fun to cook together, but if he hasn't learned his lesson, we'll no longer be able to."

About Steven, 78th week or 18 months

"Recently, she has abandoned her toys for the things that she's not allowed to touch, like the tablet."

About Laura, 78th week or 18 months

"He is a real clown. He pays no mind to anything, just does his own thing. He loves to kid around. We call him the 'little elf."

About James, 80th week or 18 months

"Her personal awareness grows daily. She indicates what she wants and what she doesn't want. She blows kisses when bidding farewell, and if she gives something to you, it's a conscious decision."

About Ashley, 83rd to 86th week or 19 to 20 months

I Can Decide for Myself

Now that your toddler has discovered their sense of self, they realize they can make their own decisions, and that is what they are busy doing now. These examples from other parents will give you an idea of what you should pay attention to as your toddler exercises the ability to decide for themselves.

"She starts to laugh already when she's planning something naughty."
About Eve, 76th week or 17 months

"He announces everything he does. He always points to himself."
About Kevin, 76th week or 17 months

"She really knows that it's 'yucky' when she has messed her pants. She comes up and says, 'Yucky.' If she can choose the spot where she gets changed, then she doesn't make a scene and will consent to it. She finds the strangest spots to be changed. Changing clothes is the same: 'Find your spot,' and there she goes."
About Nora, 86th week or 20 months

"He wants to pick out his own clothes these days. He really has certain preferences. His comfortable jogging pants with mice print is 'out.' Sometimes he puts Daddy's jacket on with a tie and goes and wakes Mom up."
About Thomas, 86th week or 20 months

I Want Power

Now that your toddler has rediscovered their own will, they will also find new ways to find "power." Power is a fairly abstract concept when it comes to toddlers. Read these experiences from other parents to see ways that toddlers try to exercise their "power" at this age.

"The temper tantrums have really picked up. She can really scream loud. It's short but powerful. She also watches her brother very carefully when he misbehaves. It looks like she's taking mental notes."
About Victoria, 72nd week or 16 months

"He scares me with snakes and mice and does the same to the girl next door."
About Frankie, 74th week or 17 months

"He constantly hits and sometimes pinches if he doesn't get his way. If he's angry, he punches hard, softer when he's joking. The general idea is that I try to break his bad habit by calmly correcting him, and offering him a pillow to pound or by urging him to calm down. I do sometimes get angry if he really hurts. This makes him sad and then he starts handing out kisses."
About Luke, 76th week or 17 months

"He insists on eating and drinking what I have, even if he already has the same. He wants what I have. He takes my food and drink from me. We sometimes fight it out like two children."
About Gregory, 76th week or 17 months

"He has gotten notably rougher. He also forcefully throws things and really can't stand not getting his way. He sometimes throws things at the cat, like the alarm clock."
About Matt, 77th week or 17 months

LEAP 10

"If she has to come inside from the yard, she cries and stamps her feet. In these cases, I give her a timeout."
About Vera, 79th week or 18 months

"He throws everything to the ground and away from himself. He bites and hits. I really got angry this week when he smeared his food and drink all over the floor."
About John, 79th week or 18 months

"If I leave the room briefly or neglect her in the slightest, she starts digging in my plant."
About Laura, 80th week or 18 months

"He terrorizes the cats. He constantly keeps tabs on where they both are. Then he has to and will pet them."
About Jim, 83rd to 86th weeks or 19 to 20 months

"She doesn't want to be seen as 'small.' We went to get ice cream in a nice place, where the scoops are pricey and Dad said: 'Elisabeth can have some of ours.' When the ice cream came, she could lick it but she wasn't allowed to hold it. That brought on a temper tantrum. She wanted to leave. She was insulted that she was thought to be small. Dad then went to a cheaper ice cream parlor for some more ice cream. She held it but didn't eat it. Her tantrum continued all the while. She was deeply insulted. For the next half hour to 45 minutes, she was no fun. She hit Dad, too."
About Elisabeth, 86th week or 20 months

Me and the Notion That Someone Out of Sight Still Exists and Can Move

Because your toddler now understands that they are a separate system, they also understand that the same principles that apply to them also apply to the people and objects around them. They understand that people and objects continue to exist, even though they may not be in their field of vision. They also understand that they still exist for their mom and dad even when their parents can't see them. Furthermore, they now understand that other people don't necessarily remain in the same place when they are out of sight. It starts to dawn on them that they can move about and change their positions. When they look for their dad, they now understand that they may have to look elsewhere than where they last saw him.

> "He liked to crawl into closets and wanted to shut all the doors."
>
> **About Steven, 81st week or 18 months**
>
> "She hides in the closet, slides the doors shut, and then calls, 'Mom.' It really makes her laugh when we finally find her."
>
> **About Josie, 85th week or 19 months**

Me and You

Now that your toddler sees themselves as an individual, they will start using terms like "me" and "you." They grasp that their mom and dad are individuals, too, who lead their own lives. They start to compare themselves with them and map out the similarities and differences to a tee.

> "She has discovered that her father has a penis. She calls it 'Pino.'"
>
> **About Victoria, 72nd week or 16 months**
>
> "These days he points first to himself and then to me, as if he wants to point out the difference."
>
> **About Mark, 75th week or 17 months**
>
> "If I propose: 'Shall we go out together?' she points to herself as if saying: 'You mean me?' as if there are other people in the room."
>
> **About Nina, 75th week or 17 months**
>
> "He loves it when I make special reference to him. He points to himself to distinguish himself from me and as a confirmation that it's for him."
>
> **About Luke, 77th week or 17 months**
>
> "If I imitate certain stereotypical statements or behavior of hers, it makes her laugh."
>
> **About Hannah, 78th week or 18 months**
>
> "As his father, I am seemingly his role model. He is very interested in me—in the shower, in bed, on the 'john.' He follows me everywhere and always talks about me."
>
> **About Frankie, 79th to 86th weeks or 18 to 20 months**
>
> "This week, she learned the terms 'me,' 'you,' and 'yours.'"
>
> **About Juliette, 86th week or 20 months**

Now that your toddler can distinguish between themselves and others, they can also put themselves in another person's position. In a simple experiment, it was shown that toddlers of 13 to 15 months were unable to fathom that another person could make a choice that was different from theirs. They will be able to do this for the first time at 18 months. That has all kinds of consequences.

> *"We came out of the store and there was a helicopter ride for the kids there. If you put money in, it moves around for a while with lights flashing. Nora loves it and was allowed to go on once. But there was already a kid in it, who didn't want to get out after his turn. Nora looked around and ran to a mini-shopping cart and started pushing it around. The other kid came out of the helicopter right away and wanted to push that cart around, too. Nora shot over to the helicopter and got in."*
>
> **About Nora, 87th week or 20 months**

Me and My Mimicry

Just like they are an actor onstage, your toddler will mimic body postures and actions they have seen others perform.

> *"He re-enacts moods. He says, for instance, 'Stop!' in a way that a girl does, a bit sassy. He imitates certain gestures, like turning his head and body away and putting his hand up in a dismissive motion."*
>
> **About Taylor, 80th week or 18 months**
>
> *"Imitating certain postures and movements is a favorite pastime. She even tries to imitate the cat."*
>
> **About Maria, 83rd to 86th weeks or 19 to 20 months**
>
> *"He observed the monkeys and how they open nuts. We collect hazelnuts in the neighborhood and at home he really gets into shelling them."*
>
> **About Bob, 83rd to 86th weeks or 19 to 20 months**
>
> *"She imitates the other children quite a bit. If they climb a fence, she tries, too. If they knock on a window, she does the same. If they do it, she copies it."*
>
> **About Vera, 87th week or 20 months**

Me and My Fantasy Play

In their make-believe play, they start to treat their toys as if they are independent people capable of doing things. Your toddler can do this in many ways; they have boundless imagination and this fantasy play is an important part of their development. Join in with their games and watch them grow and enjoy their world.

"She grabbed an imaginary something from her hand and put it in her mouth. She did it a couple of times. It was very peculiar. It looked like her first game of make-believe."
About Josie, 71st week or 16 months

"Suddenly she has become more independent. She plays by herself very well. Now and then, it looks like she's in a dream world. She fantasizes. I had yet to see her do that. She plays the game with her doll. Sometimes she tells me her fantasies."
About Victoria, 75th week or 17 months

"He made a drawing of a turd and then stamped on it. I don't allow him to stamp on turds in the street."
About Paul, 77th week or 17 months

"After having seen his baby pictures one afternoon, he decided that all his animals were his babies and played with them the whole afternoon in his bed."
About Gregory, 84th week or 19 months

"She indicates much more clearly what she wants and gets visibly frustrated if I don't get what she means. Playing make-believe has much to do with it. She gives me a dog and I have to understand that the dog needs to be breastfed."
About Emily, 86th week or 20 months

"He does play make-believe a lot, like having a tea party, sitting together somewhere, in his toy car, on the steps. He pats the ground beside him in the most inviting way and loves if we sit there together."
About Thomas, 86th week or 20 months

"Our daughter tells us that we have to cry and then she gives us a kiss and pets our faces."
About Jenny, 79th to 80th weeks or 18 months

Other Living Creatures

Other living creatures are all separate systems with their own behavioral rules and programs. Your toddler is fascinated by this fact. Each child will explore the systems of other living creatures in their own way, depending on what interests them and what they encounter. Take your child outside and allow them to come into contact with other living creatures.

LEAP 10

"This week she was very interested in birds. She laughed when a bird she was watching returned from out of sight. She laughed more when she saw where the sounds came from, the sounds she had heard before even seeing the bird. It's the same with airplanes. She also likes to investigate how plants smell."
About Eve, 73rd week or 17 months

"He saw a snail in the street and then, before I noticed it, he said that the snail was dead. It turned out that he and his father had covered this topic a few times."
About Harry, 79th week or 18 months

"She cracked up when she saw a snake eat a mouse in a nature film."
About Laura, 84th week or 19 months

"This week he was really interested in an ant outside in the garden."
About Matt, 84th week or 19 months

"She likes watering the plants these days. She starts by making smacking noises as if the plants are hungry: 'The plants want to eat.' Preferably, she feeds them twice a day. For Ashley, it's the filling up and pouring out of the watering can that makes her feel she has done her deed for the day."
About Ashley, 85th week or 19 months

"She laughs really hard when we play with the cats, or if the cats get riled up."
About Jenny, 71st to 76th weeks or 16 to 17 months

I Live in a Nuclear Family

The nuclear family is a system like other human organizations.* It's the first human organization that your toddler experiences from the inside, right from the start. However, it is only now that they begin to see that a nuclear family is a unit, a system. Once again, we have a collection of other parents' inspiring experiences for you to read.

"She now has a strict division of tasks. Dad has to get the drink and Mom puts the glass down."
About Victoria, 73rd week or 17 months

"He points to his father, to me, and to himself. Then I am supposed to say that we all are separate people and yet we belong together. Then he nods approvingly 'yes' and sighs in contentment."
About Frankie, 76th week or 17 months

* We are using the term to mean the smallest unit in the extended family, referring to the unit of parent(s) and child(ren). That includes father-mother-child(ren), mother-mother-child(ren), father-father-child(ren), and single parent-child(ren).

"When we would take her brother to school or pick him up, she had a hard time with me calling other women 'mom of so-and-so.' There was only one mom, me. Now she understands that there are other families and that those women are mothers of other children. She still protests though if she hears them called 'Mom.' The only unequivocal mom is her mom."
About Julia, 79th week or 18 months

"Now she grasps that ours is not the only family. Recently, we went to pick up her brother, who was playing at a friend's house. We stayed to have coffee. She was clearly upset and kept calling the name of the boy's sister and asking where she was. But the sister was playing at a friend's. The family was incomplete without the sister and that troubled her. She saw that as being wrong."
About Victoria, 84th week or 19 months

"James sometimes gets left out by his brother and sister when they want to play a game. They put him in the hall and shut the door. He comes to me shattered and needs to be consoled."
About James, 87th week or 20 months

Me and My Family or Friends

Just as a nuclear family unit is a system, so too is the extended family and the circle of friends, which you might think of as your "tribe." Your toddler starts to recognize that now as well. They also learn the differences between their family and their friends' families.

"She came to me with the telephone and a picture of her grandparents and signaled that she wanted to call them."
About Juliette, 78th week or 18 months

"If I speak about his friend, he knows who that is and he says his name enthusiastically. He certainly knows his friend."
About Steven, 78th week or 18 months

"Grandma and Grandpa live around the corner. We stop by often and naturally we don't always go inside. If we pass by, she always calls out 'Ama' or 'Apa.'"
About Victoria, 82nd week or 19 months

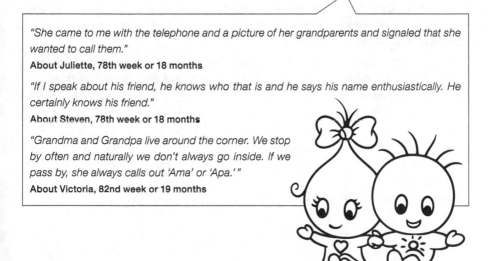

Finding My Way Around My House and My Neighborhood

Your own home is a system, as is the surrounding neighborhood. Your toddler learns to recognize that now and starts learning how to find their way. They construct a map in their head of their surroundings. Such a mental map is actually a system, too.

"He's finding his bearings. Even when he's not in really familiar surroundings, he recognizes things, and he looks for other points of recognition and he's very pleased when he finds them. He wants to share this immediately, as well as announcing what's coming up."
About Harry, 74th week or 17 months

"He knows where we are going. If I ask him, he answers correctly."
About John, 79th week or 18 months

"He knows the way from the campground to the sea."
About Jim, 80th to 81st weeks or 18 months

"Taylor and I have moved to another floor in the same building. Taylor felt at home in his new abode and after settling in, started going around with his wagon. He was familiar with the house because the previous inhabitants had two kids of their own. He seemed used to it already."
About Taylor, 82nd week or 19 months

"He has a good map of the vicinity in his head. He knows exactly where to find things at home, outside, or at Dad's work. He can point me the way to the grocery store or the way to Dad's work as well as the way inside the building to his office. He also knows the next-door neighbor's house very well. He knows where everything is, the grapes and so on. She usually has them in the house. He gets disappointed, though, if they are not in the right place."
About Thomas, 83rd week or 19 months

"If we let the dog out in the neighborhood, she says 'Ama' or 'Apa' [Grandma or Grandpa] and points in the right direction to their house, even though the house is still out of sight around the corner. Clearly, she wants to visit."
About Victoria, 86th week or 20 months

"This summer, my friend and I went to the beach regularly. Our two boys got along well. They are still good friends. Jim had expected to meet up with his friend before we went. He kept asking where he was; he wasn't at our normal meeting place. This time, they were waiting for us at the beach."
About Jim, 87th week or 20 months

Me and My Belongings

In a family system there are all sorts of principles, among which there are values, norms, and rules. Consider, for instance, "We will share fair and square" or "Thou shalt not steal." There are rules for what belongs to whom and what we are entitled to. Your toddler learns these rules by doing. Sometimes they pick it up unnoticed, and it's a pleasant surprise to find out what they've learned on their own. Other times, it takes some persuasion.

To clearly show how toddlers demonstrate "Me and my belongings," we have again collected quotes from other parents sharing their experiences. The quotes are divided into the categories "Me and my clothes" and "Me and my stuff." As you can imagine, the list of "Me and my . . ." is endless, so we have only included a few examples.

Me and My Clothes

"She knows exactly which bags, coats, and whatnot belong to which kids, and when we leave she fetches our things."
About Nina, 82nd week or 19 months

"When I empty the washing machine, I lay out every piece on the machine and pull them into shape before I put them into the dryer. She is right on top of everything, sorting things in her own way. She knows precisely who everything belongs to: 'Is Thomas,' 'Is Mommy,' 'Is Mita (Victoria).'"
About Victoria, 83rd week or 19 months

"He seems aware of his new clothes—underwear and undershirt instead of onesies. He finds it very interesting. He loves his new shoes."
About Paul, 83rd to 86th weeks or 19 to 20 months

Me and My Stuff

"While visiting a friend, Robin played with one of his toy cars, which he wasn't allowed to take home with him. He cried the whole way back to the house and at home, he threw away his own cars."
About Robin, 76th week or 17 months

"She remembers where she left things. If I ask where something is, she remembers."
About Emily, 78th week or 18 months

> *"She finds one 'diamond' after the other. Her brother collects nice stones and lays them out in his room. So she scavenges for rocks, too. Pieces of gravel go into her pocket one after the other and absolutely none of them can be thrown away."*
> **About Victoria, 78th week or 18 months**

> *"One day she came up to me, took my hand, and led me to the room where all the toys are. She pointed: 'Is Thomas, is Thomas, is Thomas . . . and Mita?' This was a hefty protest. Recently, Thomas hadn't allowed her to touch his toys, because she had broken some things. And indeed, this left her with very little to play with!"*
> **About Victoria, 83rd week or 19 months**

> *"When her cousin Lisa (now 25 months) comes to visit, it's terrible. Lisa isn't allowed to play with anything. If Lisa has anything in her hands, Hannah grabs it right from her."*
> **About Hannah, 87th week or 20 months**

> *"He no longer wants to share his toys with other children. He gets angry and passionate if they grab his toys."*
> **About Robin, 88th week or 20 months**

I Want Everything Tidied Up(!)

You've never seen anything like it before. They can't stand a mess. Enjoy it while it lasts; it won't last long and won't be back for a number of years—if it ever comes back at all. They want everything tidied up systematically.

> *"He can't handle messiness. It upsets him. So I said to my parents, 'What you never managed to achieve, my son did. Now I always clean up.' In the evening, we always clean up the blocks. Every time we have finished reading a book, he puts it back before taking another one."*
> **About Thomas, 86th week or 20 months**

Toys as Systems

Certain toys are also systems, made up of small parts that are all related and that form a whole together. The most literal example is a puzzle, consisting of puzzle pieces. It is an organized unit (the whole puzzle as a drawing/photo) that is a whole due to the interdependence (which piece fits where?) of the components (the pieces of the puzzle) from which it is comprised. There are countless other toys that are also systems. When you know what to watch for, you will see what your toddler is doing.

> *"What he likes to do is put animal puzzles together. One is 12 pieces, the other is seven. He knows exactly how to do it; he does it quickly but has no patience to put the pieces in properly. He even recognizes the back side of the piece."*
> **About Kevin, 72nd week or 16 months**

> *"Her motor skills continue to improve. This week, she enjoyed putting beads on sticks and then the sticks in holes. She also likes to take my money out and spend it."*
> **About Anna, 73rd week or 17 months**

> *"I pretended that I couldn't do the puzzle. Every time I went astray, he said: 'No, no,' and then told me where I should put the piece. After repeating this act several times, I'd had enough. I pulled the puzzle apart and put it back together in a flash. I acted like I was very proud and said: 'See, I can do it, too.' He responded with: 'No.' It turned out that a tiny corner of a piece of the puzzle was sticking up. He pushed it in and then it was right!"*
> **About Thomas, 80th week or 18 months**

Making Up a Game Myself

A puzzle is a system devised by someone else. Your toddler is now able to think up systems by themselves; for instance, a game where they make up the rules, or magic tricks.

> *"He made up a game himself, taking turns throwing dice. One person throws, the other has to pick it up. He's strict in keeping the sequence. He keeps looking for tight corners to throw the die."*
> **About Mark, 83rd to 86th weeks or 19 to 20 months**

> *"Today she did a magic trick she had come up with herself. She watches her brother doing tricks a lot. She put a marble into a bottle and said: 'Uh, oh.' She shook the bottle up and down and said: 'No.' She meant that the marble was stuck. Then she turned in a circle (like a magician does) and held the bottle upside down. Tada."*
> **About Victoria, 83rd week or 19 months**

LEAP 10

Me and My Art

After a year and a half, your toddler starts to use toys in a way that signifies they know what the toys stand for, what or who they represent. In their play, it shows that they are familiar with the people, the objects, and the situations from everyday life that are represented by the toys. The toys symbolize someone or something from the real world. Your toddler can play with these symbols in their fantasy games.

Their ability to symbolize enables them to create drawings that are completely different from their earlier drawings, representing something from the real world—for example, a car, a dog, or even themselves. This new ability did not emerge gradually, it came into being all of a sudden with a leap and is a new quality. Art is born. If your little artist loves making drawings, you will have a hard time keeping them supplied with paper. The beginning of a huge collection is at hand. If they experience something exciting, such as fireworks at New Year's Eve, it's likely they will make a drawing to capture the moment. Not only do they start making drawings, but they start building constructions as well. And if you have a little music lover, they will be playing their keyboard and can listen to music for quite a long time and enjoy it.

"Her drawings are very different now. The big scribbles have made way for small circles, tiny, tiny. She is really into details. She now colors in her drawings, too. She is very precise and hardly colors outside the lines."
About Victoria, 78th week or 18 months

"He draws horses and boats now, and this morning, he meticulously drew a circle and a square and then pointed to himself. He had drawn himself."
About Luke, 79th week or 18 months

"He has started building more, whereas he used to be more into destruction."
About Taylor, 83rd week or 19 months

"He drew a car. It was a good drawing of a car. He can only do this if he is lying down on his side with his head resting on his other outstretched arm. What does his car look like? It's two circles, the wheels, with a line in between. Circles are 'vroom vroom.' He also draws airplanes and just recently, legs. A spiral is a steering wheel—a steering wheel turns."
About Thomas, 83rd week or 19 months

"He loves music. He likes playing his electric keyboard. He puts on a certain rhythm to accompany his lead. At the store, he listened to practically a whole CD of classical music while sitting in his stroller. It lasted almost an hour. He was upset when I disturbed him halfway through to go on with our shopping. He had to listen to the end."
About Thomas, 86th week or 20 months

"He said that he was going to draw Grandpa. He drew a head four times and said: 'Wrong.' He wasn't satisfied. The fifth time, when he got the goatee in the right spot, he was satisfied and said: 'Grandpa!'"

About Thomas, 101st week or 23 months

DO REMEMBER

When it comes to drawing, it is not about creating a great piece of art, but about the fact that your toddler is exploring a new skill and the goal they have in mind. So when your toddler scribbles a few lines on a piece of paper and tells you it is a horse, then that is what it is, even if you can't make heads nor tails of it. People have often commented to us that it is ridiculous to say that children of this age can draw a horse, or something else, but we stand behind our belief (or should we say the toddler's) that when they say they have drawn something, well, that's exactly what it is. And that's actually quite logical, is it not?

Me and My Sense of Time: Past, Present, and Future

Your toddler starts to develop a sense of time now. Their memory of past experiences improves and they get better at anticipating future events.

"I can't tell her anymore in the morning that we are going to do something fun in the afternoon. Otherwise, she reminds me the whole day until it happens: 'Now Apa Ama [Grandma Grandpa] to?'"
About Victoria, 78th week or 18 months

"She makes plans. When we sit down for dinner, she asks if she may draw. I tell her that first we're going to eat. Then, she tells me where her pen and paper will need to be for later. I am supposed to say that I understand and that it will happen. If I forget after dinner, she gets very angry, and she is offended."
About Victoria, 80th week or 18 months

"He remembers promises. If I promise that we'll do something after his bath, he reminds me. When he wakes up in the morning, he refers to what we did before he went to sleep."
About Gregory, 82nd week or 19 months

Basic Physics

If you observe their play well, you cannot ignore that toddlers are busy with the basic phenomena of physics. That sounds more complicated than it actually is; read on and you will see.

"He dunks things like a ball under water to experience the resistance. He also disassembled a small electric telephone. He now looks at it differently than he did before when it just made noise. It doesn't work anymore after his experiment. He finds throwing things and taking them apart really interesting. He is trying things out."
About Harry, 77th week or 17 months

"She can spend hours pouring some liquid from one vessel into another. She uses bottles, glasses, plates, or cups. While she's busy, she likes to add the necessary commentary."
About Ashley, 78th week or 18 months

"She pays close attention to colors: green, red, yellow. Red and yellow go together. I was kidding with her when I told her that it's supposed to be that way."
About Josie, 78th week or 18 months

With principles, we have seen how your toddler started to "think about thinking." Once they have entered the world of systems, for the first time they can hone their principles into a system, principles they have learned through experience. It's quite possible they are doing this while taking their "thinking break."

"Sometimes he likes to be alone. He says, 'Bye,' and goes to sit in his room to be alone. He's pondering life. Sometimes he does that a half hour at a time, with a toy. Other times he stares and thinks for 10 minutes like a 50-year-old. He just wants a bit of peace after having such fun playing. After he's taken his break to collect his thoughts, he returns cheerful, says 'hi,' wants to nurse a bit, and then goes to sleep or to play a bit. He really needs his privacy."
About Thomas, 80th week or 18 months

"Initially, he was afraid of the electric toothbrush, but now that he's gotten used to it, it's fine and he says 'on.'"
About John, 83rd week or 19 months

"She grasps that the train takes batteries, and understood that they were drained. She went and found new ones."
About Hannah, 86th week or 20 months

Basic Architecture

Their interest in the phenomena of physics extends to more systems than simply physics. They are also interested in basic architecture. They can spend hours watching builders, and you will notice their play will produce more structures since their latest leap, such as towers of cups pushed together, and more elaborate constructions.

"My husband cemented the fish pond this week. He explained to my eldest son how to mix cement. My son then explained the same to Victoria. Now they are together the whole day long mixing sand and water for cementing. She does everything he does. She looks up to Thomas."
About Victoria, 79th week or 18 months

"Cars have fallen out of favor. Now it's more the alternative transportation, like motorbikes, semis, dump trucks, trolley cars. He loves to watch the builders."
About Mark, 80th week or 18 months

"He tries putting the small Lego blocks together these days. He can't quite manage because it takes a bit of strength. But he tries. He doesn't use the bigger blocks."
About Matt, 86th week or 20 months

Me and My Talking

Between 17 and 22 months, toddlers start using the adult language system with an explosive increase in the spoken vocabulary and the average duration of a speaking turn. They also start combining words to form sentences. They are now able to distinguish two different languages from each other and ignore one of the two. Furthermore, there is an impressive increase in verbal language comprehension around 18 months.

There is large individual variation in the budding development of speech. Some toddlers don't use many words (approximately six) around the time this leap takes place. The parents know that they actually know and understand many more words, which can cause some frustration. Other children use many words, repeating after you (sometimes just the first syllable) or taking the initiative, but no sentences yet. They can make themselves understood, though, literally with hands and feet. They mime their part. A third group already produces sentences, while they are still miming. This variation is very normal, so don't concern yourself with it, just as you shouldn't with the race to walk first. It is about time that we all stopped seeing children's development as a competition.

> *Was ready to file today under "barely surviving parenting two toddlers," with my littlest being more clingy and whiny than usual, a couple of boo-boos (very minor), and a seriously never-ending pile of laundry. Then I snatched my little one up for bedtime, yelling behind me for hubby to grab me an apple for a snack, when— boom—my little one (who really only whines the words "mom" and "mumum" as code words for, "Mom, feed me!") looks at me and says, "apple," clear as day with the biggest grin, so proud of herself. And just like that my whole day was changed.*—**Instagram post**

Understands a Lot, Says a Few Words

It is clear that your toddler understands a lot already. They will start talking more and using more words themselves now. But what they initially make of those words and how they pronounce them can be highly entertaining. It is fun reading the words other toddlers use, but even nicer if you write down the words your child uses (see page 444). You will not be able to remember them all at a later date.

"The words he now uses are limited: 'cookie,' 'bottle,' 'ouch,' 'thank,' 'Mom,' 'Dad,' 'bread,' and 'pel' (= apple; he only pronounces the last syllable). He understands everything and follows instructions well."

About James, 76th week or 17 months

"He puts his arms up in the air at 'hip, hip, hooray' and shouts something like 'oora!' He knows all the gestures, too, like 'clap your hands.' And if he doesn't succeed he says 'oot' (shoot)."

About Robin, 76th week or 17 months

"He says three words: 'di dah' is tick-tack, 'moo' is moon, and 'hi hi' is horse."

About Robin, 80th week or 18 months

"He doesn't say much yet, but he understands everything! And he communicates exactly what he wants."

About James, 81st week or 18 months

"He understands everything you say and ask. He is very enterprising, always doing something, walking through the house all day long singing or mumbling something."

About James, 83rd week or 19 months

"He picks up more and more words. Now he knows 'Dad,' 'Mom,' 'cheese,' 'ow,' 'boom,' 'ant,' 'more,' 'di dah,' 'moon,' and 'sars' (= stars)."

About Robin, 84th week or 19 months

"He definitely uses more words now. He answers sometimes now with 'yes.' 'Eese' (cheese) and 'food' are now part of his repertoire. In general, he's not yet very talkative. By pointing and a few oohs and aahs, we understand him. He gets what he needs."

About James, 86th week or 19 months

"A great moment this week was the comprehensive contact we had when we were playing a game making noises. It was really funny. We tried to stick our tongues in and out of our mouths while making noise. Later, we tried to push our tongues against the back of our front teeth to produce the 'lll' sound as in: 'Lala.' She found it exciting and challenging and wanted to do what I did. At the same time, it looked like she was thinking, 'I'll get you.' I saw so many different expressions in her face. We both loved it and the laughter grew, especially when she said 'lala' spontaneously with a kiss."

About Ashley, 73rd week or 17 months

LEAP 10

Understands a Lot, Many Words, a Lot of Mime, No Sentences

This is the stage between saying individual words and making sentences. The rhythm, interpretation, and intention of a sentence are there, but instead of using a series of full words, the sentence is "told" in rhythm with gestures and individual words. And yet, you understand your toddler because you know them so well.

"The way he talks has changed again. Even though his speech is, for the most part, incomprehensible, it does seem that he's forming more sentences, and I think: 'Heck, I'm getting this!' He explains clearly through gestures and 'words' what has happened to him in my absence. For instance, when he was at Grandma's in the kitchen and I asked him what he'd done. He said something I couldn't understand with the word 'cheese' in it, which led me to understand that he had gotten a piece of cheese from Grandma. When asked, he nodded yes."
About Taylor, 74th to 77th weeks or 17 to 18 months

"The way he communicated this week was interesting. He seems to be forming sentences in his own language. He keeps it up until I understand him. An example: we walk across the street to the sea for the second time, Luke on Daddy's back. I had the bag with gear and the sand shovel was sticking out. All of a sudden he shrieks: 'Da, da, da.' It takes a bit before I get that he means the shovel. When I say, 'The shovel?' he says, 'Ya,' and points from the shovel to the sea. I repeat in words: 'Yeah, we're taking the shovel to the beach.' He sighed contentedly and leaned back. We have this type of conversation often."
About Luke, 74th week or 17 months

"She makes sentences that seem like a long word but missing some letters. But I can understand her even if I don't pay close attention. She saw that the stoplight was red and pointed to it. I hadn't seen it yet, but heard her say it, and she was right, although I don't know exactly what she said. Rather strange! It was like she herself didn't know what she was saying, but did utter some sounds that seemed to fit the picture."
About Ashley, 76th week or 17 months

"He uses a lot of words, but mainly only the first syllable. He's saying more and more words that he starts himself. The joy he gets from speaking is so touching."
About Bob, 77th week or 17 months

"He comes up to me with his index finger pressed to his thumb and that means 'money.'"
About Taylor, 84th week or just over 19 months

Understands a Lot, Many Words, and Sentences, Too

At this age, some toddlers not only understand all words, they can also say many words, and even use sentences themselves. But just like with all motor skills, every baby and toddler does things at their own pace.

> "She really 'reads' books now. She tells a story while she looks at the pictures. Can't understand a word, but very touching. Moreover, she can speak in intelligible sentences, too."
> **About Victoria, 75th week or 17 months**
>
> "If she wants the cat to come to her, she calls: 'Wittie, come here.'"
> **About Jenny, 75th week or 17 months**
>
> "She says several things together, like 'that's good,' 'not now' or 'Mommy and Daddy.'"
> **About Emily, 81st week or 18 months**
>
> "He wanted the soap. But I didn't feel like reacting to 'eh, eh' and said: 'Tell me what you want?' Then he said: 'Yes, that that, me.'"
> **About Thomas, 82nd week or 19 months**
>
> "She now puts two and three words together."
> **About Emily, 83rd week or 19 months**

Show Understanding for "Irrational" Fears

When your toddler is busy exploring their new world, and working out their new-found ability, they will encounter things and situations that are new and foreign to them. Those things may scare them at first. But once they start to understand better what is going on, they'll stop being afraid. Until that happens, try to be sympathetic with them.

> "She is afraid of thunder and lightning. She says: 'Bang, boom.'"
> **About Maria, 71st week or 16 months**
>
> "He really disliked the vacuum cleaner and a running tap. They had to stop."
> **About Paul, 72nd week or 16 months**
>
> "He is scared of balloons. He also won't go between the sheep and goats at the petting zoo. He wants to be picked up then. Nor does he like sitting on an animal at the carousel. He does like to watch, though."
> **About Matt, 73rd week or 17 months**
>
> "He's been frightened of the vacuum cleaner for a while. He used to get on top of it when I turned it on. Now he gets well out of the way in a corner until the chore is done."
> **About Steven, 85th week or 19 months**
>
> "He was afraid of a spider in the garden and of flies."
> **About Harry, 88th week or 20 months**

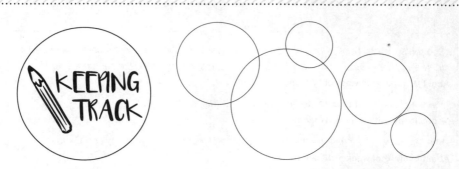

YOUR FAVORITE GAMES: THE WORLD OF SYSTEMS

These are games and activities that your toddler may like now and that help them practice their newly developing skills.

Instructions to Fill In This List:

Check off your toddler's favorite games and take the time to look for the connections between what interested your toddler most in What You've Discovered: The World of Systems and the games they best enjoy. You may have to think about it, but by doing it you will gain a unique insight into your toddler's personality.

- ☐ Playing silly games together by pronouncing words differently and making silly movements
- ☐ We make a game of recognizing certain people
- ☐ Standing on your head, scrambling about, practicing balance
- ☐ Drawing
- ☐ Blowing bubbles
- ☐ Jumping and balancing on walls
- ☐ Playing the fool
- ☐ Tickling and physical play
- ☐ Play-wrestling and joking around
- ☐ Playing outside
- ☐ Other children, playing and messing around
- ☐ Balls
- ☐ Ghost games
- ☐ Twirling around and getting dizzy and being thrown on the bed
- ☐ Playing circus
- ☐ Riding horse game
- ☐ Playing tag

- [ ] Hide-and-seek
- [ ] Reading stories
- [ ] Tongue games: your father or mother pushes their tongue against the inside of their cheek; you push their cheek in, whereby your parent sticks their tongue out

YOUR FAVORITE TOYS

- [ ] Cars
- [ ] Modeling clay (that you like chewing on more than anything)
- [ ] Children's TV
- [ ] Books
- [ ] Small trinkets, pots, and bottles (things that belong together)
- [ ] Garages with cars
- [ ] Toy airports with various parts
- [ ] Coloring pencils and paper
- [ ] Bucket with sand and water
- [ ] Push cars/cars to sit on
- [ ] Plastic chairs
- [ ] Balls
- [ ] Bicycle
- [ ] Stuffed animals and dolls
- [ ] Stickers
- [ ] Sandbox
- [ ] Digging in the yard
- [ ] Children's songs
- [ ] Slides
- [ ] Tractor with trailer
- [ ] Blowing bubbles
- [ ] Trains
- [ ] Rocking chair and other objects to rock back and forth on
- [ ] Rocking horse
- [ ] Swings
- [ ] Puzzles (up to 20 pieces)
- [ ] Clickers for spokes on a bike

Your Toddler's Choices: A Key to Their Personality

All toddlers have gained the ability to perceive and control systems. They need years to completely familiarize themselves with it all, but the world of systems opens up to them now. In this world, they take their first, tentative steps. For instance, at this age, a toddler may choose to focus on getting the hang of using their body and leave talking for later, using just a few words and no sentences. Or they may be very busy with their family, friends, house, and neighborhood. Or they might prefer the arts, drawing endlessly and listening to music. Just like every toddler, they choose what best suits their inclinations, mobility, preferences, and circumstances. The very first choices become apparent when they are 75 weeks, or just over 17 months. Don't compare your child with other children. Each child is unique and will choose accordingly.

Observe your toddler. Figure out what their interests are. By now, you can readily see which talents and capacities they have, as well as their strong points. If your toddler has a high musical intelligence, for instance, that will now become clear. In What You've Discovered: The World of Systems there is room to cross off what your child selects first. You can also see whether there are some systems that you think your child could use or learn.

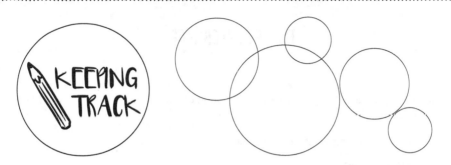

WHAT YOU'VE DISCOVERED: THE WORLD OF SYSTEMS

These are the skills your toddler can develop once they have made this developmental leap. As you check off your toddler's skills on the lists, remember that no toddler will do everything listed.

Instructions to Fill In This List:

Now that your toddler has made the 10th leap at the end of the so-called sensorimotor period, they have laid all the foundations for their further mental development. Everything they learn during the rest of their life will build on all the mental insights they have gained through the 10 leaps. This 10th leap, in your toddler's mental development forms an overarching layer, as it were, over the previous leaps. Everything that is still to come rests on the top layer of those foundations, so this leap has an enormous impact and is fairly complicated. You may notice how children deal with the development of the corresponding skills in a variety of ways. Their individual characters have never been as clear as they are now. This does mean this list can be difficult to complete, because there is a big chance that your toddler will not exhibit many of the skills and you will need to be more specific than ever. But we have made it a bit easier for you by listing many examples seen by other parents with toddlers making this leap. Your toddler very well may not do these things, but they will give you an idea of what to watch for and steer you in the right direction to help you see how your toddler goes through this leap. Read the list and the previous quotes from parents through regularly to refresh your memory. You will discover more about your toddler than you may imagine.

You made this leap on: _____

On _____ the sun broke through again and now, at the end of the leap, I see you can do these new things.

THE CONSCIENCE

Date:

☐ You get scared and blurt out a loud "NO" when caught doing something you know is not allowed.

☐ You test me by doing what's not allowed.

☐ You imitate behavior from the TV.

☐ You are hurt and confused by unjust sanctions.

☐ You are able to "lie."

☐ You test other people's limits. It may sound negative but it is actually a healthy development, much like the fact that I set boundaries. You need them, after all.

☐ An example of how you test the boundaries:

_____

_____

_____

THE NOTION OF SELF

Date:

☐ I notice you grasp the concept of "I."

☐ You have control over your body and realize that it is your body.

☐ You want to do things by yourself.

☐ You have your own will.

☐ You can decide for yourself.

☐ You want . . . power. And that isn't meant negatively; it is all part of the healthy development of the notion of self.

☐ This is how I noticed your growing notion of self:

_____

_____

_____

OUT OF SIGHT BUT NOT OUT OF MIND

Date:

☐ You hide and want to be found.

☐ You really look for people. You look everywhere and not only the place you saw that person last.

ME AND YOU

Date:

☐ You grasp that your parents are not the same person.

☐ You size up similarities and differences between people to a T.

☐ You want to be recognized as your own person.

☐ You can put yourself in the place of others. This is an amazing breakthrough, as you can interact with people in a completely new way now.

☐ You can realize that another child wants something different and that other people can like different things from those you like.

☐ You can console another person.

☐ You love mimicry and do it yourself.

☐ Your fantasy play has really taken off. For example:

_____

☐ You treat toys as autonomous people able to act.

OTHER LIVING CREATURES

Date:

☐ You like waving at birds and planes in the sky.

☐ You explore how a plant or a _____ smells.

☐ You like feeding the chickens, or the _____ .

☐ You are interested in tiny creatures, such as bees, ants, ladybugs, or

_____ .

☐ You want to water the plants.

NUCLEAR FAMILY

Date:

- ☐ You grasp that members of the family are separate people but still belong together.
- ☐ You play the whole day long with dolls and stuffed animals. You feed them and put them to bed.
- ☐ You grasp that there are other nuclear families with other parent(s), brothers, and sisters.

FAMILY AND FRIENDS

Date:

- ☐ You grasp the difference between your own family and that of your friends.
- ☐ You know exactly who belongs to who.
- ☐ You want to phone Grandma or Grandpa, or: _____.
- ☐ You indicate that you want to visit Grandma or Grandpa, or _____ by: _____.

HOUSE, NEIGHBORHOOD, AND FINDING THE WAY

Date:

- ☐ You have a good idea of the lay of the land in your surroundings. For example, you know the way to _____ or to _____.
- ☐ You know exactly where to find things in and around the house.
- ☐ You recognize your own house and that of _____.
- ☐ You can point the way to the supermarket or park.
- ☐ You recognize things even if they are in less familiar surroundings.

OWNERSHIP

Date:

☐ When I am sorting the laundry, you know perfectly well whose clothes are whose.

☐ You know exactly which bag and jacket belongs to which child.

☐ You know exactly which toy belongs to whom and what's off limits.

☐ You no longer wish to share your toys with other children.

☐ You collect things and insist they're not to be thrown away.

☐ You do not like mess. You want everything systematically put away.

PUZZLES AND LITTLE THINGS

Date:

☐ You are now good at doing puzzles, those consisting of 7, 12, or at the most 20 pieces.

☐ Your motor skills are increasingly more refined than before. I notice that through:

_____

☐ You find boxes containing collections of small objects interesting. Boxes you like examining are, for example:
  ☐ Tool boxes
  ☐ Boxes with sorted nails or colored pencils, etc.
  ☐ Boxes of beads
  ☐ Other:

  _____

  _____

☐ You are a stickler for detail. For instance:
  ☐ _____
  ☐ _____
  ☐ _____

MAKING UP YOUR OWN GAMES

Date:

☐ You make up a game with its own rules.

☐ You make up your own magic tricks.

ART

Date:

☐ You grasp that toys symbolize real-world things or people.

☐ You have started drawing in a completely different way. Random big scribbles have made way for circles, squares, and _____.

☐ Although, if I am honest, I can't identify what you have drawn, you are clearly trying to draw something. You tell me what you have drawn and you are right: if you say it is a horse, it's a horse. You like drawing:
    ☐ _____
    ☐ _____
    ☐ _____

☐ You also like it when I draw with you.

☐ You listen to music for quite a long time and fully concentrate. Children that do this now, out of pure interest, often have more of an affinity with music later on.

☐ You like playing with the following (toy) instruments:
    ☐ Keyboard
    ☐ Drums
    ☐ Other:

    _____
    _____

☐ You build more "constructions" than you used to.

SENSE OF TIME

Date:

☐ You remember past experiences. For instance:

    ☐ _____

    ☐ _____

    ☐ _____

☐ You can "predict" what is about to happen because something happens or we are doing something.

☐ You remind me the whole day of a promise I have made. For instance, that we will to go to _____ .

☐ I notice you make plans in your head. If I promise to do something and I do not keep my promise, for example, because I forgot something, you get upset and I notice you even feel insulted.

☐ You sometimes remember in the morning what you did before going to bed.

BASIC PHYSICS

Date:

☐ You hold things underwater to watch them pop up again, such as a ball. You like to experiment with the feeling of resistance.

☐ You are endlessly occupied by pouring fluid from one glass to the next.

☐ You pay attention to various colors and sometimes look for a specific color.

☐ You find new things a bit frightening all of a sudden. For instance:

    ☐ The first time you saw snow

    ☐ A new electric toothbrush

    ☐ Other:

_____

_____

☐ You like other experiments or investigating things, such as:

_____

_____

_____

BASIC ARCHITECTURE

Date:

☐ You really enjoy watching builders. You study how they _____
_____ .

☐ You want to imitate things builders do:
    ☐ You make "cement" with sand and water
    ☐ You "plaster" walls
    ☐ Other:
_____

☐ You lay down a simple train track.

☐ You try building with small blocks (such as Lego blocks).

LANGUAGE

Date:

☐ You understand most of what is said.

☐ For children brought up with two languages: you can distinguish between the two languages/language systems. Your preference is for the _____ language. You sometimes ignore the other language: yes/no

☐ You are producing more and more words.

☐ You can combine words to form short sentences.

☐ You imitate animal noises.

☐ You mime a lot and can imitate things with your hands and feet.

☐ You love books. You listen to short stories to the very end while concentrating fully.

Your Words

"Real word"   What you say

_____   _____

_____   _____

_____   _____

_____   _____

Help, My Toddler Can't Do Everything!
No, Of Course Not, That's Impossible!

The first phase (clinginess) of this leap is age-linked and predictable, and starts around 71 weeks. Most toddlers start the second phase of this leap 75 weeks after the due date. The first perception of the world of systems sets in motion the development of a whole range of skills and activities. However, the age at which these skills and activities appear for the first time varies greatly per child. For example, the ability to perceive systems is a necessary precondition for "being able to point the way to the supermarket or park," but this skill normally appears at any time from 75 weeks to many months later. The difference between the mental capacity (ability) to do something and actually doing it (skill) depends on your toddler's preferences, their desire to experiment, and their physical development. The skills and activities in *The Wonder Weeks* are presented at the earliest possible age; that is the age children gain the new ability and become fussy, so that you can watch for and recognize skills (they may be rudimentary at first) as soon as they are performed for the first time. It would be a pity if any would go unnoticed. All toddlers gain the same ability at the same age, but they differ greatly in what they do with it and when. That is what makes every toddler unique.

THE EASY PERIOD: AFTER THE LEAP

After 79 weeks or just over 18 months, most toddlers become a little less troublesome than they were, although their budding notion of self and a tendency to want to get their own way and the struggle for power are not making it any easier. However, those behaviors make them troublesome in a different way. They are not difficult in the sense of the three Cs: crying, clinginess, and crankiness. They are occasionally just plain difficult. The trick is to place yourself above it all. Stop and count to 10, remember that your little darling is progressing, and do your best to manage the situation. After all, this is a very good opportunity to phase in some rules (of conduct) for your toddler so they learn that the world doesn't revolve around them, and that they must take others into account as well.

It's good to know that for adults, thinking and reasoning or logic are not the highest attainable goals, as some people like to think. Logic belongs in the world of programs and is subordinate to the worlds of principles and systems. If you really want to make a change, you will have to change your principles, and to change your principles, you will first have to change the accompanying system. The problem is that concepts at system level are not easily changed in adults. That is due in part to the fact that every change at the system level has far-reaching effects for all levels under the world of systems. And that doesn't happen without a struggle. History has taught us that such upheaval often brings with it revolutions or wars using words or even arms.

Concepts at the system and principle level are more easily formed than they are changed. Children learn them by observing their surroundings and then start to use them themselves. Sometimes adults place emphasis on certain principles and system concepts. This is a textbook example of socialization and upbringing.

Your toddler is, of course, new to the show. Their world is still very small and close to home. It will be many years, until after their childhood, before they have developed what we adults call an outlook on life, but a tender start has been made. It's an important step with far-reaching consequences. Among other things, a beginning is made by forming a conscience and learning norms and values. If a poor start is made here, the negative consequences will be most noticeable a few years down the road. If you give this all your attention, it will be a very good in-depth investment. It will save you, your child, and everyone around them a lot of misery.

The importance of this early start applies, of course, to all the other domains in the world of systems. Whether your toddler likes music, likes to build, talk, play with physical phenomena, or practice body control, give this rising star a chance. You will be amazed at the pleasure you will have together.

Postscript

Every parent will, at some time, have to deal with a baby who is tearful, cranky, or fussy; a baby who is difficult to please; a baby who, in fact, just needs a "daddy or mommy refill." Those parents are not alone. All their colleagues have had to deal with this when their infants reached certain ages. All parents forget—or would like to forget—these trying times as soon as possible; as soon as the difficult phase is over, in fact. It's human nature to play down the misery we have to go through, once the dark clouds have parted.

When parents understand that their child's difficult behaviors and the parents' anxieties and irritability are all part of a healthy and normal development toward independence, they feel more secure and confident. Parents know there is no instruction manual for bringing up a child. After each leap, every baby will "explore" the possibilities in each "new world" in their own individual way. And all you can do is help them on their way. The baby's parents know that the best person to help them is the one who knows them best. They know their baby unlike anyone else does. What the parents could use is information about what is going on in their baby's head with each leap. We have shared that information in this book. It will make it easier for you to understand and support your baby. In our Dutch parental support and education program *Hordenlopen* [Leaping Hurdles], and book of the same name, we showed that understanding and supporting your baby using this program makes a huge, positive difference to the parents themselves and for the further development of their babies. So your baby's development is partly in your hands, the person who cares for that baby and who knows best what the baby needs, and not in the hands of your family, neighbors, or friends. Everyone's baby is completely different. We have made this clear in this book and we hope that we have empowered parents to be immune to unwelcome and conflicting advice from others.

We have shown that every baby is "reborn" 10 times in the first 20 months, or the so-called sensorimotor period. Ten times over, their world was turned upside down. Ten times over, they were bewildered and did everything in their power to cling to their mom or dad. Ten times over, they touched base. And 10 times over, they took a "mom or dad refill," as it were, before making the next leap in their development.

Obviously, your toddler still has a long way to go. Research into the development of brain waves (EEG) of children aged one and a half to 16 years old has shown that major changes suddenly occur in the brain waves at the transition between well-known stages in their mental development. The beginning of puberty is one such leap at a later age. For a long time it has been common knowledge that surging hormones trigger the onset of puberty. But recent discoveries have shown that big changes in the brain also co-occur with the onset of puberty. These are not only changes in brain waves, but also sudden and extremely rapid increases in the volume of certain parts of the brain. For the umpteenth time, these youths enter a new perceptual world, and gain a new perceptual ability and insight that they could not possibly have developed at an earlier age. Teenagers are not keen to admit this, because they think they are on top of the world already—in much the same way that babies are of the same opinion. Further leaps occur several more times before a child becomes fully independent. There are even indications that adults experience these phases, too.

As the Colombian author and journalist Gabriel García Márquez wrote in *Love in the Time of Cholera:*

> Human beings are not born once and for all on the day that their mothers give birth to them, but . . . life obliges them over and over again to give birth to themselves.

Further Reading

Readers who want to know more about the scientific literature behind the book *The Wonder Weeks* can consult the literary sources listed below.

Aldridge, J. W., Berridge, K., Herman, M., and Zimmer, L. (1993). Neuronal Coding of Serial Order: Syntax of Grooming in the Neostriatum. *Psychological Science*, 4, 391–395.

Alink, L. R. A., Mesman, J., van Zeijl, J., Stolk, M. N., Juffer, F., Koot, H. M., Bakermans-Kranenburg, M. J., van Ijzendoorn, M. H. (2006). The Early Childhood Aggression Curve: Development of Physical Aggression in 10- to 50-Month-Old Children. *Child Development* 77(4), 954–966.

Bell, M. A., and Wolfe, C.D. (2004). Emotion and Cognition: An Intricately Bound Developmental Process. *Child Development* 75(2), 366–370.

Bell, M. A., Wolfe, C. D., and Adkins, D. R. (2007). Frontal Lobe Development During Infancy and Childhood: Contributions of Brain Electrical Activity, Temperament, and Language to Individual Differences in Working Memory and Inhibitory Control. In D. Coch, K. W. Fischer, and G. Dawson (eds.), *Human Behavior, Learning, and the Developing Brain. Typical Development*, Chapter 9. New York: The Guilford Press.

Bever, T. G. (1982). *Regressions in Mental Development: Basic Phenomena and Theories*. Hillsdale, NJ: Erlbaum.

Cools, A. R. (1985). Brain and Behavior: Hierarchy of Feedback Systems and Control of Input. In P. P. G. Bateson and P. H. Klopfer (eds.), *Perspectives in Ethology* 109–168. New York: Plenum.

Diamond, A., and Goldman-Rakic, P. S. (1989). Comparison of Human Infants and Rhesus Monkeys on Piaget's AB Task: Evidence for Dependence on Dorsolateral Prefrontal Cortex. *Experimental Brain Research*, 74(1), 24.

Diamond, A., Werker, J., and Lalonde, C. (1994). Toward Understanding Commonalities in the Development of Object Search, Detour Navigation, Categorization, and Speech Perception. In C. Dawson and K. Fischer (eds.), *Human Behavior and the Developing Brain*, 380–426. New York: Guilford.

Feldman, D. H. and Benjamin, A. C. (2004). Going Backward to Go Forward: The Critical Role of Regressive Moment in Cognitive Development. *Journal of Cognition and Development* 5(1), 97–102.

Fischer, K., and Rose, S. (1994). Dynamic Development of Coordination of Components in Brain and Behavior: A Framework for Theory and Research. In G. Dawson and K. Fischer (eds.), *Human Behavior and the Developing Brain*, 3–66. New York: Guilford.

Heimann, M. (ed.) (2003). *Regression Periods in Human Infancy*. Mahwah, NJ: Erlbaum.

Horwich, R. H. (1974). Regressive Periods in Primate Behavioral Development with Reference to Other Mammals. *Primates* 15, 141–149.

Jusczyk, P. W., and Krumhansl, C. L. (1993). Pitch and Rhythmic Patterns Affecting Infants' Sensitivity to Musical Phrase Structure. *Journal of Experimental Psychology: Human Perception and Performance* 19(3), 627–640.

Krumhansl, C., and Jusczyk, P. (1990). Infants' Perception of Phrase Structure in Music. *Psychological Science* 1, 70–73.

MacLaughlin, S. (2016). New Infant Sleep Recommendations and Strategies, www.zerotothree.org, accessed February 16, 2017.

Mansell, W. (ed.). *The Handbook of Perceptual Control Theory.* Amsterdam: Elsevier, forthcoming.

Mansell, W., and Huddy, V. (2018). The Assessment and Modeling of Perceptual Control: A Transformation in Research Methodology to Address the Replication Crisis. *Review of General Psychology* 22(3), 305–320.

McKay, P. (2014). The Myth of Baby Sleep Regressions—What's Really Happening to Your Baby's Sleep? www.pinkymckay.com, accessed May 3, 2015.

Mizuno, T., Yamauchi, N., Watanabe, A., Komatsushiro, M., Tagaki, T., Iinuma, K., and Arakawa, T. (1970). Maturation of Patterns of EEG: Basic Waves of Healthy Infants Under 12 Months of Age. *Tokyo Journal of Experimental Medicine*, 102, 91–98.

Ockwell-Smith, S. (2015). *The Gentle Sleep Book: A Guide for Calm Babies, Toddlers and Pre-schoolers.* London: Piatkus.

Plooij, F. (1978). Some Basic Traits of Language in Wild Chimpanzees? In A. Lock (ed.), *Action, Gesture and Symbol: The Emergence of Language*, 111–131. London: Academic Press.

———. (1979). How Wild Chimpanzee Babies Trigger the Onset of Mother-Infant Play and What the Mother Makes of It. In M. Bullowa (ed.), *Before Speech: The Beginning of Interpersonal Communication*, 223–243. Cambridge, UK: Cambridge University Press.

———. (1984). *The Behavioral Development of Free-Living Chimpanzee Babies and Infants.* Norwood, NJ: Ablex.

———. (1987). Infant-Ape Behavioral Development, the Control of Perception, Types of Learning and Symbolism. In J. Montangero (ed.), *Symbolism and Knowledge*, 35–64. Geneva: Archives Jean Piaget Foundation.

———. (1990). Developmental Psychology: Developmental Stages as Successive Reorganizations of the Hierarchy. In R. J. Robertson and W.T. Powers, (ed.), *Introduction to Modern Psychology: The Control-Theory View*, 123–133. Gravel Switch, KY: Control Systems Group, Inc.

Plooij, F. X. (2003). The Trilogy of Mind. In M. Heimann (ed.), *Regression Periods in Human Infancy*, 185–205. Mahwah, NJ: Erlbaum.

———. (2010). The 4 WHY's of Age-Linked Regression Periods in Infancy. In B. M. Lester and J. D. Sparrow (eds.), *Nurturing Children and Families: Building on the Legacy of T. Berry Brazelton*, 107–119. Malden, MA: Wiley-Blackwell.

Plooij, F., and Van de Rijt-Plooij, H. (1989). Vulnerable Periods During Infancy: Hierarchically Reorganized Systems Control, Stress and Disease. *Ethology and Sociobiology* 10, 279–296.

———. (1990). Developmental Transitions as Successive Reorganizations of a Control Hierarchy. *American Behavioral Scientist* 34, 67–80.

———. (1994). Vulnerable Periods During Infancy: Regression, Transition, and Conflict. In J. Richer (ed.), *The Clinical Application of Ethology and Attachment Theory*, 25–35. London: Association for Child Psychology and Psychiatry.

———. (1994). Learning by Instincts, Developmental Transitions, and the Roots of Culture in Infancy. In R. A. Gardner, B. T. Gardner, B. Chiarelli, and F. X. Plooij (eds.), *The Ethological Roots of Culture*, 357–373. Dordrecht: Kluwer Academic Publishers.

———. (2003). The Effects of Sources of "Noise" on Direct Observation Measures of Regression Periods: Case Studies of Four Infants' Adaptations to Special Parental Conditions. In M. Heimann (ed.), *Regression Periods in Human Infancy*, 57–80. Mahwah, NJ: Erlbaum.

Plooij, F., Van de Rijt-Plooij, H. H. C., Van der Stelt, J. M., Van Es, B., and Helmers, R. (2003). Illness Peaks During Infancy and Regression Periods. In M. Heimann (ed.), *Regression Periods in Human Infancy*, 81–95. Mahwah, NJ: Erlbaum.

Plooij, F. X., Van de Rijt-Plooij, H., and Helmers, R. (2003). Multimodal Distribution of SIDS and Regression Periods. In M. Heimann (ed.), *Regression Periods in Human Infancy*, 97–106. Mahwah, NJ: Erlbaum.

Powers, W. T. (1973). Feedback: Beyond Behaviorism. *Science* 179(4071), 351–356. (William Powers is the developer of the Perceptual Control Theory that inspired the research underlying the Wonder Weeks.)

———. (1973). *Behavior: The Control of Perception*. Chicago: Aldine. Second edition (2005), revised and expanded, Bloomfield, NJ: Benchmark Publications.

———. (1978). Quantitative Analysis of Purposive Systems: Some Spadework at the Foundations of Scientific Psychology. *Psychological Review* 85(5), 417–435.

Powers, W. T., Clark, R. K., and McFarland, R. L. (1960a). A General Feedback Theory of Human Behavior, Part I. *Perceptual and Motor Skill* 11(1), 71–88.

———. (1960b). A General Feedback Theory of Human Behavior, Part II. *Perceptual and Motor Skill* 11(3), 309–323.

Sadurní, M., and Rostan, C. (2003). Reflections on Regression Periods in the Development of Catalan Infants. In M. Heimann (ed.), *Regression Periods in Human Infancy*, 7–22. Mahwah, NJ: Erlbaum.

Sadurní, M., Burriel, M. P., and Plooij, F. X. (2010). The Temporal Relation Between Regression and Transition Periods in Early Infancy. *Spanish Journal of Psychology* 13(1), 112–126.

Schwab, K., Groh, T., Schwab, M., and Witte, H. (2009). Nonlinear Analysis and Modeling of Cortical Activation and Deactivation Patterns in the Immature Fetal Electrocorticogram. *Chaos: An Interdisciplinary Journal of Nonlinear Science* 19(1), 015111–015118.

Sears, Dr. (2016). 8 Infant Sleep Facts Every Parent Should Know, www.askdrsears.com, accessed December 19, 2016.

Seehagen, S., Konrad, C., Herbert, J. S., and Schneider, S. (2015). Timely Sleep Facilitates Declarative Memory Consolidation in Infants. *Proceedings of the National Academy of Sciences* 112(5), 1625–1629.

St. James-Roberts, I., Roberts, M., Hovish, K., and Owen, C. (2015). Video Evidence That London Infants Can Resettle Themselves Back to Sleep After Waking in the Night, as Well as Sleep for Long Periods, by 3 Months of Age. *Journal of Developmental & Behavioral Pediatrics* 36(5): 324.

Tremblay, R. E. (2004). Decade of Behavior Distinguished Lecture: Development of Physical Aggression During Infancy. *Infant Mental Health Journal* 25(5), 399–407.

Trevarthen, C., and Aitken, K. (2003). Regulation of Brain Development and Age-Related Changes in Infants' Motives: The Developmental Function of Regressive Periods. In M. Heimann (ed.), *Regression Periods in Human Infancy*, 107–184. Mahwah, NJ: Erlbaum.

Van de Rijt-Plooij, H., and Plooij, F. (1987). Growing Independence, Conflict and Learning in Mother-Infant Relations in Free-Ranging Chimpanzees. *Behaviour* 101, 1–86.

———. (1988). Mother-Infant Relations, Conflict, Stress and Illness Among Free-Ranging Chimpanzees. *Developmental Medicine and Child Neurology* 30, 306–315.

———. (1992). Infantile Regressions: Disorganization and the Onset of Transition Periods. *Journal of Reproductive and Infant Psychology* 10, 129–149.

———. (1993). Distinct Periods of Mother-Infant Conflict in Normal Development: Sources of Progress and Germs of Pathology. *Journal of Child Psychology and Psychiatry* 34, 229–245.

Van de Rijt-Plooij, H., Van der Stelt, J., and Plooij, F. (1996). *Hordenlopen. Een Preventieve Oudercursus Voor de Eerste Anderhalf Jaar.* Lisse: Swets & Zeitlinger.

Woolmore, A., and Richer, J. (2003). Detecting Infant Regression Periods: Weak Signals in a Noisy Environment. In M. Heimann (ed.), *Regression Periods in Human Infancy*, 23–39. Mahwah, NJ: Erlbaum.

Index

Note: *Italicized* pages refer to skills checklist.